UCL INSTITUTE OF ARCHAEOLOGY

VOLUME 7

GW01471527

Inclusive Visions

The Museum Experience of Young Blind and Partially Sighted Visitors

RAFFAELLA CECILIA

BAR BRITISH SERIES 672 | 2022

BAR
PUBLISHING

Published in 2022 by
BAR Publishing, Oxford, UK

BAR British Series 672

UCL Institute of Archaeology PhD Series, volume 7
Inclusive Visions

ISBN 978 1 4073 5965 6   paperback
ISBN 978 1 4073 5966 3   e-format

This book is available electronically on the BAR Digital Platform

DOI https://doi.org/10.30861/9781407359656

A catalogue record for this book is available from the British Library

BAR
PUBLISHING

BAR titles are available from:

BAR Publishing
122 Banbury Rd, Oxford, OX2 7BP, UK
EMAIL   info@barpublishing.com
PHONE   +44 (0)1865 310431
FAX   +44 (0)1865 316916
www.barpublishing.com

UCL INSTITUTE OF ARCHAEOLOGY PHD SERIES

Series Editor: Ruth Whitehouse (Chair of the IoA Publications Committee)

The aim of this series is to offer rapid publication of largely unaltered PhD theses. It covers the full range of subject areas studied at the Institute, including world archaeology, archaeological science, cultural heritage, conservation and museum studies. It makes data, analyses and interpretation available promptly to a wide audience.

The UCL Institute of Archaeology is one of the oldest, largest and most prestigious archaeology research facilities in the world. Its extensive publications programme includes the best theory, research, pedagogy and reference materials in archaeology, cultural heritage and cognate disciplines. Through its publications, which also include a General Series and a Critical Cultural Heritage Series, and a number of associated journals, the Institute brings together key areas of theoretical and substantive knowledge, improves archaeological and heritage practice and brings archaeological findings to the general public, researchers and practitioners.

Volumes in the Series

Of Related Interest

Commemorating Coal Mining Worldwide
International museums, heritage centres and sites related to coal mining
Margaret Lindsay Faull

Oxford, BAR Publishing, 2022   BAR International Series **3076**

Visitor Experiences and Audiences for the Roman Frontiers
Developing good practice in presenting World Heritage
Nigel Mills

Oxford, BAR Publishing, 2021   BAR International Series **3066**

Conservation of Classical Monuments in the Mediterranean Region
A Study of Anastylosis with Case Studies from Greece and Turkey
Kalliopi Vacharopoulou

Oxford, BAR Publishing, 2016   BAR International Series **2800**

Dispute Management in Heritage Conservation: The Case of in situ Museums
Kalliopi Fouseki

Oxford, BAR Publishing, 2015   BAR International Series **2774**

Current Trends in Archaeological Heritage Preservation: National and International Perspectives
Proceedings of the international conference, Iaşi, Romania, November 6-10, 2013
Sergiu Musteaţă and Ştefan Caliniuc

Oxford, BAR Publishing, 2015   BAR International Series **2741**

La musealización del patrimonio arqueológico in situ
El caso español en el contexto europeo
Víctor Manuel López-Menchero Bendicho

Oxford, BAR Publishing, 2013   BAR International Series **2535**

Archaeological Heritage: Methods of Education and Popularization
Roksana Chowaniec and Wieslaw Wieckowski

Oxford, BAR Publishing, 2012   BAR International Series **2443**

The Good, the Bad and the Unbuilt: Handling the Heritage of the Recent Past
Sarah May, Hilary Orange and Sefryn Penrose

Oxford, BAR Publishing, 2012   BAR International Series **2362**

Acknowledgements

I want to thank my supervisors, Dr Theano Moussouri and Prof. Catherine Holloway, for their support, encouragement and precious advice. I am grateful to my PhD examiners, Prof. Richard Sandell and Dr Jessica Hayton, for their input, kind words, and for encouraging me to disseminate my work. My deepest gratitude goes to the participants who generously offered their time to take part in my study – I wish I could name and thank them one by one. Their generosity made this research project possible and meaningful.

My heartfelt appreciation also goes to my family and friends, my parents, Marco and Pina, and my partner Gorjan for their support and affection.

Finally, I would like to dedicate this book to all the disabled people who have been struggling beyond imagination during the COVID-19 pandemic. Their lives, rights, and well-being have often been challenged, neglected, disregarded and forgotten. It has been encouraging to see cultural institutions reaching out to disabled people during the national lockdowns. However, the work ahead is still long, and now it is essential more than ever. I hope this work can make a small but tangible contribution because disabled lives matter and deserve to be heard, acknowledged, and represented.

Contents

List of Figures

List of Tables

Abstract

This book explores the embodied experience, situated interactions and identities of blind and partially sighted (BPS) visitors unfolding in the museum space. It investigates how BPS visitors make meaning and form identities by physically encountering objects, resources, and the environment together with their companions and other visitors. It presents different aspects of the visit experience of BPS participants at three London-based museums, the Victoria & Albert Museum, the Wallace Collection and the Museum of London. The embodied experience of BPS visitors is analysed through the lenses of Interpretative Phenomenological Analysis methodology. Using qualitative audio, fieldnotes, and video-based research methods, it answers the following research question 'How do BPS visitors' social embodied practice contributes to meaning-making and identity formation in museums?'. Based on the theoretical framework bringing together embodiment and situated learning, this research looks at meaning-making and identity formation as a result of the social and embodied practice of museum visitors. This book looks at how meaning-making and identity unfold in perceptual experiences through bodily states, and shared situated action. Based on the research findings, the discussion provides a holistic context for understanding how the different characteristics of the embodied practice of BPS visitors unfold during the visit and how they enable meaning-making and identity formation.

Foreword

The World Health Organisations reported that 'globally, at least 2.2 billion people have a near or distant vision impairment'. The impact vision impairment has on a personal and economic level for individuals and societies can be wide-ranging and long-term. Yet, these impacts are not an inevitable consequence of having an impairment. Instead, they are the consequence of how impairment has historically been conceived and applied in the way we have organised society. Indeed, disability studies research, scholarship and activism has demonstrated how society disables and excludes people with disabilities.

The majority of previous studies about disabled museum visitors centred on access and representation, often framed in terms of 'barriers' that prevent disabled people from visiting. That led to museums employing a number of 'mitigating measures' to eliminate these barriers. Notwithstanding the well-meaning motivation, these measures did not translate into higher visitation numbers, nor did they offer any insights into why and how disabled people are excluded from museums.

'Inclusive visions: the museum experience of young blind and partially sighted visitors' by Raffaella Cecilia is an innovative analysis of the museum experience of visually impaired visitors. It is a nod to disability studies, an embrace of its emancipatory research tradition, but it also takes it a step further. Offering an insightful study of the embodied lived experience of visually impaired visitors, Cecilia re-examines visual impairment through the lens of embodiment and critical disability to reflect on spatial inclusion/exclusion in museums and the agency of the visitor. This approach enables her to frame her study in the context of a social responsibility and rights-based call for change in museums and other cultural institutions.

Cecilia's conceptualisation of visual impairment allows her to identify different characteristics of the embodied practice of visually impaired visitors and the possibility for them to participate in museum and other cultural experiences to the same extent as other visitors. Using a mixture of date sources, from fine-grained field notes, visitor conversations and images, which situate the body at the centre of the museum experience, Cecilia deconstructs the museum visit and tells the story of the visitor journey, identity construction and meaning making. She creates a highly engaging and sophisticated account of the impaired visitor museum experience as a bidirectional interaction between the body and the physical and social environment of the museum.

'Inclusive visions: the museum experience of young blind and partially sighted visitors' has implications for future academic research and applications in museum practice that can lead to meaningful and authentic museum experiences for visually impaired visitors. The theoretical discussion around embodiment and disability couple with the use of interpretative phenomenological analysis of the museum visit can be applied in the investigation of how disabled visitors make use of museum collections. In particularly, the video recording method can be used to investigate the embodied experience of disabled visitors and the impact this can have on the design of fully accessible museum environments. It also highlights the importance of taking a participatory approach when considering assistive technology, and involving visually impaired people in the decision-making and development process. Cecilia clearly demonstrates the impact such an inclusive approach can have on the development of environments where visually impaired people can perform and express themselves, bringing up their voices and affirming their self-presence.

On the personal level, the research presented in this book has been one of the most rewarding projects I had the pleasure to supervise. It has been a joy to see this project evolve and mature, from the initial idea for a doctoral research through to its current form as a monograph.

Theano Moussouri
28 April 2023

Introduction

This book considers the way blind and partially sighted people (BPSP) make meaning and form identities through embodied experience in the museum space. It explores BPSP's situated interactions with companions, other visitors, objects, and the environment. This book examines the wider social and cultural context of disability and the museum visit, particularly concerning accessibility for BPSP. By drawing on empirical findings, I argue that museum accessibility is part of a wider issue of providing access to environments, institutions, geographies, and information. The finding that BPSP have developed visiting strategies for themselves and their community further highlights the leadership role that museums could play in addressing the gap of seeing themselves as part of a larger infrastructure, as well as paving the way for a wider cultural shift.

1.1. Research context

When I started the research for this volume, I began by asking what it means for someone with a vision impairment to be physically in a museum. The lack or loss of sight usually means that BPSP need to navigate, approach, and understand the environment differently compared to sighted people. The most obvious questions that come to mind when one thinks of BPSP in a museum are 'how do they walk around?' and 'How do they experience objects if they cannot see?'. Both questions imply that the physical impairment of sight loss and blindness directly affects the way BPSP access and make sense of museums through their bodies.

The focus of this book on the body and the embodied experience comes from the fact that there is a significant debate in the UK around physical access to museums for disabled people. For a long time, concerns seemed to be primarily related to tokenistic access resources like ramps for wheelchair users or tactile replicas for BPSP. This can be defined as being part of a 'culture of compliance' (Candlin 2010; Sandell and Nightingale 2012; Smith et al. 2012). Until recently, the debate rarely focused on the effect of embodied practices on meaning-making and the overall learning experience of disabled people. Recently (2021) the Science Museum Group advertised the position of Head of Access and Equity within the Department of Learning. This position, one of the first of its kind in a large national institution, formally brings together the realm of accessibility with that of learning. This can be seen as a public acknowledgment of how accessibility and inclusion of disabled people is not a mere access issue of 'how to get in and how to get around'. Access and inclusion are deeply connected to the way disabled people make sense of the space, how they develop cultural capital, and how they form and refine their identities. This suggests that the social and cultural shift underway across institutions and society, of which museums are a part, should broaden its scope.

In order to acknowledge the embodied and situated nature of the experience and the learning of BPSP in museums, my research is informed by sociocultural situated perspectives on meaning-making as well as the embodiment theoretical framework. The nature of the research is interdisciplinary; the theoretical framework is formed of different theories and existing literature from museum studies, disability studies, visitor studies, learning science, and urban studies that are brought together to examine visitors' meaning-making and identity formation processes. This research adopts the embodiment and sociocultural framework, arguing that BPSP's practice and identity is an embodied, social, situated, and mediated process.

1.2. Disability and museums

Over the past 20 years, the issue of equality in museums and the inclusion of disabled people have been discussed among scholars and practitioners within the frameworks of human rights and social justice. Museums and other heritage institutions have been reframed as institutions purposefully bringing about social change (Janes and Sandell 2019). Museums have made efforts to recognise disabled people as under-represented and traditionally neglected audiences, and have also worked towards a better understanding and representation of disabled people and disability-related themes in their collections and exhibitions. Scholars like Sandell, Dodd, Garland-Thompson and Janes have shown how museums have the potential to 'engage in activist practice, with explicit intent to act upon inequalities, injustices and environmental crises' (Janes and Sandell 2019).

Restrictive opening hours, expensive admission rates, and elitist access and authority remained common exclusionary practices in many museums long after they were deemed incongruent with contemporary social standards (Saunders 2014; Silverman 2010). Nowadays, museums increasingly face greater critical scrutiny from the public. Museums are increasingly called to create inclusive and accessible experiences and to reach out to audiences who have been traditionally left out of the museum discourse (Candlin 2010; Fleming 2002; Smith et al. 2012). As Silverman has argued, 'museums are embracing starkly bolder roles as agents of well-being and as vehicles for social change' (2010, 3). In light of social and governmental pressure, as well as new legislation, museums are improving accessibility in order to justify their place within society according to a re-evaluation of their role as educational and social environments (Spence 2007). In this sense, accessibility must be re-examined in relation to institutional change and a shift of values in the museum context.

Museums have the unique opportunity to embrace advocacy and activism roles, and to support the diverse communities in which they are embedded (Sandell 2002). Sandell has argued that it is essential for museums to develop 'awareness and understanding of their potential to construct more inclusive, equitable and respectful societies' (2002, 4). This is due to the greater understanding of the authority and impact of museums on the cultural and social experiences of individuals and communities that systematically face injustice. Museums have the potential to provide educational opportunities that compensate for exclusion from, and different treatment experienced within, traditional learning settings like schools (Ainscow and Sandill 2010; Hayhoe 2013a). Scholars have examined how the social component of being able to visit museums plays a crucial role in the life of disabled people (Candlin 2010). Others have discussed how museums can offer a fresh perspective on physical and mental differences which prompted visitors to engage in discussions informed by the non-discriminatory and rights-based narratives they encountered there (Dodd *et al.* 2010).

This book sits within such framework. Museums have the potential to be inclusive settings that can host, inform, and stimulate inclusive conversations and embodied practices among visitors. It is necessary to look at how these conversations and practices unfold in the experiences of disabled visitors (Hayhoe 2017). Listening to the voices and amplifying the lived experiences of disabled people is the first step towards the development of an inclusive and non-discriminatory museum experience that has a positive social impact. Hence, I aim to investigate the way BPSP make meaning and form identities through their interactions with, and embodied experiences of, the museum environment and collections. A deeper understanding of their experience has the potential to inform practice for the development of non-discriminatory, inclusive, and to empowering spaces, which reflect and shape the lived experiences of visitors.

1.3. Book structure

The introductory chapter has presented the rationale for conducting this study, the research context, the legislation around disability and sight loss in the UK, and the research questions.

Chapter 2 lays out the overarching theories of my research: the embodiment theory, the concepts of habitus and capital from the theory of practice, and the situated learning and identity theories. The combination of these theories allows me to devise the framework with which to answer the research questions, and specifically frame the context of embodied and social practices of BPS visitors. The chapter builds the theoretical framework for this research, providing insights which will be elaborated on in Chapters 4, 5, and 6. The chapter begins with a discussion of embodiment theory, focusing on how the interaction between the body, the physical actions, and the perceptions of the environment have a meaningful role in learning and identity formation. It continues with a discussion of impairment and embodiment, considering what it means to have an impaired body, and outlining the links between embodiment and two concepts from Bourdieu's theory of practice, capital, and habitus. I also examine the situated nature of embodied practices, drawing from Lave and Wenger's situated learning theory to frame my research within the concept of meaning-making and identity formation. Here, I discuss learning as situated and as a continuous process deeply rooted in bodily activity.

Chapter 3 discusses the different characteristics of the embodied practice of BPSP in museums. It turns to empirical studies and it reviews existing literature to situate the study of BPSP experiences and meaning-making. The chapter opens with a discussion of normative practices, namely a repository of behaviours and conducts that visitors are supposed to enact in the museum space. This is particularly relevant as it aids understanding of how visitors move in the space, and how they perceive their movements in relations to objects and other visitors. The discussion of normative practices encompasses how the physical impairment of BPSP influences and shapes their embodied practice and their social interactions with other walking and standing bodies. The remainder of the chapter follows the different characteristics of visitors' embodied practice: from gesturing, walking, seeing and being seen, to looking at and touching objects. These are characteristics of the embodied practice of sighted and BPS visitors according to existing literature, which helped shape the analysis of my findings. The discussion of these characteristics provides insights for my investigation of the perceived roles of museums for disabled people, and specifically BPSP. I draw from a broad range of studies on embodied practices, both in museums and other contexts, which offer insights for my discussion on embodied practices and meaning-making.

Chapter 4 sets out the nature of the research, presenting the methodology, research methods for data collection, and research design. I present my recruitment strategy, as well as the rationale for selecting case studies and participants.

Chapters 5–7 present findings from my three case studies and my analysis and discussion of the results. Chapter 5 presents findings from the Victoria & Albert Museum; chapter 6 from the Wallace Collection; and chapter 7 from the Museum of London. Each provide a cross-analysis of findings gathered via interviews, video recordings, and fieldnotes. Findings are presented and discussed following six themes which mirror the categories of the embodied practice of participants that emerged during the coding of data: co-walking, scaffolding, identity formation, looking, touching, and using resources. This structure allows me to perform a comparative analysis of the three case studies, discussing how the embodied practice enables meaning-making and identity formation.

In chapter 8, I summarise key findings and conclusions, discussing them in relation to the body of literature on embodiment, practice, disability and situated learning. The chapter provides an overview of the implications and recommendations for practitioners and scholars on how BPSP experience the museum space, make meaning, and form identities. Additionally, I provide a reflection on the limitations of my research, and issues to be considered for future research. The chapter ends with a short section on the effects of the COVID-19 pandemic and its implications for the access and inclusion of BPSP in museums.

2

The Embodiment Framework

2.1. Introduction

Museum-studies literature has been interested in the embodied experience of non-disabled visitors. Previous studies have considered bodies as inscribed in a deeply social space during the museum visit and were concerned with how bodies interact with other bodies and the environment. The debate around embodiment has flourished in the past twenty years thanks to the work of several scholars including Rees Leahy, vom Lehn, Heath, Levent, Pascual Levone, and many others. This book brings together perspectives and discussions around embodiment in museums, and access and inclusion of BPSP.

To understand how BPSP make sense of their visit, it is necessary to first examine what it means for BPSP to be physically in the museum and to understand how their bodily experience unfolds. This chapter situates my research within the existing literature on embodiment and the museum visit, literature about embodiment, and disability studies. The theoretical framework of this book is informed by the recent work in a variety of disciplines such as museum studies, disability studies, sociology, learning sciences, and phenomenology. This chapter discusses the influence of embodiment theory and situated learning in understanding the museum experience and links it with the concepts of habitus and capital from theory of practice. It centres the embodied nature of the museum experience and the situated character of visitors' encounters with objects and the environment.

This chapter sets the theoretical framework on which my research was based. I start with a presentation of the theory of embodiment (section 2.2), followed by a discussion of what it means to have an impaired body, and of the theoretical discussion around impairment and embodiment section (2.3). Section 2.4 briefly presents Bourdieu's theory of practice, and outlines the links between embodiment and the concepts of capital and habitus. Finally, section 2.5 focuses on the sociocultural and situated nature of embodied practices, drawing from Lave and Wenger's situated learning theory.

Combining embodiment theory and situated learning offers a better understanding of learning in and through embodied activity and practice. My theoretical framework develops a holistic approach to learning. Learning is seen as an aspect of engagement in social practice that involves the whole person - mind and body. The two theoretical perspectives allow me to conceptualise learning as a way of being in the social world and collecting social practices.

The combination of embodiment and situated theories facilitates a comprehensive analysis of the visitor as a whole person and the world within which they live as they engage in 'activity with and in the world' (Lave and Wenger 1991). This conception of learning as inseparable from social and cultural development is grounded in Bourdieu's theory of practice (1977; 1990). Lave and Wenger (1991) claim that situated learning is essentially a theory of social practice. The concept of practice refers to human activity in the social and natural world (Bourdieu 1977). Participating in social practice indicates a conceptualisation of the person-in-the-world as a legitimate member of a sociocultural community (Bourdieu 1977). Therefore, learning involves perception and understandings embodied through participation in social interactions (Bourdieu 1977).

2.2. Embodiment

Over the past thirty years, the debate about cognition and learning has shifted significantly. The traditional idea was that cognition essentially happens in the mind, that is largely unaffected by contextual elements, and that mind and body operate seperately (Farnell 1999; Rowlands 2010; Port and van Gelder 1995). The shift away from these three principles led primarily to the conceptualisation of situated cognition and situated learning (Lave 1991; Lave and Wenger 1991). It led to an increasing awareness that mind and body cannot be separated and affect and depend on each other (Clark 1997; Cox 2018; Rowlands 2010; Varela *et al*. 1991). Embodied approaches to cognition argued that the interaction between the body, the physical actions, and the perceptions of the environment have a meaningful role in learning and cognitive development. Embodiment scholars working in different disciplines have looked at the various definitions of embodiment, the nature of embodied practice, and the implications for learning (Chrisley and Ziemke 2002; Drodge and Reid 2000; O'Loughlin 1998; Rambusch and Ziemke 2005; Rohrer 2007; Rowlands 2010; Wilson 2003; Ziemke 2002). Despite the differences, there is a consensus that the body has a central role in learning, and that it is connected with practices like the use of tools and objects, social interactions, and physical approach to the environment. Nevertheless, there is a lack of literature on the embodied reality of human bodies in museum environments. According to Harris (2015) visitors' bodies have occupied a conceptually lower place in traditional museum literature compared to museum objects. Neglecting the physical reality of bodies results in a poor understanding of how bodies behave, how visitors perceive and think about their bodies while in the space, and how objects are physically encountered. While there exists strong tradition of discussing the interpersonal and object-mediated museum experience, visitors' bodies remain marginalised (Rees Leahy 2012).

The concept of embodiment invites an analysis of the bodily aspect of the museum visit, understanding that visitors enact their narrations while they move through the space (Harris 2015, 114). It enables scholars to acknowledge and liberate bodies from the 'awkward and unwelcome' category imposed by traditional literature that fails to recognise the embodied experience's physical and textual reality (Rees Leahy 2012, 12). In doing so, it reveals that the body inscribes thoughts, feelings, emotions, meanings, and memories in the space (Tiwari 2010, 18).

The embodied nature of social interactions is a growing area of study. Its role in cognitive development was noted in the 1960s and '70s (Merleau-Ponty 1962; Vygotsky 1978). For example, Merleau-Ponty stated that individuals' corporeal realities were the basis of social interactions between them. Merleau-Ponty argued that the mind was embodied (1962). Thus, it interacted with the surrounding world, including individuals (ibid). The embodied nature of the mind, according to Merleau-Ponty, signified that it was the body that provided meaning and intentionality due to the social nature of its interactions (1962; -1963). In section 2.5, I explore the role of the body in social interactions and meaning-making in museums when I present the theory of situated learning in relation to embodiment. Indeed, throughout this volume, the deeply social nature of embodied practices of BPSP in museums repeatedly emerges as a key concept.

For the purpose of this research, the concept of 'embodiment' does not simply refer to the physical realm of the body. Embodiment here is understood as social bodily practices regarding objects, the environment, and other individuals. As Tiwari posits, it encompasses ideas of the physical and mental sphere and the individual, social and political body associated with it (2010). This research recognises the embodied visitor and acknowledges the museum as a site of social and corporeal practice. Visitors' bodies are seen as real and discursive as they move through the gallery while inscribed in social space and practice (Grosz 1994, 14). The body is the key through which individuals access and experience the world (Merleau-Ponty 1962). The body inhabits the space, and therefore it is the first point of contact with the environment on a corporeal level (ibid).

In museum discourse, the body has been traditionally disenfranchised and reduced to 'eyes only' (Buck 1997; Harris 2015; Rees Leahy 2010). This bodiless 'vision' stems from Enlightenment ideas and principles and it is a way of thinking about visitor experience which museums tend to retain despite the substantial body of criticism of the past thirty years (Bennett 1995; Buck 1997; Garoian 2001; Rees Leahy 2010; Walsh 1992). In particular, this vision-over-body can be traced to the Cartesian division of the corporal and the cognitive (Descartes 2008 [1637]). Indeed, Descartes perceived the body as a weak

and fallible instrument (ibid). Museums have tended to replicate this mind-body dualism by overemphasising the value and importance of vision at the expense of the bodily reality. This decontextualises the visitor from the body, reinforcing the idea that vision is the primary, if not the only, sense used to access knowledge in museums (Belova 2012). 'Ocular centrism' reinforces a long-held Western perception that seeing something equals understanding it rationally and objectively. Contrastingly, the corporeal is associated with bias, subjectivity, and less rational and logical modes of knowledge.

Over the past thirty years, the ocular-centric perspective has been challenged. Cartesian dualism has largely been abandoned for an embodied perspective of individuals as corporeal and cognitive realities within, and as a part of, the material environment. This emerges from new philosophical conceptualisations of the body and of knowledge. In particular, from Merleau-Ponty's conceptualisations of how individuals engage physically with the material environment and how knowledge does not derive solely from the visual investigation, but rather from the physical realm and the disquiet of the physical (1962).

Museum practitioners have challenged this ocular-centric vision by acknowledging visitors not as bodiless and distant viewers but as active and engaged participants. As a refult, they have developed multisensory, hands-on, tactile and perceptual elements in exhibitions. Creating stimulating activities does not, however, fully acknowledge the embodied presence of visitors. This would require understanding and embedding emotional and bodily responses and recognising that visitors' bodies introduce multiple narratives that unfold in the museum space. In short, this entails a shift from an informing to a performing museum where visitors use their bodies to engage with the museum collection (Buck 1997; Harris 2015; Kirshenblatt-Gimblett 2000). In reality, this embodied act is not neither new nor unusual: the embodied practice of describing and understanding is an already well-used and familiar everyday practice, albeit mostly unacknowledged.

2.3. The impaired body

The previous section focused on analysing the concept of embodiment and the corporeal reality of bodies in the museum space. This section shifts the focus to BPSP visitors. I discuss what it means to have an impaired body, how it is perceived, and how the impaired body comes together with other bodies. The concepts and theories discussed in this section mainly emerge from the discipline of disability studies, and I adapted them to the museum context.

In one of the earliest definitions of embodiment, Hirose (2001) borrows an image from Merleau-Ponty (1962), that of a blind person's walking cane as an example of how a certain tool might extend the body and become part of it in an act of embodiment. The choice of a blind person is peculiar since it raises the question of what embodiment means for people with physical disabilities, especially those with vision impairments. Arguments for acknowledging embodied realities in museums (see 2.2), must avoid thinking about a single generic 'visitors' body'. The embodied perspective on museum visitors should encompass the plurality and individuality of visitors' bodies, their differences and similarities. This approach fosters a common way of understanding the visitors' experience. Impaired bodies move in museums alongside non-impaired bodies: some feel welcome, others unwelcome. The impairment is part of the identity, and the knowledge people bring inside the museum. Hence, the embodied experience of BPSP in museums needs to be placed into the context of what it means to have an impaired body.

Disability studies is an academic discipline that investigates disability not only as a condition or a synonym for deficits, but as a form of social oppression (Abberley 1987). Debate between the Medical Model and the Social Model has characterised the discipline since the 1980s (Abberley 1987; Barnes and Mercer 2002; - 2010; Barnes *et al.* 1999; Barnes *et al.* 2002; Barton 1998; Oliver 1996; Shakespeare 1998; -2005). The former explained disability as a biological condition, a personal limitation, a dysfunction, a disturbance, a disorder or abnormality of the health condition, and above all, a personal tragedy (Barnes and Mercer 2010; Barnes *et al.* 2002; Barton 1998; Campbell and Oliver 1996; Oliver 1990; -1996, -1998; Shakespeare 1998; -2005; Shakespeare and Watson 2001). The disability was conceived as a functional lack that had to be compensated to provide the individual with life as close as possible to what is perceived as 'normal' (Barnes *et al.* 2002). The Model looked at disability in terms of the single individual whose quality of life and the opportunities to participate in society are diminished because of the bodily impairment.

In contrast, the Social Model of Disability overcame the vision of disability as an individual tragedy that happened to an unfortunate minority of the population, and it interpreted disability as a consequence of social factors (Barnes *et al.* 2002; Barnes and Mercer 2002; -2010; Barton and Armstrong 2001; Campbell and Oliver 1996; Goodley 2004; Martiny 2015; Oliver 1990; -1996, -1998). Emerging in the early 1990s, the Social Model revolutionised disability studies in Britain, shifting the causes of social restrictions from the 'personal dysfunction and tragedy' narrative to social oppression (ibid). The Social Model succeeded in overturning the medical assumption that inequality was caused by physical disability (Hughes and Paterson 1997). The Social Model emphasised social discrimination and prejudice as the real causes of social inequalities and barriers (Shakespeare 1994). In doing so, it established a radical politics of disability (Shakespeare 2005). 'Disability' is seen within this Model as a burden not in and of itself, but because of how people with impairments are isolated and excluded from participation in society (Goodley 2004). Therefore,

the causes of disability cannot be identified with the individual impairment but rather by economic, social, and cultural barriers which must be removed for disabled people to participate equally in society.

These two opposing models dominated the debate for a long time. However, in the second half of the 1990s, other schools of thought were established, and disability began to be viewed as a more elaborate, dynamic and multifaceted phenomenon. This required scrutinising the way disability studies research was carried out. Moussouri (2007, 93) summarised the principles of emancipatory research as follows (table 2.1):

Within the emancipatory research framework, scholars started to criticise the Social Model and advocate for a sociology of impairment, which takes the Social Model a step further and calls for an embodied understanding of disability (Hughes and Paterson 1997, 326). Their main criticism of the Social Model is that it failed to offer interpretations to account for the different ways in which disability can be experienced (Owens 2015). For example, illness and impairment were examined as two separate entities, neglecting the social nature of the two (Charmaz 2010; Bury 1991; Locker 1983; Owens 2015). Thomas took the criticism further by asserting that the impairment itself becomes disability through the experience of 'structural oppression; cultural stereotypes, attitudes, bureaucratic hierarchies, market mechanisms, and all that is pertaining to how society is structured and organised' (2010, 42). The Social Model fails to recognise that impairment and its embodied values have a distinct impact on individuals' everyday lives and social relationships (Bury 1991).

Criticism of the Social Model is primarily centred on a social interpretation of disability, arguing for the consideration of embodied experiences in disability accounts (Owens 2015). Advocating for a sociology of impairment, Hughes and Paterson criticised the Social

Table 2.1. Principles of emancipatory research (Moussouri 2007)

1. Control: People with disabilities and the organisations representing them should be involved and have a say in the research process.
2. Accountability: Researchers should be accountable to people with disabilities and their organisations by establishing and reporting to an advisory group consisting of people with disabilities.
3. Choice of methods: This should reflect the needs of the project and take into account the agenda and goals of the organisation involved in the project either directly or indirectly
4. Empowerment, dissemination and outcomes: Emancipatory research should aim to produce knowledge that will benefit people with disabilities and assist them in overcoming barriers. Research findings should be shared with people with disabilities and the organisations that represent them and disseminated widely. People with disabilities should feel ownership of the information and use it to their benefit

Model as they argued it deprived the disabled body of its social dimension by failing to account for embodied experiences (1997, 325). While they acknowledge that separating the body from culture led to political gains, they claim that this happened at the expense of disabled people's identities since the bodily dimension was relegated to the medical sphere (Hughes and Paterson 1997). The Social Model did not account for how the impairment is constructed (Paterson and Hughes 1999). Oliver (1990, 4), one of the main scholars that theorised the Social Model, argued specifically that 'Disablement has nothing to do with the body', a belief that is clearly visible in the distinction made by the Social Model between disability and impairment. While disability is taken from the realm of medicine, impairment is left reduced to a biological condition (Turner 2001). The Social Model reduces impairment, and therefore the body, to the medical sphere (Shakespeare 1994). As argued by Hughes and Paterson, it reduced impairment, and therefore the body, to the medical sphere, following the Cartesian' mind over body' dualism (Imrie 2001; Shakespeare 1994). As argued by Hughes and Paterson, it reduced impairment, and therefore the body, to the medical sphere, following the Cartesian' mind over body' dualism. Oliver himself responded to this critique by stating that the Social Model did not aim to be an 'all-encompassing framework within which everything that happens to disabled people could be understood or explained' (2013, 1024).

It is important here to present a historical overview of 'impairment' and how it has been conceptualised. Doing so reveals how the Social Model has failed to address the social nature of the bodily impairment, leading to theorising a sociology of impairment.

According to the World Health Organisation (2001), impairment is one of three dimensions of disability:

1. Impairment in a person's body structure or function, or mental functioning; examples of impairments include loss of a limb, loss of vision or memory loss.
2. Activity limitation, such as difficulty seeing, hearing, walking, or problem solving.
3. Participation restrictions in normal daily activities, such as working, engaging in social and recreational activities, and obtaining health care and preventive services.

Impairment has been traditionally conceptualised as a physical characteristic, trait or attribute of a disabled person (Thomas *et al.* 1997). Thomas *et al.* (1997) conceptualised three characteristics of impairment. Firstly, it was seen as affecting the disabled person's appearance 'in a way which is not acceptable to society' (Thomas *et al.* 1997); as limiting the cognitive or physical functions of the disabled person 'either because of or regardless of society'; and as causing pain and fatigue or affecting communication and consciousness (ibid). Within this framework, impairment is not seen as the cause of or a justification for disability (ibid). Instead, this perspective considers people with impairments as 'subject disability' that can also experience other forms of oppression at the same time (ibid).

The reassessment of the body's agency is central to advocating a sociology of impairment (Paterson and Hughes 1999) which recognise that impairment is produced by the junction of body, mind, and culture (Imrie 2000, 18). A sociology of impairment overturns the idea that impairment is a medical issue, and instead perceives it as an experience itself and a discursive construction (Hughes and Paterson 1997). The ultimate difference between the social Model and a sociology of impairment is that the latter does not exclude impairment, and therefore the body, from sociological and cultural consideration (Paterson and Hughes 1999). The starting point of a sociology of impairment comes from the phenomenological framework that looks at the disabled body as a historical, social, and cultural phenomenon, as much as a biological one (Hughes 1999; Imrie 2012).

As seen in the previous section (2.2), scholars have theorised a phenomenological conceptualisation of embodiment that transcends the Cartesian mind/body dualism. Merleau-Ponty (1962) conceptualised the body as the key through which individuals access and experience the world. Therefore, the body is the base for all knowledge, experience, and perception (ibid). Hence, the sociology of impairment theorises that the impaired body has a subjective experiential ontological dimension (Hughes and Paterson 1997). In other words, the impaired body actively creates meaningful expression and significance (Edwards and Imrie 2003; Imrie 1996a; Imrie 2000).

The impaired body is an experiencing agent, a site of meaning and source of knowledge (Merleau-Ponty 1962; Paterson and Hughes 1999). Impairment is experienced as an enveloping situation of oppression and affliction (Hughes 1999; Hughes and Paterson 1997). The impaired body becomes the site of oppression itself, not because of its dysfunction, but because of the social limitations that are imposed upon it (Abberley 1987). Given that the body is at the same time experience and the foundation of experience, it becomes the first point of access to the world (Crossley 1995). Impairment is itself a social phenomenon and is analysed within the phenomenological perspective. It becomes the phenomenological symbol of perceptual unity of the corporeal, emotional, cognitive, and cultural domains. Following this concept of impairment, Crossley (1995, 43) and Hughes and Paterson (1997, 336) argue that the social realm is embodied, and the impaired body is itself social.

A central concept in the sociology of impairment is that of dys-appearance which comes from the phenomenological idea that the impaired body is a lived and embodied experience (Paterson and Hughes 1999). Dys-appearance is the product of socio-spatial exclusion, not through physical restrictions but through oppressive social process that devalue or dismiss the impaired body (Imrie

2001). The concept of dys-appearance comes from the phenomenological notion that the body (impaired or not) disappears from conscious awareness (Leder 1990). While the body maintains its corporeal dimension, it actively experiences the world with a passive dysfunctional attitude (Paterson and Hughes 1999). Such 'disappearance' is typical of ordinary working bodies, and bodies that are impaired also enter the realm of the 'dys-state' (ibid, Leder 1990, 84). Dys-appearance is a social concept; the body dys-appears when it experiences disabling cultural and socio-spatial experiences (Imrie 2001; Kitchin 1998; Valentine 1999). Nonetheless, although the body does not dys-appear in relation to one's physical impairment, the oppressive socially constructed barriers and dys-abling practices are felt bodily because when the impaired body feels socially produced prejudice and other oppressive behaviours, it dys-appears (Paterson and Hughes 1999; Valentine 1999). The dys-appearance is structured by the socially constructed process that is hostile to non-conforming forms of physicality (Paterson and Hughes 1999, 604). The dys-appearing bodies cannot contribute to the social environment, and therefore do not have a place in it (Edwards and Imrie 2003). Of course, disabled bodies (and thus, disabled people) can challenge socially-constructed restrictions., and chapter 3 discusses normative bodily practices to explore how disabled bodies resist dys-appearance within the museum context.

2.4. The body, habitus, and capital

In this section, I explore the sociocultural framework of the embodied experience of disabled people (and in particular BPSP) through the lens of Bourdieu's theory of practice and the concepts of habitus and capital. While Bourdieu's theory does not deal with impairment and disability directly, it provides insights into the social interpretation of cultural practices. Specifically, it usefully frames the embodied nature of impairment as it helps to consider the embodied experience of disabled people in cultural and social practices.

In his work 'Outline of a Theory of Practice', Bourdieu presents a theory of the production of practice and the way it depends on social structures (1977) which explains individuals' relationship to other individuals, their culture, and their environment (Bourdieu 1977). Bourdieu's theory of practice posits that cultural practices (like visiting museums) depend on educational, cultural and social levels (1984). He linked cultural practices with individuals' upbringings, inclinations, socialisation and personal interests (ibid). Hence, cultural practices appear to be regulated by a person's habitus, a combination of internalised experiences that are used when facing a particular situation, and 'cultural capital', the set of dispositions internalised through socialisation (Bourdieu 1977). Both concepts shed light upon the sociocultural practice of participation in the museum.

Habitus is the generating and unifying principle that regulates practice (Bourdieu 1977). It includes deep-rooted social habits, assets, skills and inclinations (ibid). Habitus involves individuals internalising experiences and reformulating them into action when confronted with a particular situation (ibid). It configures the way individuals understand, experience, and react to the environment (Bourdieu 1990), and is conceptualised as a process of internalising dispositions to generate action (Swarts 1997). Bourdieu described it as:

A system of durable, transposable but also mutable dispositions, structured structures predisposed to function as structuring structures, that is, as principles which generate and organise practices and representations that can be objectively adapted to their outcomes without presupposing a conscious aiming at ends or an express mastery of the operations necessary in order to attain them (Bourdieu 1990, 53).

Therefore, habitus is the acting principle that individuals exert based on strategies developed and acquired through social practice. Bourdieu argued that habitus encompasses both the cognitive realm of mental habits and the 'hexis', namely the predisposition to use the body in a certain way, such as gesturing, posture etc. (1977). Individuals' habitus consists of social, economic, and cultural capital. Habitus determines an individual's behaviour in a given social context, and is reflected in their physical behaviour. Bourdieu located the habitus in the body's active engagement in its environment, in tasks which are part of everyday practice, involving typical postures, positioning, and gestures (1977, 87).

The concept of capital refers to the idea that individuals acquire resources to create values for themselves or other individuals (Resnick 2002). There are several types of capital, as theorised by Bourdieu, mainly economic, social and cultural. Cultural capital refers to the set of knowledge and values transmitted from the family, and the intellectual and social skills acquired in educational and cultural systems which form part of the habitus (Bourdieu 1986; 2006). According to Bourdieu, cultural capital includes individuals' expertise to appropriate and consume cultural products like art, music, science etc. (ibid). Bourdieu developed the concept of cultural capital from research into unequal academic accomplishments of children from families with comparative social origins but diverse educational background (Swarts 1997). Bourdieu rejected the notion that academic success or failure depended on natural dispositions like intelligence and giftedness (ibid). He argued that they depended on cultural capital acquired within the family environment (ibid). Bourdieu conceptualised cultural capital as cultivated dispositions, cultural abilities, and familiarity with culture (1984). It is acquired through upbringing, familiar milieu, and schooling, and it is consolidated through prolonged and repeated participation in educational and cultural activities (Bourdieu 1984). It is, therefore, an advantage of educated middle and upper classes, who are physically exposed to music, artworks, literature etc., institutionalised and legitimised through the education system and the cultural apparatus of theatres, museums and other institutions (Bennett *et al.* 2009).

Bourdieu (1986) identified three types of cultural capital: embodied cultural capital, meaning the set of cultivated dispositions internalised through socialisation; institutionalised cultural capital, as in educational qualifications and credentials; and objectified cultural capital, in the form of material possessions, resources, and transmissible assets. In brief, cultural capital determines the global cultural level of the individual and, at the same time, the possibility of success in the social environment.

Cultural capital manifests through taste, inclinations, manners, preferences, and lifestyle (Merriman 1989). The practice of acquiring cultural capital mirrors the effect of cultural capital: it pervades the choices the individual makes in regard to everyday life which implytaste and lifestyle (Bourdieu 1984). Bourdieu argued that the way cultural capital is acquired is visible in the

> ordinary choices of everyday existence such as furniture, clothing or cooking, which are particularly revealing of deep-rooted and long-standing dispositions because, lying outside the scope of the educational system, they have to be confronted, as it were, by naked taste, without any explicit prescription or proscription (Bourdieu 1984, 77).

In brief, it is clear that members of the middle and upper social and educational backgrounds benefit from higher levels of cultural capital compared to less socio-economically advantaged people. Therefore, they are more likely to experience and consume culture in ways which corresponds to what is considered appropriate and legitimate by cultural and educational institutions.

According to Bourdieu, individuals are always socially positioned (1977). Museum visitors, for example, must have had a meaningful existence before entering the museum and before becoming part of the visiting experience. Through these prior experiences, individuals develop the dispositions that make up the habitus. Dispositions include attitudes, motivations, interests, and habits and a sense of embodied reality, like gesturing, performing, ways of behaving, etc. (Hodkinson *et al.* 2007). These generally unspoken dispositions determine and orientate individuals in relation to all of their actions, and can, therefore, either enable or inhibit certain forms of learning. In this sense, learning can be understood as a process through which the habitus' dispositions are confirmed, developed, challenged or changed (Hodkinson *et al.* 2007). Learning dispositions are generated through acquired experience in different contexts, like familiar settings, educational settings, professional settings, and leisure and local communities (ibid). Hence, the dispositions that make up habitus directly relate to active social and embodied learning. In this sense, as stated by Bourdieu, habitus develops meaningful practices and 'meaning-giving perceptions' (1984, 170).

The concepts of habitus and capital allow us to better understand the impaired body in the museum space. The body holds a crucial role in Bourdieu's theory of practice: it is a bearer of value in society (Bourdieu 1990; Edwards and Imrie 2003). Social inequalities, and more generally, socially-constructed conditions, are understood in connection with bodies as bearers of value and bodily tendencies (namely, walking, speaking, gesturing, touching, sitting, etc.) (ibid). The body and its social relations are intertwined because the body holds power and status and because the management of the body within social relations with the environment is the way to acquire status and power (Bourdieu 1977; -1990).

At the core of Bourdieu's theory of practice is the idea that habitus is the key through which the body is understood (Bourdieu 1990). Bodily tendencies like ways of moving and speaking, and general conduct, are a core part of habitus (Bourdieu 1977; -1986; -1990). Hence, the concept of habitus refers to the peculiar habitual way in which the body relates to the environment (ibid). Habitus covers the knowledge that comes from the everyday embodied interaction with certain cultures or subcultures and seeks to understand social structures by understanding social relations and embodied interactions between individuals (Bourdieu 1977; -1986; -1990).

Understanding social structures through habitus is the key to understanding the production and reproduction of social inequalities (Bourdieu 1990; Edwards and Imrie 2003). Socially constructed inequalities experienced through embodied and corporeal experiences are at the core of the sociology of impairment. The notion of habitus offers a way to understand inequalities of the lives of disabled people through their production and reproduction within social structures through the analysis of bodies as bearers of different values. According to Bourdieu's theory of practice, social practices are neither regulated by the personal decisions made by a single individual's free will nor by objective social rules (1977; -1986; -1990). Social practices are influenced and regulated by how individuals' bodies habitually interact with sociocultural and political environments (Painter 2000). Habitus is the embodiment of individuals' responses to different social interactions, which are often cyclical, consistent, and sometimes unconscious practices (Edwards and Imrie 2003).

The notion of habitus as embodiment of social practices (and therefore social inequalities) can be used to analyse the socio-spatiality of the impaired body (Allen 2004a). The concept of habitus can be employed to examine how impaired people develop strategies to respond to socially constructed restrictions within different environments and how social elements like cultural, economic, and social class backgrounds can make certain impaired people more inclined than others to resist socio-spatial restrictions and dys-appearance. The strategies developed by impaired people to respond to social exclusion can be analysed in light of the effects that impairment has on habitus. Individuals' responses to different social interactions are often spontaneous and unconscious. However, for disabled people, these habits and practices must often be learned, unlearned, adapted, reassessed in conscious ways (Edwards and Imrie 2003).

Social practices are influenced and regulated by how individuals' bodies habitually interact with sociocultural and political environments. Hence, it seems reasonable to argue that social inequalities are the product of the encounter between social forces and the bodies of non-disabled individuals. Non-disabled bodies bear different values compared to disabled bodies, and the structured inequalities coming from the dominant bodily forms and values of the non-disabled monopolise political, social, cultural, and physical capital. As Joppke puts it, the tension between the values borne by disabled and non-disabled bodies is 'a reflection, acknowledgement and legitimation of a given distribution of economic, cultural, and social capital' (1986, 60).

The concept of habitus allows us to understand how social variables are an integral part of the embodied experience of socio-spatial exclusion. Therefore, the inclination to resist or accept socio-spatial exclusion is not universally determined for all disabled people, but it is class-specific and heavily influenced by habitus. According to this theoretical framework, the impaired body-in-space is conceived regarding its agency to overcome disadvantage, prejudice, and resist dys-appearance (Allen 2004b). The resistance/acceptance of socio-spatial exclusion and dys-appearance constitutes a social-class habitus related to the continuous exposure to a privileged or deprived sociocultural and economic status (Allen 2004a). The social class background is itself part of the embodied experience of socio-spatial exclusion of disabled people. Therefore, it directly impacts the inclination to accept it or resist it (ibid).

In section 2.3, I discussed examples of resistance to the dys-appearance of the impaired bodies, which emphasises that disabled people are not passive victims of socio-spatial exclusion (Allen 2004a; -2004b; Edwards and Imrie 2003). However, while the concept of resistance to dys-appearing bodies is universally attributed to all disabled people, this appears ill-fitted to Bourdieu's concept of social habitus. Resistance inclination appears to be socially distributed according to social class habitus and is specific, not universal (Allen 2004a).

Habitus makes individuals define and develop an unconscious understanding of the personal 'place-in-the-world' and 'reasonable expectations' about it, which derives from the social class and background in social place (Bourdieu 1977; Creswell 2002). On the relation between habitus, social space, and expectations, Allen (2004a, 492) writes:

> The habitus 'belongs to', is 'possessed by' and thus 'attuned' to that social space to such an extent that it is able to formulate practical responses that are

appropriate to situations as they present themselves, and without having to undergo an express process of rational calculation, choice and statement of intention.

Disabled people from deprived habitus tend to be more inclined to accept the physical and social exclusion derived from their impairment (Allen 2004a). The social exclusion derived from their impairment does not seem to affect or threaten their expected place-in-the-world (ibid). On the contrary, disabled individuals from the privileged habitus tend to be more inclined to resist the physical and social exclusion derived from their impairment (ibid). In this case, resistance is necessary to maintain their expected place-in-the world including the wide-ranging possibilities to which their background accustoms them (ibid). The social class of the privileged habitus chiefly inspires the effort to expand bodily possibilities and challenge spatial boundaries (ibid).

The habitus and cultural capital of BPSP play a crucial role in their embodied experience of museums. In fact, if the visitor's body indicates the ability to interiorise the museum's message, it also becomes the indicator of cultural habitus (Rees Leahy 2010). The way the body responds to the museum environment and the normative bodily practices reveals the visitor's familiarity with the museum's dynamics, which is part of the visitor's habitus. The cultural habitus provides the visitor with a range of potential situated actions (Merleau-Ponty 1962). Hence, body-space relations generate situated opportunities for cultural consumption (Rees Leahy 2010). Chapter 3 expands on the relationship between habitus and the capital of BPSP and how they enable meaning-making in the museum environment.

2.4.1. Technology and capital

This section discusses connections between technology, habitus, and capital before. considering technology as an enabler of technical capital.

The path traced by Bourdieu through the definition of habitus and capital provides a powerful sociological perspective to give meaning to social stratification, as cultural consumption is increasingly mediated by technological devices (Bourdieu 1986). Technical capital requires his theoretical framework to evolve from the partial autonomy of the use of technology in social processes towards a more holistic vision of the phenomenon (1986).

Yardi initially developed the concept of technical capital, following the concept of cultural capital and social capital theorised by Bourdieu. Technical capital is 'the availability of technical resources in a network, and the mobilisation of these resources in ways that can positively impact access to information and upward mobility' (Yardi 2010, 1). It recognises that individuals have different access to resources embedded in relations with network members (or, for the purpose of this research, community of practice) (Bourdieu 2005; Coleman 1988; Lin 2001). Technical capital aims to be a subset extension of cultural capital that specifically focuses on the skills and knowledge related to the approach to and use of technology (Yardi 2010). The concept refers to the availability of technological resources in a network and the mobilisation of those resources to positively impact access to knowledge and trigger the acquisition of skills and education (Yardi 2009). Technical capital is formed through the availability and accessibility of technology as well as familiarity with technology in familial and social environments such as schools. (Yardi 2010).

Individuals use their technological expertise to participate and to gain power. The accumulation of technological expertise makes up technical capital, and depends on the access an individual has to technology (Brock *et al.* 2010). In turn, access depends on other forms of capital: human capital (education), economic capital, social capital etc. (ibid). The use of technical capital enhances opportunities to develop further these other forms of capital, and vice-versa (Hayhoe 2015b). Furthermore, technical capital can trigger resistance to lower social capital and habitus (ibid). In fact, the use of online resources (generally more available and less expensive than physical ones) enables users to empower themselves by communicating information that would otherwise be unavailable to them (Brock *et al.* 2010; Yardi 2009).

Hayhoe (2015a) accounts for disabled people and the issues of equality and inclusion in his Inclusive Technical Capital model (ITC).

2.4.1.1. Inclusive technical capital

The ITC model employs inclusive traditional and mainstream technologies to promote inclusion in cultural, social, and economic capitals by enabling habitus in education, information and training. ITC originates from the concept of technical capital (Yardi 2010), and therefore from the concept of cultural capital theorised by Bourdieu (1986), both of which promote equality of opportunity achieved through equal access to education, information and training. ITC posits that exclusion from the use of technology produces disadvantage and forms deprived habitus, as non-users are less able to participate, access education, or improve their social and economic status.

ITC develops the argument that equal access to technology, and the skills derived from it, now underpin social inclusion (Hayhoe *et al.* 2015). The skills provided by technology in the current mainstream culture are not only confined to education and training but also include the development of communication, literacy, and political capital (ibid). Applied to the realm of disability, ITC claims that lack of access to technology in general, but also to accessible (or assistive) technologies, represents a social, cultural, and economic disadvantage for disabled people (ibid). ITC claims that technological literacy (in particular digital literacy) is crucial to assist social inclusion of disabled people. ITC is developed by enhancing learning

skills, which develop other types of capital and therefore promote inclusion (Hayhoe 2015a).

ITC criticises how certain aspects of traditionally-defined assistive technologies are employed. In fact, Hayhoe (2014a; 2014b) claimed that while technologies like magnifiers, braille devices, wayfinding aids, and audio-descriptive technologies facilitate the daily lives of BPSP, they do not promote inclusion. This is because these 'special' technologies draw attention to disabled people in mainstream settings like educational ones (Hayhoe 2013b). Such attention culturally and physically excludes from able-bodied people in the same setting (Hayhoe 2014a). ITC on the other hand, avoids this problem since modern assistive technologies are usually embedded in tablet devices. Whether intentionally or involuntarily, tablet devices lend themselves to redefinition as inclusive technology or mainstream technology that can be used by disabled people with little or no adaptation (Hayhoe 2014a, 2014b). Such devices constitute a crucial tool for social inclusion, as they have inclusive applications in educational contexts and are used by learners to create and share information (Hayhoe 2013b).

Over the past 20 years, technologies (especially digital ones) have helped disabled students access and produce knowledge and communicate more easily (Baga 2012; Gkatzidou and Pearson 2009). Advanced software and digital resources such as audio descriptions of books and artworks, magnification or recolouring of text on screen, and representation of sound as text have helped reduce barriers to education (Hayhoe 2013b; 2014a; 2014b). Inevitably, this technology has led to a contemporary philosophy of inclusive technology (ibid). Technological approaches that support cultural inclusion are developing rapidly, particularly three-dimensional and tactile objects as well as web applications and audio resources. For example, Celani and her colleagues (2013) created a system of tactile architectural models to teach urban environment to BPS students. Similarly, Ziebarth (2010) discussed the development of tactile technology in inclusive information. These include maps of galleries, Braille texts, and talking tactile models (ibid). Moreover, Wilson and his team (2020) have recently discussed the application of 3D technology to support cultural inclusion. Similar work is being done by the London-based company 'Museum in a Box' who are developing accessible and portable audio-touch devices (2021). These are just a few examples of museums and organisations creating inclusive technology to support accessible learning and cultural inclusion.

The previous sections (2.4 and 2.4.1) brought together the embodiment framework with the concepts of habitus and capital which allowed me to frame the embodied experience of the impaired body in the museum. I discussed how impaired people develop bodily strategies to respond to socially constructed and imposed restrictions and showed how cultural, economic, social class, and technology backgrounds trigger different levels of resistance to socio-spatial restrictions and dys-appearance. The next section (2.5) presents a perspective around meaning-making in relation to embodiment and cultural capital within the framework of situated learning theory.

2.5. Sociocultural framework

In the previous section (2.4), I examined how visitors' habitus is linked to perception and action, and argued that the encounter of the body and the museum space creates situated opportunities for cultural consumption. In this section, I look at meaning-making in relation to embodiment, and I explore the situated nature of the embodied practice in museums in further detail through the lens of identity formation and the situated learning theory.

This book aims to analyse the situated meaning-making of BPS visitors through the lenses of embodiment, and my working definition of learning brings together the theory of embodiment and situated learning. Learning is described here as meaning-making grounded in sensory-motor activities and bodily participation. When we look at the learning processes of BPSP, it is necessary to acknowledge both the embodied and the sociocultural nature of learning. Bringing these approaches together is essential for better understanding how, and how far, the body is involved in the learning process. The embodied nature of situated learning allows knowledge to be framed as framing knowledge as the achievement of the whole body in its interaction with the environment.

Situated learning is a theoretical approach based on the work of Vygotsky (1978) which looks at the deeply sociocultural nature of learning and cognition (ref). Situated learning is 'a conceptual framework for thinking about learning' as it occurs 'in the context of real-world environment, […] perception, and action' (Wenger 1998b, 11, Wilson 2003, 627). Within it, learning and knowledge are understood as the product of the social activity in context (Lave 1991; Lave and Wenger 1991; Rogoff 2003) and in relation to bodily activity, participation, practice, and experience. By underlining this connection, situated learning theory overcomes the mind-body dualism according to which the cognitive sphere is detached from the bodily experience (Lave and Wenger 1991; Rogoff 1990).

Situated learning looks at the relationship between learning and the social context in which it takes place. Instead of defining learning as a passive acquisition of external knowledge, Lave and Wenger (1991) placed learning in the context of specific forms of social participation. The learner does not acquire a quantifiable amount of abstract external knowledge, which they then re-use in other contexts. Instead, Lave and Wenger postulated that the learner acquires the ability to act in the situated context. Learning and activity can be regarded as processes that occur in a network of social relations (St Julian 1997). Through the process of learning, characteristics

of the learner's (individual and collective) habitus are communicated, shared, expressed, and redefined. The learning participation actively shapes the learning process through the context, the tools, and the culture in which learning takes place. The practice of learning is a dynamic co-construction of meaning, which continually reflects on the learner's habitus, prior knowledge, and experience.

Wenger (1998a; -1998b; -2009) expands the notion of participation further in his 'community of practice' concept, referring to social groups of individuals who share common interests and histories, which is developed through regular participation and interaction (Wenger 1998a; -1998b; -2009). The members of a community of practice engage in a 'process of collective learning in a shared domain of human endeavour' and draw value from their participation (Wenger 2009, 1). Because the meanings of members' actions are continuously negotiated (1998a; -1998b; -2009). Practice can be understood as a source of knowledge. Learning is conceptualised as embedded in the different communities and mediated by social participation to produce or share knowledge (dynamic tools) and shared resources (Barron 2006).

Within the situated learning framework, learning involves an active process of participation in a community of practice. Learning is conceptualised as meaning-making, the social process whereby habitus, social situation, activity and knowledge converge and co-exist (Silverman 1995). Situated learning approaches take the location where learning occurs as a starting point rather than the individual from a cognitive perspective (Mason 2007). Over the past twenty years, this learning framework has been widely applied in the museum context. As a result, visitors take a more active role in the making of meaning which is seen as malleable and dynamic rather than based on pre-established categories and outcomes (Allen 2002; Rowe 2002). It is a joint activity of a group of visitors, where individuals get together and make meaning as they interact (Allen 2002; Silverman 1995).

The role of the body within situated learning and meaning-making has been re-evaluated in light of neuroscientific knowledge related to the body's role in social interaction practices and the social use of tools (Rambusch and Ziemke 2005, 1803; Ziemke 2002). Consequently, Hodkinson *et al.* (2007) have called for a more sustained focus on learning as embodied and as part of the situation in which it occurs, understanding learning from the dual perspectives of the individual learner and the learning situation.

Looking at learning as embodied allows better acknowledgment dispositions like a repertoire of bodily practices, corporeal techniques, and embodied skills (part of an individual's habitus) that visitors bring to the museum. These bodily practices are acquired, culturally specific, and learned techniques (Mauss 1973, 21). Bodily practices implicate different layers of knowledge. For instance, knowing 'how to look' at a display means knowing 'where and how to stand' in relation to it, 'how fast and where to walk' in the space, 'what to say or not say and what to touch or not touch' (Rees Leahy 2012, 6–7). These practices are distinctive of the visitor's social habitus and are acquired and developed through participation in a community of practice. Hence, practised visitors are more likely to display socially acquired and approved embodied modalities (Mauss 1973). Embodied modalities, once acquired, become part of the habitus of the visitor, and they come 'naturally, functioning as structuring structures' (Bourdieu 1990, 53). If we look at learning as situated meaning-making, these acquired embodied modalities (such as looking, gesturing, positioning, walking, sitting etc.) are an integral part of visitors' practice.

Since learning is grounded in activity, exploring the link between activity and the body is necessary. Within sociocultural and situated frameworks, the dependency of learning and activity is a core concept. However, Rambusch and Ziemke (2005) argued that, within these frameworks, activity is relegated to a process of cultural and social relations between the learner and their environment. They claimed that this conceptualisation of 'activity' disregards the role of the body (Rambusch and Ziemke 2005). In this sense, the environment (tools, physical space, other people) seems to be considered a 'container' in which actions and activities are performed. Fenwick (2003) argues that this view disregards the issue of learning from an embodied perspective.

Situated learning theory places the community of practice as the context in which individuals develop practice (e.g. values, norms, knowledge, and relationships) and identities that are appropriate to that community. The situated learning approach tends to focus on the sociocultural aspects of learning like its social nature, social participation, and identity formation in the community of practice. An embodied perspective of situated learning allows sociocultural elements to expand to take into account the nature of the social-material interactions (Clancey 1997). Embodiment perspectives offer an additional layer by reconsidering the body and its role in learning and meaning-making, focusing on social interaction and the use of tools (Dawson 2014). As the body and the environment play a mutual role in the learning process, learning is distributed across the body, the mind, and the environment (Clark 1997).

Situated learning theory conceptualises learning as a collaborative, dialogical, and socially mediated process which takes place through participation within a community of practice and brings together learner's habitus and capital. Communities of practice detain the knowledge which is shared among its members. This research looks at learning as meaning-making, and examines it in terms of embodied activity and participation in a community of practice. Ultimately, this situated framework allows me to systematically analyse the intersection of learning components: community, practice, meaning and identity. This provides a conceptual framework for exploring learning as social participation.

2.5.1. Learning & identity

Learning involves participating in the community's practices and offers opportunities to develop identities that offer a sense of belonging and commitment (Handley *et al.* 2006). Wenger (1998b) identified community, practice, meaning, and identity as the four 'deeply interconnected and mutually defining' components of learning (Wenger 1998b, 5). He defined them as follows: community as social intersections in which practice is defined and participation is identifiable as competence; practice as the shared frameworks, perspectives, and social resources that enable shared engagement; meaning as the ability to experience the world as meaningful; and identity as the way learning changes who we are (Wenger 1998b).

The last of these, identity formation, closely correlates with practice (Wenger 1998b). The negotiation of identities is of equal importance to the negotiation of meaning within a community of practice (ibid). Identity formation in practice is enabled by social participation in communities of practice, and it is constructed through the negotiation of meaning which is produced through relationships and shared identities (ibid). The dynamic between the development of identity and forms of participation is essential to understand how individuals internalise, challenge, or reject the existing practice of their community (ibid). Identity, within situated learning, is seen as 'living relations between persons and their place and participation in communities of practice' (Lave and Wenger 1991, 53). Learning is, therefore, a complex, multi-layered and ongoing process, tightly interrelated with identity formation and deeply situated within social and cultural contexts (Lave and Wenger 1991).

Interpretations of Situated Learning theory offer critical perspectives on identity construction. Individuals construct their identity and understanding of the 'self' based on the level, nature, and outcome of their participation in the community (Handley *et al.* 2006). Depending on the resonance with their current senses of identity, individuals embrace or reject occasions to participate more or less fully (ibid). There is a constant negotiation between the community of practice's efforts to regulate identity and individuals' situated and ever-evolving sense of self (Alvesson and Willmott 2002). Through participation in the community of practice, individuals continuously define, shape, adapt, maintain, or revise their perceptions of self (Handley *et al.* 2006).

When recognising identity formation as grounded in embodied practice, Oyserman's (2001; -2015) situated approach furthers how visitors perceive actions and difficulties in relation to identity. She argued that people make sense of specific situations and difficulties they encounter in the space in a way that is congruent with their identity and their situated perception of the self (Oyserman 2015). Additionally, they tend to prefer identity-congruent to identity-incongruent actions and practices (ibid). When a specific action is perceived as identity-congruent, an individual is more likely to engage with it since they feel the action is meaningful to them (ibid). On the contrary, when action feels identity-incongruent, the same difficulty makes the action appear pointless and 'not for people like me' (Oyserman 2015, 4). People use their embodied perception of the immediate social situation to make sense of how they perceive their identity and then act in a way that makes sense for the interface between their situated identity and what that seems to mean in context (Oyserman 2015). Oyserman's work is particularly relevant within the CoP framework, as individuals act and form their identity based on the situated context of their interaction with other members of their CoP.

This social aspect of learning and identity-formation emphasises how the individual is a participant in meaning-making who draws on the social world as a resource for constituting their identity (Wenger 2010). Wenger (2010, 180) defined this meaning-making entity as a 'whole person, with a body, a heart, a brain, relationships, aspirations, all the aspects of human experience', thereby going beyond the cognitive. The individual's experience in all these aspects is actively constituted, defined, and interpreted through learning, as the individual is constantly negotiating meaning (Wenger 2010, 181). Identity formation happens through learning (ibid). As well as acquiring skills and sharing knowledge, learning means becoming 'a knower': a certain person in a context in which the meaning of knowing is negotiated with the level of competence of the community of practice (ibid). In this sense, 'a community of practice is a living context that can give newcomers access to competence and invite a personal experience of engagement by incorporating that competence into an identity of participation' (Wenger 1998, 214). Wenger (2010) argued that, based on competence, learning could be defined as the process of readjustment between socially defined competence and personal experience. Such a process can cause both identification and dis-identification with the community depending on the balance between competence and experience (Wenger 2010).

The following two sections (2.5.2 and 2.5.3) present two sociocultural concepts: funds of knowledge and scaffolding. These illuminate how visitors develop, acquire, and share knowledge within the community of practice

2.5.2. Funds of knowledge

Funds of knowledge is a socio-cultural concept grounded in cultural practice and usually associated with families and family development, although it can also be applied to individuals and other communities (Gonzalez *et al.* 2005). Groups develop different sets of skills and understanding accumulated through lived experiences, situated social interactions, and embodied practices which are necessary for their members' everyday lives, including their work, family, interests, and wellbeing (Gonzalez *et al.* 2005; Moll *et al.* 1992; Hogg 2011). Funds of knowledge are also 'tools' built, consumed, distributed and shared

among the community of practice - across individuals, the environment and situated situations (Moll *et al.* 1992) and refers to the body of knowledge and expertise that community members develop due to their role in the family, community, and culture (ibid). Every community has meaningful educational resources acquired through everyday practices, knowledge sharing, cultural beliefs, and values (Rodriguez 2011). Similarly, visitors can draw from funds of knowledge to identify and read the museum 'script' (see chapter 3, section 3.2) and develop embodied practice to navigate the museum space.

Funds of knowledge move away from a focus on deficits and barriers by highlighting the reservoir of knowledge, skillset and experiences that under-represented and disadvantaged groups and communities have (Gonzalez *et al.* 2005; Moll *et al.* 1992). Hence, the concept can frame how BPSP develop and acquire educational tools, techniques, and strategies through everyday practices in order to overcome socially-imposed barriers. 'Funds of knowledge' is employed in this book to consider meaning-making in museums among BPSP. The embodied and socially embedded interactions of BPSP occur within varied social and physical contexts, like family, school, and the workplace. Because these contexts often overlapexperiences, strategies, knowledge, and insights gained in one context can potentially be employed within another (Gonzalez *et al.* 2005).

This conceptualisation of funds of knowledge suggests that BPSP can actively create resources and strategies to read the museum script. They can adapt to perceived normative physical practices by drawing from everyday experiences of navigation through unfamiliar spaces, encounters with and use of unfamiliar objects, and access to 'inaccessible' information. In the case of BPSP, tangible tools like mobility aids (for instance, white canes) or assistive technology (for instance, screen readers) can be considered as funds of knowledge. BPSP from less privileged habitus, however, with lower cultural or technical capital, may lack the frame of reference to interact with museum environments, objects, and activities. Additionally, the lower levels of empowerment, of self-confidence and a lesser ability to navigate unfamiliar spaces and barriers they might encounter. This through their directly impacts the way they approach the museum and its contents.

2.5.3. Scaffolding

The socio-cultural concept of scaffolding helps show how guidance is sought, developed, shared, and fades among communities of practice. It also aids our understanding of the role of bodily communication and guidance in negotiating the response to the museum environment and exhibitions.

The concept of scaffolding was initially theorised in formal education environments (Pea 2004) and subsequently adapted by Mai and Ash (2012) to the museum context. The traditional conceptualisations of scaffolding are varied and sometimes difficult to group together. The concept is broad in meaning within the educational field, and its significance is not always defined (Pea 2004). The concept of scaffolding comes from Vygotsky's (1978) argument that socially-mediated interactions enable learning. In these interactions, a less experienced person is assisted by a more expert one in reaching a better understanding and greater independence in the making of meaning (Wood *et al*. 1976). Scaffolding is a temporary system of support that enables members of a social group or community of practice to perform in a particular activity (ibid). As a working summary of the concept, scaffolding is a way of looking at episodes where learning skills and abilities are assessed, and guidance is subsequently given in a formal environment (Cazden 2001; Granott 2005; Mascolo 2005; Pea 2004; Wood *et al*. 1976). As the learner's skills develop, guidance eventually diminishes or fades as the learner becomes more competent (ibid). According to Ash and her colleagues (2012, 24–25), scaffolding activity includes specific elements including:

a. several individuals participating in joint activity;
b. typically, one individual asking for or receiving some form of question or guidance (oral or gestural);
c. the exchange occurring between individuals who are cross-age or cross-generational (for instance, parent to child or sibling to sibling); and
d. support and guidance eventually diminishing or fading completely.

Mai and Ash (2012) adapted the concept of scaffolding as the foundation of the social practices in museums which included how to approach the exhibition and then understanding the content (in their case, science) of the exhibit (ibid). They used the concept of scaffolding scenes to illustrate how the members of a family scaffold their understanding and actions in the museum's informal learning environment (ibid). This perspective included individuals interacting with each other and museum educators, exhibitions, displays, and signs. The latter are considered tools of the scaffolding scene (Ash *et al*. 2012; Mai and Ash 2012). Mai and Ash (2012) argued that scaffolding interactions constitute the base of the social practice of families as they determine 'how to do' the exhibition, what they perceive the content to be, and how they make sense of that content. A typical scaffolded interaction included at least two individuals and scaffolding elements of guidance, instructions, supervision, teaching, questions and comments, with successful or unsuccessful educational outcomes (Ash *et al*. 2012; Mai and Ash 2012). Mai and Ash observed how guidance tended to be more evident at the beginning of the exchanges and then started to fade (2012). 'Exchanges' were defined as the start of talk or a gesture that called for physical or verbal guidance (ibid).

Mai and Ash's work showed how guidance unfolded during the exhibition in family groups (2012). They observed shifting roles in guidance and support among different family members (Mai and Ash 2012). Parents and children

took turns adopting authoritative roles to explain elements of the exhibitions and, at times, children positioned themselves as an authority by showing specific display elements to their parents or siblings (ibid). Price and her colleagues observed similar scaffolding interactions in their analysis of family collaboration supported by interactive tabletops (2021). These instances of scaffolded guidance and shifting roles reveal a complex social activity that is at the core of how collaborative groups make sense of the museum exhibit. Reciprocal guidance becomes the key to analysing how members of a group engage with one another in scaffolded meaning-making in a museum context.

Mai and Ash's study is relevant to this research for several reasons. Firstly, because they investigated meaning-making from learners' perspective, focusing on how they act in the space. Secondly, their research included culturally and ethnically diverse families not traditionally considered a mainstream audience of museum exhibits (Mai and Ash 2012, 101); BPSP are also an 'underserved community'. Thirdly, their analysis of scaffolded guidance naturally applies to the experience of BPSP, where physical and verbal guidance is required not only as an element of the social activity but often due to the physical impairment itself. Finally, they defined scaffolding as a key socio-cultural concept, which naturally fits within the situated framework of learning I explored in section 2.5. I look at the interactions between visitors, other individuals, and tools as an expression of the socio-cultural, situated and embodied activities. The scaffolding use of tools, in this sense, facilitates an understanding of how individuals construct their own agenda and the goals of their visit, as they see it.

Scaffolding is used in this book as a hanger concept to analyse the bodily practice of participants after which I investigate how bodily practices enabled meaning-making. Within the scaffolding framework, 'practice' accounts for the individual participant, or group of participants, that are increasing their expertise as they change their category in the community of practice. I adapt the concept of scaffolding to analyse bodily techniques and tools that are part of practice to understand the function that a particular tool or technique appears to play in enabling meaning-making. My research started with the assumption that visitors' participation happens through the body. The concept of scaffolding is then used to describe what the body does and how it makes sense of the museum environment. This allows us to look at strategies and practices visitors rehearse in the museum and other parts of their social and cultural everyday lives, labelled here as 'everyday practices'.

For this research, I refined the concept of scaffolding further to bring up the bodily element (research question 1) and the use of resources (research question 3). Tools play a crucial role, as BPSP use tools as part of scaffolding techniques to minimise frustration due to inaccessible spaces and resources, and also to be independent. Scaffolding allows me to analyse participation in a joint activity, the dynamics of participants' interaction with other individuals, and the physical interaction between individuals and the environment, and individuals and tools.

2.6. Conclusion

This chapter discussed the embodiment theory, concepts of impairment within the sociology of impairment theory, concepts of habitus and capital from Bourdieu's theory of practice, and situated learning theory, and reflected upon the research questions posed in the Introduction. Each theory presented helps create my theoretical framework which is applied to research findings in chapters 5 to 7.

This chapter situated the museum experience within the context of embodiment which, combined with situated learning, and identity-formation theories allow me to confirm that the embodied practice of visitors is deeply situated. Everything that a visitor does while in the museum space, including interpersonal interactions as well as interaction with exhibits, is examined through embodiment lenses, which allows its sociocultural and situated dynamics to be captured.

Characteristics of visitors' embodied practice presented and discussed in the following chapter (Chapter 3) help form 'building blocks of meaning-making' (Silverman 1995) which they develop through active participation in the community of practice.

The Embodied Practice of Museums' Visitors

3.1. Introduction

The previous chapter presented the theoretical framework of my research. This chapter expands upon the previous one by providing an overview of the characteristics of the embodied practice of BPSP during the museum visit. It presents empirical research conducted in museums and other settings and critically reviews characteristics of BPSP embodied practice. The research discussed in this chapter focuses primarily on studies from the UK and, particularly, London-based institutions but also includes several studies carried out in North American and European contexts.

After having framed the overall research within the embodiment and the situated learning traditions, the focus now turns to BPSP as museum visitors. The discussion encompasses the characteristics of their embodied practice, looking at how BPSP make sense of the exhibits through their bodies inscribed in social spaces. It begins with concepts analysed by Helen Rees Leahy in her book 'Museum Bodies: The Politics and Practices of Visiting and Viewing' (2012), where she investigates the corporeal practices (techniques, skills and methods) that visitors enact in the museum and that are usually taken for granted.

The chapter starts with two sections (3.2 and 3.3) exploring literature around these corporeal practices, discussing how visitors acquire, enact, and in some cases resist them. These sections frame the embodied practice as part of a set of normative practices, namely a repository of behaviours and conducts that experienced visitors are supposed to enact in the space following the museum 'script'. From section 3.4 to 3.8, I examine the characteristics of the embodied practice. Section 3.4 looks at gesturing, focusing on how BPSP acquire and use this particular practice despite their sight loss. Section 3.5 discusses walking, drawing on the concepts of co-presence and co-awareness. Additionally, it looks at the meaning of walking with other visitors while having a vision impairment. Section 3.6 considers the issue of 'being seen' in museums, elaborating on the issue of impairment visibility and what it means to be 'stared at' if one has a physical impairment. Section 3.7 turns to look at visitors' visual practice, and it focuses on how BPSP make sense of visual concepts and perform the act of looking at objects despite their sight loss. Finally, section 3.8 discusses multisensory encounters with objects and, in particular, the practice of making sense of objects through touch.

3.2. Museums and the body

Embodiment directly influences the way museum collections are rendered meaningful for visitors and the way visitors make meaning of them. Visitors' reality is shaped by their bodily practice, movements, orientation, and the form of their interaction with objects (Johnson 1987). Over the past thirty years, several researchers focused on the bodily practice of visitors in the field of museum studies. In particular, this research direction has been conceptualised as a shift towards sensory museology (Classen 2005; - 2016; Classen and Howes 2006; Dudley 2010; Howes 2014; Levent and Pascual Levone 2014; Rees Leahy 2010; - 2012). One of the major trends within sensory museology has been the re-evaluation and rehabilitation of the sense of touch in museums (Black 2005; Chatterjee 2008a; Candlin 2010; Classen 2005; - 2012; Dudley 2010; Gadoua 2014; Jewitt and Price 2019; Pye 2007). It is important to highlight here that such rehabilitation, together with research on the sensory tradition of early museums, has opened up a deeper understanding of visitors' embodied and multisensory experience.

Another major trend in sensory museology is the healing value and therapeutic benefit of museum objects (Howes 2014, 263). Research has shown how handling cultural heritage objects enhances wellbeing (Chatterjee 2008b). While Chatterjee's research (2008b) did not specifically focus on BPSP, several studies have shown how sensory encounters with objects can help those who have lost or are losing sight in their normalisation process.

This body of literature examining sensory museology and embodiment in museums contributes to our understanding of the different characteristics of the embodied practice of museum visitors, such as walking, pacing, looking, sitting, speaking, gesturing, and standing at the 'correct' distance from objects. These embodied practices (or corporeal techniques, as defined by Rees Leahy) are deeply situated, acquired, and culturally specific (2012). They enable visitors to make meaning of museums' collections and environments (Rees Leahy 2012). Findings from Rees Leahy's work show how museum visitors orientate their bodies to build new relations with the environment and other visitors (2010).

Embodied practices identified by Rees Leahy can be seen as part of the visitors' habitus, as they contribute to the way visitors make meaning in the space. Examples of the embodied practices she discusses are walking, standing, pacing, gesturing, and looking (2012). These embodied practices are part of a series of normative practices that visitors' bodies are expected to perform in the museum space (Rees Leahy 2012). This section presents Rees Leahy's discussion on normative practices and critically reviews how they are acquired, what they mean in the space, how they contribute to meaning-making, and what they mean for BPSP.

The discussion of normative practices originates from Merleau-Ponty's assumption that visitors position themselves in museums in relation to objects in order to 'achieve an optimal balance between the inner and outer horizon' (1962, 302). This means that experienced visitors are able to position themselves in such a way which allows them to maximise the meaning they make of the object. According to Merleau-Ponty, visitors' bodies respond to the implicit requirements set by the objects on display (1962).

This idea comes from the 'vision over body' tradition. If vision is the highest sense, then optimal viewing is the best practice (Classen 2007). Visitors are, therefore, expected to position their bodies in order to achieve the best possible viewing. The ability to position themselves correctly for optimal viewing comprises taken-for-granted embodied techniques that visitors bring inside the museum (Rees Leahy 2012). Rees Leahy defined them as 'taken for granted' as they are part of a repertoire of embodied practices that have become incorporated in practised visitors (2012).

These normative embodied practices directly respond to the museum's 'script' which Noordegraaf defined as how museums communicate with their audiences through displays, exhibitions, presentations, choice and positioning of objects and resources (2004). She applied a Film Studies framework to argue that museum exhibitions are based on a 'script' that defines the action framework within which the environment, its curators, and the audience interact, similar to the script of a film (Noordegraaf 2004). The script encompasses elements including the layout of the environment, the disposition and arrangement of objects, the different display techniques, and communication strategies (ibid). These elements mediate between the museum and its audience. The script is also embedded in the rhythm of the displays that controls the visitors' pace, the direction of walking, looking modality, and other embodied practices (Kirshenblatt-Gimblett 1998). Kirshenblatt-Gimblett argued that museums arrange displays and objects in the space to direct the visitor in relation to them (1998). Hence, practised visitors know how to behave in museums, as they have internalised the correct reading of the museum script (ibid). If we look at embodied practices as situated, these walking and looking modalities (along with other corporeal techniques) are clearly acquired and developed while enacting them in the museum space. Reading the museum script is an acquired practice, part of the visitors' habitus. Rees Leahy argued that the museum itself inculcates and accommodates these techniques by offering verbal and physical guidance, explicit and implicit regulations, and visual and physical deterrents that aim to regulate visitors' performance (2012). A notable example is a general guideline that explicitly forbids touch (usually through signs) or the use of ropes to cordon off areas near objects. Even less

experienced visitors are quick to recognise such deterrents and capable of restraining their behaviour in the gallery accordingly (Rees Leahy 2012).

However, normative practices go beyond mere adherence to guidelines and respect of deterrents. Rees Leahy argued that these corporeal techniques involve how to look, where and how to stand in relation to objects and others, where and at what pace to walk, when to talk and what to say, what to touch and how, and what not to touch (2012). Following the museum display means adhering to different norms of environment-body and object-body relations which require the skills to 'read the exhibition script' (Noordegraaf 2004). Some exhibitions may require the observer to look at the display both vertically and horizontally, such as paintings in a historic house. Others require the visitor to follow a specific direction, as is the case for chronological displays. Reading the script requires embodied skills acquired through time and experience and shared among groups of visitors. The experienced museum observer and walker has mastered these bodily techniques and is 'embodied within a repertoire of actions that reflect and respond to the space of display, the conditions of viewing and the presence of other spectators' (Rees Leahy 2012).

As I mentioned before, these corporeal techniques are acquired, and part of visitors' habitus. Merlau-Ponty described them as the overall familiarity or habit acquisition with the museums' 'ways', which provide a repertoire of appropriate and situated actions to enact in different contexts as required by the display (1962, 142). As these practices are acquired, the experienced visitor can draw upon this repertoire of relevant viewing and moving habits, demonstrating the familiarity, ease, and experience with the institution's script, both to themselves, to others from their same group, and to visitors and museum staff (Rees Leahy 2012, 49). Automatically adopting the posture and embodied habits of an experienced visitor means aligning consciously with the display's institutional intention. Mastering the art of understanding how to read the objects within the narratives they have been inscribed is the outspoken social demonstration of socially acquired bodily techniques.

Once these normative 'correct' practices are acquired, they are taken for granted (Bourdieu 1990, 53). After all, they are drawn from the habitus that visitors bring inside the museum, and they are unthinkingly employed in the different situated opportunities, as required. Therefore, these embodied normative practices are distinctive of the social habitus of the visitor (Mauss 1973, 73). Visitors from a privileged social habitus tend to have learned what to expect and how to behave 'correctly' and 'appropriately' (Rees Leahy 2012).

3.3. 'Normative' bodily practices

The question now turns to how visitors 'acquire' and 'learn to master' these techniques. Official explicit guidance on how to walk, how to look, how to touch, and in general 'how to do' an exhibition is often missing from museums (Rees Leahy 2012). These practices are not straightforward, and less experienced visitors are often lost as they are not provided with guidance on how they are supposed to approach the space (Rees Leahy 2012). One clear example of this is visitors' issue when they decide what to 'look at'. Although looking at everything in a given museum is usually not feasible, Harbison argued that no guidance says that visitors are not supposed to do so (2000, 145). He argued that it is difficult for visitors (even experienced ones) to negotiate what to prioritise (Harbison 2000, 149). His findings demonstrate that visitors experience difficulties in selecting or prioritising particular objects compared to others (ibid). These difficulties are due to the uneasiness visitors feel in relation to the historical and intangible values the objects embody (ibid).

Rees Leahy asserted that this provokes contrasting feelings in the visitor, who can suddenly feel lost, overwhelmed, and excluded (2012). Ironically, the only explicit guidance that museums tend to offer is related to what the visitor is not supposed to do: 'Do not touch', 'do not sit', 'do not eat', 'do not take pictures'. In theory these prohibitions regulate visitors' behaviour, but do not equip the visitor with enough guidance to approach the display (ibid). The rules can suggest an approved mode of walking (for example, it is usually forbidden to run) (ibid), but this rarely increases visitors' confidence and agency in the space (ibid).

Several researchers have argued that if the museum succeeded in making visitors learn how to walk the space effectively by providing explicit guidance, visitors would also develop skills to effectively approach objects and plan their visit (Bennet 2006; Rees Leahy 2007; - 2010). It seems reasonable that this would increase less experienced visitors' confidence in the space, as they would be able to focus on the meaning they make of their visit rather than worrying about their walking practice. This lack of explicit guidance is follows from a tendency of disregarding the physical realities of visitors' bodies (chapter 2, section 2.2). As museums are fundamentally visual institutions, the bodily techniques are taken for granted in favour of what Bourdieu described as the 'pure aesthetic gaze which is capable of considering the work of art in and for itself' (1993, 36).

In the absence of explicit guidelines, visitors naturally tend to look at others in the space to guide their embodied practice indirectly. Several studies pointed at emulation and mimicry as a pivotal aspect of the social and bodily training of normative embodied practices. Mauss referred to the acquisition of normative corporeal techniques as 'prestigious imitation' (1973, 73). Through this imitation, the novice visitor emulates the behaviour that has succeeded and has been successfully performed by other members of the community of practice in whose authority they have confidence (ibid). A direct effect of embodiment is that bodily mimicry is produced by the perception

and awareness of the embodied state in other visitors (Rambusch and Ziemke 2005). Research in psychology disciplines has shown that individuals tend to mimic and emulate the bodily behaviour of others, including facial expressions (Barsalou *et al.* 2003; Cappella and Planalp 1981; Chartrand and Bargh, 1999; Meltzoff 2002; Rizzolatti *et al.* 2002; Rueff-Lopes *et al.* 2015). This embodied and social emulation and mimicry can take the form of synchronising one's movement with another person (Barsalou *et al.* 2003; Chartrand and Bargh 1999).

Once acquired, these techniques are inscribed in the body and build the now-experienced visitor's self-awareness as a viewing subject within the museum (Rees Leahy 2012). The ability to perform a certain degree of bodily self-discipline and adhere to normative practices allows visitors to navigate the environment with ease. Studies within the discipline of social psychology have shown how there is a direct correlation between mastering correct bodily techniques and social stimuli (Barsalou *et al.* 2003; Cappella and Planalp 1981; Chartrand and Bargh, 1999; Rueff-Lopes *et al.* 2015). In particular, Barsalou and his colleagues (2003) examined social stimuli using embodiment theory. They observed that social stimuli produce bodily and cognitive states (Barsalou *et al.* 2003). The former, perceived in others, produce, in turn, bodily mimicry in the self (Barsalou *et al.* 2003). For example, individuals who receive gratification for 'correct' behaviour (for instance, a good grade) tend to adopt a more erect posture than those who underperform (Barsalou 2003; Barsalou *et al.* 2003). Barsalou and his colleagues (2003) argued that feelings tend to be expressed with bodily posture and movements. Accordingly, it is possible to look at visitors' posture, movements and walking in order to identify higher or lower levels of self-confidence and ability to perform in the museum. Embodied practice can therefore show 'a flexible power of action and reaction' in the way visitors approach the space (Crossley 1996, 109). Contrastingly, failure to master normative practices provokes censure and anxiety (Merlau-Ponty 1962).

Negative emotions like censure, anxiety, and lack of confidence, derived from the idea that one is unable to master normative corporeal techniques trigger cultural, social and physical exclusion. Rogoff looked at the issue of participation and exclusion in the context of the 2001 contemporary art exhibition 'Shadows and Silhouettes' that took place within the corridors of the Courtauld Institute rather than in the Courtauld Gallery (2005). She observed visitors' reactions to entering a space that was usually barred to the general public (Rogoff 2005) and found that they seemed generally unimpressed by the space itself and underwhelmed by privileged access (ibid). Rogoff stated that the intent to democratise access to the space produced instead 'an embodied manifestation of the mythical and phantasmatic which kept them at a distance' (2005). In this sense, the performance of exclusion has nothing to do with entrance or access and far more to do with 'perceptions of the possible' (Rogoff 2005, 120).

Museums have made similar efforts to increase 'democratisation' and 'accessibility' and to encourage broader participation while overcoming cultural exclusion. However, for people with a physical disability in particular, access is both a social and a spatial problem. Rogoff argued that attempts to democratise and open up exhibitions which focus on their content only, can, in fact, produce spatial and embodied exclusion (2005). Such was the case of the exhibition at the Courtauld Institute. While visitors did perform a breach of privilege and cultural exclusion, they still ended up trying to figure out what had kept them outside of the space rather than participating in the cultural experience offered (Rogoff 2005, 121). In this sense, the embodied practice of visitors can create spatial exclusion, which then generates cultural and social exclusion. If the visitor senses that their corporeal techniques are 'incorrect' or non-compliant it triggers spatial exclusion, as the environment is perceived as exclusive, intimidating, or barred. Spatial exclusion, in turns, triggers social and cultural exclusion, as social and cultural participation are dependent on the situated opportunities that the body creates while it walks.

Rees Leahy developed the argument of spatial exclusion further by focusing on the inability of visitors to adhere to normative practices despite being aware of them (2012). Knowing 'what to do' in theory does not necessarily mean that all visitors have the physical abilities, desire, or energy to do it in practice. Disciplined walking and visual concentration trigger what Gilman describes as 'museum fatigue' (1916) while walking creates bodily fatigue. The process of walking from one object to the other, the exercise of standing still while looking, the effort to maintain a posture that facilitates the social learning experience, and the effort to digest objects and content deprive the body of energy as the visit progresses. The quality of the 'felt' bodily experience changes as the walking continues, and the status of the body-in-space is variable. In the case of temporary or permanent physical impairments, the effort required is often more significant, in some cases impractical or even impossible.

'Museum fatigue', together with impairments, trigger the dys-appearance that has been examined in chapter 2, section 2.3. Rees Leahy argued that bodies in museums are 'recalcitrant', and they 'rebuke' the museum's normative practices and 'resist the official script' (2010, 163). She stated that bodies, precisely due to the situated nature of the museum experience, do not fully comply with the norms and goes as far as defining normative practice as 'fashions' that non-compliant or tired visitors' bodies struggle to follow (2010, 164). While on the one hand, non-compliance to normative practices may trigger social exclusion, if we look at bodily practices as forms of authoritative speech and affirmations of self-presence (Butler 1993), resistance to normative practices must be understood as a form of self-affirmation and an exercise of binding power. Defiance of conventional museums scrips and imposed practices become a form of political resistance where traditionally excluded bodies reclaim their right to participate and re-appropriate of the space. The affirmation of intractable and untrained bodies and the resistance to imposed behaviours and practices must be read as a cultural appropriation and spatial self-affirmation. Although the attempt to organise and regulate visitors' movements is a crucial goal of museum design, it is necessary to acknowledge the unfolding of non-conforming bodily engagements as part of the museum narrative (Tzortzi 2014).

In the case of BPSP, the spatial exclusion, subsequent dys-appearance, and possible resistance to it depend on several factors. Firstly, it depends on the type and the level of vision impairment and its effect on the body (vom Lehn 2010). This directly links to the level of comfort and discomfort experienced in the space (Hayhoe 2017). Impairments, for instance, can be linked to other conditions that debilitate the body. Secondly, it depends on the habitus of the individual, the level of confidence and independence in performing everyday tasks that the visitor brings in the museum (Kleege 2018). The process of building confidence in the space can be entirely undermined while experiencing socio-spatial exclusion. Finally, it depends on the support and guidance that the BPS visitor has access to during the visit from their companion, the museum staff, and other visitors (Hayhoe 2017). The familiarity of the BPS visitor with the museum environment plays a crucial role in developing confidence and expertise on 'how to do the museum' (Candlin 2010). Due to the vision impairment, it is more challenging (if not impossible) for BPSP to acquire the 'normative' bodily techniques through the process of emulation, and to negotiate the 'correct' positioning while walking through the environment. There is a lack of research on how BPSP learn 'how to behave', how to walk, orientate, and position their bodies in the museum, and this volume aims to help fill this gap.

In this section, I looked at implicit and explicit guidance from the museum – or lack of thereof – that visitors draw from to improve their embodied practice in the space. The section presented an account of the lack of explicit guidance on walking and looking in museums. The following sections expand on the embodied practices of visitors in museums, critically discussing key embodiment characteristics in museums, like gesturing, walking, looking, touching and using resources.

3.4. Gesturing and pointing

In section 3.3, I mentioned emulation and mimicry as one of the methods to acquire corporeal techniques in museums. Then, I briefly presented how different vision impairments can hinder emulation, and I discussed the need to obtain data about BPS visitors embodied experience in museums to understand how they 'learn' to move in the exhibition space and read to the museum script. I present gesturing as one characteristic of embodiment, which is part of visitors' practice in the museum and can potentially be hindered by vision impairments.

Pointing at, mimicking, orienting the body towards a certain object or a person are gesturing activities that visitors perform in the museum. Gestures have been analysed as a repository of practices that employ the hands and body to make meaning in situated social contexts (Streeck 2009a; -2009b). Different studies have categorised gesturing in different ways, both in regard to hands gesturing and body gesturing (Kendon 2004; McNeill 1992; Steier *et al.* 2015.). However, there is a consensus among more recent studies to categorise gesture as situated, according to their function in context (Kendon 2004; Steier *et al.* 2015).

Goldin-Meadow and her colleagues performed several studies analysing how adults and children gestured while solving cognitive tasks (in particular basic mathematical problems) (Alibali and Goldin-Meadow 1993, 484; Goldin-Meadow *et al.* 2001). They monitored the relationship between gesture and speech in each explanation and solution of the mathematical problem (ibid). Findings were consistent among adults and children. Individuals who learned to solve the mathematical problem correctly matched gestures to their speech (Goldin-Meadow *et al.* 2001, 519). They also observed how individuals who initially came up with incorrect answers also did not gesture (Alibali and Goldin-Meadow 1993, 485). However, as soon as they started gesturing, they would correct their initial response to ensure that their words matched their gestures, giving the correct response (Alibali and Goldin-Meadow 1993, 485; Goldin-Meadow *et al.* 2001, 521). This is consistent with the conceptualisation of learning as profoundly rooted in embodied experiences. Gesturing can be understood as a practice that enables meaning-making and contribute to the experience of understanding (Roth and Lawless 2002). Gesturing provides a significant cognitive purpose for the speaker as it allows them to think and communicate things clearly and understandably (Roth 2002).

Iverson and Goldin-Meadow (1997; -1998; -2001; Iverson 1999) discussed the function of gesturing for blind people within a mainstream approach to gesturing research. Their research showed how even people who were blind since birth gesture while they talk, in the same way sighted people do (ibid). The framework of their study was to analyse how people learn how to gesture (ibid). Their study concluded that gesturing has a function beyond the mere scope of communication (ibid). In fact, for congenitally blind people, it would be impossible to learn gesturing movements from watching others move their hands while talking. However, despite their lack of a visual model to emulate, their study showed how blind people still gestured, even in the presence of other blind people (ibid). Blind people did not appear to need experience receiving or observing gestures before they spontaneously gesture on their own (ibid). Iverson and Goldin-Meadow (1997; -1998; -2001; Iverson 1999) suggested that this is because speakers, both blind and sighted, gesture both because of their understanding that gestures can convey information to the listener and because gesturing facilitates the speaking process. Gestures do not seem to depend on a model or an observer, but they appear to be an integral part of the speaking process (ibid). Therefore, Gesturing is a deeply situated embodied practice, which BPSP can draw from to make sense of normative corporeal techniques in the space and position their bodies according to the museum script.

3.5. Walking

While the previous section discussed the embodied practice of gesturing in relation to learning and, in particular, learning how to read the museum script, this section turns to look at another characteristic of embodiment in museums: walking. Walking is one of the primary aspects of embodiment in museums. Harris (2015, 102) argued that museums are places of various narratives which walking visitors bring in. If museums are seen as social spaces it is necessary to acknowledge the presence of visitors' walking and looking bodies (both individuals and groups). Walking facilitates a visitors' understanding of the space through accessing objects and interacting with other visitors. Groups of people walking to the museum, walking together through the exhibition space, and stopping in front of exhibits scaffold how they do the exhibition by setting a pace and negotiating spatial priorities.

Walking as an embodied practice shapes the museum experience. The deep relationship between and thinking (or meaning-making) dates back in the Western tradition to the Peripatetic philosophers like Aristotle, who performed teaching while walking (Fontana-Giusti 2007, 258). In the museum, individuals and groups choose to follow different paths which shape the narratives (and the way visitors make meaning through their bodies) as they guide the walking bodies but are at the same time shaped as the walk progresses (Harris 2015). Different stories or narratives offer a different atmosphere. In some cases, narratives flow evenly and horizontally, but other times the path can be chaotic and even unruly depending on how the walking body approaches the route (Lund 2012). Therefore, walking narrates the landscape as a phenomenological aspect of life (ibid). As a situated practice, walking can be seen as social and embodied.

Harris asked, 'what does it mean to walk [in a museum] […] behind the disembodied eye?' (2015, 106). Within the vision-centric museum narrative, walking is often a taken-for-granted corporeal technique and situated practice that visitors bring with them (Rees Leahy 2012). Mauss (1973) described walking as a learnt, acquired, and culturally specific corporeal practice. As seen in the previous chapter (section 2.5), Mauss (1973) looked at these 'techniques of the body' as part of the habitus of individuals. Ingold (2000) argued that walking and specifically learning to walk is an acquired skill within the social and cultural environment. Since walking is a practice influenced mainly by the social and physical environment in which it takes place, it must be examined as a situated practice that contributes to the way individuals make meaning in the space.

Walking is a conscious or unconscious act of exploration; visitors decide the direction from, and pace at which, they discover their surroundings (Lund 2012, 226). As visitors walk, they simultaneously create opportunities to learn about the environment and about their own bodies (ibid). In this sense, the practice of walking through the space shapes directly how individuals make meaning and scaffolds the way groups make sense together. The body, through walking, brings together the 'inner world' of the visitor with the 'outer world' (Harris 2015), and by doing so, induces an 'intense feeling of self-presence' (Rees Leahy 2012, 79).

According to Rees Leahy (2012, 79), this 'feeling of self-presence' enables a higher awareness of oneself within the environment. She specifically described the unforeseen and undesirable behaviour of visitors in Tate Modern's exhibition 'Shibboleth' (2007) as an affirmation of self-presence that ran counter to museum authority (Rees Leahy 2012, 112). In this case, visitors were expected to walk along the line of artist Salcedo's fissure that ran across the floor of the museum's Turbine Hall (Rees Leahy 2012, 111). However, visitors' bodies did not respond to the museum script and started to trip, fall, touch, and consciously or unconsciously refuse to commit to walking the entire length of the fissure (ibid). Rees Leahy discussed these behaviours as going explicitly against normative bodily practices (ibid). She argued that visitors' made their meaning through a series of social embodied performances: 'hands were held across the crack at its widest points. Children stood arms akimbo over it, peering downwards. Groups clustered as if in consultation at the points where it deepened or changed direction' (Rees Leahy 2012, 111). Meaning-making was effectively an embodied and social performance.

This combination of walking, thinking, exuding self-presence and cultivating self-awareness and empowerment serves to encounter the space. In the museum context (and in public spaces generally), the walker asserts their self-presence and becomes self-aware of the positioning of their body within the environment and also in relation to other walking bodies. Walking can be seen as an empowering practice, as it makes the walker central in the spatial reality and in relation to other bodies. In this sense, the walker enunciates themselves in the space as they become aware of their physical reality and assert their presence in the environment.

As well as a social and embodied practice, Solnit (2001) described walking as a cultural act. She traced a connection from the writings of Peripatetic philosophers to Rousseau, all of whom associated the ability to think, meditate, teach, and speak to the act of walking. This type of walking described as a 'kind of unstructured, associative thinking', fits within my conceptualisation of walking as situated (Solnit 2001, 21). Walking can be considered a cultural act as it creates situated opportunities where walking enables the integration of the inner and outer worlds of the person who walks (or the groups who walk) and allows the walker to 'perceive their environment and react to external stimuli' (Rees Leahy 2012, 79).

In the following subsections, I expand upon the practice of walking, and specifically walking in a museum with a vision impairment. The focus shifts from what it means to walk to how BPSP learn to walk in the museum and how they adapt their walking rhythm to that of others.

3.5.1. *Walking with a vision impairment*

In the case of BPS visitors, the walking practice is deeply connected to their type of vision impairment and use of different walking aids. If we look back at Hirose's (2001) metaphor of the walking stick of the visually impaired person that becomes part of the body in an act of embodiment, it is clear how critical walking aids are in the discussion of embodied walking. BPSP use multiple navigation and walking aids, usually based on the type, level, and severity of the vision impairment they have (Giudice and Legge 2008; Worth 2013). Those with enough residual vision usually do not use navigation aids but instead rely on low- and high-tech resources (ibid). People with more severe impairments might opt for white canes (also called walking sticks), guide dogs, a sighted guide, handheld sensors, and different assistive technology devices. The purpose of these aids is to help BPSP walk through familiar and unfamiliar environments by orientating them, providing information about obstacles, and helping them picture the physical surroundings. Thus, the walking practice of BPSP outside and inside the museums is directly shaped by the use (or lack thereof) of mobility aids.

Previous research has shown how BPSP tend to visit museums in the same range of ways as sighted people, that is accompanied by another person, in groups, or independently (Asakawa *et al.* 2018; Candlin 2010; Hayhoe 2017; Kleege 2018). However, there is little research and evidence on how BPSP tend to use navigation aids in the museum. This lack of data on whether they enact the same familiar techniques or everyday practices that they use outside the museum makes it challenging to understand their walking practice in the space.

Several museums in London and across the UK formally offer guiding services for BPSP which are bookable-in-advance, with smaller museums often offering walk-in services. For instance, the V&A offers one-hour private touch tours bookable in advance with a trained guide who accompanies the visually impaired visitor and their companions (V&A 2021). Similarly, front of house staff at the Charles Dickens Museum (London) and the Museum of Cambridge offer to guide visually impaired people around if they require it when the museum is not particularly busy (from personal communication). Some museums also offer digital guidance and technology to facilitate the visit. For example, the British Museum's self-guided touch tour of the Egyptian Gallery uses specifically designed audio-description devices (British Museum 2021). Another example is the series of free audio-described tours offered by the Wellcome Collection, which can be downloaded or streamed directly on visitors' mobile devices (Wellcome Collection 2021a). In general, guide dogs are allowed in most museum buildings, and carers are often allowed to escort BPSP free of charge. In addition, staff members are usually trained to assist BPSP and provide information on the available resources (Ginley 2013). I am not going into details about the effectiveness of these resources; however, it is worth pointing out that previous research has outlined how the museum environment can be unfamiliar and difficult to navigate with a vision impairment (Asakawa *et al.* 2018; Candlin 2010; Hayhoe 2017; Kleege 2018; vom Lehn 2010).

Museums' layouts and floorplans are not straightforward. Objects, cases, benches, panels, mounts, and other exhibitions elements are scattered throughout the rooms, usually without a specific (or at least intuitive) order (Candlin 2010). Paths are irregular and confusing (Ginley 2013). In several cases, rooms do not have set routes and visitors are encouraged to walk freely (Hayhoe 2017). Bumping into an object or a case is not unusual (Manduchi and Kurniawan 2011). Learning how to position the body in relation to space, content, and other people is complex, even for sighted visitors (ibid). Cecilia's (2021b) study on BPSP's motivation showed that all participants in her research claimed that navigating through the unfamiliar museum space was a primary concern before their visit. The attention of previous research on the experience of BPSP traditionally focused on the concept of inclusion from a political perspective, and of access to content and information (Candlin 2010; Hayhoe 2017; Kleege 2018; vom Lehn 2010).

Vom Lehn (2010) employed marketing research and video recording methods to investigate how BPSP examine and make sense of artworks through tactile resources and how they interact with sighted companions and guides. He carried out the study in a London-based museum where BPSP visited an exhibition accompanied by a sighted guide (vom Lehn 2010). The exhibition featured several tactile objects and vom Lehn observed how the guide and the BPS visitor organised their access and examination of the object (2010). His study focused on the social action and the techniques used by BPSP to orient themselves among, and make sense of the actions of others. He analysed how the interaction between BPSP and their sighted guides produced shared experiences of the museum content (ibid). Hence, the analysis focused on the ways in which the participants established shared perspectives and experiences of the exhibits in and through their talk and interaction with and around the works of art (vom Lehn 2010). While the employment of video recordings as a method represents a significant contribution to the understanding of participants' shared orientation and shared experience of touch, vom Lehn's discussion focused primarily on the social situation and

social action, rather than reflecting on the embodied nature of meaning.

While there have been studies about access to space and content (Asakawa *et al.* 2018; Ginley 2013; Mesquita and Carneiro 2016; vom Lehn 2010), these tend to present them as a spatial issue, disregarding the social nature of the problem, or vice versa. All the barriers that BPSP face when they enter a museum have been detailed, but little research has been conducted on the actual embodied practice of BPS visitors' walking practice.

If walking is a situated practice and people learn how to walk as they walk, how are BPSP supposed to learn if they do not have visual access to the walking practice of other individuals? Despite Kwon and Sailer's argument (2015) that all senses can provide some awareness of others s in the space, there is little clarity on whether or how this can happen if someone has a vision impairment. So, how do BPSP learn to walk in the museum? What kind of pressures does the museum environment place on the practice of walking, especially for BPSP? In order to answer these questions, it is necessary to take a step back and to look at the discussion around co-presence and co-awareness.

3.5.2. Co-presence, co-awareness & co-walking

While bodies walk in the space and become aware of their embodied reality, they also have to negotiate their walking practice in relation to other walking bodies. In order to present the walking practice of visitors in relation to other walkers, it is necessary to look at the concept of co-presence, a concept that comes primarily from urban planning studies, geography, and urban design disciplines. It explores how different individuals approach and co-exist in public spaces and target issues like urban segregation (Lageby 2013). Furthermore, it is used to understand how public spaces facilitate co-existence and how individuals position themselves in relation to others in the space (Jacobs 1989). This latter conceptualisation is especially useful for studying how people walk in museums together with others. Co-presence can be adapted for this research as 'co-walking', namely the practice of walking through the space together with other walking individuals and social groups. Lageby (2013, i) argued that 'by sharing space and being co-present with others, which does not necessarily imply focused interaction, we gain information and knowledge from our fellow citizens and participate in processes that negotiate social structures, acceptable behaviours and identities'. This applies to the museum context: if we look at learning and participation as situated, sharing the space, being co-present, and co-walking contribute to creating situated learning opportunities within the community of practice.

Sharing the museum space with other walking bodies becomes a central part of the museum social experience. Thobo-Carlsen's (2016) autoethnographic study in the exhibition 'Riverbed' shows that 'walking is a social activity even if you walk alone' (2016, 145). He argued that walking through the unfamiliar Icelandic landscape featured in the exhibition made him aware of the different ways of walking and looking promoted in the unspoken exhibition script (Thobo-Carlsen 2016). He described the meaning he made in the space by 'touching the stones, stepping into the stream of water, listening to the sounds, looking at the others, gaining eye-to-eye contact, watching their movements, listening in on their conversations' (Thobo-Carlsen 2016, 146). Although he visited 'Riverbed' alone, the fact that he did not know 'how to walk' in that specific environment made him more aware of other walking and performing bodies (ibid). These findings support the idea that walking bodies are constantly reactive to the other moving bodies in the surrounding environment (Ingold 2011). In order words, bodies are co-present in the space.

Co-walking has a direct impact on learning and meaning-making. Understanding the way spatial configurations relate to the social practice of visitors offers a better understanding of how they make meaning of the environment together, and how they access objects and resources. In this sense, it is essential to ask how the physical space relates to the social space. Applying the concept of co-presence it can be argued that the community of practice in the museum is dependent on social relations and social networks that, in turn, are dependent on the physical space (Jacobs 1989; Lageby 2013). In the museum, visitors encounter other visitors in the situated context of interaction (Giddens 1984, 64). This interaction happens with others who are physically co-present in the space (ibid). In some cases, visitors employ different modalities, which Goffman terms 'involvement shields' by Goffman (1963, 39), to minimise or avoid social contact and exchanges with other co-walkers.

Co-walking, like co-presence, is a deeply embodied practice grounded in the perceptual and social modalities of the body. Visitors become co-present, and co-walk as they feel they are in close proximity to be perceived while acting and walking, as they experience others, and as they sense being perceived (Goffman 1963, 17). Co-walking aims to enable a deeper understanding of the bodily experience and embodied activity within co-presence. In the case of museums, co-walking focuses on how visitors adapt their walking practice in relation to the other visitors walking in the space. People who are co-present can be seen as 'the raw material for community' (Hillier 1996, 141). When visitors are co-present and co-walk, they use their bodies to indirectly communicate with each other, and they adapt the way they move.

An example of this is Rees Leahy's finding that visitors adapt their walking rhythm in relations to others (2012). In her discussion of walking as an institutionalised and inculcated bodily technique, she explored how this adaption of pace and rhythm (in other words, being co-present) is symptomatic of cultural competence (Rees Leahy 2012, 75). Rees Leahy drew a comparison between walking in a modern-day gallery and art galleries in private houses

in the 19th century (Rees Leahy 2012). While in modern-day galleries (especially large institutions), visitors often complain about the amount of walking required to see the collection, 19th-century private galleries were often specifically used for walking exercises (Rees Leahy 2012, 78). The collections were added for the purpose of entertaining walkers during their journey along corridor-like gallery structures (ibid). The galleries themselves were considered social spaces for the consumption of social walkers: people were expected to walk together and calibrate their pace with those around them (ibid). Despite complaints about the amount of walking, she argued that social walking remains unaltered in modern-day galleries as visitors still calibrate their walking practice to that of others (ibid). In other words, they are co-present with other bodies that walk the same space.

Hence, if co-presence is the primary form of awareness of others (Hillier 1996), it is reasonable to argue that visitors become aware of how others walk around them in the museum. Doxa (2001) describes this as 'co-awareness'. Kwon and Sailer (2015) clarified that co-awareness could be felt through all senses, including vision, touch, sound or smell. Of course this is relevant for BPS visitors who primarily rely on non-visual sensory experiences.

According to Rees Leahy (2012) co-awareness of the presence of other walking bodies makes visitors walk in company and at a pace rhythmically aligned to that of others, both in their group and around them. According to Ingold and Vergunst (2008, 1), walking is a deeply social activity which concerns 'timings, rhythms and inflections' as the body responds to the pace and stride of other walkers (Ingold and Vergunst 2008). They applied a phenomenological framework to analyse the walking practice of anthropologists conducting ethnographic studies (Ingold and Vergunst 2008, 3). They argued that ethnographers rarely reflect on walking itself despite the fact that the essence of the ethnographic investigation is walking around with participants, and that the topic often appears in fieldnotes (Ingold and Vergunst 2008). Their analysis showed how everyday practices all 'takes place, in one way or the other, on the move' (Ingold and Vergunst 2008, 4); walking with others and being aware of others walking around them is the foundation for practice (Ingold and Vergunst 2008). The fact that people are social while they walk is what makes walking social (ibid).

Following Ingold and Vergunst's framework, Curtis (2008) analysed the walking practice of classes of primary school children whom she escorted along the streets of Aberdeen (Scotland) to enhance their awareness of the city's architectural heritage. She observed how children followed a trail and frequently stopped to make observations (ibid). Observations happened when children stopped, failing to acknowledge walking as a practice of observation (ibid). Failure to acknowledge the social role of walking reduces it to the act of getting from point A to point B. Curtis argued that the walking practice of children is instead deeply social: while walking, children are expected to behave in a particular way, following social rules and calibrating their practice to that of their peers (2008). While their attention was supposedly focused on road safety, children made sense of their surrounding as they walked (Curtis 2008, 153). Curtis argued that children gathered and processed information when they stopped walking, through the act of walking together, and by being aware of the surrounding environment about which they were learning (2008).

The same analysis can be applied in the museum context. As Rees Leahy puts it, 'whether or not we talk to, or even meet the eye of, our fellow visitors, we keep pace with each other, overtake, then fall back, and take turns to stand in front of successive exhibits' (2012, 78). Co-awareness produces a conscious or unconscious response from those in the same perceptual range (Christidou and Diamantopoulou 2016; Goffman 1981; vom Lehn 2013).

Christidou and Diamantopoulou's (2016) investigation of co-presence within family engagement in the Wellcome Collection's exhibition space (London) shows how the presence of others in the space influences visitors' embodied practice. Visitors start negotiating their co-presence when members of the same group disperse and re-join, and they calibrate their co-presence when they encounter strangers (Christidou and Diamantopoulou 2016, 23). Specifically, these researchers looked at the interaction of a family group comprising a mother and two daughters using the museum family activity pack (ibid). They observed how one of the daughters took the lead following the pack instructions (ibid). The child at first focused her attention on the activity leaflet and subsequently shifted her attention to look for the rest of her group (ibid). Christidou and Diamantopoulou (2016, 23) observed how her bodily positioning, gestures, and gazing represent an embodied performance of her shift in attention to monitor the co-presence of her group. Within the same 'participation framework' (Goffman 1981, 226), another adult (not part of the family group) walked near the child (Christidou and Diamantopoulou 2016, 23). In order to exclude the newcomer from her encounter, while still monitoring her group's co-presence, the child positioned her body away from the newcomer and used person-reference verbal cues to attract the attention of her mother (Christidou and Diamantopoulou 2016, 26). These interactions support the claim that visiting an exhibition is a deeply social activity as both the mother and the daughter were constantly responsive to the presence and movements of others in the surrounding environment (Christidou and Diamantopoulou 2016, 27). Visitors seem to orient their bodies towards or away from others to include or exclude them (Christidou and Diamantopoulou 2016, 26). In doing so, they maintain control and negotiate their co-presence in the space.

Similarly, Heat and his colleagues (2002) looked at how exhibitions can facilitate co-participation and collaboration between groups and also between people who happen to be in the same 'perceptual range' (Goffman 1981, 226). They analysed visitors' interactions at the mixed-media installation 'Deus Oculi' at the Chelsea International Crafts Fair in 1999 (Heat *et al*. 2002). They observed the interaction of two couples who did not previously know each other but happened to be in the same place, experiencing the installation (Heat *et al*. 2002, 24). The installation featured two fake mirrors connected to CCTV cameras and a main painting of a Renaissance scene (Heat *et al*. 2002, 13). When someone looked at one of the fake mirrors, their face appeared in the Renaissance painting (ibid). While the woman from the first couple looked at the fake mirror, her face appeared in the main painting, which the woman from the second couple was looking at (ibid). This forced co-presence, facilitated by the installation itself, provoked initial surprise and amusement (ibid). This then evolved into the two couples shifting positions in the space to figure out how the installation worked (ibid). Their co-presence then evolved into an act of co-participation, as they temporarily interacted to make sense of the object. These findings suggest that the co-presence of others in the surrounding environment influences the way people orient their bodies, what they choose to look at, and how they make meaning of objects and interactions (Heat *et al*. 2002, 23). Furthermore, certain interactive exhibitions can facilitate a shift from co-presence to co-participation, where people who happen to be in the same perceptual range temporarily interact to make sense of specific objects or exhibits.

Co-presence can therefore be seen as both a resource that visitors can draw up onto inform their interpretation and meaning-making, and also a factor which informs their behaviour, conduct, and movement in the environment 'moment-by-moment' (Christidou 2016). Visitors can monitor co-presence, thus allowing interacting individuals to monitor others who are present and adjust their conduct and movement accordingly (Cahagan 1984; Christidou and Diamantopoulou 2016; Goffman 1963). Monitoring co-presence enables visitors to mediate, negotiate, adjust, regulate and refine the way they move and perform to achieve an 'ideal behaviour' in the space.

3.5.3. Walking as placemaking

The act of co-walking is deeply situated in the context in which it occurs. Therefore, the concept of placemaking can help us understand how co-walking through the museum impacts visitors' relationships with places and the process of forming such relationships. Placemaking has been referred to as the sense of being-in-the-world (Merleau-Ponty 1962). It is conceptualised within Urban Studies as marking and shaping place (Kyle and Chick 2007; Lalli 1992). Walking through museums makes people develop a layered, lived experience of the museum as a place. This occurs through day-to-day negotiations as visitors navigate physical spaces through social practices (Cresswell 2004). As visitors walk and move their bodies through a place, they make meaning and establish a sense of belonging (Cresswell 2015). For the purpose of this research, placemaking contributes to understanding the role of place within the context of the museum experience and its impact on the formation of BPSP's identity as museum visitors.

By walking in the museum, visitors make their own personal and shared meanings of place within the social context of the museum. These meanings are negotiated and refined through ongoing situated interaction with co-present visitors and the environment (Kyle and Chick 2007). Visitors' cultural and individual identities are formed through the meanings visitors ascribe to places (Stokowski 2002). The embodied act of walking makes people develop social and cultural identities that contribute to meaning-making and, therefore, to learning (Hay 1998).

Budge (2020) used placemaking to look at how museum visitors mark place as meaningful through digital interactions via the social media platform Instagram. Her performed qualitative analysis on the Instagram posts of visitors to the Museum of Contemporary Art in Sydney and Cooper Hewitt Smithsonian Design Museum in New York as markers of placemaking. The analysis demonstrated that Instagram posts created and shared by visitors are 'creative and productive acts' which reflect place as being meaningful (Budge 2020, 14). Furthermore, Budge argued that posts and tags reflected moments of engagement between visitors and with the environment where encounters held a level of significance (Budge 2020, 14). These encounters and the meaning visitors made of them was then shared with their digital communities (Budge 2020, 15).

While this book does not focus on digital and social media interaction, Budge's findings help refine how placemaking contributes to meaning-making and identity formation. For example, Boy and Uitermak (2017) previously observed that visits through museums shared in the form of tags could be seen as markers of identity and lay a claim to the place. Similarly, Gerges (2018) proposed that by using museums place tags on social media platforms, visitors from BAME backgrounds challenge 'invisibility' and amplify their voices.

If we apply the embodiment and situated framework discussed in chapter 2, the act of walking itself through the museum space can be considered as a placemaking practice that impacts visitors' meaning and identity-formation. By walking through the museum environment, visitors establish connections with the place, make meaning, and perform an affirmation of self-presence (Rees Leahy 2012). Thus, walking enhances visitors' understanding of the place, their sense of belonging, and allows them to claim the place. Additionally, it also enables visitors to establish a relationship between the museum as a place of national or municipal importance and as an institution that has an essential role within their community. In this sense, walking can be conceptualised as an act of agency and authority (Budge and Burness 2018). Agency, in this sense, comprises identity work from the visitor, including embodied practices that aim to destabilise the authority of the museum through the use of humour (Kozinets *et al.* 2017) or the defiance of normative practices (Rees Leahy 2012).

3.6. Seeing and being seen

The previous section discussed the concepts of co-presence and co-awareness and the practices of visitors in the museum space in relation to walking, standing, positioning, orientation and gesturing. In this section, I expand on the concept of co-awareness by exploring what it means to be simultaneously an active viewer and a viewing subject in the space.

Christidou and Diamantopoulou (2016) argued that while the acts of seeing, and being seen, seem grounded in the ocular centric realm, they actually are multimodal events and deeply embodied practices that contribute to meaning-making. While I discuss the ocular centric perspective and the dominance of vision in museums in more details in the following section about visual culture (section 3.7) and tactile encounters with objects (section 3.8), here I focus on the reality of bodies being at once viewers and viewing subjects in relation to other visitors in the space.

The emergence of situated learning and embodiment perspectives favoured a growing interest in embodied practices like walking, gesturing, posture, and looking as modalities of engagement employed by visitors to communicate during their visit (Christidou and Diamantopoulou 2016; Heath and vom Lehn 2002; -2004; Levent and Pascual Levone 2014; vom Lehn *et al.* 2001; vom Lehn and Heath 2007; Steier *et al.* 2015). Movements (including standing) are a key element of seeing in the museum, just as much as talking. However, while the visitor 'sees' the exhibition, they are at the same time 'being seen' in the space (Christidou and Diamantopoulou 2016; Kwon and Sailer 2015). The mutual co-awareness in the space and the consciousness of being the subject of other visitors' observation makes visitors negotiate and regulate their positioning and movements in a choreography of socially organised bodies (vom Lehn *et al.* 2001). The visitor and their groups in close proximity share the space and form a participation framework (Goffman 1981). Within this participation framework, those who are in the same spatial context as bystanders form the 'perceptual range' (ibid). Visitors negotiate and regulate their embodied practice both in relation to their participation framework and their perceptual range as they view both subjects. Heath and his colleagues argue:

> the conduct of others within the same space can influence how people orient themselves, what people choose to look at and how they experience particular objects, artefacts and events (2002, 23).

Kwon and Sailer examined the issue of inter-visibility in an interesting comparison between museums and department stores (2015). They analysed spatial usage patterns and interaction between visitors in the V&A (London) and a famous London-based department store (Kwon and Sailer

2015). They drew upon the connection between co-presence and the act of seeing and being seen, looking at co-presence as an interaction-enabler and as a 'by-product of seeing and being seen among visitors' (Kwon and Sailer 2015, 1). Their study defined the visitors who happen to share the space in museums as spatial communities characterised by proximity, as opposed to transpatial communities formed by non-spatial relationships (families, friendships, schools, professions, and similar interests) (Hillier 1996; Kwon and Sailer 2015). In this sense, transpatial groups of visitors (for instance, a family who decides to visit a museum) are also transformed into spatial communities by the museum space itself (ibid).

The act of 'seeing and being seen' is an embodied modality of communication, interaction, and representation, which is rehearsed, employed, mediated, and regulated within the social framework of the visit (Christidou and Diamantopoulou 2016). Through co-awareness, visitors develop a level of awareness of themselves and their bodies as viewing subjects, as subjects that are viewed by others, and as subjects of monitoring by the museum. (Rees Leahy 2012). In this sense, the visitor becomes aware of their relationship to the objects and starts 'sensing' that their performance in the space is the object of external scrutiny.

Because visitors are constantly scrutinised, both formally and informally (Rees Leahy 2010), the individual develops an awareness of the significance of being seen as evidence of their ability to respond to the museum's 'silent message' (or the museum script) (Wilson 1994). The duality of seeing while at the same time being seen directly affects the embodied practice of visitors, as this awareness forces them to perform as a viewing subject (Bagnall 2003). Being looked at has the potential to make one feel objectified, scrutinised, judged, and put on the spot. Previous sections have shown how visitors use embodied practices like gesturing, pointing, walking, and standing to establish themselves as social entities. This section discussed how the co-awareness of others in the museum space affects how visitors scaffold their movements, that of their group, and that of other bystanding visitors (Christidou and Diamantopoulou 2016). This further shows the situated and social nature of the embodied practice.

3.6.1. 'Being seen' as disabled

'Being seen as disabled' is something that disabled people experience throughout their lives, and it becomes part of their identity (Spirtos and Gilligan 2020). In particular, adolescents and young adults experience their disability in relation to their social groups (family, school, friends, and workplace) as they transition out of childhood disability services (ibid). Being seen as disabled is part of the process by which young disabled people define themselves in relation to their position within a social group (Hutchinson et al. 2018). An integrated identity and sense of belonging to a social group can foster feelings of self-confidence, self-worth, and empowerment (Connors and Stalker 2007).

Several studies have shown that disabled people tend to avoid others recognising their disability by physically or verbally hiding the impairment (Connors and Stalker 2007; Eisenhauer 2007; Frances 2014; Hutchinson et al. 2018; Spirtos and Gilligan 2020). Negative past experiences, and a desire to avoid ableism – whether internalised or external - influence the way disabled adults face 'being seen'. Many try to manage their disability in new social contexts by deciding in advance how and with whom they would reveal having an impairment, or by acting in a way that makes their embodied practice resemble that of non-disabled people (Campbell 2019; Dunn and Burcaw 2013; Frances 2014; Hutchinson et al. 2018; Keary 2009).

Keary (2009) observed how the self-perception of people with physical impairments (including her patients and her daughter) is significantly shaped by the public's furtive, confused, and at time openly hostile looks (Keary 2009, 170). Applying a body psychotherapy framework, she argued how 'being the object of […] gaze is hard [for the disabled person], as the difficulty around looking is the very thing that embeds the discrimination that follows on the heels of difference' (2009, 170). For example, Keary observed how one of her participants, Anne, was a lively, confident and extroverted person, but her body language did not match these traits (2009, 152). Keary concluded that her bodily practice appeared to be deliberately planned and cautiously performed (ibid).

Both Keary (2009) and Frances (2014) discussed the damaging effect of the 'do not stare' instruction often given to young children when encountering a visibly disabled person. While the intention is usually good, the effect is potentially damaging. Frances argued that children's compliance with looking away has the effect of physically distancing them from whatever was their first impression upon seeing a 'different-looking' person (2014, 200). Furthermore, when looking is not reciprocal, 'looking at' reduces the person looked at to state of abjection.

Hutchinson and her colleagues (2018) discussed the experiences of adults who acquire neurological impairments within the social model of disability framework. They observed them in their communities, analysing the factors that affected their capacity to accept the impairments as part of who they are, and recognised a pattern between participants' normative expectations for health and abilities and how they felt observed by others. They argued that the way participants were 'stared at' shaped their perception of their impairment, leading to lower levels of self-worth (Hutchinson et al. 2018, 185). If the looking was hostile, this resulted in experiences of dys-appearance as well as a 'loss of social status and lack of self-worth' in the community (Hutchinson et al. 2018, 183).

In the case of BPSP, navigation aids usually disclose their condition, and the individual has little agency on whether they want to share or hide their impairment. This visibility increases the social pressure that BPSP face when they approach unfamiliar and potentially unfriendly environments like museums. As well as trying to adhere to ableist normative practices, they face another layer of difficulty: that their disability is disclosed to other visitors in their perceptual range. While BPSP may not be visually aware of others' gazes studies have shown that they nonetheless are aware of when they become viewing subjects (Durham-Wall 2015; Ostrove and Crawford 2006; Ostrow Seidler 2011). Casual social encounters are important because cultural attitudes to disability are deeply linked to how disabled visitors experience their impairment in the museum space. For instance, Kleege (2018) explained that turning her face in the speaker's direction is often misunderstood as 'eye contact' as her eyes line up more or less with the speaker.

Garland-Thompson's (2000; -2009) research provided a powerful account of what it means for disabled people to be 'stared at', which we might consider as an 'evolution' of the status of 'being seen' that disabled and non-disabled visitors traditionally experience in museums. Staring is an intense, situated, one or two-way visual exchange that makes meaning (Garland-Thompson 2009, 9). According to Garland-Thomson, the act of staring is voluntary, but it depends on the surrounding social context (2009). Staring is the product of the embodied separation between the disabled person observed and the viewing starer. Garland-Thomson argued that understanding the act of staring is the key to unpacking why certain bodies (in this case, disabled bodies) are stared at (2009). She claims that 'the sight of a radically unusual body provokes cognitive dissonance' (Garland-Thomson 2009, 166) since a different body, one that sticks out of the crowd, violates the ableist social script, resulting in the urge to stare unapologetically (Garland-Thomson 2009). The act of being stared at is experienced as a form of violence which transforms the viewed body into an 'other' (Garland-Thomson 2009). Bodies socially marked as 'stareable' include those that are disabled and genderqueer, racially or ethnically diverse, poor, and female, and are constantly subject to this discriminating violence in several social contexts, including museums (ibid). The stare triggers a deep feeling of vulnerability and of being at fault, which generates the need for a defence, shield or escape from the look. Being stared at can be then seen as a microaggression, and even just the fear of it is being considered a disabling experience.

The reaction of disabled people who become subject to staring depends on several factors. These include age, the social context in which the staring takes place, the nature and the length of the stare, the level of empowerment of the individual, and the way they are used to dealing with stares related to their disability as part of their everyday practice (Frances 2014). Reactions are diverse. Some disabled people try to resist the staring by disguising their disability, or dys-appear under the pressure of being recognised and singled out as disabled. Others find the social dynamic of staring as intensely 'liberating assertions and representations of the self' (Garland-Thomson 2000,

335). For example, Kleege described how making her disabled body 'transgressively visible' allowed her to affirm her identity against the patriarchal and ableist order (1999). By 'being there' and 'being visible', disabled people can resist social pressure to accept limitations and to 'stay at home, out of sight and out of mind' (Kleege 2018, 9). Kleege (2018) argued that when BPSP visit museums, they assert their place in society and their right to access and participate in public institutions.

3.6.2. 'Being seen' as representation

The idea of 'being seen' in museums has gained prominence in the past twenty years in relation to the issue of representation of marginalised groups, which include disabled people. From 1998, the work of Sandell, Dodd, and their colleagues prompted conversations about social justice and equality in museums, not only in relation to access but also as an issue of cultural and political representation (Dodd *et al*. 2004; Dodd *et al*. 2008; Dodd and Sandell 2001; Janes and Sandell 2019; Sandell 1998; -2002; -2007; -2017; Sandell *et al*. 2005; Sandell *et al*. 2010; Sandell and Nightingale 2012). Representation and communication, in this sense, comprise the modalities that museums started to use to respond to the insufficient or inaccurate representation of certain cultures and specific communities in their collections and exhibitions (Sandell 2007).

'Being seen' mainly refers to the spatial response to co-presence, but can also be conceptualised as the advocacy of disabled people to be represented in museum collections, exhibitions, and narratives. The issue of representation includes all problems concerning the unequal inclusion of certain groups and subgroups, often associated with ethnicity, races, genders and in general with disadvantaged subjects (Sandell *et al*. 2010).

The experimental and mixed-method research project 'Buried in the Footnotes' by Dodd and her colleagues (2004) provided a fascinating account of how museums understand and interpret disability-related materials. Findings showed a wealth of this material in the collections, rarely displayed in a way that meaningfully acknowledges its relation to disability (Dodd *et al*. 2004). The project also found out that if disability-related material was presented and included, it mainly was displayed within a negative and stereotypical representation framework (ibid).

The 'Re-thinking Disability Representation' project further revealed the richness and diversity of responses from visitors to the representations and interpretations of disability, disabled people, and disability-themed narratives (Dodd *et al*. 2008). It included findings from nine further projects that showed how most visitors saw the issue of inclusion and disability as meaningful, and recognised the museum's role as a place for reducing prejudice and changing attitudes (ibid). The project further showed how the inclusion of the lived experiences of disabled people was essential to amplify disabled people's voices and inform and challenge negative views of disability (ibid).

Sandell and Dodd (2010) argued that there is an emerging 'activist practice' in museums in the form of raising awareness of the social and political effect that museums have when they foster human rights-based narratives. Dodd and her colleagues (2010) carried out an audience research study to analyse visitors' responses to museum projects that aimed to change attitudes towards disability-related themes. Patterns that emerged from findings showed how the museum narrative influenced the way visitors spoke about disability (Dodd *et al*. 2010). Within this framework, Sandell (2007) argued that museums could host, stimulate, shape, and inform conversations about disability among visitors.

Museums play an essential role in reframing how society perceives disability (Sandell *et al*. 2010). They do so by 'reframing, informing and enabling society's conversations about difference' (Sandell 2007, 173). When museums take a moral stance on disability and enable conversations that support human rights, they act as agents of social change (Dodd *et al*. 2010; Sandell 2007). They also inform how visitors make meaning related to disability in and outside the museum by representing disabled people in more equitable and respectful ways (Dodd *et al*. 2010). By presenting the plurality of disability experiences and addressing 'difficult stories' from disability history, museums the significance of these stories to society in the past, present and the future (Sandell *et al*. 2005). In doing so, they create an inclusive and empowering environment where, by 'being seen' in the collection, disabled people feel adequately represented and develop a new sense of belonging.

Within the debate on representation, museums are called to reconsider ways of presenting disability and the lived experiences of disabled people in their collections. They are called to listen to the voices of disabled people, to include them in the decision-making process and policy developments, and recognise the value of the history and narratives of disabled people. This book does not provide a comprehensive account of the debate around representation in museums collections, as this goes beyond the scope of this research. However, it is important to acknowledge that the lack or inaccuracy of representation of disability in museums can alienate and exclude disabled people. On the contrary, adequate representation and the inclusion of disability-related narratives are a critical empowering tool for disabled visitors as well as representing educational opportunities for all other visitors (Dodd *et al*. 2010).

While the focus of the chapter is on access and the encounter of BPSP with objects and with the environment, it is crucial to bear in mind that disabled people face other barriers. In order to create genuinely inclusive environments and empowering experiences, museums must take a holistic approach and re-assess both the content of their collection, the way it is presented, and access-related issues.

3.6.2.1. The normalisation process

The normalisation process within the disability studies framework means making everyday life practices and living conditions as close as possible to those available to disabled people (Nirje 1969). In the case of people who lose sight later in life, the normalisation process means retaining and restoring normative living conditions as close as possible to the life before sight loss (ibid). For the scope of this research, the normalisation process is understood as the possibility for visitors who lost their sight to participate in the museum experience (and in cultural activities more generally) to the same extent as their sighted companions or to before they lost their sight.

Despite the progress discussed in the previous chapter, the message that society sends to BPSP and disabled people in general remains that the 'correct' behaviour is for them is to accept their limitations graciously and to make peace with the renunciation of past interests and activities (Kleege 2018). Visiting the museum space and facing the difficulties and barriers that come with it means actively resisting dys-appearance, and creating a bridge between life before sight loss and life after. Through participation in the museum visit and other cultural activities, BPSP can retain, develop, and adapt their funds of knowledge from which they can draw to perform in the museum successfully. Being able to carry out museum-related interests despite losing sight tests BPSP identity, and it is always at least in part about their sight loss and what it represents. Additionally, participation in museum activities facilitates regular engagement with sighted people without feeling excluded by conversations about visual art and artefacts (Candlin 2003).

However, this process takes time. While museum encounters can be beneficial at an emotional level, they can also trigger a traumatic and painful experience of re-living distressing and ghastly aspects of sight loss, especially to newly disabled people or to less experienced visitors. For individuals whose sight is deteriorating, the museum experience takes a heavy emotional toll, as they have to recognise to an ever-evolving transition to a blind identity. BPS visitors are often torn between their sight loss or progressing sight deterioration and desire to continue interacting with museum collections through visual practices (Hayhoe 2017). To overcome this tension, they employ creative strategies, drawing from their funds of knowledge to adapt their practice and participate successfully and gain a rewarding experience

Harrys argued that embodied experience gives rise to strong physical responses and highly emotional engagements, as opposed to decades of the hegemony of viewing detachment (2015). She suggested that if museums acknowledged the embodied presence of visitors, the intense emotionality bound to result would be anticipated and therefore could be worked into exhibitions (Harris 2015). Latham (2012) and Soren (2009) give an example of highly emotional museum encounters turning on feelings of transportation within and mystical connection with the environment. These studies showed how visitors experienced unsettling and deeply moving moments through their bodies during their museum experience (Latham 2012; Soren 2009).

3.7. Looking

The previous sections discussed how visitors are aware of the presence of others in the space, how they look at them, and how they perceive being observed by others. This section focuses on another characteristic of the embodied practice of looking: that of looking at objects. Here, I discuss how visitors, particularly BPS visitors, encounter visual culture in museums.

Different types of vision impairments have different effects on what and how people see. 'Blind' and 'partially sighted' are generic terms that refer to a broad spectrum of different characteristics of vision. The type of vision impairment has a direct effect on the following aspects of the visual experience:

- Visual memory: People born congenitally blind or who became blind very early in life usually do not have a visual memory from before starting to lose sight. They might have an understanding of shapes and some light perception but do not usually have a visual memory of colours and other visual characteristics. People who are partially sighted with good residual vision or have lost sight later in life usually retain a good visual memory and understanding of visual concepts.
- Residual vision (or usable vision): People who are partially sighted with congenital or acquired vision impairment can retain some vision that allows them to see some or most visual characteristics.

The idea that people with sight disabilities cannot process visual concepts has been repeatedly challenged in the past decades. Traditional theoretical frameworks on understanding visual culture by BPSP are mainly based on traditional scientific epistemologies of cognition and perception, coming from medicine, cognitive psychology, and physiological approaches (Hayhoe 2017). BPSP and museums grounded in visual culture are often described as mutually incompatible within these frameworks (Hayhoe 2017). This is due to the idea that benefiting from the encounter with museum objects, especially artworks, is syllogistically connected to the performance of sight (ibid). Research has shown that BPSP enjoy museums and make meaning of their encounter with objects, suggesting that traditional logic is flawed (Hayhoe 2017; Kleege 2018). This signifies that there is a purpose for art and visual culture beyond perception (ibid). Empirical studies have found that blind people can reproduce visual metaphors and perspectives without prior education in these concepts (Kennedy 2008; Kennedy and Juricevic 2006; Heller *et al.*

2006; Hayhoe 2017; Kleege 2018). Other studies have found that perception of visual characteristics is multi-modal, and that all senses work together to form holistic images of phenomena (Bertelson and De Gelder 2004). Therefore, touch cannot be considered the only sense to inform the perception of BPSP, as erroneously believed in the past. In light of this, accessibility in museums cannot simply focus on making objects available to touch but rather on creating a comfortable environment where BPSP – as well as sighted visitors – can easily employ all their senses to access visual culture.

The concept of visual culture is grounded in the disciplinary framework of art history, aesthetics, and visual studies (Pierroux 2003). As seen in previous sections, museums are visual institutions in which vision has been traditionally viewed as the primary sense to access, experience, interpret, aesthetically judge, appreciate, and make sense of collections of objects and artworks. For centuries, the spectrum of visual experience has had a blind person at one end representing the complete absence of sight, and an artist at the other, was deemed to possess extraordinary – even magical – powers of vision (Kleege 2018). However, this view has been overturned in favour of a more embodied and multisensory experience of visual culture which acknowledges the ability of BPSP to understand, conceptualise, and even make and perform visual concepts. This section focuses on the embodied ability of BPSP to understand visual culture and concepts, rather than the performative and creative abilities of BPS artists However, it is important to note that BPS artists' performances and works significantly destabilised misconceptions about blindness and visual culture.

Following Merlau-Ponty's phenomenology of perception (1962), 'looking at' objects is an ontological process that happens at the junction between the visitor's embodied subjectivity and the museum's materiality. Heavily vision-based activities like looking at objects are deeply embodied: the viewer's body performs the action of looking and it is physically absorbed in the aesthetic qualities of the object. Carroll and their colleagues described how visitors make sense of visual culture as 'the way viewers acquire, represent and manipulate information embedded in the formal and compositional structure of artworks to recognize and evaluate their content' (2012, 48). Steier and his colleagues used the framework of embodied interpretation to analyse how visitors (in their case, non-disabled people) made sense of visual culture through embodied practice (Steier 2014; Steier *et al.* 2015). They discussed the experience of young adults aged 17–18 years old at the National Museum of Art, Architecture and Design (Oslo) (Steier *et al.* 2015) and looked at how physical actions like movements or positioning contribute to the understanding of visual culture (ibid). While their methodology and findings referred to people who primarily use vision to access visual characteristics of artworks, it is clear from their discussion that vision is not the only sense through which it is possible to make sense of visual culture (ibid). Before artworks and objects started to be mass-reproduced through photography and other reliable reproductions, a wide range of techniques was employed to describe them for readers who could not view them for themselves (Kleege 2018). We could say that before reproductions were widely available, all those who were reading about art in books were blind in some way, yet their understanding of aesthetic properties and visual appreciation of artworks was rarely challenged.

Understanding and perceiving visual culture is grounded in people's habitus just as much as it is in their sight abilities. To illustrate this point, it is helpful to look at Kleege's experience as the blind daughter of visual artists (1999; 2018). Kleege described how growing up with her parents' work, their materials, tools, conversations about visual arts, visual techniques, visits to art galleries and museums (all part of her family habitus) contributed to the knowledge she developed about art, visual culture, and visual concepts (2018). She explained how the most significant contact she had with artworks remained through touch, but that her ability to touch and use touch to understand visual concepts was a skill developed through her habitus and participation in her artist parents' community of practice (ibid). As Bourdieu argued, looking at and studying objects in museums (he specifically referred to artworks) enables the acquisition of highly formal cultural capital (1986). Cultural capital becomes then part of the habitus with social and cultural value to the individual who develops it.

BPSP who were formerly sighted tend to have a certain degree of prior knowledge of visual art, art history, and familiarity with visual terms and concepts (Kleege 2018). Depending on the condition and level of sight impairment, partially sighted people can, to differing extents, still perceive visual concepts like light and darkness, some colours, motions, outlines, shadows, forms, and shapes against surroundings (Kleege 2018). Hayhoe looked at the way BPSP with different levels and histories of impairment approached artworks (2017)[1]. The verbal content of the imaging (through audio descriptions, labels, or companions' guidance) can fill in the gaps that are missing from BPSP's immediate visual perceptions (Hayhoe 2017). Hayhoe has observed how even visitors with 'partially functioning vision' tend to be drawn to the biographical value of the object, even though, in general, their primary focus remains the aesthetic nature of artwork (2017). Hayhoe refers to this as a preference for the artworks 'aesthetic capital' (2017, 145). Blind visitors who have a congenital condition and cannot see tend to place higher importance on artwork's historical and biographical details (ibid). The values they ascribed to artworks then become objects of politics, history, or religion (ibid).

Kleege claimed that BPSP who have grown used to their impaired condition rarely rely on residual vision

to perform daily tasks since this is often unreliable and inadequate (2018). Instead, employing well-established strategies like technology, mobility devices, or relying on companions to perform everyday tasks is more efficient and painless (Kleege 2018). Perhaps, therefore, the same or similar strategies can be performed in the museum when encountering elements of visual culture. Interpretative resources like labels, audio guides, and descriptions by companions enhance the impressions that BPS visitors form ideas and opinions through their perception, even if impaired (Kleege 2018). Experienced and empowered BPS visitors do not necessarily suffer from lack of sight when approaching visual culture in specific institutions like museums can employ and rely on their learnt techniques (or funds of knowledge) to attend to their non-visual senses in different ways as during everyday practices (Kleege 2005).

Kleege stated that 'a totally blind person, even one who has never had any visual perception at all, can nevertheless conceptualize features of visual experience […] because they live in the same visual culture as the rest of us' (2018, 8). Someone totally unfamiliar with terms associated with vision and visual culture must have led a very isolated devoid of contact with any element of visual culture (2018). Kleege presents this as a paradox. If we look at the example of colour (the most basic visual concept), even congenitally blind children are exposed to the names and characteristics of colours since early childhood in schools and familiar contexts (Hayhoe 2018; Kleege 2018). The names of colours are usually associated with concepts that explain their meaning through colour-related idioms that provide accessible associations. For instance, they learn to associate blue with the sky or the sea and green with grass. They learn that colours change as the grass can turn yellow or brown, and the sky can get darker. They learn how to make paint by understanding the colour spectrum and mixing different colours together. These associations are acquired from external sources beyond immediate perception, and used for memorisation purposes by both BPS and sighted children (Kleege 2018).

Similar associations, though more complex, happen in the museum space when a visitor approaches visual culture. Visual concepts like colours or shades of paintings, for instance, are discussed and understood in relation to the style and the technique of the artist (Hayhoe 2018). The texture and appearance of sculptures can be interpreted in relations to their materials. Meaning-making happens through perception but also the discussion and interpretation of these associations. Hayhoe argued how the lack of sight provides BPS visitors with an opportunity to engage with artworks on a deeper level (2017) which allows situated relationships to be formed with the artworks and feelings of cultural ownership to develop through depth of knowledge (Hayhoe 2017). The lack of knowledge about a particular style, artist, or period can affect meaning making just as much – if not more – as the lack of sight. Hence, museums play an essential role

---

[1] This book does not necessarily distinguish between 'artworks' and 'museum objects', as its purpose is to understand how visitors physically experience and make sense of museum collections in general. Hayhoe's discussion of artworks is useful here to illustrate how BPSP make sense of visual concepts.

in developing visual cultural knowledge and forming a cultural identity beyond perception (Hayhoe 2017).

This section presented studies showing how visual culture can be potentially understood virtually and perceptually by all blind people, irrespective of their impairment. Not seeing some or all visual concepts like colour, visual depth, shapes, or shades pushes BPSP to creatively understand visual objects through a multisensory approach and to draw on their prior knowledge, habitus, and social experience of the objects in the space. The following section presents a more detailed analysis of the tactile practice of BPSP visitors as a key way in which they physically encounter objects in the space.

3.8. Touching

There has been a significant shift from museum visits based only on vision towards multisensory experiences in the past decades. Philosophically, the value of tactile experiences has been recognised as a means to understand and appreciate objects and materials (Classen 2007; Clavir 1996). In addition, touch is seen as a resource for learners to make their meanings from contact with objects (Clavir 1996; Spence and Gallace 2008). According to a survey from the UK Royal National Institute of the Blind (2005), touch is an essential element of teaching and learning for BSPS in museums (Hillis 2005).

Itis necessary to summarise the historical evolution of touch as a sense in museums to understand the role it currently holds. Touch was traditionally allowed (or at least tolerated) before the 19th century. In most cases, it was deemed a legitimate and even essential way to understand and enjoy objects and artworks. In the later part of the century touch became increasingly forbidden in museums (Saunders 2014). This coincided with the period in which museums became increasingly open to a broader section of the public whose 'untrained' or untrusted touch seemed to pose a greater threat than the 'rational' contact of the upper-classes.

Thereafter, touch remained largely forbidden for safeguarding and conservation purposes until the second half of the twentieth century (Candlin 2004; -2007; 2010; Pye 2007; Silverman 2010).

Museums have traditionally tried to regulate visitors' bodies and mould 'ideal visitors' through techniques of control such as forbidding eating, limiting the volume of talking, and prohibiting touch. Reducing sensory impact have had a profound impact on how museums function. Several scholars have analysed the social, philosophical, economic, political and cultural reasons behind such prohibitions in the Western-European museum environment after the second half of the 19th century (Candlin 2010; Chatterjee 2008a; Classen and Howes 2006; Pye 2007; Saunders 2014). Firstly, touch was considered inferior to sight following the Cartesian mind/body dichotomy. It was also thought to have no intellectual role and present risks regarding conservation and security including theft and vandalism. Finally, curators and conservators were reluctant to share their cultural privilege of creating intimate relations with objects through tactile experience (Candlin 2010).

When working class visitors were admitted through museums' doors, they were not credited with the ability to learn or enjoy through rational touch (Anderson 2003; Classen and Howes 2006). In fact, they were considered unruly, destructive, and potentially dangerous for the safeguarding of collections (Appleton 2001). Their exclusion from cultural institutions was perpetuated in light of the elitist privileges of the upper classes (Classen and Howes 2006; Silverman 2010). The ban of touch was perpetuated during the 20th century in almost every European museum, a notable exception being the 1976 tactile exhibition held at the Tate Gallery in London (Hetherington 2003; Saunders 2014). Tactile restrictions in museums are still the norm nowadays, mostly due to preventive conservation and curatorial reasons (Candlin 2004; -2006; -2010; Saunders 2014). However, these are constantly challenged and resisted through the implementation of multisensory museum experiences.

The role of multisensory experiences (especially tactile ones) has been reassessed in light of national and international legislation that aims to facilitate access to museums for disabled people; of public funding regulations that require museums to be more accessible; and of a shift in the value of material culture in the communication of cultural heritage (Candlin 2006; Chatterjee 2008b; Classen and Howes 2006; Gadoua 2014; Pye 2007; Romanek and Lynch 2008). The revaluation of touch began by examining the sensory history of 18th and 19th-century museums (Howes 2014; Rees Leahy 2012) and it is now recognised as a way to enhance understanding of objects and materials (Classen 2007; Clavir 1996). Literature has primarily focused on objects' visual nature, highlighting the emotional importance of being able to touch objects (Hayhoe 2017; Levent and Pascual-Leone 2014; Wojton *et al.* 2016). Four main reasons for tactile engagement were identified: learning about the object, aesthetically appreciating the object, experiencing a feeling of intimacy, and healing (Classen 2005; -2012; -2016; Candlin 2010; Chatterjee 2008b; Dudley 2010; Howes 2014). The revaluation of touch trend began as part of a general direction to make museums more engaging and interactive for visitors (Hooper-Greenhill 1994; -1995) and make museum collections accessible for BPSP (Candlin 2010).

Traditional approaches to accessibility in museums for BPSP have developed the practice of offering special courses and tours largely based on touch (Axel and Levent 2003; Hayhoe 2017; Kleege 2013). Both Hayhoe (2017) and Kleege (2013) reflected that special separated activities that are usually structured and require guidance separates BPSP from sighted visitors and, therefore, from the museum's social context. Guarini (2015) and Davis (2008) stated that access and inclusion could not be reduced to merely providing information or tokenistic 'special' tours or handling sessions. They advocated for a universal policy to offer parity of exhibitions in the museum for disabled and abled bodied people (ibid), and pointed out that inclusion relates to the intangible just as much as the tangible sphere of practice in the museum (ibid). Davis specifically claimed that 'access means that there is an equal opportunity for the disabled to enjoy any public presentation' (2008, 21). Hayhoe (2017) carried out interviews with BPSP in several US museums. He observed how one of his participants, who identified as blind, shunned the touch tours offered by his local museum as he felt that they defeated the point of his visit (Hayhoe 2017, 181). For this participant, visiting museums was an opportunity to connect and share an experience with his friends and family, whether blind or sighted (ibid). Hence, being removed from this social space in favour of a special separated activity triggered feelings of exclusion (ibid).

An inclusive, holistic approach was first advocated and implemented by Ginley (2013) at the V&A (London) and Krantz (2013) at the Guggenheim Museum (New York). They advocated for removing physical barriers to touch in the galleries, specialist staff awareness training, the development of technology, and the employment of disabled people as access and inclusion officers (Ginley 2013; Krantz 2013). Their approach overcame the separation between BPSP and sighted visitors, as it allowed them to share the space, enabling a social experience of the collection and the environment. This holistic approach included the possibility of touching specific objects that were deemed risk-free or at lower risk by conservators (Ginley 2013; Krantz 2013). These objects could[?] be put on open display for everyone to touch, usually paired with interpretation about the material and the manufacturing techniques (ibid). This can happen in the form of hands-on desks, or the objects might be exhibited as part of the permanent displays (Ginley 2013). In the case of contemporary art, often visitors were invited and encouraged to engage with artworks physically (Krantz 2013). Finally, several studies have started to look at 3D prints and other types of replicas as access strategies when objects cannot be touched due to conservation reasons (Ballarin *et al.* 2018; Cecilia 2019; Sandberg 2016; Wilson *et al.* 2018; Wilson *et al.* 2020)[2].

In section 3.5.1, I briefly presented vom Lehn's (2010) study on how BPS museum visitors examine and make sense of artworks through tactile resources and interaction with sighted companions and guides. His work offers an interesting contribution to the understanding of the value of touch and tactile resources not only to access objects, but also to facilitate the social situated experience between the visitor and the sighted companions (vom Lehn 2010). Specifically, vom Lehn (2010) argued that visitors and their sighted guides or companions orient

to the different ways in which they have access to the artworks through touch. He considered this mutual orientation as a collaborative effort to understand how the other person accesses the artworks. He observed how BPS visitors adapted their tactile examination to the verbal guidance offered by sighted guides and, in turn, how sighted guides used observations of the tactile experience to adapt their verbal guidance (vom Lehn 2010). Touch can therefore be considered as an enabler of social interactions and as a tool to scaffold the learning experience.

Despite remarkable developments and innovations in creating and offering multisensory experiences, work remains to recognise how multisensory experiences can be incorporated into everyday museum practices (Hayhoe 2013a). A multisensory experience is not only a powerful vehicle to prevent BPSP from being defined only in relation to their disability when accessing objects (Candlin 2003; Grandjean 2000), but is also a meaningful resource for all visitors (Wojton 2016). In fact, touch leads back to the stimulus of exploring material through a multisensory approach that fulfils curiosity about what an object is, how it feels like, how it is made, and how it functions (Davidson *et al.* 1991). Several studies have shown the positive impact of hands-on exhibits, tactile resources, and tactile engagement activities for BPS and sighted people (Cavazos Quero *et al.* 2018; Cecilia 2021b; De Coster and Loots 2004; Wilson *et al.* 2020; Udo and Fels 2010).

Tactile encounters in most museums are conceived as an additional way to look at the objects from a closer perspective (Candlin 2006; Pye 2007; Saunders 2014). However, this view underestimates the potential of touch as a standalone learning tool. While some of the information provided by the sense of touch can overlap with that of sight, touch grants details that are inaccessible to sight alone, like the quality of the fabric, its texture, shape, actual dimensions, temperature, the way different materials interact with one another, flaking or powdering, moisture, dryness, waxiness, or stickiness (Jones 2007). Touch supplies information that sight cannot detect (McGlone 2008).

Spence and Gallace (2008) argued that tactile investigation does not aim to create the mental image of an object as vision. It is essential to understand that touch is not a surrogate of vision (Spence 2007). Material culture properties such as texture, weight, temperature, shape and size create a different understanding of an object and the message that it embodies (Gadoua 2014). Handling enables the development of a spatial and tactile figure that is otherwise incomplete and sometimes misleading (Spence and Gallace 2008). In light of this, tactile experiences should not be relegated to a mere 'quick touch': touch needs to be examined as a sense, and BPSP should be taught and guided to touch (Gallace and Spence 2008). Learning and mastering tactile techniques can be seen as part of the normative practices of the experienced museum visitors examined in section 3.3.

---

[2] Since this research focuses not on the authenticity of museums objects but rather on how visitors make meaning, I do not make a formal distinction between visitors touching original objects and replicas.

Although mental images are often associated with sight alone, tactile experience plays a crucial role in their formation (Spence 2007). Given the limited role of sight for BPSP, other senses become necessary in forming mental images (Spence and Gallace 2008). Therefore, touching becomes a primordial need in the museum context to create those mental images that foster understanding of objects (Spence and Gallace 2008).

Tactile investigation is often put on the same level as vision investigation, disregarding the different epistemology of the two sense (Landman *et al.* 2005). Unlike vision, touch is mostly analytical and sequential and requires an elaboration of the elements perceived by adding them together to obtain a structured set of information (Lancioni 2006). Because of the serial nature of tactile processing, it demands a wider working memory and a considerable degree of processing (Garip and Bülbül 2014). Therefore, it is necessary to design communicative strategies that consider the specific amount of time required for tactile appreciation and the different information it conveys. Similar to walking, no official guidance on how to touch is given in museums unless one is part of a specifically organised touch tour Such guidance (formal or informal) would be beneficial for both BPSP and sighted visitors.

A general misconception can be identified when it is assumed that tactile exploration aims to recognise the shape of an object by tracing its outline (Kleege 2018). This comes from the misconception that viewing an object was solely a matter of identification. Tactile exploration encompasses and engages the wider spectrum of touch sensation, including forms and shapes, texture, temperature, and resiliency (Kleege 2018). Tactile exploration rarely focuses on the mere translation of visual features. Rather, it draws attention to characteristics that cannot be detected by the naked eye (Kleege 2018). Kleege argued against the over-determined analogy which relates touch in BPSP to sight in sighted people (2018) for failing to acknowledge the presence of other senses and the skills of BPSP to draw analogies from nonvisual experiences in order to develop concepts about visual culture (Kleege 2018). Touch in BPSP is not more sensitive or more developed than touch in sighted people. The main difference is that experienced BPSP learn to interpret their tactile perceptions with higher conscious awareness during everyday lives (Kleege 2018). This ability becomes part of the funds of knowledge that BPSP can draw from during the museum visit.

Experiencing objects through the body does not necessarily mean touching them. Following Merlau-Ponty's embodiment framework, visitors perceive museum objects through their bodies, and the body holds an 'intentional perspective' in regard to the surrounding environment (1962). This 'intentional perspective' means that visitors do not experience objects through their appearance or the tactile exploration only, but rather through a holistic multisensory perception. The body perceives intangible values associated with objects through their imagined materiality such as the perceived weight, material, texture,

temperature or smoothness. These sensations do not solely arise from directly touching objects but also from how visitors perceive objects from the point of view of handling them (Heidegger 1962 [1927]).

3.9. Conclusion

This chapter discussed the different characteristics of the embodied practice of visitors, and it started to analyse what it means for bodies to perform in the museum space with other performing bodies. Different embodied practices like gesturing, walking, looking at, talking, standing, positioning, scaffolding guidance, physically interacting with each other, and with objects and resources contribute to the making of meaning and the production and sharing of knowledge among the community of practice. Here, the museum space was conceptualised as a space that allows visitors to constantly move and negotiate the distance and the positioning between themselves, the exhibits, and other people. Shifts in posture and gaze, pointing and showing, and standing and walking characterise visitors' embodied practice and influence how they make sense in the space with other visitors.

First, I discussed the problem of how normative practices forwards perceived 'correct' behaviours in exhibition spaces and how visitors are expected to learn these taken-for-granted corporeal techniques in response to the museum 'script'. This discussion was followed by a closer examination of the different characteristics of embodied practice, which constitute the essence of shared meaning-making: gesturing, walking, seeing and being seen, looking at and touching objects. These characteristics will be micro-analysed in Chapters 5 to 7 through the detailed analysis of participants' embodied practice and making of meaning across the three case studies that I now present in chapter 4.

Methodology

4.1. Introduction

This chapter outlines the methodological approach chosen to address the research questions. It gives details about the rationale behind selecting case studies and the selection and recruitment of research participants. It illustrates the research design, the methods, and the strategies employed to analyse the data. The methodological approach is qualitative, and it aims to understand the social and embodied practice of blind and partially sighted visitors. Eight participants were recruited, and five of them visited the Victoria & Albert Museum (V&A), three of them the Wallace Collection, and three of them the Museum of London (MoL) (some participants visited more than one museum).

4.2. Qualitative research: IPA

The focus of this book is the meaning that visitors make through social and embodied practice in the museum space. Hence, the nature of this research is qualitative, as it is a flexible approach to study embodied practice and meaning-making in a natural context (Denzin and Lincoln 2005). My research questions place emphasis on the embodied experience of BPSP in the museum space. Additionally, the diversity of the people involved, both in terms of vision impairments and sociocultural backgrounds, made it necessary to find lenses through which I could gain a holistic overview of their actions and the meanings of participants in the social context of the museum. The involvement of BPSP determined the necessity to find a flexible approach that would let participants describe their experience in the museum on their terms. The focus on the body required the development of a methodology that allowed capturing evidence around how the body moved and made sense of the different elements of the museum experience. The methodological approach aimed to examine how people talked about the body and how they experienced what the body did, offering a direct perspective on the embodied practice. The inclusion of BPSP made it necessary to find a methodological approach that involved both types of data (self-reported speech data as well as visual fieldnotes data) because due to the vision impairment, the way participants perceived their bodies in the space was just as important as the actual bodily actions and movements.

The interpretative phenomenological analysis (IPA) methodological approach seemed to satisfy all the above requirements. This orientation aims to describe a specific phenomenon or experience from the perspective of specific participants (Creswell 1998). Phenomenology provides qualitative research with a starting point to immediate

social experiences (Crotty 1998). IPA aims to discover and describe the essence of a phenomenon (Larkin *et al.* 2011). It investigates phenomena from the subjective point of view of individuals and assumes that fundamental truths are mediated by each person's lived experience (ibid). IPA allows analysing details and nuances of the particular instances of the lived experiences (Smith *et al.* 2009, 38).

I mainly employed the hermeneutical interpretative approach of IPA developed by Heidegger (1962), as it aims to understand the meaning attributed to the lived experiences by the individuals that have lived them.[3]. The hermeneutical approach of phenomenology investigates the essence of phenomena by first analysing their outward manifestation. The benefit of this approach in the context of this research is that it allows addressing the participatory and multi-contextual sense of the embodied experience under the lens of situated learning perspective. Additionally, it aims to provide descriptions of the phenomenon and explanations and meanings of the phenomenon based on situated data. By drawing upon this methodological framework, my research investigates the essence of the phenomenon as the central underlying meaning of the experience shared within the different lived experiences (Holstein and Gubrium 1994). Accordingly, this approach facilitates addressing the meanings and perspectives of BPS participants (Schwandt 2000), as I approach the museum experience from the perspective of those 'who act, while they act' by using their quotations and descriptions (Firestone 1987). The target of this phenomenological enquiry is to acknowledge the diversity and nuances of possible meanings (Daly 1992, 22–23), to explore the different ways in which BPSP construct their experience in museums, and to critically assess how the body experience resources in the space and how they can facilitate the museum experience.

4.3. Methods

The research methods comprised of qualitative semi-structured interviews, video recordings, and fieldnotes. The interview protocol was developed, reflecting on the broad themes that emerged during the literature review. Semi-structured interview and fieldnotes protocols were constantly tested and refined before, during and after each visit. Semi-structured interviews were conducted with participants after their visit to provide in-depth information about the visitor and their experience of museums. Interviews were conducted in a quiet separate space, inside the museum.

---

[3] As opposed to the descriptive approach developed by Husserl that aims to understand the essence of the phenomenon as described by individuals.

While interviews offered an account of the visitor experience as expressed directly by the participants, the focus of the research on the body and the embodied practice of visitors also required in-depth accounts of what the body did, how it responded to the different elements of the exhibition, and how it made meaning of the exhibition. This was achieved through observation in the form of fieldnotes and video recordings.

In this research project, participants visited the museum of their choice independently. Participants were free to decide how and with whom to visit the museum. When I recruited them, I informed them that I would be present in the gallery as a researcher and that I was going to take notes of their behaviour.

The focus of the fieldnotes was how participants moved, their gestures and shifts in postures, how they positioned their bodies in relation to objects and other people, how they touched objects, and in general, how their bodies reacted to and made sense of the different elements of the visit. This allowed to create a rich record of actions, movements, reactions, and interactions and their sequence in the space. The combination of observations and interviews (together with video recordings, where applicable) provided a greater insight into how participants made meaning during their visits.

Video recording is an established method in qualitative phenomenological research, and it has a long tradition in IPA. Video recordings offer credibility due to the possibility to repeatedly access the generated data (Silverman 2006; vom Lehn *et al.* 2002). Vom Lehn (2010, 753) argued that interviews and fieldnotes methods alone 'do not generate sufficiently fine-grained data that allow the researcher access to the social organisation of actions in and through which the participants configure each other's orientation to exhibits'. He argued that video recordings are the most suitable method to fully capture details of the interaction between BPS visitors and their companions (vom Lehn 2010).

One participant, Jane, who decided to visit the V&A, asked not to wear a camera as it would have made her feel uncomfortable, and she felt that she would have changed her behaviour with her partner if she was being recorded. After making sure that she would not mind being observed, we decided to go ahead with the visit. Her visit took place after the other four visits had already been completed (five participants chose to visit the V&A); hence I had time to refine the fieldnotes and interview protocols in light of the things that emerged during the visits, the interview transcripts, and the segments of video data that had already been gathered. The fieldnotes protocol for Jane's visit was far richer and elaborate than the other ones, as I tried to capture gestures and actions that the camera would have typically captured. Additionally, I employed an audio recording device paired with a timer to track her visit. After Jane's visit, I transcribed the interviews and the fieldnotes, and it was clear that despite the embodied

first-person view was missing, the data collected still offered a detailed and rich perspective on Jane's experience.

Owing to the nature of the research, there was a range of options that participants were given in terms of methods (the case of Jane is an example), and this was extended to also include museums as key stakeholder. After initial meetings with the Museum of London, a decision was made not to grant permission to collect video recordings quoting visitor privacy concerns. This posed a serious methodological challenge, as the data collection process could be potentially different across the three case studies. The decision to go ahead with the visits to the MoL despite the lack of permission to collect video data came primarily from methodological reasons. In the first place, the visits to the MoL would have occurred after Jane visited the V&A; hence I had already carried out data collection without using the camera. From an initial analysis, the lack of video recordings did not negatively impact the data collected in that specific case. The focus during that visit was more on the speech data and the fieldnotes taken in the galleries. Secondly, participants that were contacted expressed enthusiasm at the idea of visiting the MoL. In particular, while two of them (Fred and Lily) agreed to visit other museums, another one, Anna, specifically said that the Museum of London was the only museum that she was interested in visiting and that it was her condition to take part in the study. Anna had a particular connection and a solid motivation to visit the MoL; asking her to visit another museum would have altered her experience.

Additionally, data collection at the MoL took part only after all the visits to the V&A and Wallace were completed. The initial transcription of interviews, and analysis of fieldnotes and video recordings, allowed me to evolve, change and refine the fieldnotes protocol to the point that I felt confident enough to carry out the visits without video recordings. Due to the lack of video data, the analysis of the MoL visits focused more on how participants perceived their bodies in the space and how they perceived what their bodies did. Fieldnotes focused on how participants positioned themselves in relation to other people, objects, and other elements of the exhibit.

The combination of the three methods provided a rich perspective and a holistic picture of the visitor experience. Interviews provided data on the way participants talked about the body, communicated the sense they made of the exhibit. Video recordings captured the experience from the unique angle of the visitor, and they enabled to observe in detail the different kinds of interaction. Fieldnotes offered an insightful perspective on what the body did, as observed by me.

4.4. Recruiting participants

The research included eight adult BPSP participants: five participants visited the V&A, three, the Wallace Collection, and three, the MoL (some visited more than one museum). Qualitative methodology IPA enquiries suggest a low number of participants, usually between five and ten (Hefferson and Gil-Rodriguez 2011). Due to the study's time and resources' limits, I decided to focus on a specific group of visitors: BPS millennials born between 1981 and 1996 (Rauch 2018). The criteria behind this choice are several. Firstly, as mentioned in chapter 3, previous studies about BPSP in museums tended to focus on younger people primarily (<18), usually children, pupils and school groups, or older people (60+) (Kleege 1999; -2018). Hence, there is a significant gap when it comes to the visitor experience of BPS millennials.

Additionally, as the third research question of this project looks at the use of technology and its impact on meaning-making, BPS adults were considered potentially more familiar with the use of technology, and therefore more eager to use it in the museum environment. Finally, after informal conversations with several London museums accessibility managers, consultations with the RNIB and VocalEyes, it seemed clear that young to middle-aged BPS adults visit museums less frequently than BPS school groups, children, and older people who are often part of the museum's special programmes.

Participants in the study lost their sight at different stages of life, and have different cultural and social prior experiences of engaging with museum collections and environments. There was a balance between participants who were already museum enthusiasts, participants who were technology savvy, and those who were simply interested in exploring new experiences. This recruitment distinction is theoretically driven, as it allowed to obtain a balance between people who have a higher cultural capital and those who have a higher technical capital. This allowed to gather richer and deeper data, as it allowed to analyse the embodied experience from different perspectives, reflecting on the heterogeneous nature, often neglected in museums, of people with vision impairments (chapter 3).

The following table (4.1) presents an overview of participants.

Despite several difficulties reaching out to young adult BPS millennials, eight people agreed to take part in this research. Two participants visited more than one museum (Fred visited all three, Lily visited the Wallace Collection and the MoL); hence eleven museum visits were recorded: five in the V&A, three in the Wallace Collection, and three in the MoL. The difficulties and the reluctance of young BPS millennials to visit museums were mainly due to time-commitment issues, lack of interest in museums as free-time activities, and a general feeling that museums are not for or welcome BPSP.

4.5. Data analysis and coding scheme

This section looks at the analytical framework employed to analyse and code data. The starting point of IPA is an interest in participants' experience (Smith and Osborn 2003). For the purposes of this research, the meanings BPSP assign to their museum experience was central, and the research goal was to attempt to understand the content and complexity of these meanings. This understanding required me to engage in an interpretative relationship with the data. Hence, findings were consistently analysed with research conducted within a phenomenological framework (Creswell 1998). A phenomenological bottom-up, inductive coding approach was employed. I began data analysis with repeated readings of the interview transcripts and watching several times the video recordings, through which the full spectrum of themes and patterns in the conversations, the recordings and the fieldnotes became clear. While I started the analysis with three broad categories coming from the theoretical framework in mind, during the coding process I refined and added categories and subcategories emerging from the data, in order to prioritise participants' own perceptions (Corbin and Strauss 2008). This analytical approach highlighted what was important to the participants, and how they viewed and interpreted their own experiences.

4.6. Categories of embodied practice

The data analysis revealed six major categories of embodied practice addressing different aspects of the

Table 4.1. Overview of participants

	Vision impairment	Frequency of museum visiting	Museums visited
Fred	Visually impaired	Frequent	V&A, Wallace Collection, MoL
Ravi	Blind	Rare	V&A
Asif	Blind	Regular	V&A
Jane	Visually impaired	Rare	V&A
Susan	Visually impaired	Regular	V&A
Lily	Blind	Frequent	Wallace Collection, MoL
Davide	Visually impaired	Frequent	Wallace Collection
Anna	Visually impaired	Regular	MoL

visit's social context: co-walking, scaffolding, identity formation, looking, touching, and using resources.

Firstly, co-walking includes all those practices that visitors carried out to explore the space and negotiate the co-presence of others in shared meaning-making in their encounters with the exhibits. Additionally, I look at co-walking as the enabler of identity formation, as it allowed participants to affirm their self-presence in the museum. Co-walking is a theoretical category borrowed from embodiment theory, explored in chapter 3, section 3.5. In the three findings chapters, the discussion on co-walking is preceded by an initial section where I present how participants arrived at the museum. This section helps identify how participants' everyday embodied practice shaped their walking practice in the museum.

Scaffolding is the sociocultural concept theorised by Mai and Ash (2012) that I discussed in chapter 2, section 2.5.3. I used it as a hanger concept to analyse how visitors' bodies interacted with others in scaffolded meaning-making of the museum content and environment. Scaffolding instances are analysed starting from scaffolding techniques that participants enacted interacting with each other's and using tools.

The third category is defined as 'identity formation', following Lave and Wenger's situated learning and community of practice frameworks, as explored in chapter 2, section 2.5. This category contributes to understanding the correlation between identity and practice, discussing how participants negotiated their identities together with the negotiation of meaning. This category looks at how meaning is developed through social relationships and shared identities.

The looking category comes from Hayhoe's (2017) and Kleege's (2018) discussion on 'visual culture' that I presented in chapter 3, section 3.7. I discuss how participants made meaning of visual concepts, despite their vision impairments. I look at participants' visual practice to prolong their museum experience and as a way to focus on historical details of the objects. In response to Hayhoe's (2017) 'aesthetic capital' (chapter 3, section 3.7), I create the concept of 'historic capital' to discuss participants' preference for the historical and biographical details of objects.

The touching category comes from the discussion on the way visitors, and BPSP in particular, make sense of museums' collections through the sense of touch and other visitors (chapter 3 section 3.8). I refer to this practice of touching together as 'co-touching', a category I created to conceptualise the social and situated nature of touching objects in the museum. Co-touching, here, is seen as a practice that enables scaffolding activity and shared meaning.

The final category, using resources, brings together the interactions that participants had with resources in the space. This category looks at how participants used resources and how their technical capital (presented in chapter 2, section 2.4.1) facilitated the shared meaning-making.

4.7. Ethics

The data collection was carried out in compliance with the UCL Institute of Archaeology ethical guidelines. The research involved adults with full capacity to consent. The ethical concerns of the project and health and safety issues were discussed in consultation with the three institutions. In order to guarantee participants' anonymity, their names and those of their companions were changed with pseudonyms, and the details of their works were not disclosed.

Victoria & Albert Museum

5.1. Introduction

This chapter presents the findings from the first case study, namely the Victoria & Albert Museum (V&A). Five participants agreed to visit the V&A and be interviewed afterwards from December 2017 to February 2018: Fred, Ravi, Asif, Jane, and Susan. Findings from this chapter provide evidence that the embodied practice of participants was deeply social and situated. They adapted their embodied practice to respond to the museum script and the presence of other walking and looking bodies. The characteristics of their embodied practice directly impacted their meaning-making and the development of their identity as museum visitors, art learners, and disabled people.

5.1.1. Description of the museum

Founded in 1852, the Victoria & Albert Museum (V&A) was named after Queen Victoria and her husband, Prince Albert (V&A 2020). The V&A is the world's largest decorative arts and design museum, located in London. Its collection includes over 5,000 years of art, from antiquity to the present day, from the cultures of Europe to North America, Asia and North Africa. In addition, it houses a permanent collection of over 4.5 million objects. The V&A offers a wide range of resources for BPSP both in the galleries and with a series of designed events and workshops. In the galleries, the museum provides a self-guided touch tour of museum touch objects in various rooms, mounted to be handled by visitors without supervision (V&A 2019). These objects are accompanied by tactile booklets, large prints, and audio descriptions accessed from the museum website.

The V&A states that its mission is to make its collections and sites relevant and accessible to more people (V&A 2020). 'Outreach' and 'inclusion' are two of the main goals in the future plan of the museum. Therefore, while a plurality of access resources is available for BPSP, resources are embedded as part of the collection to benefit all visitors and offer an inclusive experience to all.

5.2. Visitor profile

Different vision impairments and backgrounds are crucial recurring elements that inform and influence the characteristics of participants' social and embodied practice. These elements continue to emerge in conjunction with how participants moved in the space and how they made meaning with their companions.

5.2.1. Visitors' demographics

Five participants visited the V&A (Table 5.1). Fred, Susan and Jane are British. Asif has dual nationality, Pakistani and British, and has lived in both countries. Ravi is from Pakistan; he studied in Saudi Arabia for his undergraduate degree and moved to London to pursue a postgraduate degree.

Two participants (Fred and Susan) have university qualifications at the undergraduate level. One, Ravi, has a postgraduate qualification. Asif is studying for a Business Diploma, and the fifth participant, Jane, graduated from high school and works full time. Thus, three out of five participants are in full-time occupations, one is a student, and one is a volunteer. These profiles begin to show a discrepancy with the national statistics. According to the RNIB (2021), only 27% of all registered BPSP of working age in the UK are currently employed. Several statistics also show how disabled people, and BPSP in particular, represent a relatively small percentage of the total number of higher education students in the UK (Croft 2020). As of 2017/2018, only 3,170 students across all levels of study registered to UK universities identified as blind or partially sighted (HESA 2019).

Table 5.1. Visitors' profile

	Gender	Nationality	Occupation	Highest educational qualification	Other museums visited[4]
Fred	M	British	IT developer and blogger	BSc Computer Science	Wallace Collection Museum of London
Ravi	M	Pakistani	Engineer and banker	MSc Technology Management	/
Asif	M	Indian and British	Student (Business Diploma)	High school	/
Jane	F	British	Professional athlete	High school	/
Susan	F	British	Volunteer at a local charity	BA English Literature	/

---

[4] As part of this research project

Table 5.2. Participants' vision impairments

	Vision impairment and residual vision	History of vision	Navigation aid
Fred	Diagnosis: Aniridia and Nystagmus. Issues: sensitivity to sunlight and glare; poor distance vision; shaky eyes, making it hard to focus on things unless they are close or enlarged.	Impaired since birth. Vivid visual memory.	No aid Uses phone and monocular
Ravi	Diagnosis: Congenital Glaucoma. Issues: totally blind, no residual vision.	Impaired since birth, blind since 7 years old. No visual memory.	White cane
Asif	Diagnosis: Retinitis Pigmentosa. Issues: totally blind with some light perception.	Turned blind when 28 years old. Vivid visual memory	White cane
Jane	Diagnosis: Retinitis Pigmentosa and nystagmus. Issues: night blindness, difficulty to see things if they are far and no peripheral vision, double vision, colour-blind.	Impaired since 10 years old. Weak visual memory.	Guide dog
Susan	Diagnosis: Macular Degeneration. Residual vision: slight peripheral vision in her right eye.	Impaired since 16 years old. Vivid visual memory.	White cane

While this book does not examine in detail the reasons behind these low levels of education and employment (see Croft 2020 for a detailed discussion), it is clear that the participants in this research are not fully representative of the UK demographic of BPSP, and that they mostly come from socially advantaged backgrounds. As mentioned in Chapter 4 (section 4.3.3), the recruitment of participants presented several difficulties, and this resulting unbalanced demographic is an initial indication of the audience that museums manage to attract.

5.2.2. *Vision impairments*

At the beginning of each interview, participants were asked what type of vision impairment they had and how long they had been visually impaired. Two participants are blind: Ravi turned blind when he was 7 years old, and Asif at 28 years old. Two participants have severe sight loss: Susan has been impaired since she was 16 years old, and Jane since she was ten years old. Fred has been impaired since birth, but his residual vision is 'still good enough, to the point that I can go around and do stuff almost like anyone else'. Their conditions (or combination of conditions) are different, as well as their residual vision. Ravi's eyes were replaced with a prosthesis; hence he cannot see anything. Asif is blind with only some light perception. Susan, Jane and Fred are partially sighted with residual vision but with different visual abilities.

Describing the different needs associated with diverse levels of vision loss helps understanding how this diversity impacts every aspect of the museum experience. There is a crucial difference between people who have been blind from a young age as opposed to someone like Asif, who had sight for 28 years. The former group lacks previous experiences with sight in museums as points of reference.

Nevertheless, it was clear that Ravi, who has been blind for longer than Asif, had more time to adjust his lifestyles and was more comfortable navigating the museum space.

Table 5.2 presents a summary of the different vision impairments of participants.

5.2.3. *Visiting habits*

As part of the recruitment process, participants were asked about how frequently they visited museum and with whom they usually visit. My definition of frequency comes from Merriman's (1989, 49) framework: frequent visiting defined as three or more visits per year; regular as one to

Table 5.3. Visiting habits

	Frequency	Typical companion	Companion on this occasion
Fred	Frequent	Friends; members of social groups; partner; alone	Alone
Ravi	Reluctant	He mentioned two previous visits, one with family and one with a friend	Alone, escorted by a museum guide
Asif	Regular	Family or friends	Alone, escorted by a museum guide
Jane	Reluctant	/	Partner (fully sighted)
Susan	Regular	Friends or family	Friend (fully sighted)

two visits; occasional as last having been to a museum between one and four years before; rare as to last having visited more than five years before.

Participants were free to decide how to visit the museum and with whom. While Fred visited on his own, Ravi and Asif asked for a guided tour, Susan came with a friend, and Jane visited with her partner. Both Ravi and Asif asked for the assistance of a guide. The preference to visit with a companion seemed to come primarily from logistic reasons, as it is often difficult to arrive at the museum (either with public or private transport) (section 5.4) and to navigate the museum space alone (section 5.5). Visiting with a companion and spending time together were also important elements of the social practice of Jane and Susan. Additionally, Asif mentioned that he usually goes to museums with his family, and when asked why he visited on his own on this occasion, he responded that he primarily agreed to help me with my research and that he wanted to do it on his own. This desire to perform certain practices and experiences independently is analysed in section 5.7.1.

5.3. Categories of the embodied practice

The analysis follows the six categories of embodied practice presented in chapter 4, section 4.4: co-walking, scaffolding, identity formation, looking, touching, and using resources. In table 5.4, the six categories are presented with the sociocultural characteristics associated with them in the instances analysed for the V&A case study.

Table 5.4. Summary of the characteristics of sociocultural practice identified within each category

5.5 Co-walking
- Planning
- Co-presence and co-awareness
- Affirmation of self-presence

5.6 Scaffolding
- Guidance and support
- Intimacy and humour

5.7 Identity formation
- Looking disabled
- Cultural identity

5.8 Looking
- Looking forward: expanding learning
- Looking back: historic capital

5.9 Touching
- Professional guidance
- Co-touching

5.10 Using resources
- Accessing content
- Sharing meaning

5.4. Getting to the museum

This section describes how participants arrived at the museum. In order to reach the best possible understanding of participants' navigation in the museum, it is necessary to consider how they arrived at the museum. Everyday practices (like using the underground, taking a taxi or walking to an unfamiliar place) influenced participants' embodied practice in the museum. Everyday practices developed outside the museum space (especially those effective and successful) are applied in the museum and enable BPSP to gain access to environments, institutions, geographies and information. Findings from this section show that elements like planning, technology, being with friends or family members, guide dogs, and travelling independently are characteristics of the embodied practice of participants outside the museum. I identified similar ones in their museum practice.

During the interviews, I asked them how they got to the museum and how their journey was. Fred, Ravi, and Jane explained that they used the underground, which is also their main transport mean in their everyday lives. They all described the strategy that they employed to minimise risks due to their impairments. In the following section (5.5), I look at how they employed similar bodily strategies in navigating the museum space.

Fred explained that getting to the museum was easy for him:

> I mean, I visit museums quite a lot in this area. I planned and checked out where the V&A was on Street View[5] just so that I knew when I was coming out of the station where it was in relation to everything else. [...] I use this monocular[6] if I can't read the signs at the station, [...] or if I need to check platforms and directions.

After prompted, he elaborated on how he normally uses the application Google Street View:

> Mainly to explore the buildings and the surrounding area. You see? I plan in advance. I can create benchmarks in my head before I go.

Similarly, he also carefully planned the route of his visit. Planning routes in advance is a key strategy that Fred seemed to employ in his everyday life to minimise difficulties. Similarly, planning was key element of Fred's walking practice in the museum.

Ravi explained how he normally uses the underground on a daily basis:

> I go to most places on my own with the tube. If I am familiar with the place, then I would get out and go

---

[5] Street View is a software technology part of Google Maps and Google Earth, which provides interactive panoramas from positions along streets.
[6] A monocular is a modified refracting telescope used to magnify the images of distant objects

on my own as well. If I'm not, I either ask my friend or someone to meet me at the station, or I use Google Maps, which isn't always very successful.

In this case, he asked me to meet him at the South Kensington underground station,[7] and I guided him to the museum. As he was unfamiliar with the museum space, he asked to be accompanied during his visit by a guide. Travelling independently, using technology, asking for assistance, and being with someone are all part of Ravi's everyday navigation practice. He seemed to replicate the same successful navigation strategy he typically employs in other unfamiliar contexts.

Jane used the underground as well, and her guide dog and her partner accompanied her:

> I take the tube all the time. I live far from [the location where she trains], so that's the only way. I'm all the time with [her guide dog], so it's really not that difficult. If it's a station I don't know, I might ask for assistance from the staff.

Although she did not have troubles during her journey to the museum on this occasion, she explained that the underground can be a frustrating and challenging environment for her:

> Most people do not understand how guide dogs work. Have you looked at the video, I think it was on the Guardian or the Independent […] where a man with a guide dog gets rude comments? […] That happens all the time; people don't get that guide dogs are trained not to move on escaladers. I get rude comments, too, all the time. I always react if that's the case, […] but it can be very frustrating. I hate looking disabled. I don't like lecturing people, and that's what you have to do. It belittles you. It's even worse when my partner is with me. He gets really annoyed and responds angrily, and it makes me want to cry.

Jane's remark about 'hating to look disabled' sheds light on her identity as a disabled person and is contextualised within the framework of 'being seen as disabled'. Being seen as disabled is part of how Jane defines herself in relation to her social position within a certain context. Her desire not to look disabled is in line with studies on how disabled people tend to resist external viewings of their disability trying not to disclose their impairment (Eisenhauer 2007; Hutchinson *et al.* 2018; Spirtos and Gilligan 2020). Her remarks show how disability can become apparent during casual social encounters, as they can happen on public transport (Spirtos and Gilligan 2020). Jane was conscious of this potential visibility of her impairment, and she acted accordingly. This is linked to how she normally experiences her impairment in the space. When prompted ('How do you typically react?'), she explained:

> To be fair, I always get quite angry and nervous. I get shaky if people are rude, and I really want to teach them a lesson. But you know, at the same time I hate it. I hate that you really get in that. Those things are just awful. I usually say why what people are doing is wrong. And to be fair, it's always the best way, I mean, you can react, but I overreact. I really try to prove my point.

While moving through unfamiliar and unfriendly environments, Jane's defensive disposition appears to be a deep-rooted habit that she has developed through her life and has become part of her identity as a disabled person. As I show in the following sections, she carried the same disposition in the museum space, which she saw as unfamiliar and potentially unfriendly. She was inclined to act in a similar defensive way. Her body seemed to have internalised strategies and defensive mechanism, which were enacted to actively resist and deconstruct socially constructed oppressive practices (Shakespeare 2005).

Asif came to the museum with a pre-arranged taxi. The taxi driver left him outside the V&A, where he had asked me to pick him up. At the end of the visit, the same taxi driver picked him up from the museum. In the interview, Asif voiced his lack of confidence in moving independently:

> If I'm not familiar [with a place], I rely quite a lot. If I'm alone, definitely on cab. If I'm with someone, I will see. Like I said, I rely on them (his family) and what they choose: cab, public transport. If I am with my family, most of them have a car. I always prefer being with someone.

Susan came with her friend who drove from Milton Keynes (near London). She explained that her work is close to her home, and she walks there. Therefore, she is not used to using public transport:

> I don't really use the car or the bus. Work is only 20 minutes walk from my flat. I'm not really that independent when it comes to moving around. It's a struggle. […] Usually, my family or some friends make arrangements for it [journeys to unfamiliar spaces]. I also use cabs sometimes, if I'm on my own.

While she claimed that transport is not her primary concern, it is clear that she usually takes time to make special arrangements with her family or friends. Later in the interview, she added considerations about the issue of navigation and the need to make special arrangements:

> I would not mind being a bit more independent in moving around. […] I should probably find a way to use the tube on my own if I had to live here [in London]. Taxis are too expensive.

Overall, Susan and Asif seemed less confident and less eager to resist bodily restrictions outside and inside the museum space. Instead, Jane, Ravi, and Fred actively challenged and resisted oppressive bodily practices, and they asserted their self-presence through their actions in the space. Susan and Asif's different level of confidence and empowerment could be traced back to their different history of vision loss and habitus. In fact, they both lost sight later in life and they both live less independent lives. Jane, Ravi, and Fred were highly empowered individuals who are used to challenge and resist dys-appearance (Imrie 2001), with their bodies in their daily lives (Jane as an athlete; Fred as an advocate blogger and at his work in computer science; Ravi as an engineer, public speaker, and athlete). On the contrary, Susan and Asif seemed more reluctant to challenge socially constructed spatial and physical inequalities.

Overall, two main findings need to be highlighted from this section, as they contribute to the understanding of everyday embodied practices of BPSP. The first finding is that participants were confident about their everyday navigation strategies. They all knew which assistive tools worked for them and the best possible strategy to reach an unfamiliar place. In the following section, I draw parallels between these everyday navigation strategies and those in the museum during their visit. In most cases, they opted for similar tools to what they use in their everyday lives, and they seemed to replicate successful navigation strategies. The second important finding to highlight emerged from Jane's interview, where she mentioned her discomfort at the idea of 'looking disabled'. This continues to emerge throughout this chapter and the following two chapters in relations to how participants walked in the museums, how they touched or looked at objects, what they perceived as correct positioning, and how they interpreted difficulties that arose during their visits in relation to their identity as museum visitors and as disabled people.

5.5. Co-walking

In the previous section (5.4), I argued that elements and strategies of participants' everyday walking practice align with their walking practice in the museum. Here, I present a systematic analysis of how visitors walked in the museum space in relation to objects, their companions, and other visitors. I focus on the embodied elements of the visit, and I discuss how the practice of co-walking enabled meaning-making and identity formation.

This section is divided into three different parts, which explore the different characteristics that were identified as part of the walking practice of participants: planning (5.5.1); co-presence and co-awareness (5.5.2); and affirmation of self-presence (5.5.3).

5.5.1. Planning

This section looks at Fred's strategy to navigate the space and respond to the museum script. Fred's route mirrored his desire to learn and explore the museum content. He spent almost 3 hours in Gallery 7 Europe 1600–1815. He looked at every object and only managed to explore

one room before he completed his visit. Fred's walking was a learning practice. He embraced the space and systematically engaged with cultural and digital tools. Meaning-making happened as he walked through the galleries. Hence, it is deeply connected with his walking practice. The following quotes present 'planning' as a key element that enabled him to respond to the museum script effectively and to make meaning of the exhibit. In the interview, he described how he planned his visit:

> I looked online to see what was available, yeah. I liked the fact that the Europe exhibition had like an audio guide on the website to go with it, so I was obviously trying that.

Moving around the gallery and accessing information seemed to be his primary concern before the visit. He explained that he downloaded the museum map and checked in advance the location of the gallery he wanted to visit:

> I knew roughly where the Europe exhibition was but it's quite a big elaborate museum; I checked online. I used their map, and I benchmarked where I wanted to go and what I wanted to see.

Fred carefully planned his visit to the museum. He used all the resources available for him to facilitate his visit to be able to focus on accessing information. Planning was a crucial characteristic of his visit. As seen in section 5.4, it was also a recurring element in his everyday life. On the one hand, this can be attributed to his vision impairment. Planning activities in advance is a common strategy among BPSP to minimise difficulties in relation to navigation and access (Montarzino *et al.* 2007; Wang *et al.* 2017; Worth 2013). The main aim of planning in advance is to familiarise with surroundings and unfamiliar environments. In Urban Planning studies, planning was identified as promoting independence, with route planning, awareness of facilities, and knowledge about the different services available becoming a 'second nature' for BPSP (Montarzino *et al.* 2007). Planning the journey and taking the time to familiarise with the museum's new surroundings are identified and discussed as important activities part of Fred's practice.

On the other hand, Fred is an experienced museum visitor, and planning was one way he responded to the museum script. Planning is recognised as a common pre-visit strategy among museum visitors, and websites are identified as the primary resource where visitors look for information to familiarise themselves with the environment and the content (Marty 2008). As such, planning can be considered a strategy part of experienced visitors' funds of knowledge (Gonzalez *et al.* 2005). Planning as a form of funds of knowledge is part of the repository of techniques that allow visitors to acquire information to respond to the museum's script (Rees Leahy 2012). Findings from this section suggest that planning is grounded in Fred's cultural practice. Careful planning allowed Fred to focus on the visit's cultural aspect and minimise disruption in his encounters with objects.

Planning, in this case, was the strategy that allowed Fred to identify a gallery of interest on the museum website before his visit. In doing so, he drew on a successful everyday practice (planning) to maximise his situated learning opportunities in the space. Fred also used this strategy to adapt to perceived normative practices. He did so by investigating the space in advance, looking at online maps and creating benchmarks to his places of interest. He drew from his everyday navigation experiences through unfamiliar spaces and adapted them to the museum environment. Finally, he used scaffolding tools like digital audio guides and access resources from the website to facilitate his experience in the space. He effectively learned 'how to do the exhibit' before entering the museum, thus minimising difficulties that could have arisen due to his impairment or the exhibit's characteristics.

Fred used tools, namely the museum website, online maps, online benchmarks to places of interests, digital audio guides, and accessible resources during his planning activity. If we look at how he used these tools in his planning activity, they can be viewed as funds of knowledge in their own right. Fred mentioned how he used similar tools and techniques in different contexts; hence these can be considered educational tools acquired through everyday practice (Moll *et al.* 1992). Fred used tools to access objects, facilitate his learning experience and make meaning of the environment and the exhibit. Therefore, in Fred's visit, walking was a situated cultural act, enabled by his planning activity (Solnit 2001).

5.5.2. Co-presence and co-awareness

Co-presence and co-awareness are two key characteristics of Susan's and Fred's walking practice. These findings contribute to understanding how visitors perceive the museum environment and how they make meaning in the space through their embodied performance. Co-presence refers to how visitors walk in relation to objects and other visitors who share the same space and how they are aware of these other walking bodies. The first element to consider within the category of co-presence is that participants' mobility practice was directly affected by their vision impairments.

Susan mentioned the issue of 'correct positioning' in the gallery in relation to other visitors and objects when she explained the value of having someone to rely on for navigation:

> I always misjudge where an object is, I might think something is really close to me but it's actually further or closer than I expected. This usually results in me crashing into objects, which is quite embarrassing if I'm out in public. Imagine in a museum! [...] I was happy Sally was with me. It gives me anxiety the idea

of being somewhere like this on my own. I used to, but since I lost my sight... It is too much.

The choice of visiting the Ceramic and Furniture galleries derived specifically from the fact that on Sundays[8] the museum tends to be busier than usual, and the galleries on the lower floors are more likely to be busier:

> I hate to walk around when there are so many people, I'm hyperaware. I never know where to stand, where to go. It's panicking. There are children and I hate the idea of tripping over a child and hurt him or myself. So scary! We thought that the upper floor was quieter. [...]It was nice to go around a gallery not too crowded, without bumping into people. [...] I like that I don't have to worry about other people around me

The fourth-floor galleries are less visited and offer the opportunity to move more freely and use resources without worrying about other visitors' presence. In fact, during the visit, Susan and Sally were never close to other visitors, which made Susan relax. Susan clearly stated how she was aware of other looking and standing bodies, which triggered concerns and worries, making her feel uneasy.

Susan mentioned that she often feels anxious when navigating an unfamiliar place, especially if she has to do so independently. She explained that when she lost her sight, she convinced herself that it is too much of a daunting skill to master. Susan also explained how in the past years, her confidence has grown when it comes to going out and that this kind of social outings with her friend boost her confidence. In the quotes above, she explained how she is self-conscious about how she is 'supposed to' move and how others see her. The quotes show how this makes her feel: she expressed embarrassment, anxiety, overwhelm, panic, fear, and awkwardness. These feelings seem to be connected to an element of how other people in the gallery see her. Susan was aware of her body in the space, and was afraid that incorrect positioning due to her vision impairment would make her look awkward or inexperienced. She explained that she did not want to be seen as inexperienced by others.

Susan seemed comfortable while moving in the Ceramic and Furniture galleries, both guided by her friend and independently exploring each object. However, instance 5.1 below show how aware she was of other visitors in close proximity:

Instance 5.1:

Source: fieldnotes
In Gallery 139, Susan touched a clay vase while Sally was on her left-hand side, reading a panel. Susan and Sally were the only two people in the gallery.[9]

---

[8] The day on which they visited.
[9] I was in the gallery as well, but I observed them from a distance.

Four visitors (two adults and two children) entered the gallery from gallery 138, on Susan's right-hand side. The group was particularly loud, with one adult shouting at the children not to touch a computer monitor near the entrance.
Susan immediately stopped touching the object and removed her hands from it. She sharply turned her head towards the newcomers, and she shifted her body to face them, giving her back to Sally. Her posture stiffed, and she squinted her eyes to look better at the group.
The newcomers started looking at a nearby table, close enough to Susan and Sally to attract Sally's attention, who asked Susan if everything was ok. Susan nodded yes.
Susan moved her body closer to Sally, positioning herself between the newcomers and Sally. She turned her back to the newcomers, and she faced Sally directly, rather than the table and the objects they were looking at. Susan did not resume touching objects but instead kept her attention focused on Sally, looking at her directly. At times, she would slightly turn her head in the direction of the voices of the other group. Sally explained to her the information about manufacturing techniques she had been reading on the panel.
After 6 minutes, the group left the gallery passing next to Sally and Susan. Susan followed them with her head. As soon as they exited the gallery, she took a step back and resumed her position before they entered the gallery (less close to Sally), and she resumed touching the same vase she was touching before.

Susan seemed to be particularly aware of normative bodily techniques, mostly the presence of other 'walking and looking bodies' (Rees Leahy 2012, 75). For Susan, walking in the 'right direction' and conforming to what she seemed to perceive as the normative behaviour practices was a constant concern while in the space. Her body articulated the shape of her visit. She was careful to calibrate her pace to that of her companion, to negotiate the distance between herself and the display, and she was always conscious of the presence of others.

Walking for Susan was a practice shaped by the social and physical environment where it happened. It was her act of exploration of walking through the space; she set the direction and the pace at which she discovered the environment and objects (Lund 2012). As she walked, she created situated opportunities to learn about the exhibit, and she and Sally directly scaffolded the way they made sense together (Harris 2015). Instance 5.1 shows how Susan negotiated her walking practice in relation to Sally's and other walking bodies (Lageby 2013). Susan said in the interview that sharing the space with other people made her uneasy and insecure. While I explore in section 5.6.1 the reasons for this uneasiness and insecurity, it is important to discuss how her body reacted when she happened to share the space with other visitors.

Firstly, a noteworthy incident was her reaction to the parent's suggestion towards their children not to touch the nearby computer monitor, as described in the instance above (instance 5.1). Susan immediately reacted to the 'do not touch' order and stopped touching the object in front of her, despite the order came from a stranger and

was not directed at her. This is a clear example of where co-awareness and perceived normative bodily practice meet. Susan's co-awareness of the newcomers made her more aware of her own bodily movements. She instantly responded to an 'order' that she perceived as 'normative' – do not touch – despite she was allowed to touch the object in front of her.

Susan and Sally's spatial configuration was directly linked to their social practice (Ingold 2011). They negotiated and scaffolded the way they made meaning together of the environment, of objects, and of resources. Susan negotiated her being co-present with Sally in different ways based on the configuration of the space and the presence of other visitors. Instance 5.1 shows how, as soon as she became aware of other visitors entering the gallery, she stood closer to Sally, relied on her guidance, limited her movements and positioned her body between Sally and the newcomers. Co-awareness of other walking bodies made her employ 'involvement shields' to minimise the social contact with and create a barrier from the other co-walkers (Goffman 1963, 39). Co-awareness produced Susan's conscious response to those who happened to be in the same perceptual range (Christidou and Diamantopoulou 2016; vom Lehn 2013).

In doing so, her physical reaction to Sally's presence also changed. They both re-adapted their embodied practice to include the physical presence of the other one in their perceptual range, thus affecting meaning-making (Ingold and Vergunst 2008). Susan re-negotiated her co-presence when she dispersed and then re-joined Sally, calibrating her co-presence as she became aware of the newcomers (Christidou and Diamantopoulou 2016). In doing so, Susan effectively monitored the co-presence of her group and took a leadership role to monitor the co-presence in her immediate surroundings. If we look at Susan and Sally's learning and participation as situated, being co-present and co-walking together, as well as being aware of other visitors, enabled situated learning opportunities (Lageby 2013). This happened as she oriented her body towards Sally's to include her in their interaction, while at the same time she positioned both their bodies away from the newcomers (Christidou and Diamantopoulou 2016, 26).

Despite her outspoken lack of confidence, these findings actually show that Susan mastered bodily techniques in the museums and was able to control and negotiate co-presence dynamics in the surrounding environment. Additionally, as I discuss later in section 5.9, she seemed experienced in how to touch objects: she knew where to position herself to observe the display and what kind of elements and objects to prioritise. Her bodily practices are acquired, culturally specific, and depend on her habitus (Bourdieu 1984; Rees Leahy 2012). They come from her experience as a museum visitor before losing her sight and the visits she performed with her friend after losing her sight. Being in a friendly space, without the presence of too many other visitors and with the possibility to sit down, also seemed to increase Susan's confidence and willingness to independently explore the space and to enable sociability (Worth 2013). The combination of Susan's expertise as a practiced visitor and the inclusive nature of the space created situated opportunities, where Susan made sense of the exhibition with her friend (Christidou 2013; Rees Leahy 2012).

Furthermore, Susan seemed to be conscious of her sight loss condition throughout her visit and during the interview. Her disability seemed to be at the front of her mind while she was visiting. The quotes above show that she was concerned that she might 'look disabled' in the eyes of other visitors. On the one hand, successful visits appear to be a way for her to keep her mind off her condition (Hutchinson *et al*. 2018). On the other hand, the museum seemed at the same time to be the element that allowed her to embrace her condition, turning it into a positive experience (Hayhoe 2017). Her impaired body-in-the-space was no longer defined by the impairment but rather by the opportunities to perform in a positive way. Despite the tension due to her disability that she mentioned in the interview, video findings and fieldnotes show that spending time with her friend exploring their mutual interest and interacting with objects allowed Susan to make meaning of the visit.

Similar to Susan's visit, several instances could be identified in Fred's visit where co-presence emerged as a crucial characteristic of his walking practice. Contrary to Susan, he visited the museum on his own. However, several instances show how he was aware of other visitors' bodies, and he negotiated his positioning in relation to the other visitors in his immediate surroundings. This was particularly clear when he approached objects, and other visitors were standing nearby looking at them. Owing it to his habitus as an experienced museum visitor, Fred responded to their presence abiding by what I have discussed as 'normative bodily practices' (Rees Leahy 2012). From video findings, it is clear that he was conscious of people around him, as well as physical barriers. Fred positioned himself at a certain distance from every object, and in case other visitors were looking at the same object, he waited until they moved away before getting closer and observing with his monocular. Figure 5.1 below shows how he negotiated a correct distance between himself and the other visitors, waited until they had finished looking at objects and had left his perceptual range, and only then he got closer to the object. His vision impairment, possibly due to his considerable residual vision, did not seem to make it difficult for him to negotiate co-presence. On the other hand, the fact that he needed to get quite close to objects and to use his monocular to observe them better (figure 5.1) was a factor that had an impact on the way he negotiated his waiting time in relation to other visitors.

Walking and standing for him meant respecting normative trajectories of the museum (Rees Lehay 2012). In the interview, he mentioned that he had been to several

Figure 5.1abc. Fred's different distances between himself and the object when other visitors were looking at it (a & b), and when he looked it on his own (c).

museums since moving to London. From his posture, gestures, and pace observed through video findings, it was clear that he enacted specific corporeal techniques acquired during previous visits. In addition, he seemed aware of the non-verbal bodily regulations and practices typical of the habitus of more experienced and practiced visitors.

His bodily techniques of attentive viewing and self-restrained posture seemed incorporated in his embodied practice. He seemed to embrace the space and everything it had to offer. He vigorously but systematically engaged with objects and resources but seemed restrained by physical barriers and his awareness of other visitors. He seemed to know how to look and how and where to stand, the supposedly correct distance from other visitors, and how fast and where to walk. These bodily practices create specific object-body relations, which I explore in the following section (5.5.3), but they also show that Fred knew how to read the 'script of the display' in relation to others (Rees Lehay 2012). Fred's experience of co-presence resonates with Thobo-Carlsen's argument that walking is a social activity even if one walks alone (2016, 145). Walking, in this sense, created situated learning opportunities. The visitor learns while walking, and, reflectively, the walking shapes the learning experience. Based on Fred's awareness of other walking and standing bodies, Fred's encounters can be viewed as a situated context of interaction (Giddens 1984, 64). Findings from Susan and Fred's experiences support the argument that walking bodies are constantly reactive to the other moving bodies in the surrounding environment (Ingold 2011). In order words, bodies are always co-present in the space, shaping each other's meaning-making.

5.5.3. Affirmation of self-presence

This section looks at Jane's distinctive walking practice in the space with her partner Max and her guide dog. Findings from fieldnotes and the interview suggest that being able to walk around the museum and perform the visit independently (although Max accompanied her) was an important part of Jane's experience. Furthermore, the findings presented below suggest that her guide dog allowed her to retain that independence in the same way it typically grants her independence in her everyday life. It can therefore be argued that Jane's dog is a tool and was in some way part of the funds of knowledge she drew from navigating the unfamiliar environment.

As seen in section 5.4, Jane usually walks with her guide dog during her everyday life. She explained that despite walking with the guide dog allowed her to move around independently, it can also be frustrating because of the public's reaction to guide dogs. When I recruited her, she expressed nervousness at the idea of navigating the museum with a guide dog. When I asked what her concern was, she mentioned that she was worried that security would have stopped her because of the dog; that other members of the public would not know how to behave in the presence of the dog; that the dog might find the environment distressing; and thatmshe would not feel welcome because of it. During the interview, she explained that she carefully thought about whether to take her guide dog with her or not:

> I thought about it a lot. I was wondering whether it was too much for [the dog]. I was nervous about it because they have stopped me in the past. Or people start touching [the dog]. I think it was my biggest concern. Max phoned the museum and they said they were fine with it and that it's not a problem to bring the dog, so I did. […] I feel, I don't know, that I wanted to prove something. I go everywhere with [the dog], why not here?

During the visit, Jane was primarily guided by her dog that followed her partner (instance 5.2). Her partner often held her hand or placed his hand on her shoulder but did not actively guide her. Her dog followed Max, and she relied entirely on the dog for moving around.

Instance 5.2:

Source: fieldnotes
When she arrived at the museum, she seemed tense, and she walked very close to her partner, grabbing his arm. She appeared very cautious of where the dog was going, and she kept him closer to her. Max proposed going and asking for a map from the information desk, but Jane refused to be left on her own. Hence, they started walking together. Jane heavily relied on her dog that was following Max. A staff member from the museum saw them and greeted them, asking if she could help them. Max responded that it was the first time at the museum, and the lady advised them on how to read the museum map. She mentioned the activities that were taking place for Friday Late and that they could have drinks and food from the museum café. After this encounter, Jane seemed to relax: her posture seemed less tense, her pace slowed down, she stopped grabbing her partner's arm, and they laced their hands instead. She continued to hold her dog's handle, and she relied on the dog for guidance, giving him directions to follow Max.

Despite Jane encountering several problems with other visitors often stopping by to pet her dog[10], it was clear that being able to walk with the dog in the museum triggered a sense of accomplishment and independence. Overall, despite a clear annoyance, Jane seemed used to dealing with these kinds of public interactions. The fact that the members of the staff of the V&A were welcoming to the dog seemed to make her experience a pleasant one. Guidance by the dog appeared to be the tool that allowed Jane to have an independent and successful experience in the space, as she could walk, she could find her way around, and she knew how to move without relying on her partner. The dog was both aid and, at the same time, the instrument that allowed Jane to be independent in the museum space.

The importance of 'being independent' for Jane became evident in some of Jane's interview passages:

> When you first messaged me to do this [take part in the research] I told Max and he was like 'you're never going to do it, we never go to museums anyway' and I was like 'yes because you know I don't really like museums' and he was like 'no that's not true'. He was making fun of me and he kept saying how I didn't want to go because museums are difficult for the visually impaired, and I don't do well with difficulties. But I was sure that I was going to overcome them and I was going to succeed. I knew it. Yeah museums are difficult, but I have faced worse. So at that point it was basically a challenge. I had to show him that he was wrong and that I could do this and so I did it. All on my own. He basically never really helped me.

---

[10] Petting working guide dogs in the UK is considered as a serious hazard for the safety of the handler.

The interview response where she talked about the challenge to her boyfriend gives a good idea of the importance for Jane of 'doing the museum visit independently' and 'overcoming difficulties for BPSP': she overcame a vision impairment thanks to the tool (the dog) that allowed her to regain that independence.

Arguably, the progressive confidence she displayed through her movements seemed to represent an affirmation of self-presence in the environment and a bodily enunciation that she belonged to the museum space (Butler 1993). Jane's bodily performance was deeply situated: she adapted and learnt to walk while walking in the galleries. She enacted her narration of the museum as she was walking through it. Her walking practice, enabled by her dog, became a form of political response where her traditionally excluded body (as she perceived it, due to not considering the museum a welcoming environment) reclaimed her right to participate and performed a re-appropriation of the space.

5.6. Scaffolding

Elements of scaffolding were recurring in all participants' experiences. In this section, I look at two particular scaffolding characteristics identified following Mai and Ash's (2012) theoretical framework: 'guidance and support' (section 5.6.1) and 'intimacy and humour' (section 5.6.2). Due to participants' vision impairments, I adapted the key elements of scaffolding to mirror the different needs for guidance and assistive tools that BPSP require.

5.6.1. Guidance and support

Guidance and support are critical characteristics of scaffolding, as seen in chapter 2 (section 2.5.3). The findings presented in this section show instances of scaffolded guidance and shifting roles (Mai and Ash 2012) that occurred while participants walked together and approached objects in the gallery. Additionally, this section highlights how guidance took place and faded differently based on the different types of participants' vision impairment, their personal preferences, and their relations with their companions.

The museum guides used their expert knowledge to guide Ravi and Asif's interactions with the objects. If we frame their interactions within the scaffolding perspective, we can consider the guides as the scaffolders, and we can identify several elements typical of scaffolding. Firstly, micro scaffolding instances observed throughout both visits always happened between the scaffolder and the participant in front of an object. They can be considered traditional scaffolding interactions, similar to that in formal education settings, as guidance was always given from the scaffolder to the participant, and no instances of shifting roles were identified (Mai and Ash 2012). Most instances can be considered socially mediated interactions where the scaffolder guided the participant in understanding or gaining more independence in the learning process. Guidance was

given verbally and physically, and it enabled participants to progress activity (in most cases touching) and make sense of the objects. Verbal guidance on how to touch objects and in the form of descriptions continued throughout the visit, also due to the nature of the guided touch tour. The instance below (5.3) shows how in Ravi's case, physical guidance eventually faded as he acquired skills and confidence to make sense of the objects and navigate the space independently. In the case of Asif (instance 5.4), the scaffolder continued to provide guidance throughout the visit, and the scaffolding element of guidance never faded. Essentially, the scaffolder supported Asif's meaningful engagement in the tasks of making sense of objects and navigating the space, which he could not have done unaided (Belland 2014).

Instance 5.3:

Source: video	Source: fieldnotes
	The guide met Ravi by the information desk at the entrance of the museum. She explained to him how long the tour was going to be and what kind of objects they would see. She also explained that all the objects that they were going to see were tactile objects.
	The guide asked Ravi if he had any preferences on how he wanted to be guided. He explained that he was comfortable to just follow her by grabbing her left elbow with his right arm. Ravi folded his white cane and kept it in his left hand (figure 5.2).
When they approached tactile objects, the guide took Ravi's hand from her elbow and guided it to the object (figures 5.3 ab). While Ravi mainly touched the objects independently (figures 5.4 ab), she also guided his hand to touch particular features of the objects (figures 5.5 ab).	
	When they came across a flight of stairs, the guide asked Ravi whether he preferred to walk up the stairs or take the adjacent lift. Ravi opted for the stairs.
The guide took him to the beginning of the stairs. Ravi removed his hand from the guide's elbow, reached for the handrail, guided by his guide (figure 5.6) and walked up the stairs unassisted considerably fast[11] following the handrail (figure 5.7).	

---

[11] Both the guide and I struggled to keep pace with Ravi while he was walking up the stairs.

| | Ravi often removed his hand from his guide's elbow when in front of objects and explored them on his own without guidance. |
| | When they reached the upper floor, the guide commented that he walked very fast and that she struggled to keep up with him. He explained that he is very active in general and that he plays many sports. |

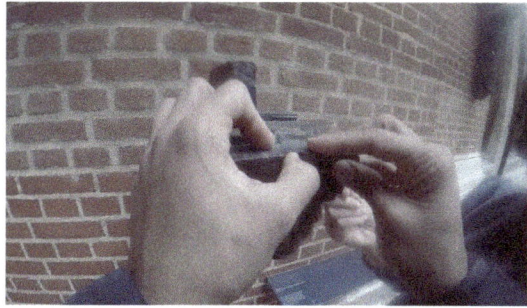

Figure 5.2. Ravi holding his folded white cane.

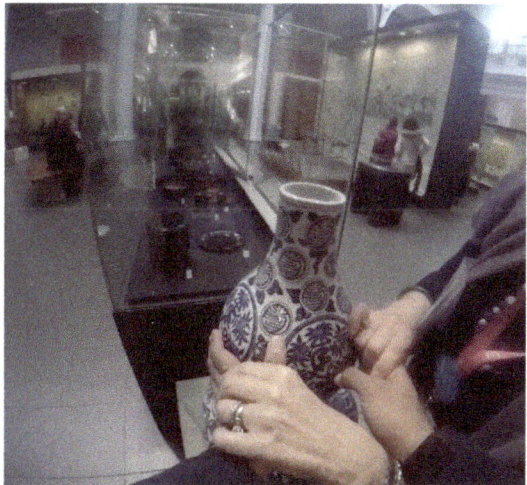

Figure 5.3ab. The guide guiding Ravi's hand to reach the objects.

Figure 5.4ab. Ravi touching objects independently.

Figure 5.5ab. Ravi touching objects with guidance.

Figure 5.6. Ravi reaching for the handrail, guided by his guide.

Figure 5.7. Ravi walking up the stairs unassisted, following the handrail.

Both instances where Ravi walked through the galleries and instances in which he approached objects present scaffolding characteristics. The guide provided physical and verbal guidance and support at the beginning of the visit, scaffolding Ravi's sustained engagement. Ravi progressively took the lead as he acquired confidence and familiarity with his guide, with the environment and with the objects. He started making physical explorations and walking independently as guidance faded. As Ravi took the lead, the guide (the 'scaffolder') better understood 'where to scaffold' and focused on the verbal descriptions to support Ravi's making of meaning (Ash *et al*. 2012, 41).

Similar to Jane's experience in section 5.5.3, it is arguable that the progressive confidence Ravi enacted through his movements seemed to represent an 'affirmation of self-presence' in the environment (Butler 1993), a bodily enunciation that he belonged to the museum space. Ravi's bodily performance was deeply situated: he adapted and learnt to walk while he was walking in the galleries. He enacted his narration of the museum as he was walking through it.

The following instance (5.4) shows how the scaffolding experience of guidance for Asif was different compared to Ravi's.

Instance 5.4:

Source: fieldnotes	Source: interview
Similar to Ravi's visit, the guide met Asif by the information desk, and she explained how the tour was going to work. She also explained that all the objects that they were going to see were tactile.	
The guide asked Asif if he wanted to grab her elbow and fold his cane. He took her elbow but decided to keep his cane unfolded (figure 5.8).	[Prompt: why did you decide to use your cane even if [your guide] was guiding you around?] You know, is difficult. I mean hard to walk and it helps [the white cane].
Asif kept his white cane unfolded and his arm on the guide's elbow throughout the visit (figures 5.9 abc). He only removed his hand from the elbow while he was touching objects. On two occasions, his guide took his white cane momentarily to allow him to touch two objects with two hands (figures 5.10 ab).	

The following figures (5.11 and 5.12) respectively summarise how Ravi and Asif's scaffolding guidance evolved during the visit. In the case of Ravi, guidance eventually faded, allowing him to actively contribute to meaning-making and taking ownership of his visit (figure 5.11). However, in the case of Asif, it never faded, and he continued to be guided by the scaffolder as a passive recipient rather than an active maker of meaning (figure 5.12).

Figure 5.8. Asif walking with his white cane unfolded and grabbing his guide's elbow.

52

Figure 5.10ab. Asif's guide holding his white cane while he touched the 'Metalwork bench' (a) and the 'Fallen Angel' sculpture (b).

These examples from Ravi and Asif's visits show how scaffolding guidance was determined by the participant's vision impairment, personal preferences, and confidence level. The scaffolders (the guides) tailor-made their guiding approach by adapting their bodily practice and the descriptive part of the tours. Ravi seemed to be more confident compared to Asif. Hence, he folded his white cane, relied on his guide, and often walked or explored objects on his own with guidance fading, following a classic scaffolding pattern (Mai and Ash 2012). Asif, on the other hand, generally seemed less at ease in the space. He kept his white cane unfolded, and he used it despite his guide was also guiding him. He kept his arm to that of his guide even when they just stood in front of objects. He always touched objects with only one hand, as he held his white cane in the other hand.

If we compare these findings with self-reported findings from section 5.4 (how they got to the museum), it is clear

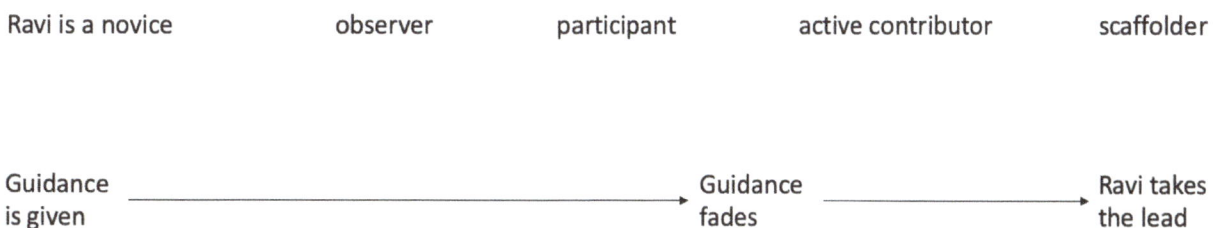

Figure 5.9abc. Asif holding his white cane throughout the visit.

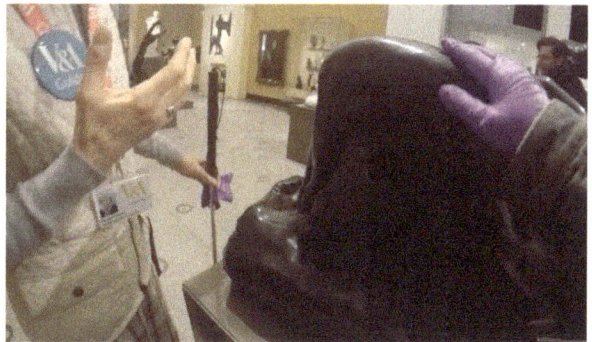

Ravi is a novice	observer	participant	active contributor	scaffolder

Guidance is given		Guidance fades		Ravi takes the lead

Figure 5.11. Progress of Ravi's guidance.

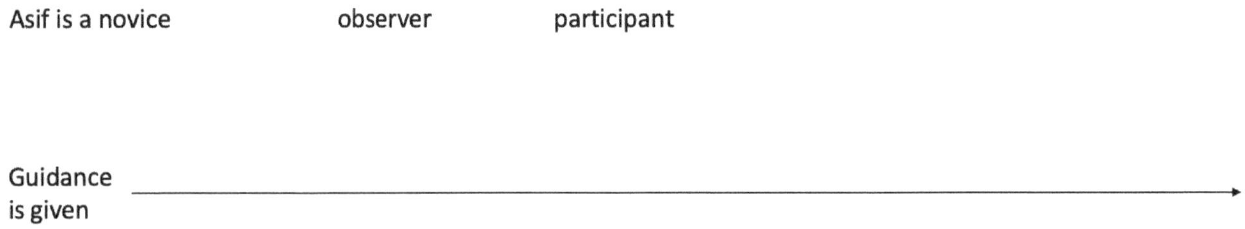

Asif is a novice   observer   participant

Guidance ———————————————————————————————————————→
is given

Figure 5.12. Progress of Asif's guidance.

that they both acted in the museum in a similar way to when they navigate unfamiliar environments in their everyday lives. Ravi acted with extreme confidence. While he recognised that he needed guidance because of his impairment, he often resisted it, performing on his own 'acts of explorations' of the space. Fading of guidance enabled Ravi to develop the confidence, the skills and the expertise to read the museum script independently. Guidance seemed to be an important part of his navigation practice as well. Instances above clearly showed that guidance was scaffolded and eventually faded. However, while guidance started at the beginning of the visit due to Ravi's vision impairment and the initial unfamiliarity with the environment, it faded at times where Ravi seemed to feel more confident to walk and move on his own. However, it never faded entirely due to the nature of Ravi's vision impairment (Gibbons 2015; Rickard *et al.* 2019; Williams *et al.* 2006). To a certain extent, and certainly less than Asif, Ravi always relied on his guide. When he stopped relying on her physical guidance, he continued to follow her for directions and the content of the touch tour. The scaffolding guidance facilitated Ravi within the context of the museum shifting from peripheral participation to central participation (Lave and Wenger 1991).

On the contrary, Asif seemed to rely more on his guide. This mirrored his preference for guidance that he expressed when he explained how he usually navigates unfamiliar environments. Relying on his guide seemed the tool that enabled Asif to make meaning during his visit. Not having to worry about where he was going allowed him to focus on the objects entirely. In this case, the guidance did not follow a typical scaffolding pattern as it never faded, not only because of Asif's vision impairment, but also due to his lack of confidence and his preference to be guided. This aligns with other studies that looked at scaffolding embodied interactions for BPSP in different contexts (Gibbons 2015; Rickard 2013; Rickard *et al.* 2019).

5.6.2. Intimacy and humour

During the visit, Jane and Max shared several moments of intimacy (instance 5.5). As mentioned above, Jane

asked not to wear a camera specifically because she did not want to feel limited in sharing moments of intimacy with her partner. Instances of shared intimacy are discussed within the scaffolding framework of Mai and Ash (2012), who similarly identified intimate physical gestures as elements that scaffolded visitors' activity and meaning-making.

Instance 5.5:

Source: fieldnotes
After they finished their meal, they wandered around galleries 27–26–45–47f-47e-44. They held hands for the whole duration of the visit, even when they were touching objects together. Max took Jane's hand to guide her to touch the architectural features of the building like the bas-relief decoration on the wall near the stairs by the café (figure 5.13), the column decorations in the café (figure 5.14), and wall decorations. He used his hand to guide Jane's, and he positioned his body behind Jane's to physically guide her towards the objects they were touching.

Instance 5.6:

Source: fieldnotes
When they encountered the tactile object Bodhisattva Head (figure 5.15), Max took Jane's right hand with his right hand, and he placed his left hand on her hip to move her towards the object so that they were both facing it. At the beginning, she stood still, looking uneasy and confused - her shoulders and neck stretched, looking tense. Then, he took her hand to touch each feature of the object, quizzing her on what she thought the object was. They laughed together after she identified that the object was a human head. As she was laughing and touching the object guided by Max, her posture relaxed, her shoulders lost their tension, and she leaned her body towards Max's.

Jane came to the museum seeking fun and pleasurable things to do as part of a date. Her socially mediated interaction was shaped by the characteristics of the museum experience and the characteristics of the dating occasion. The combination of the two resulted in several moments of intimacy. They shared moments of physical contact, while touching things together and talking to each other, holding hands, and hugging each other. Other moments of intimacy consisted of shared laughter and jokes.

Figure 5.13. Bas-relief decoration on the wall near the stairs by the V&A café.

Figure 5.15. Bodhisattva Head, China gallery 44, V&A.

Figure 5.14. Column decoration in the V&A café.

Interactions facilitated by jokes and intimacy presented a higher degree of 'emotional intimacy' and 'intuitive understanding' (Maybin *et al.* 1992, 23) compared to the other couples of visitors (Asif and Ravi with their guide, and Susan with her friend Sally). This deeper emotional interaction significantly contributed to how they scaffolded each other's learning. Their interaction mirrored a traditional scaffolding pattern on a macro level: Max acted as a guide that facilitated Jane's approach to objects with interventions consciously informed by his professional expertise. However, the microanalysis of the instances above (5.5 and 5.6) shows how the shared intimacy directly scaffolded meaning-making. Joking and laughing together contributed to creating a positive environment in which Jane and Max experienced feelings of mutual interdependence. Research has shown how situated feelings of mutual interdependence allow people to engage in higher-quality interactions and, therefore, higher quality learning experiences (Johnson and Johnson 2008; Vogelzang *et al.* 2019).

The physical acts of holding hands, touching each other and laughing together directly affected Jane's body, as it is evident in instance 5.6. Physical intimacy allowed her to relax her posture and release the tension in her body. She progressively became more engaged in the shared making of meaning with Max. The laughter and the intimate moment actively scaffolded how she made sense of the object as they enabled her focus to shift to the object and the explorative act of touching it with Max. Similarly, research from the fields of Neuroscience, and Positive Physiology has shown how humour and laughter directly benefit education (Davidhizar and Bowen 1992; Gonot-Schoupinsky *et al.* 2020; MacDonald 2004; Miles *et al.* 2016). In addition, they are increasingly discussed as an approach that can assist students in meeting educational goals and objectives (Davidhizar and Bowen 1992). Finally, they have been observed as tools to enable, facilitate, and mediate interactions among family members or the same community (Gonot-Schoupinsky *et al.* 2020).

In the museum context, Mai and Ash (2012) argued how jokes and humour are key parts of scaffolding and understanding the exhibition. They discuss it as part of the complex and intense social activity that enables shared meaning-making by effortlessly mixing object-related and non-object-related talk (Mai and Ash 2012). The social and the exhibition-related activity coming together enabled Jane and Max's shared activity of 'figuring out' what the object was (instance 5.6). This type of interaction encouraged participation and enabled a sense of agency (Wilson 2016). Intimacy and humour were an 'enabling factor' in Max and Jane's shared scaffolding process (Morcom 2015). They scaffolded Jane and Max to make connections with each other, their understanding, and their emotions. This enabled them to make sense of the objects together.

5.7. Identity formation

This section discusses the category of 'identity formation'. Identity is analysed within the situated framework of community of practice theorised by Wenger, as presented in chapter 2, section 2.5. While instances of identity formation are discussed in other categories throughout this chapter, this section contributes explicitly to understanding the correlation between identity development and practice. It does so by discussing how participants negotiated their identities as museum visitors and disabled people. It links the development of shared identity together with the negotiation of meaning. This section is divided into identity and disability (5.7.1) and cultural and social identity (5.7.2).

5.7.1. Identity and disability

Susan decided to visit the museum with her friend, Sally. She was confident in navigating the space thanks to Sally's guidance. However, Susan expressed her concern about navigating an unfamiliar complex environment several times before the visit and during the interview. These concerns seemed to come from insecurities related to the visibility of her disability. The instance below (5.7) helps to understand how these concerns related to her identity and the perception she had of her disability.

Instance 5.7:

Source: video	Source: fieldnotes
	Susan and Sally walked through the ground floor from the information desk through the Medieval galleries to reach the lift to go to the fourth floor. Susan looked around while walking, both to her right and left, and not in Sally's direction. She only looked in Sally's direction when standing.
Sally walked slightly ahead of Susan while their arms were loosely linked until Susan accidentally bumped into a pushchair (figure 5.16).	
	The pushchair was standing on their left-hand side, and Susan walked straight into it. Sally did not seem to notice it or to warn her. Susan took a sudden step back, and she looked around, looking disoriented. Then she started to apologise to the person guiding the pushchair.
	After this episode, Susan better linked her arm to Sally's, and she walked very close to Sally while they had their arms linked. While Sally often looked in Susan's direction when they talked, Susan looked straight ahead, concentrating on her route.
In the lift, they stopped linking arms and faced each other while they were talking[12].	

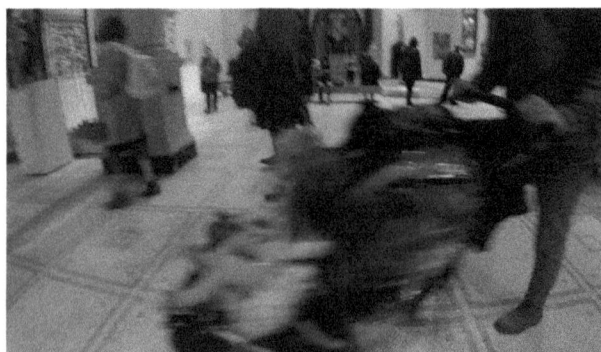

Figure 5.16. Susan bumping into a pushchair

---

[12] Images not included as Sally would be recognisable.

In the interview, Susan explained how the possibility of bumping into children made her feel uneasy:

> I would hate that. I did at some point. Imagine if I had hurt the child? Thank the Lord nothing happened. It would be really bad. I would indeed feel quite awful. Can you imagine? I hate when these things happen because I know it's not my fault because I can't really assess distance well, but how do I explain it? It's awful.

Similar to Jane's desire to 'not look disabled' expressed in relation to using public transport in section 5.4, the episode above shows that Susan had difficulties negotiating her identity as a disabled person during the visit and accepting the idea of 'being seen as disabled'. Susan was deeply concerned about the possibility of experiencing issues with other visitors because of her impairment. She was conscious of her disability throughout the visit, and she relied on Sally's guidance to limit the difficulties related to her impairment. When we look at this through the lenses of identity formation, it is clear how her impairment and the perception she had of the difficulties related to it impacted her identity and how she perceives herself and her body. Susan's example supports the argument that there is a deep correlation between identity and practice (Wenger 1998b). In general, Susan's identity formation in practice was enabled by the social participation in the museum visit, and it was constructed through the 'negotiation of meaning' (Handley *et al.* 2006). She developed meaning through the social relationship with Sally and the situated learning opportunities (Wenger 1998b). However, her disability – or better, how she faced difficulties related to her disability – impacted her practice, identity formation, and, therefore, her learning experience (Oyserman 2015).

'Being seen as disabled' was something Susan started to experience later in life when she started losing her sight. It was slowly becoming part of her identity, and she was in the process of negotiating it in relation to the other characteristics of her identity (Spirtos and Gilligan 2020). Her disability impacted Susan's situated and ever-evolving sense of self, particularly in relation to how other people perceived her and her impairment in a social context (Alvesson and Willmott 2002). Susan experienced difficulties in museums in relation to how she perceived herself as a disabled person. The way she experienced these difficulties was strongly influenced by the context in which they occurred (Smith and Collins 2010).

If we look at how she acted and reacted to the pushchair incident, it is clear how the situatedness of the museum experience took on a different dimension for Susan. Susan was aware of her surrounding environment. She experienced the environment and what was happening in it as she walked with Sally. She did not assess the distance between herself and the pushchair correctly, thus causing a minor collision. In that moment, Susan lost control. She seemed disoriented by the sudden change

in her surrounding environment caused by the collision. After the initial confusion and the apology, she processed what happened while they continued to walk to the lift. Her bodily response changed to adapt to the new situation and to make sense of what happened. She walked closer to Susan, linked their arms and concentrated on what was happening in front of her by never turning her head around. Therefore, Susan's bodily response to the episode can be considered situated, just as the identity characteristic triggered by it (Oyserman 2015). Her identity and self-perception of her impairment influenced judgement, action and behaviour (ibid).

Even before the visit, Susan was apprehensive about the possibility of causing injury to other visitors, in particular children. Her embodied practice observed in instance 5.7 shows how distressed bumping into the pushchair made her feel. After that episode, she became insecure and heavily relied on Sally's guidance. Only after they reached the fourth floor of the museum (emptier compared to the ground floor), her body and posture relaxed, and she stopped relying as heavily on Sally's physical guidance. An interesting interplay can be identified between identity (or better, threats to identity) and scaffolding practice. In fact, this incident directly impacted on the nature and amount of scaffolding required by Susan and offered by Sally. As Susan became insecure and progressively lost her confidence, she increasingly required guidance. Susan's body was fine-tuned to changes in activity and these findings show the role that the body plays in perceiving change and adapting to it.

Moreover, Susan's physical concerns in relation to her disability were also among the reasons why she and Sally decided to visit the fourth floor of the museum. This recurring concern relates to studies showing that disabled people tend to resist external viewings of their disability (Connors and Stalker 2007; Eisenhauer 2007; Frances 2014; Hutchinson *et al.* 2018; Spirtos and Gilligan 2020). Common mechanisms to do so include trying to hide it, avoiding situations and contexts in which impairment can become apparent, and being conscious of how actions can disclose it (ibid). A noteworthy finding that needs to be highlighted here is that the strategy Susan enacted to minimise occasions in which her impairment was disclosed, was acting to make her embodied practice resemble that of non-disabled people. She linked her arms to Sally's, who guided her through the gallery so that Susan did not have to use her mobility aids. Additionally, they planned which gallery to visit to minimise the risk of sharing the space with a crowd.

Creating these strategies to minimise the impact of her perception of self and her impairment directly affected the situated learning opportunities and her shared meaning-making with Sally. Avoiding the co-presence of other walking bodies in the space allowed Susan to focus on her social and cultural experience without worrying about how her practice and body looked to other visitors nearby.

5.7.2. Cultural and social identity

The previous section looked at how Susan's identity was shaped by her perception of her impairment and its impact on her embodied practice. This section turns to look at the engagement with the collection. Susan pointed out that her visits to art museums with her friend Sally made her feel a connection with her life before she started losing sight:

> I wanted to study art, to go to art school […] I lived […] near an art museum, and we used to go there during on Fridays when I was a child, with other children. I really liked going there. It was nice to spend time in the museum. […] When I lost my sight, I had to accept that I couldn't go to art school anymore. […] It was quite sad. […] I did English literature at university in the end. I quite enjoyed it, so it's not too bad. But it's nice to be able to come back to these places [art museums], especially with her [Sally]. We always loved it when we were younger.

Susan actively re-discovered and embraced part of her past identity as an art learner. In her case, learning involved an active participation process in the community of practice of art learners. She re-connected to her former self through the social encounter with objects and the shared meaning-making with Sally. The opportunity of visiting the museum with Sally contributed to Susan's normalisation process.

These findings are consistent with the idea that museums play a crucial role in developing cultural capital and cultural identity (Bourdieu 2010; Gombrich 1984; Hayhoe 2017). Learning had an impact on Susan's feelings of inclusion in cultural life through the museum. These findings show that visiting the museum made Susan feel a sense of belonging and ownership of the museum. By visiting museums, she strove to maintain the identity of the person with sight that she used to be. This effort can be interpreted as the determination to reject the imposition of her diagnosis of sight loss on her identity (Hayhoe 2017). This determination required Susan to adapt her practice and the way she encountered museum collections. She created different strategies, drawing from her funds of knowledge as a former museum visitor. The decision to visit with Sally, that of visiting galleries that better relate to her interests, the choice of avoiding crowded spaces are examples of these strategies. These enabled Susan to make meaning and, through learning, to develop a new identity related to her former one. Visiting with Sally, for instance, developed Susan's social and cultural identity through participation. This enabled her to gain acceptance from her cultural peer (Sally) (Keller 2005). The museum was a site that defined Susan's cultural identity as an art learner, and at the same time, it preserved a certain degree of her sighted identity. Visiting enabled a connection with her former sighted self, which Hayhoe (2017, 141) described as passive inclusion. In section 5.9, I expand on Susan's cultural identity development by presenting findings on how she made meaning through touching objects.

While Susan's identity formation process related primarily to her re-discovery of herself as an art learner, Fred's social and cultural identity development enabled him to assert his identity as a museum visitor. Despite visiting the V&A on his own, Fred mentioned tours organised by Vocaleyes and other London social groups. In particular, he said:

> It's been a big social part of my life. More than I expected. Especially like these VocalEyes tours and things. It's a great way of meeting [people]. Because everyone comes here for a common reason, because they enjoy visiting museums. You're going to an exhibition because you want to look at something. You have a common interest in things with people. So, you actually get chatty about it with them

Fred appreciated the opportunity of visiting museums as part of a social group. He seemed to find appealing the idea of meeting new people while exploring the museum collection. This suggests that he considered museums as places to meet new people and share meaningful experiences and interests. Visiting as part of an organised social group enabled his participation in that particular community of practice, negotiating his membership and developing a cultural identity adapting with his impairment. Being a museum visitor was a social trait that Fred linked to group membership (Oyserman 2015).

In the interview, he mentioned the value he attributed to museums, which helps to understand how he saw himself in relation to the institution:

> I enjoy coming to the Museum. Being here is nice. It's a nice building. It's an important Museum. I could watch a Youtube video or listen to a podcast. But it's not the same. This is an important place, an institution, it part of our culture. […] I guess I value the cultural aspect.

Fred regarded the museum as an institution with cultural, institutional, and national value, not just a repository of collections. This value was partially determined by his appreciation of the museum's cultural and institutional position and by the proximity to objects enabled by the museum. If we consider this in relation to Fred's identity development, it is clear that museums' social and cultural experience enabled his identity formation as a museum visitor. His very presence in the museum and proximity to objects enabled the development of his identity as a museum visitor (Handley *et al.* 2006). This was an essential aspect of his life, and it reinforced his identity as a disabled person.

Participating in the museum-goers' community of practice and developing a cultural identity by attending museum visits symbolised inclusion (Hayhoe 2017). This means that, even though he may not be able to access all the objects or information, participating was something that he valued as important and as meaningful for his personal development. Fred valued the practice of attending museums and participating in the museum experience as itself an acquisition of cultural identity (Darke 2003). This identity reinforced his sense of inclusion in the community of practice.

5.8. Looking

This section discusses the category of looking, namely participants' visual practice. It presents findings on how participants made visual sense of objects. In this section, I look at visual practice as the understanding of visual concepts like shapes, colour, visual depth, the intersection of light and shade. These visual concepts form what Hayhoe (2017) defines as visual culture. Despite their sight loss, participants still interacted with elements of visual culture through visual practice. Participants spoke at length during the interviews about how they used objects, what these meant for them, what characteristics they valued, and how they engaged with them with their companions. Making sense of objects happened differently for each participant, based equally on their different vision impairments and personal preferences.

Here I introduce the concept of 'historic capital' to refer to visitors' preference for the historical details of objects. This is a category that emerged from the data analysis. I framed the concept of 'historic capital' in response to Hayhoe's conceptualisation of aesthetic capital, focusing on aesthetic qualities of visual culture, explored in chapter 3 section 3.7.

5.8.1. Looking forward

The visual interaction with objects inspired Susan to prolong her learning experience outside of the museum. During the interview, Susan spoke of how museum visits encouraged her to continue learning about a particular topic. She emphasised how nice it was to prolong the experience and read about what she had seen:

> The best thing is that here you find out so many interesting things. New things, like I had never heard of mother-of-pear furniture. I really look forward to reading more about it. I think I will look online if there are book recommendations. [...] I find that this always happens, really. There is always something new you happen to discover during a visit. Once I started reading about bronze manufacturing techniques, or how they use brass to make musical instruments. I don't know, maybe an artist, a technique, even just a specific colour. I always go home wanting to find out more about something. You leave [the museum] but it's like you never actually leave it.

Susan's desire to extend the visit beyond the museum and prolong her learning experience is the effect of intense encounters with the objects. These encounters generated a sense of 'troubling incompleteness' (Carr 2001, 176). Susan explained how she wanted to learn more and continue the learning experience outside of the museum space. The encounter with objects provoked a sort of 'incompleteness'

feeling, a longing to prolong the experience (Carr 2001). Meaning-making happened while she was performing in an environment that leads to open-ended experiences. She desired to continue to make meaning of her experience outside of the museum environment.

Susan felt that she was motivated to revisit the museum. Although this book does not analyse visitors' motivations, it seems clear that this desire comes from her previous experience of visual culture. This was primarily due to her early attendance at museums as a child and throughout her teenage years, before losing sight. Susan had a history as a child of being part of a visual arts culture through school, family, and institutions. Susan developed the habit further as an adult. Visiting museums regularly is part of her social and cultural identity. The experience of visual culture during her visit to the V&A fed her already vivid desire to be part of the museum culture despite her sight loss.

5.8.2. Looking back

This section looks at Fred's preference for the historical details of the objects. Fred did not touch any of the tactile objects in the V&. He only explored the objects by looking at them, reading information on a large print guide and listening to audio tracks on his phone. He took time looking at each object, but he spent most of the time reading and listening to information. His responses in the interview allow us to understand better how he looked and made sense of the objects. The findings below show how he tended to 'look back', that is, to focus on the objects' historical details and make associations with his memories.

As mentioned above, Fred decided which area of the museum he wanted to explore in advance. He spent 2 hours and 12 minutes exploring gallery 7 'Europe and the World 1600–1815'. He read the large print guide; observed with his monocular every object in the gallery; and listened to the audio descriptions of every object that had one. Fred had few aesthetic preferences and preferred learning about the historical context of objects. During the interview, he highlighted how he valued putting into contexts the objects he was looking at instead of simply appreciating their aesthetic:

> It's ok to say "oh that looks nice", but putting it in context, understanding what you're seeing and the story behind it makes it so much more interesting

He often spoke of the connections he made between what he was seeing (furniture and decorations from 1600s) and his lifestyle:

> Yeah, I did. It's interesting to see how people used to live and to see the things that they used to have in their homes. And to compare it with what we have today. Things today are a lot simpler, I think. A lot more functional rather than fancy in appearance. I mean you

can still get artistic decorative things, but obviously a lot of people can't afford those things these days, so you just have much simpler cheaper things.

He also made specific connections between objects from the display that reminded him of objects from his personal life:

> There was a table in there that actually is a little bit similar to a table that we've got at home, you can pull each end to extend the table. It made me think and compare it to something at home. That was quite nice.

Learning, specifically in the form of finding out more about historical details of the museum's collection, was the key element that triggered empowerment in Fred's experience:

> It just great to be able to go out and about and learn something new, see new things. It just adds a lot more of a variety to my life I think. There is a good reason to go out and look at things, learn things, to enjoy things. It's great.

Fred constructed his knowledge from experiences he brought to the situated learning opportunity. Meaning-making took place through the habitus he brought into the museum. It is important to highlight the situated nature of meaning-making: it occurred at the junction between Fred's pre-visit expectations - the desire to learn more about a specific collection - and the situated meaning he made in the environment (Lave and Wenger 1991). While immersed in the experience, Fred reflected on knowledge he previously held. He performed in a specific space and was reminded of how he used similar objects in another context. In the case of the table, he interacted directly with the object, engaged with the information provided by the museum, and at the same time, he made references to both visual and non-visual aspects of the objects. The parallel he made was grounded in the material qualities of the object: how it functioned and how he used it. The meaning he found in the object did not rely on the explicit visual values enforced in the museum but instead on the bodily interaction he had with a similar object in his life. He initially drew meaning from the information on the large print guide, but he then reflected on how his own experience was related to the object's materiality. The objects possessed little aesthetic capital, with power and value deriving primarily from Fred being in their presence while learning historical details about them. Fred's visit was a chance to define his direction of cultural development.

5.9. Touching

While Fred spent his visit mostly looking at objects, the other four participants encountered objects through touch. This research started from the perspective that, as museums are primarily institutions of visual culture, the way BPSP access objects is different from that of sighted visitors. Participants seemed to experience objects through their bodily encounters, touch and, in general, multisensory experiences of proximity.

This section is divided into two different parts, which analyse the different characteristics that are part of the tactile practice of participants. Section 5.9.1 looks at how Asif and Ravi encountered objects with the assistance of their guides. Section 5.9.2 provides a detailed analysis of how Susan and Jane touched objects together with their companions. I introduce the concept of 'co-touching' to describe the process of physically touching together objects and sharing meaning-making

5.9.1. Professional guidance

This section focuses on the experiences of Ravi and Asif. Before their visit, they both asked for a guided tour. In their request, they both mentioned that they wanted to hear more about the V&A and its collection. Ravi and Asif asked for a guided touch tour in order to be able to touch objects while learning about their histories. They were offered touch tours of tactile objects by two museum guides specifically trained to assist BPSP.

While their desire for a guided tour also came from the needs related to their vision impairments, it is clear that personal preferences also played an important role. Neither Ravi nor Asif seemed to be familiar with the V&A, and they both expressed the preference of having a guide to help them navigate the physical environment and the content of the museum. In Asif's case, the personal preference to have a guide was also related to his general lack of confidence. In Ravi's case, he asked for a guide because he was unsure about the museum content and he had a specific list of activities that he wanted to perform during the visit. In both cases, the possibility of touching objects seemed to be the main reason for both of them to ask for a guided tour. This personal preference sits at the same level as the needs coming from their vision impairments.

Additionally, Ravi and Asif explained how the presence of accessibility features, like tactile objects, are a trigger for empowerment and inclusion:

> And thinking about accessibility and vision impairment, and how people can get the same enjoyment and fun as the others sighted people get. It's good. It makes you feel like you belong – Asif

> Museums definitely need to be more accessible. Like a million time more accessible. It was good to have touch objects. If you don't, you're saying "this place is not for you". Accessibility means that you give everyone equal opportunities. There's still so much work to do – Ravi.

Ravi enthusiastically interacted with his guide. During his visit, he asked his guide questions about the museum's history, the history of each object, the materials, and the shapes. The two often engaged in conversations where Ravi would describe what he was feeling to his guide, giving inputs on the subjects they were discussing.

In section 5.6.1, I showed how the guide guided Ravi around the museum space. Instance 5.8 below shows that while at the beginning Ravi seemed to heavily rely on the guidance of his guide, as soon as he became more familiar with the environment and confident with his abilities in the space, guidance faded (in a typical scaffolding pattern) and he moved around confidently and independently. His tactile practice in the space followed the same pattern. Instance 5.8 illustrates how the guide scaffolded Ravi's exploration of the first tactile object of the tour:

Instance 5.8:

	Source: video	Source: fieldnotes
	When they touch their first object, the Ming vase in China gallery 44 (figure 5.17), Ravi waited until his guide took his hand and placed it on the vase to start touching it (figure 5.18a). Then he waited until his guide moved his hand around the whole length of the vase (figures 5.18bc). He listened very carefully to the guide's guidance, who was explaining the shape of the vase, its rim, and the bottom, and he touched what his guide guided him to touch (figures 5.18 abc).	Ravi's guide started with an introductory talk about the vase, and while she was speaking, Ravi did not touch the vase although it was in front of him. She took his hand and placed it on the vase when she started talking about the material features of the object.
	He took a step back from the object when they stopped to touch the vase (figures 5.19 ab).	When the guide stopped talking about the material features of the vase, and she started to explain its history, Ravi stopped touching it.

Figure 5.18. Ravi's guide guiding his hand on the Ming Vase.

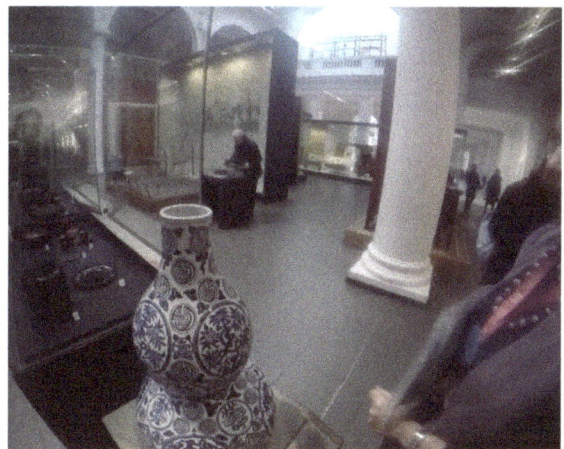

Figure 5.19. Ravi taking a step back from the object.

This initial instance shows how Ravi was less confident and seemed hesitant to touch objects on his own initially. He relied heavily on his guide, following guidance and instructions to make sense of the object. Ravi did not touch the object on his own and did not attempt to investigate other features besides those his guide pointed out. He relied on the information that his guide provided.

Instance 5.9 shows how gradually Ravi became more confident and relied less on the guidance of his guide as the visit progressed and they touched other objects together:

Instance 5.9:

	Source: video	Source: fieldnotes
		When Ravi approached Danny Lane's glass staircase (figure 5.20), his guide guided his hand, placing it on the knob of the first pillar of the staircase (figure 5.21). She verbally explained to him the shape of the staircase while guiding his hand on the knobs on top of the first two pillars (figures 5.22ab).

Figure 5.17. Ming Vase. China gallery 44, V&A.

He bent to touch the base of the pillars (figure 5.23), he kneeled to touch and feel the entire length of the pillar and the different ridges on the glass (figures 5.24ab).	As soon as he understood the staircase concept, Ravi started immediately to explore it on his own.
	He walked up and down the staircase while his guide was at the base of it, and he followed the knobs on top of each pillar for guidance (figures 5.25abcd).

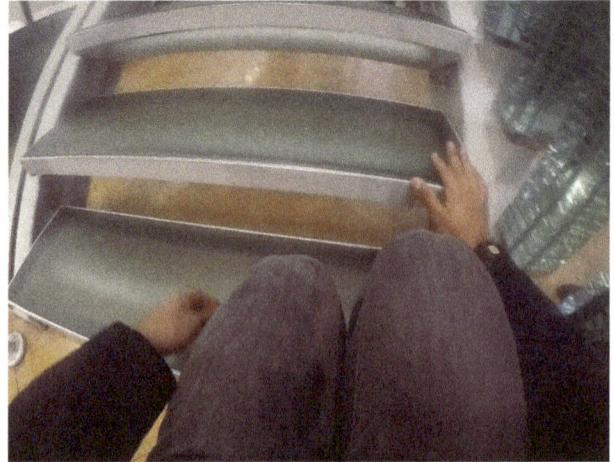

Figure 5.20. Glass staircase by D. Lane. Gallery 129, V&A (V&A 1997).

Figure 5.21. Ravi's guide placing his hand on the knob of the third pillar of the staircase.

Figure 5.22. Ravi's guide guiding his hand on the knob on top of the first pillar.

Figure 5.23. Ravi bending to touch the base of the pillars.

Figure 5.24ab. Ravi bending to touch the full length of the first pillar.

As soon as he gained confidence and became comfortable with the environment, Ravi independently engaged with the objects he encountered. Occasionally, his guide would position his hands on the features she was describing. Otherwise, she only guided him verbally. He touched with

Figure 5.25ab. Ravi touching all the pillars while climbing the stairs.

approached other objects was mostly the same. He started touching the whole object rapidly to make sense of the shape, dimensions, and materials. He then focused on one area, mainly following his guide's physical or verbal guidance. He would listen to the description and move his hands according to the verbal instruction, but he would also touch the rest of the object. At times, he tapped with his finger on the objects, presumably to get a better understanding of the materials (figures 5.26 and 5.27).

two hands, ran his hands through the entire length of each object, explored every fine detail, and kept touching while his guide was describing.

Ravi's tactile practice in the space is a clear example of scaffolding. The particular element about the tactile and embodied nature of scaffolding is the type of physical and verbal guidance required by BPSP. Guidance can be seen as the temporary system of support that enabled Ravi to perform, in this case, to make sense of objects through touch. Ravi and his guide participated in the joint activity. The guide initially offered guidance and instructions on how to touch the object to make sense of it, both verbally and by guiding Ravi's hand. As Ravi's skills and confidence developed during the visit, guidance diminished (the guide limited herself to verbal instructions) and eventually faded as Ravi became more competent. This view of scaffolding is in line with Mai and Ash's (2012) findings. They argued that guidance tends to be more evident at the beginning of the interactions and then fades (2012). Ravi and his guide's interaction followed the same pattern.

Instance 5.9 shows how he took long to explore every feature of the objects he was touching. The way he

Figure 5.26abc. Sequence of Ravi tapping on the tabernacle section with his finger.

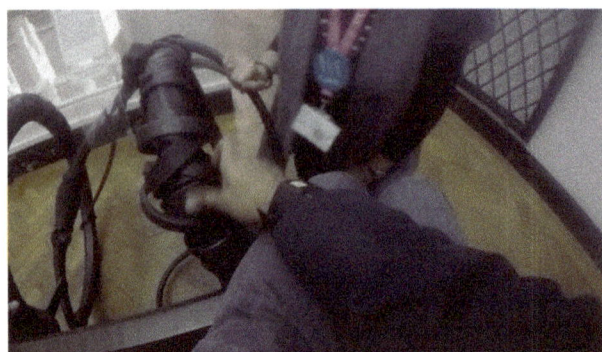

Figure 5.27abc. Ravi tapping on the metal details of the Metalwork bench with his finger.

These explorative acts seemed to respond to his need to understand the object as a whole and make sense of each feature's spatial reality. This approach to objects resembled the way he walked through the environment. He moved with confidence, striding and stomping, and he vigorously touched all the architectural features to make sense of the space around him. The combination of making sense of the space and objects was evident in how he physically engaged with the Danny Lane's glass staircase (instance 5.9). He went up and down on his own, moved around, touched the entire length of the pillars. He bent, knelt, and crouched on the floor to touch the base of the staircase. All this shows how Ravi made sense of the space, the dimensions and the context of the object first, and then he started to investigate the finer details of the object. Touch for him appeared to be an essential learning tool to establish a holistic understanding of the artwork. Handling enabled the development of a

complete spatial and tactile figure. As discussed in chapter 3, section 3.8, Spence and Gallace (2008) argued that touch cannot be understood as a surrogate of vision and that tactile examination requires significantly more time than a visual one. These findings suggest that this is what makes scaffolding different for BPSP. Ravi's practice is in line with this argument as he took a long time to handle each object to develop a complete spatial and tactile understanding. As mentioned above, at the beginning of the visit he needed guidance to develop an effective tactile strategy to fully make sense of objects. He then employed the same strategy for the rest of the objects while guidance faded.

In Ravi's experience, learning can be understood not just as cognitive and factual but also as embodied. The way he performed in the space, interacting with his guide, touching objects, and moving around, was an act of exploration and an affirmation of self-presence. His body was performing a social activity, exploring the physical environment, and a cultural act. Ravi's body regained its physical materiality by resisting dys-appearance (chapter 2, section 2.3). In doing so, he conceptualised himself as a whole corporeal entity. He made meaning through the unwavering connection between the body and the world, bringing about an 'intense feeling of self-presence' (Rees Leahy 2012, 79).

Asif had a tour similar to that of Ravi. He was guided by another specifically trained guide and was given a highlight touch tour of the collection. However, his experience was very different from that of Ravi. This was due to their different levels of visual memory, preferences, ways in which they navigated the space, and levels of confidence and cultural capital.

As Asif lost his sight later during his life as an adult, he still retained a strong visual memory, unlike Ravi. He remembered remarkably well colours and features:

> Yes you know I remember all those things, colours, what it looks like, a description. You tell me 'red' I know what 'red' is.

He described how he built up a mental image from his guide's descriptions and from touch, which constituted an essential mean to build a connection and learn from the objects:

> She tells what it is and then I touched it and it made sense. I understood what she was saying because I touch it. I got it, what the thing was.

Due to his vivid visual memory, when he explored objects, he managed to build a mental image. The way he explored objects was different to that of Ravi, as he heavily relied on the descriptions provided by his guide, and mostly used his residual memory to make sense of the object. The issue of residual memory is of paramount importance. Ravi was born with a vision impairment, and he lost his sight entirely at the age of seven. Therefore, he did not have any residual memory as he could never create visual memory benchmarks. Asif turned blind at the age of twenty-eight, which allowed him to retain a solid and vivid visual memory. Having a high level of visual memory made it easier for Asif to create mental images. On the contrary, Ravi tended to form mental images relying on his other senses, and not any form of vision. In brief, their different experiences of vision impairment meant that while their condition was the same upon entering the V&A, they drew from completely different funds of knowledge.

Unlike Ravi, Asif touched every object in the same way: he briefly touched with one hand only (he held his white cane with the other hand), and his guide guided his hand for most of the time (figures 5.28a; 5.29a; 5.30a; 5.31a). For the rest of the time that his guide talked about the object, he took a step back and stood there without touching (figures 5.28b; 5.29b; 5.30b; 5.31b). Unlike in Ravi's experience, guidance never faded, and Asif never seemed to reach a level of confidence strong enough to touch the objects independently.

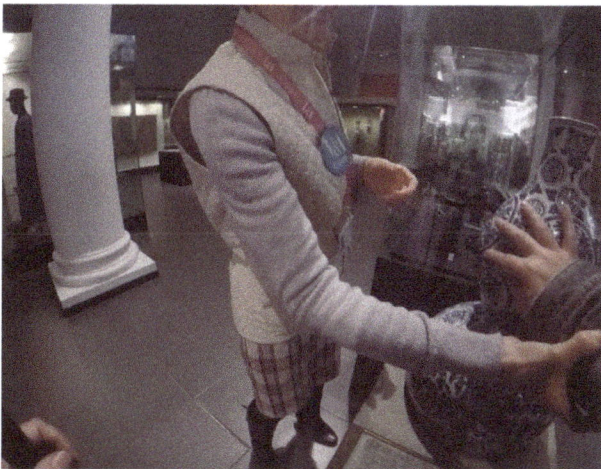

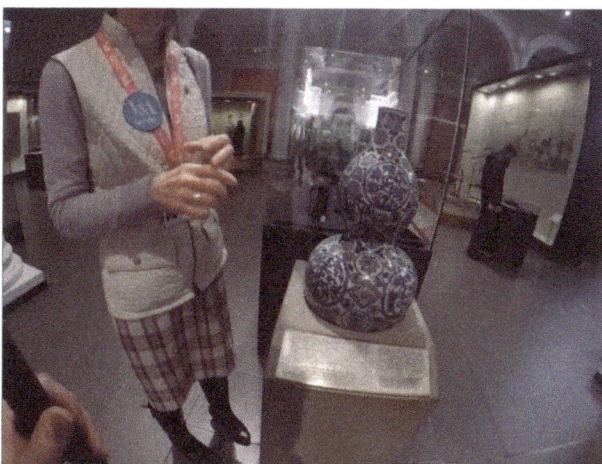

Figure 5.29ab. a) Asif's guide guiding his hand on the Bodhisattva Head; b) Asif taking a step back.

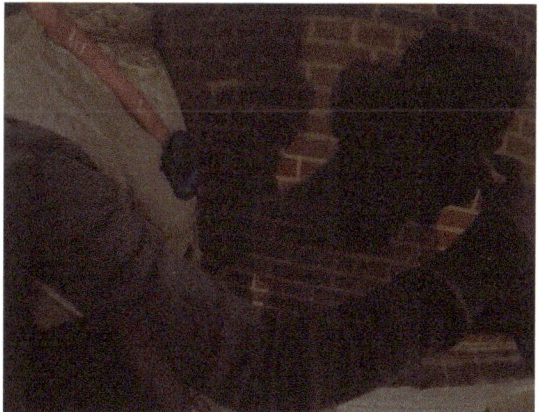

Figure 5.28ab. a) Asif's guide guiding his hand on the Ming Vase; b) Asif taking a step back.

Figure 5.30ab. a) Asif's guide guiding his hand on the Chimney bracket; b) Asif taking a step back.

Figure 5.31ab. a) Asif's guide guiding his hand on the Marble Owl; b) Asif taking a step back.

Figure 5.32ab. Sequence of Asif touching the first pillar of the glass staircase.

The way he approached the Danny Lane's glass staircase can be compared with Ravi's experience with the same object (instance 5.9). While both interactions present the traditional scaffolding element of guidance, in Asif's case, the guidance did not fade at any point. The video sequence below (figures 5.32abcde) shows that Asif only examined the first pillar of the staircase, verbally guided by his guide. He did not climb, kneel, or walk around to touch other features of the staircase. He remained still and only touched the first pillar with one hand while holding his white cane with the other hand. When his guide started sharing historical details of the object, he stood back and stopped touching it (figure 5.32e). Additionally, when his guide asked him whether he wanted to climb the stairs and feel the other pillars, he declined.

These less dynamic tactile interactions seem to clash with Asif's initial self-reported desire to touch objects and physically engage with the collection. This apparent clash between Asif's personal preferences and the actual performance in the space can be explained if we look at his level of confidence in relation to his vision impairment. If we look again at Asif demographic findings and compare

it to Ravi's, it is clear how their background is entirely different despite having the same impairment. Ravi had experienced vision loss and blindness for all of his life. He was twenty-six years old when he visited the V&A, and that essentially gave him twenty-six years of 'experience' at being visually impaired. On the other hand, Asif lost his sight when he was twenty-eight years old, seven years before taking part in this research. Being blind for 'only' seven years meant that he had less time than Ravi to adapt to the condition. Ravi started to build strategies to experience the world with sight loss as a kid and received substantial support both at school and from his family. In a certain sense, having lost sight early on in life gave Ravi a more 'privileged' habitus compared to Asif. Findings suggest that this form of habitus is peculiar to BPSP, and it can be seen as a fund of knowledge that BPSP bring into the museum. This fund of knowledge allowed Ravi to grow confident and empowered and develop strategies and capital, to apply to various contexts of his life.

On the contrary, Asif explained how he stopped working since he lost his sight and heavily relied on his family for daily tasks. He mentioned how only recently he managed to resume studies and become more independent. This is in line with national statistics that suggest that people who lose sight earlier in life and are given adequate support tend to outperform those who lose it later in contexts like work, education and sport (EBU 2020; NFB 2019; RNIB 2019).

During his touch tour, Asif was also allowed to touch with gloves two sculptures by August Rodin in gallery 21, 'August Rodin at the V&A', which generally cannot be touched. One sculpture was the head bust 'Portrait of Honoré de Balzac' (figure 5.33), the other one was 'The Fallen Angel' (figure 5.34). Asif's guide could not

Figure 5.33. Portrait of Honoré de Balzac, by A. Rodin. Sculpture gallery 21, V&A (V&A 2007).

Figure 5.34. The Fallen Angel, by A. Rodin. Sculpture gallery 21, V&A (V&A 2002).

touch the sculpture but could only guide Asif's gloved hand. Below, I compare the two interactions with the two sculptures (instances 5.10 and 5.11) to show how touch enabled Asif's making of meaning.

Instance 5.10:

Source: video	Source: fieldnotes
	His guide handed him one glove, helping him fit it (figure 5.35a), and offered to give him the other glove, but he refused (figure 5.35bc). Asif only took one glove as he was carrying his white cane with the other hand. As he wore one glove only, he touched both Rodin's sculptures with one hand only.
	His guide took his hand and placed it on the object 'Portrait of Honoré de Balzac'.
She told him that it was the face of a human being, and she verbally guided him to touch the different features (figures 5.36abc).	While she was explaining each feature, like the moustache (figure 5.36a), the hairy chest (figure 5.36b), and the chin (figure 5.36c) of the bust, Asif independently moved his gloved hand on the sculpture to touch the features his guide was mentioning. He did not seem to have difficulties identifying them, and he did not need guidance.
[the camera struggled to capture all the hand movements as Asif stood very far from the object and only touched with one hand stretching his arm to the right-hand side]	Asif never went close to the object, and he stretched his hand most of the time.
After Asif touched the object, he stepped back even further and stood listening to his guide (figure 5.37).	
	While his guide described the object, Asif asked questions about the colour and commented about the cold feel of the sculpture. He did not seem to have difficulties in understanding the object.

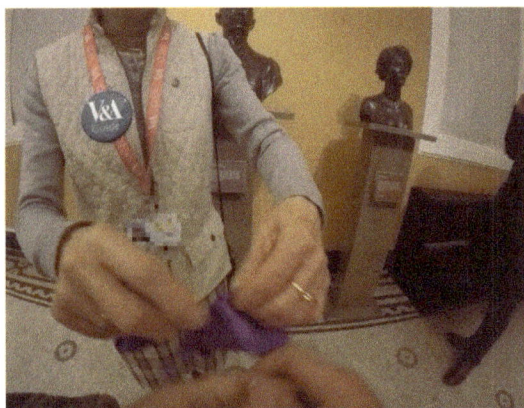

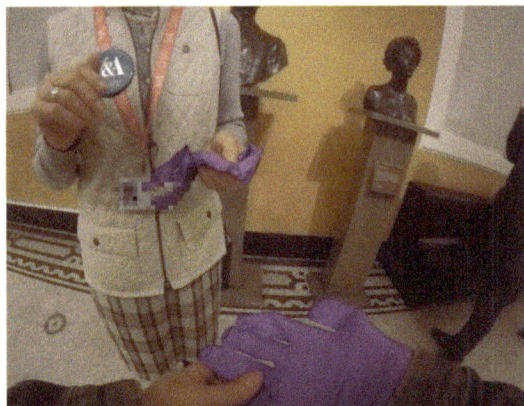

Figure 5.35ab. Asif's guide offering him gloves and Asif's wearing only one.

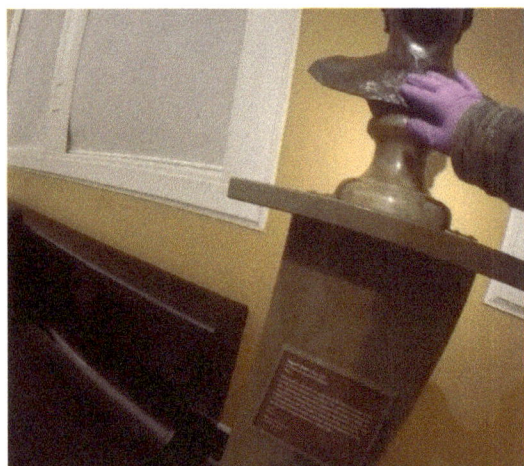

Figure 5.36ab. Asif independently touching the different features of the bust, following his guide's verbal guidance.

Figure 5.37. Asif taking a step back when his guide started explaining the significance of the sculpture.

Instance 5.11:

Source: video	Source: fieldnotes
	Afterwards, when they approached the 'Fallen Angel', his guide explained that it was a highly complex sculpture, even before they started to touch it. Before making Asif touch it, she explained the shape, the material and the concept of Rodin's art behind the sculpture.
	Asif touched with one gloved hand only, as he was carrying the white cane in the other hand, and he did not wear the second glove.
She took his arm and guided it on the sculpture (figure 5.38) without touching the sculpture herself. She verbally guided him on the different features that she explained (figures 5.39abcd), the same way she did for the previous sculpture.	
	Asif asked some questions as he did not seem to understand the shape and the concept of the sculpture despite verbal guidance.
	His guide tried to respond and guide him even more precisely verbally. However, Asif still did not seem able to follow the guidance.
As verbal guidance did not seem enough, his guide tried to guide his hand and arm on the features of the sculpture she was mentioning without touching the sculpture herself (figures 5.40).	This guidance seemed to help Asif understand the features of the sculpture better.
Asif took a step back, and he stood listening to his guide (figure 5.41).	They spent 10 minutes trying to make sense of the object together, but Asif did not seem to understand it. Hence the guide said that it was just a highly complex object, and she started to explain the style of Rodin.

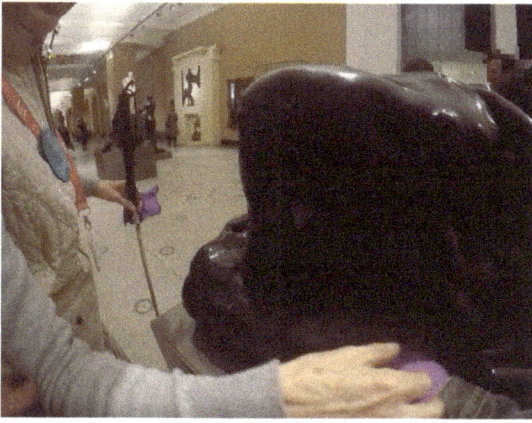

Figure 5.38. Asif's guide taking his gloved hand and guiding it on the sculpture.

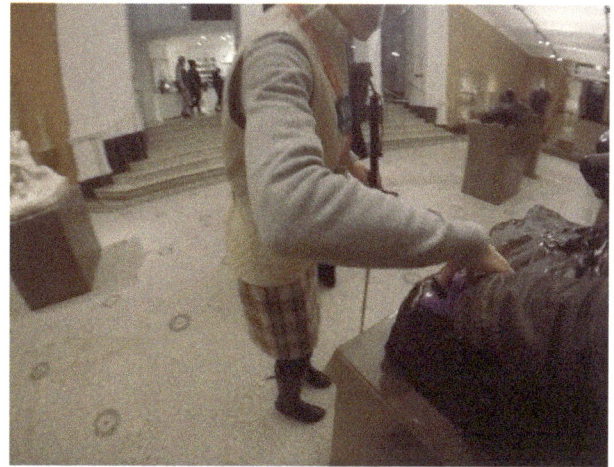

Figure 5.40. Asif's guide guiding his hand on the sculpture.

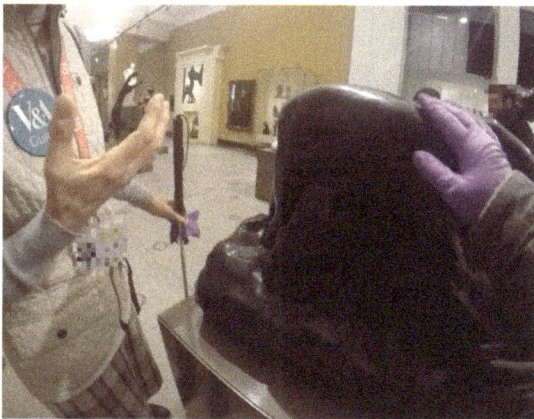

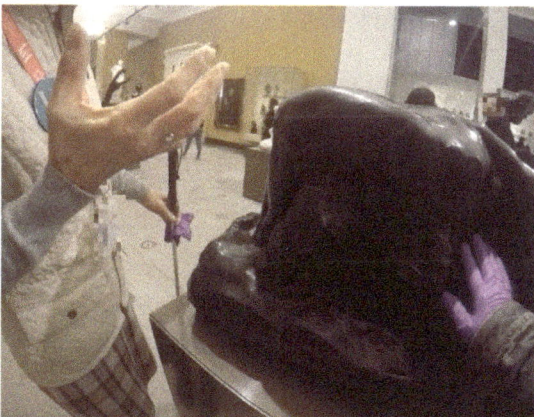

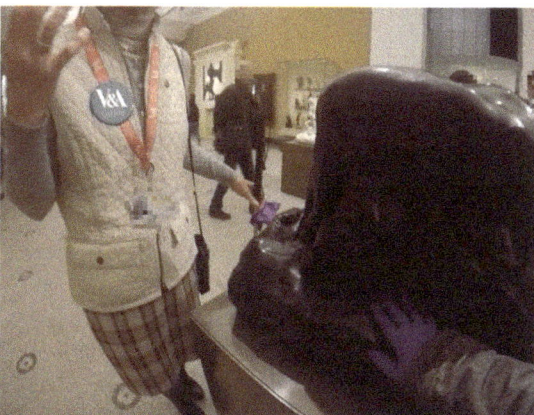

Figure 5.41. Asif taking a step back when his guide started explaining the significance of the sculpture.

Figure 5.39abc. Asif touching the sculpture following the verbal guidance from his guide.

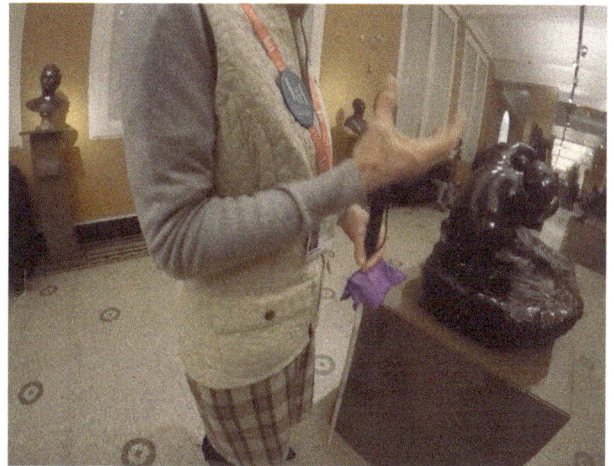

Asif had no previous knowledge of who the artist Rodin was. Despite this, he did not seem to have difficulties making sense of the first sculpture. On the contrary, during the interview, he pointed out the serious difficulties he had in understanding the second sculpture:

[when I touched 'The Fallen Angel] I thought 'what the hell'. [...] I wasn't really getting the point. Maybe I was with the gloves - I was touching it but I did not get the feeling of what it was. I didn't understand the shape. The other one [Portrait of Balzac] was quite clear, you know - the face. And this one was confusing. Two ladies, I think she [the guide] said, two men - but I don't know because normally when I touch things, I get the impression, a mental image. I create the picture in my head with imagination. But this one wasn't really clear. It was really confusing - she mentioned a male and then a female and then an animal. But the other, like I said, was quite clear. I could picture [it] in my head. [...] She [the guide] was explaining really well, but I think it was not the same impression. Maybe it was because of the gloves I had. Or maybe something else, I don't know. I didn't get the same feel of the other previous [objects that he touched] It probably was a very tough or strange object.

Despite the guide provided a description of the material, the shape, and the subject of the artwork, Asif found it hard to make sense of it because it is an intricate and complicated piece even visually (as it can be seen from figure 5.34). While other objects that Asif touched had simple, familiar shapes (animal-shaped objects, figures 5.42 and 5.43), this one appeared to be more complicated. Asif expressed the possibility that gloves made it difficult to understand the object and altered the authenticity of touch. While this is certainly plausible, he also mentioned that he had no difficulties touching the 'Portrait of Balzac', despite the material of the sculptures was the same and he touched both with gloves.

Asif did not manage to identify any of the features of the 'Fallen Angel', despite the guide's efforts to verbally guide him. He stroked the sculpture with one hand, but the complexity of the object, coupled with a superficial touch did not allow him to make sense of it. Vom Lehn (2010) observed something similar in his research. He noticed how BPS participants had difficulties to differentiate certain features of artworks for material-related reasons (vom Lehn 2010). He observed how the guides would take time to attend to the participants' difficulties by

Figure 5.43. Bronze horse. Gallery 111, V&A.

guiding their hands, in a similar way as Asif's guide did with him (ibid). Vom Lehn (2010, 761) argued that despite the guides' verbal guidance, 'the inclusion of the [BPSP] unavoidably remains partial because of [their] lack of sight'. My analysis partially confirms vom Lehn's findings, however, it takes it a step further. I argue that as well as the lack of sight, Asif's cultural capital was a key cause of his difficulties with the 'Fallen Angel'.

It is helpful to look at how he touched both sculptures by comparing the two sequences from the video findings. 'Portrait of Balzac' is simple to explore tactically: it is a realistic representation of a human face. The 'Fallen Angel', on the contrary, is the epitome of Rodin intricate style that connects the subject of the artwork with the material. Even visually, it is difficult to detect where the material ends and where the subject begins. Their tight connection and intersection are part of the object's intangible value. The material itself and how it is shaped is central in the works of Rodin, and even if Asif did not understand the subject of the artwork, he sensed that the impossibility to directly touch the material due to the gloves affected his overall experience.

When prompted both by his guide and by me during the interview, Asif admitted that he was not familiar with the Rodin's work and that he had never heard of the artist before. This probably heavily affected the understanding of the artwork, as even visually, it would be difficult to

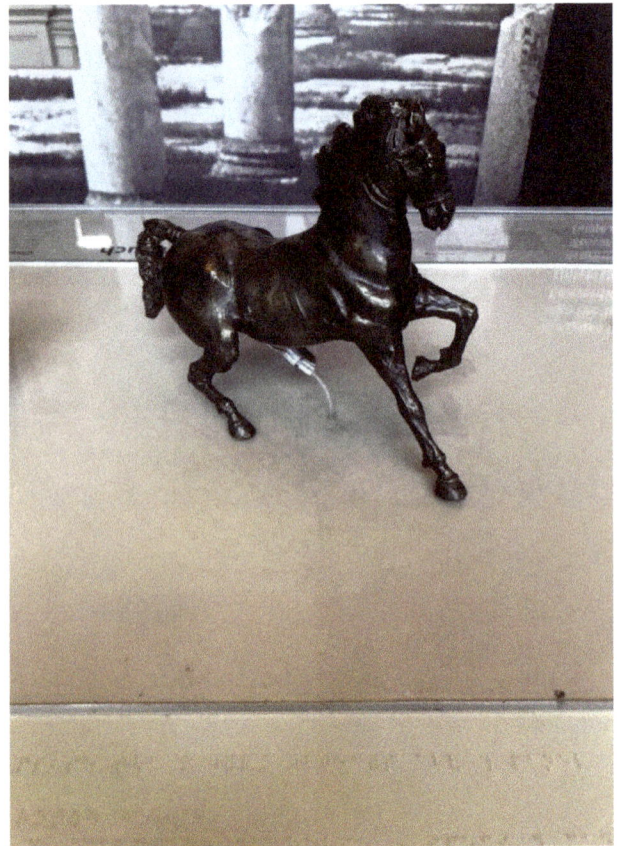

Figure 5.42. Marble Owl. Gallery 111, V&A.

understand and appreciate such an intricate piece of work with no insights into Rodin's style. Additionally, Asif decided to touch only with one hand (even though his guide offered two gloves). This probably contributed to the overall understanding (of lack thereof) of the piece. Moreover, the guide could not touch the artworks, so she could not guide Asif's hand precisely as she did with other pieces. Finally, Asif and his guide spent less than four minutes in front of the artwork. This timeframe is limited and possibly not enough to give an overview of Rodin's style, a non-visual description of the artwork, and to guide the tactile exploration.

Despite the possibility to touch objects, Asif still experienced a form of cultural exclusion which was mainly caused by the lack of knowledge about Rodin, a lack of interest in art in general, and the perceived absence of desire to make sense of the aesthetic features of the object, despite his visual memory could have helped him. On the contrary, Ravi renegotiated his inclusion in the visual culture of the museum by focusing on the non-perceptual qualities of objects rather than on their aesthetic qualities. Instead of offering some kind of gratuitous tactile experience, as the touching of the 'Fallen Angel' seems to be, it seems reasonable to argue that the museum can offer a different type of scaffolding tactile experience, which can accommodate both aesthetic and non-perceptual engagement and understanding of objects.

From a socio-cultural perspective, Bourdieu argued that the act of looking and studying art in the museum develops a high cultural capital (2010). The cultural capital then becomes part of the visitor's habitus with a solid social and cultural value. In the case of Asif, his low cultural capital made it difficult for him to access the complex artwork in a form of aesthetic exclusion. According to Bourdieu (1984, 2), 'a work of art has meaning and interest only for someone who possesses the cultural competence, that is, the code, into which it is encoded'. The lower development of Asif's visual culture and cultural capital reflected in his tactile practice was probably influenced by educational experiences of culture through family and schooling experiences.

These findings suggest that touching is part of those bodily normative practices explored in chapter 3, section 3.3, that visitors acquire and learn to master. Due to sight loss and the complex nature of touch as a sense, BPS visitors experience difficulties at different levels in mastering the techniques associated with touching. Ravi drew on funds of knowledge and capital from everyday practices. He found support in his 'privileged' habitus and initial guidance from his guide to apply strategies to successfully touch objects. He touched objects responding to the museum script by employing his body to make sense of the space and to perform socially (Rees Leahy 2012). On the contrary, Asif seemed to have difficulties mastering these 'normative' techniques. The 'Fallen Angel' case shows how touch is full-fledged, a technique that is part

of a repository of practices learnt by experienced visitors. Learning 'how to touch' an object is at the same level as learning how to look, where to position the body, or what to read (Spence 2007). Asif struggled to make sense of the object because of his inexperience as a visitor and a substantial lack of guidance on how to touch the object, which failed to compensate for his lack of capital. In this sense, the cultural exclusion experienced by Asif in the exploration of Rodin's sculpture comes both from his habitus, working class background, less developed cultural capital, and from the lack of experience due to having lost sight later in life. As Hayhoe (2017) argued, social class, more than a disabled identity, is a key factor in the meaning-making process. This is because individuals that did not receive a privileged education, or in Asif's case an artistic one, are less likely to have access to higher forms of cultural education when older and after experiencing sight loss.

5.9.2. Co-touching

Jane and her partner Max explored the ground floor of the museum. Max helped Jane touch some architectural features (the wall by the stairs near the café, the café's walls, and the decoration on the doors leading from gallery 23 to the John Madejski Garden). He took her hand and placed it on the features he wanted her to touch. He kept his hand on her hand, either guiding it or holding it. While he guided her tactile explorations, he debriefed her on notions about architecture and design and made a link to his work and other buildings they had visited together. Jane later explained in the interview:

> Max is an architect. He was describing the place, the ceiling and the outside. He was very impressed by the architecture. [...] I liked listening to him. Sometimes I get bored when he speaks about his work, but I liked it this time because he was giving me examples and he showed stuff to me.

Jane and Max's visit resonates with Rowe and Kisiel's (2012) argument that touch has a role in expanding socially-mediated interactions through demonstration and exploration. Max used touch to engage Jane in the conversation and scaffold their meaning-making, moving it 'beyond touching for the sake of touching' (Rowe and Kisiel 2012, 74) to a more prolonged and socially mediated interaction. Max used touch to move the interaction with Jane into deeper considerations of the architectural features of the building, making links to his profession. Previous research has shown how shared tactile experiences foster stronger connections between visitors who touch objects together (Wyman *et al.* 2011). It is common for visitors to be reminded through touch and share with companions how particular museum objects are intertwined with their lives (Wyman *et al.* 2011). Sometimes past life experiences can be related to objects on display, and the museum environment becomes the ideal setting for sharing memories and strengthening relations (Alvarez 2005).

In the case of Jane and Max, touch enabled the start of conversations around Max's profession and his passion for architecture. The tactile exploration made Jane interested in the conversation and kept her engaged, facilitating their social interaction and shared meaning-making.

Additionally, Max took advantage of touching to suggest comparisons between the architecture of the V&A and other buildings they had visited together. In chapter 3, I presented Barsalou and his colleagues (2003) research about touch and memory. Findings from Jane's tactile practice resonate with their work, as touch is seen as a tool Max used to enable Jane's memory. In Jane's case, the process of remembering is body-based and partially a simulation of both sensory, motor, and introspective states. In this sense, touch enabled her memory. Recalling memories of materials is an embodied practice as the individual better recalls the physical action, gesture, posture, or facial expression connected to the memory (Laird *et al.* 1982).

Susan visited the Ceramic galleries with her friend Sally. They touched objects both independently and together, and they used interpretative resources, like tactile materials, audios, and videos. Susan praised the fact that the museum offered the possibility to touch objects to everyone, and not just BPSP:

> Yes, we had a great variety of objects and resources. It is very well structured. It gives a lot of information and there are these incredible objects that are also tactile. And for everyone! Absolutely brilliant and inclusive! [...] We could both touch all the touch objects. It is indeed brilliant, you know? [...] It made me feel included. I mean, sometimes I have to stand back and listen because things are not tactile. Here I touched everything. It was marvellous. We had a great chat about what we were touching. It's a little thing, but it's brilliant. It makes you feel included because you can say 'yes, I know what you mean', you follow the story basically. And It is better for [her friend] as well. She didn't have to describe everything to me. I described things to her as I touched some of the materials, and the shape of some of the vases. We both got better at descriptions! [...] I like not feeling too dependent. It's a little thing, you know? I can touch and it's not a big thing, but it helps. Every little thing helps. I can't see anymore, but at least I can touch.

Susan pointed out that the fact that touch objects could be explored by BPSP and their companions allowed her not to feel excluded or marginalised. The presence of many different types of tactile resources allowed her to follow a narrative. She felt that she could share her experience, significantly enhancing her normalisation process after losing her sight. It also helped the interaction with Sally, and it developed hers and her friend's non-visual verbal description skills. The presence of tactile objects that could be experienced by both Susan and Sally in their own unique ways enabled them to align their perspectives and build a shared experience of the objects (vom Lehn 2010, 761).

As mentioned above (chapter 3, section 3.6.2.1), the normalisation process within the disability studies framework means making everyday life practices and living conditions as close as possible to the everyday living and social practices available to disabled people (Nirje 1969). In the case of people who lose sight later in life (like Susan) the normalisation process usually means retaining and restoring living conditions as close as possible to the life before they lost their sight (ibid). In this particular instance, the normalisation process is understood as the possibility for Susan to participate in the museum experience to the same extent as her sighted companion and as before she lost her sight. These findings are consistent with Hayhoe's (2017) discussion on how visiting museums is an opportunity to connect and share an experience with friends and family, whether blind or sighted, and that different 'special' resources (like tactile resources just for BPSP) trigger social exclusion.

The inclusive tactile objects and resources enabled Susan to develop a sense of self-identity within the broader museum-goers community of practice. Her socially mediated interaction with Sally, enabled by touching objects together, allowed both of them to retain, develop and adapt their funds of knowledge used to perform during their visit. This instance exemplifies how Susan successfully developed and adapted her funds of knowledge during the visit, moving away from a focus on deficits and barriers (Gonzalez *et al.* 2005). She drew on her funds of knowledge to initiate conversations with Sally, and they together adapted their shared repository of knowledge to created shared strategies to read the museum script.

Video recordings show that Susan and her friend acted as equals while touching the objects in the ceramic and the furniture galleries of the V&A:

Instance 5.12:

Source: video	Source: fieldnotes
	In the Ceramic Gallery, Susan touched a large tactile jar (figures 5.44). She started from the rim (figures 5.45a), and then she proceeded to touch the entire length of the jar until its base (figures 5.45bc). She continued to carefully examine the rim (figure 5.46) and touch the vase's inside (figures 5.46). She then called Sally to join her.
	Sally then read the label of the jar to Susan.
Susan took Sally's hand and guided it inside the vase to feel the texture (figures 5.47abc.).	

Figure 5.44. Susan touching a tactile large jar.

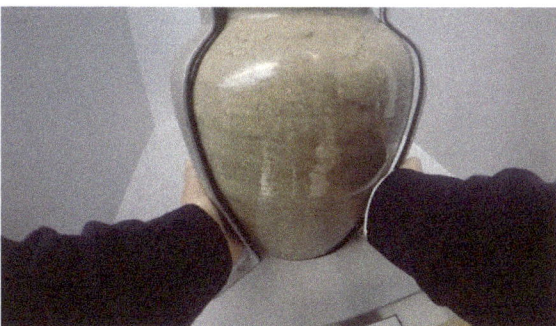

Figure 5.45abc. Susan touching the full length of the vase.

Figure 5.46. Susan touching the rim and the interior of the vase.

Figure 5.47abc. Susan and Sally touching the vase together.

Instance 5.13:

Source: video	Source: fieldnotes
	Susan and Sally start touching together examples of hand carving in the furniture gallery.
Sally showed Susan a feature of one of the carvings with a metal needle in the wood and a hole underneath (figure 5.48). Sally initially pointed at the needle (figure 5.48) and then helped Susan touch it (figure 5.49ab).	
Sally read the label, and together they started touching the horses and the human figures part of the decoration of the hand carving (figures 5.50ab).	Susan described to Sally the shapes that she was touching, like the horse muzzle and the muscled arms of the human figures.

Figure 5.48. Sally showing Susan a metal needle in the carving's wood and a hole underneath.

Figure 5.49ab. Sally helping Susan touching the metal needle in the carving's wood and the hole underneath.

Figure 5.50. Susan and Sally touching the decorations of the carving.

In the interview, she gave more details of how they scaffolded each other's meaning-making while they touched objects together:

> It was easy to understand most of them. […] The objects were not too complicated, so it was not that hard. You know, sometimes shapes can be complicated. I just asked a couple of questions […] at some point I had to show Sally the inside of a vase, because she couldn't feel it properly. […] it's normal, I'm just more used to touch things so it's easier for me.

The two instances above (5.12 and 5.13) are a clear example of how Susan and Sally shifted roles in the scaffolded exploration of objects. In instance 5.13, Susan initiated the interaction by independently exploring the jar and subsequently calling Sally to touch it with her by guiding her hand on the features she had previously examined. In instance 5.13, Sally took the lead and guided Susan's hand. They taught each other how to approach objects, scaffolding the other person's meaning-making. It is clear that scaffolding was mutual throughout their visit, in continuous back and forth interactions and negotiations between the two. These findings support Mai and Ash (2012), Granott (2005) and Mascolo's (2005) argument that scaffolding can happen reciprocally. Susan and Sally's practice uncovered a nuanced and complex layer of activity: they took turns in scaffolding each other's actions to explore objects. These 'shifting roles' and 'taking turns in leading' were the essential foundation of their social practice of approaching the museum content and making sense of objects. In their visit (similarly to Jane and Max's experience), touching can be seen as an intense social activity.

Additionally, the two instances above also contribute to the discussion on how Susan made sense of the object through touch. Susan seemed to significantly rely on touch throughout her visit. Touch appeared to be the primary sense she used to access objects, followed by audio tracks and Sally's descriptions by Sally. This is in line with Kleedge's (2018) argument that BPSP who have grown used to their impaired condition rarely rely on residual vision to perform tasks that include visual elements. Despite her residual vision, Susan relied on touch to make sense of the material properties of objects and to initiate conversations with Sally about the collection. Her tactile practice in the space suggests that she learnt to interpret her tactile perceptions with 'higher conscious awareness' (Kleege 2018). In her case, her friend Sally also developed this higher awareness of tactile perceptions due to the fact that they often visit museums together. Therefore, this ability is part of their shared funds of knowledge that both use during the museum visit to make sense of objects together in scaffolded collaboration.

Unlike Asif and Ravi's experiences – where the tour guide would guide their hands – Susan and her friend touched objects together, without a specific hierarchy of guidance.

Susan often guided the hands of her friend to make her feel certain features she identified. Sally guided Susan's hands following the descriptions on the information panels. The instances above show moments when guidance shifted between Sally and Susan in a scaffolded meaning-making. Susan and Sally's experience of touching objects is an example of the role of touching and communication in collaboration and scaffolding. Touching supported learning through their collaboration around the exhibit, and it shaped their engagement specifically in relation to scaffolding meaning-making. Susan hoped to share her experience and learn about the objects together with her friend. Touching objects together made her feel included, as it allowed her to share the experience on the same level, rather than making her companion feel like a carer.

The social element of touch created the situated opportunity where Susan and her friend made meaning of the objects while they touched them. From the analysis of the findings presented in this section, a new category of the embodied practice of participants emerged: that of touching together, which I conceptualise as 'co-touching'. This new category encompasses the social and situated nature of touching objects in the museum. Co-touching can be conceptualised within the same theoretical framework of co-walking and co-presence as a practice that enables scaffolding activity and shared meaning. I use co-touching to analyse how the social element of touch created situated opportunities where participants and their companions made meaning of the objects while they touched them together.

In summary, all participants apart from Fred engaged in tactile encounters with the museum tactile collection. They co-touched objects together with their guides and companions, and they made meaning together. Participants learnt through touch about the material culture of objects as well as their historical significance. They shifted guidance roles with their companions while touching, and they made sense together. While touch broadened access to objects and offered a wider perspective on the aesthetic and historical capital, it also appeared to be misleading and confusing at times. Guidance on how to touch objects seemed necessary during Ravi's, Asif's, Jane's and, to a lesser extent, Susan's visit. The difficulty in understanding complex objects like Rodin's Fallen Angel shows that touch cannot be considered as a substitute for vision. Guidance on how to touch objects, together with audio descriptions, seems to be of paramount importance to ensure that collections are genuinely accessible to BPSP. Findings suggest that co-touching can create social opportunities in which visitors share meaning with their companions. In particular, BPSP seem to appreciate the possibility of touching objects together with their companions, as it made them feel included and welcome.

5.10. Using digital resources

My analysis turns to focus on another category of visitors' practice in the space: how they used resources,

particularly digital ones. The following section presents a contextualised analysis of how visitors participate in social interactions mediated by resources, and therefore it contributes to the consideration of my third research question. I focus primarily on the digital element of the visit. I analyse how participants used digital tools and other types of resources to interact with the collection and environment. The overall element that I consider in this section is the possibility that digital resources provide to extend our capability to perceive information that would otherwise be inaccessible. Findings presented in this section suggest that in the case of BPSP, digital technology gives them the chance to perform far beyond what might be considered possible in terms of accessing content and information.

The V&A offers audio guides (AG) to visitors that can be retrieved from the V&A website or downloaded in advance on personal mobile devices. AG are available only for particular galleries, and while some are mainstream AG, other tracks contain audio descriptions specifically designed for visitors with vision impairments. Additionally, the museum offers built-in touch screen devices and audio devices in specific galleries. Only Fred and Susan tried the mobile AG, and only Susan used the in-built audio devices in the galleries. Ravi and Asif did not have the occasion to try digital tools, as they had a guided tour. Jane did not seem interested in using technology, as she was more focused on spending a pleasurable romantic evening with her partner.

This section comprises two subsections: accessing content (5.10.1) and enabling shared meaning (5.10.2). The first one discusses how Fred used resources as a tool to access information and develop historic capital. The second one looks at Susan and Sally's experience with resources and how they facilitated and supported their collaborative activity and shared meaning-making. These subsections draw on the combination of video and fieldnotes findings, presented as 'instances' and visitors' responses to interview questions in the form of quotes. The discussion of these characteristics is informed by Hayhoe's Inclusive Technical Capital (ITC) (2015b) framework and the definition of 'inclusive technology' (Hayhoe 2014a) (both presented in chapter 2, section 2.4.1).

5.10.1. Accessing content

In section 5.8.2, I presented findings about Fred's and Susan's preference for historical and aesthetic details of objects and their subsequent development of historic and aesthetic capital. In this section, I look at how they used resources to access information. During his visit, Fred listened to the audio descriptions from the audio guides available from the V&A website, and he used the large print booklet in room 7 of the European galleries. As mentioned above, Fred expressed his interest and preference for the historic details of objects. His entire performance in room 7 of the European galleries mirrored this desire to learn more about the objects' biographies and narratives and put them into context. By looking at the way Fred used the resources offered by the V&A, it is possible to analyse how these tools enabled him to access information and make meaning.

Firstly, a recurring element of Fred's visit is that of planning. He planned his visit from the way he arrived at the museum (section 5.4), which gallery to visit and how to visit the gallery (section 5.5). Similarly, he planned the way he was going to use resources as well:

> I looked online to see what was available, yeah. I liked the fact that the Europe exhibition had like an audio guide on the website to go with it, so I was obviously trying that. [...] I downloaded - I actually bookmarked the website where you listen to the audio, hence I made sure to have that handy. I bookmarked it on my phone. You can't download it directly to your computer, so you have to go on the website for that. [...] I listen to the introduction before coming here. So that I knew what to expect and how it worked. Here I only started to use it and listened to the objects. I can then focus on it, rather than learning how it works and wasting time. It takes a while. It's easy but not too easy.

He mentioned that he appreciated that he could access the audio from his phone both before, during and after the visit, rather than picking up a new device at the museum. The audio available from the website allowed him to choose and familiarise himself with the contents of the visit before entering the museum. This enhanced the experience since he knew what to expect, listened to the introduction ahead of the visit and focused more on the objects rather than spending time learning how to use resources.

Fred's habit of planning every aspect of the visit applies to the way he approached resources. Planning is the strategy that allowed him to perform in the space successfully and to make meaning. Following Bourdieu's (1986) sociological perspective discussed in chapter 2 (section 2.4), Fred's cultural consumption was mediated by technological devices, which allowed him to make sense of the objects by developing historic capital. One interesting element is Fred's desire not to 'waste time learning how to use the online audio guide' while in the space. If we look back at Hayhoe's (2015b) discussion of inclusive technical capital (chapter 2, section 2.4.1.1), technology resources can be considered inclusive if they grant equal access to technology, and the skills derived from it, which are crucial to develop social inclusion (Hayhoe *et al.* 2015). The fact that Fred needed time to learn how to use the resources and allocate that time before the visit shows that the technology provided does not promote 'technical inclusion' (Hayhoe 2015a). Despite Fred's literacy in the use of technology, he still required time to familiarise himself with it and to 'learn how to

use it'. His responses during the interview show that he feared that he would have taken a long time learning how to use it directly in the space, making it a detriment for his experience and, therefore, triggering social exclusion (Hayhoe 2017). In this specific case, Fred did not mention whether he encountered difficulties due to the usability of the technology or due to his impairment. In the next chapter, I expand on this, following findings from his experience with the application 'Smartify' in the Wallace Collection.

Instance 5.14 shows how Fred's highly developed technical capital enabled him to develop historic capital. Fred is a highly empowered individual who specialises in the development and the use of technology in his professional and personal life. The highly developed technical capital allowed him to make sense of the resources offered quickly and to overcome difficulties related to design, resulting in an overall positive experience.

Instance 5.14:

Source: video	Source: fieldnotes
When Fred entered the gallery, he took his phone out and plugged his headphones in. He wore his headphones, and he started using his phone (figure 5.51).	Fred took his phone out of his pocket as soon as he entered the gallery before even looking around.
Fred looked at the screen very close to his eyes. Hence, the camera failed to capture how he was using his device.	
	He picked up a large print guide, and he read the introduction. He then turned to the first object on his right. He closed the LP guide, took his phone out again, and seemed disoriented and confused about where to locate objects as he looked around for 1 minute. He then looked at two objects around the room with his monocular, and then he used his phone again to retrieve the AG (figure 5.52)
[The camera did non capture the phone's screen due to Fred's height].	When he encountered objects with an AG sign, he leaned forward to read the word, and he typed it on his phone. He listened to the AG while observing the objects with his monocular. He used the phone to retrieve AG for each object that had one.

Fred's highly developed technical capital comes primarily from the availability of technological resources in his social group, part of his habitus. The availability of technology in the V&A positively impacted his access to knowledge, enabling Fred to gain skills. It is important to remind that Yardi argues that the availability of technology

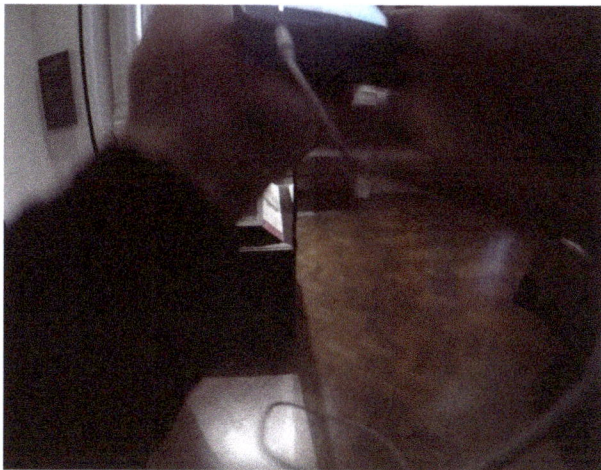

Figure 5.51. Fred starting to use his phone immediately after he entered the gallery.

Figure 5.52. Fred using his phone to retrieve AG from the V&A website.

in a network is a necessary means to develop technical capital, and it is often dependant on economic capital (Yardi 2010). As seen in section 5.2, Fred is in employment and has access to resources professionally (he is an IT developer) and recreational purposes (he has a blog). His technological expertise allowed Fred to gain access to content and information (Brock *et al.* 2010). Brock and his colleagues argued that as technical capital depends on other forms of capital, it is a key element of social inequality, as it is an indicator of economic and social well-being (2010). Fred's successful experience alone is not enough to consider the resources offered by the V&A as 'inclusive' following Hayhoe's definition of inclusive technology (chapter 2, section 2.4.1). The findings above show that using technology resources enabled Fred to empower himself by communicating information that would otherwise be unavailable to him (Brock *et al.* 2010; Yardi 2009). However, this example is not enough to assess how these resources promote inclusion in further forms of cultural, social, and economic capitals, enabling habitus in education, information and training (Hayhoe 2015a).

5.10.2. Enabling shared meaning

Susan's experience offers another helpful example to assess how participants used resources to access content and make sense of objects. Unlike Fred's experience, Susan and Sally used resources to facilitate their collaborative activity and shared meaning-making.

Susan and Sally used in-built audio in the ceramic gallery and a combination of in-built audio and the online AG retrieved on her phone in the furniture gallery. The ceramic galleries only offer in-built audio tracks that are paired with screens with videos. The audio tracks are relevant to the objects they are placed next to. Susan and Sally listened to most audio tracks they encountered.

In their case, these resources seemed to mediate their social experience and to act as tools that scaffolded their meaning-making. This was enabled because they could access the same resources and content and that Susan did not have separate resources designed explicitly for BPSP.

Instance 5.15 shows the way Susan used her body while using resources to access information to make meaning of objects:

Instance 5.15:

Source: fieldnotes
While listening to the audio track, Susan either faced Sally or shifted her body to pay attention to the object if the audio was about a specific object. After listening to each track, Susan and Sally spent time discussing the content.

In the Furniture gallery, they used a combination of in-built devices similar to the ceramic galleries' ones and AG retrieved from the V&A website on their phones. The in-built devices in the furniture gallery differed from those in the ceramic galleries, as they were paired with touch screens from which it is possible to select the type of audio track to listen to.

Instance 5.16:

Source: fieldnotes
When they approached the in-built audio devices, Sally turned towards Susan, and she told her that there was an 'audio description' track available. When Susan heard that the audio description was available, she stepped forward towards the in-built device and reached out for the headset.
Sally told her that there was only one headset, contrarily to devices in the ceramic gallery (where there were two for each device).
Susan then moved away from the in-built device, took a step towards the objects on her left, and shifted her body, turning her back to the device. She asserted that there was no point if both of them could not listen to it together.
Sally played with the touch screen while Susan was turned around, and she realised that the audio description also had a written transcription on the screen.

She informed Susan, who sharply turned around again and enthusiastically reached for the headset, saying to Sally that she could have listened while Sally could have read from the screen. Sally then selected the 'audio description' track from the touch screen menu (figure 5.53). Susan stood in front of the screen while listening to the audio, with her body slightly turned towards Sally (figure 5.54). They kept the same position at the end of the audio description while talking about it.

Figure 5.53. Sally selecting the 'audio description' track, from the touch screen menu.

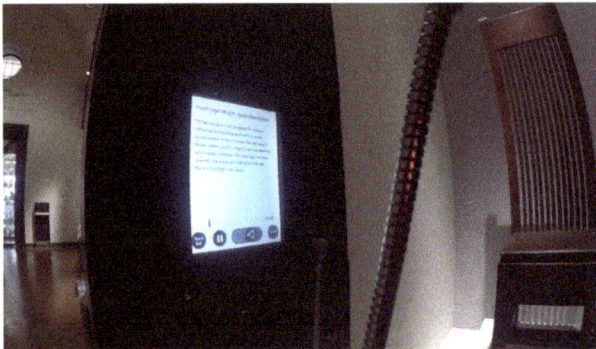

Figure 5.54. Susan listening to the 'audio description' track, using the only available headset.

Susan praised the content of the in-built devices and the fact that they were available to everyone. Similar to when she spoke of tactile objects, the possibility of accessing information together with Sally:

> The content is rich, interesting and informative. Very nice indeed. And easy to follow. We were looking at the things, and it was explaining more and adding layers of information. [...] Some of them [in the furniture gallery] had a choice for audio description. Very nice. I liked that we could use them together. It makes a difference because it's the same as for things that we could touch. It's different if I'm the only one who can touch, or I have a special tour. Here we did it together. [...] We could talk about the same thing because we listened to the same thing

Technology, in this case, supported socially mediated and collaborative interactions. The audio devices were an interactive tool to engage both Susan and Sally in learning. Collaboration was a key element of their scaffolding interaction. The design of the device and the surrounding space enabled the two friends to stand together and comfortably interact with them in pairs. While the presence of only one headset initially disrupted the interaction, Susan and Sally managed to comfortably move in the space in relation to the devices, to each other and the objects. The audio devices shaped scaffolding forms of interactions between Susan and Sally in three ways: 1. they paid joint attention to the devices facing them while listening to the tracks, 2. they explored objects letting the audio tracks' content guide their learning, and 3. they scaffolded each other's meaning-making by facing each other and having conversations prompted by the audio tracks' content. Hence, technology, in the context of Susan and Sally's visit, was used to foster scaffolding strategies.

The design of the devices paired with tactile objects and the fact that both friends could use them at the same time increased the interactivity, together with the social and collaborative activity. The interaction with the devices did not hinder the social activity but instead enhanced it. As seen in other studies, these interactive resources can promote collaboration by enabling simultaneous interactions and supporting joint meaning-making (Cecilia 2018; Proctor 2005; Seale *et al.* 2021; vom Lehn and Heath 2005).

An element that facilitated the social activity and the joint meaning-making was that the devices could be used by both Susan and Sally (even if, in the case of instance 5.16, it required adaptation). As seen in previous sections, a key element in Susan's practice was the possibility of doing things and making meaning together with Sally. Her embodied practice, in instance 5.16 show to what extent this is a crucial element for Susan. Her bodily posture reveals an initial excitement at the possibility of listening to audio descriptions. This physical momentum was a sign of genuine enthusiasm, probably since audio descriptions are usually specifically designed to facilitate BPSP's learning (Hutchinson and Eardley 2019). However, her sharp change in bodily posture when she was told that only one headset was available hints that her desire to make sense of the exhibit together with Sally was far greater than the interest in the accessible resources themselves. This suggests that Susan's perceived value of the audio track was strongly connected to the social element of using it with Sally. The initial difficulty made Susan lose interest in it despite the outspoken interest in audio descriptions. The possibility to use the device together renewed her interest and enabled the joint action of listening together. The combination of the interactive nature of the devices and the situated opportunity offered to use them together scaffolded Susan and Sally's activity and supported their shared meaning-making.

5.11. Conclusion

The analysis of the findings from the V&A revealed six major categories of embodied practice addressing different aspects of the visit's social context: co-walking, scaffolding, identity formation, looking, touching, and using resources.

Key findings showed how participants were deeply aware of the presence of others in the space, and they negotiated and adapted their walking practice to that of others in the same perceptual range. The discussion on co-walking was preceded by an initial section (5.4) where I presented how participants arrived at the museum. This section helped to identify how participants' everyday embodied practice shaped their walking practice in the museum.

Scaffolding is the sociocultural concept adapted in the museum context by Mai and Ash (2012) that I discussed in chapter 2, section 2.5.3. I used it in section 5.6 as a hanger concept to analyse how visitors' bodies interacted with others in scaffolded meaning-making of the museum content and environment. Scaffolding instances were analysed here, starting from scaffolding techniques that participants enacted interacting with each other and using tools. Key findings showed that guidance faded or did not fade in the space due to the participants' different vision impairments, confidence levels, familiarity with their scaffolders, and personal preferences.

The third category (section 5.7) was defined as 'identity formation' following Wenger's (1998b) situated learning, identity and social practice framework, as explored in chapter 2, section 2.5.1. This section contributed to understanding the correlation between identity and practice, discussing how participants negotiated their identities together with the negotiation of meaning. Key findings included the fact that meaning was developed through social relationships and shared identities. Additionally, participants saw museums as social spaces where they developed their social and cultural identity. Participants placed value on the act of visiting museums and on being able to pursue their cultural interests with their companions. Museums appeared to largely contribute to the normalisation process of sight loss and acceptance of disability-related identity. Being able to touch objects on open display with their companions enabled them to feel that they could share their experience, making them feel part of a normalised notion of enjoying the museum. This contributed to preserving their sighted cultural identity and the re-discovery of their identity as museum visitors and art learners.

The category of looking (section 5.8) came from Hayhoe's (2017) and Kleege's (2018) discussion on 'visual culture' that I presented in chapter 3, section 3.7. Here, I discussed how participants made meaning of visual concepts, despite their vision impairments. Key findings showed that participants' visual practice was a way to prolong their museum experience and focus on historic details of the objects. In response to Hayhoe's concept of 'aesthetic capital' (chapter 3, section 3.7), I created the concept of 'historic capital' as a part of cultural capital to define the type of capital participants developed when

they focused on the historical and biographical details of objects.

The category of touching (section 5.9) came from the discussion on the way visitors, and BPSP in particular, made sense of museums' collections through the sense of touch together with other visitors (chapter 3 section 3.8). I referred to the practice of touching together as 'co-touching', creating a category to conceptualise the social and situated nature of touching objects in the museum. Co-touching, here, was seen as a practice that enabled scaffolding activity and shared meaning. Key findings showed that touch facilitated participants' learning about the material culture of objects and their historical significance. Participants constantly shifted guidance roles with their companions while co-touching in a shared negotiation of meaning. While touch widened access to objects and provided a broader perspective on the aesthetic and historical capital, it appeared also to be misleading, confusing, and deceptive. The case of Asif and his difficulties clearly show how participants' cultural capital had an impact on their meaning-making just as much as their vision impairments.

The final category, using resources (section 5.10), brought together the interactions that participants had with resources in the space. This category looked at how participants used resources and how their technical capital (presented in chapter 2, section 2.4.1) facilitated the shared meaning-making. Key findings showed that technology facilitated access to content and information about the collection, supporting socially mediated and collaborative interaction. Participants used them as a scaffolding tool to negotiate and scaffold their shared meaning. Two important elements that determine participants' ability to use the resources were their technical capital and the accessibility and inclusivity of the technology itself.

6

Wallace Collection

6.1. Introduction

This chapter presents findings from the second case study, namely the Wallace Collection. The analysis is based on the post-visit interviews, video data captured from the GoPro camera attached to participants' chests during the visit, and fieldnotes. Three participants agreed to visit the Wallace Collection: Fred, Lily, and Davide. One participant's interview (Davide's) was carried out in Italian, transcribed, and translated into English.

6.1.1. Description of the Museum

The Wallace Collection is an art collection housed at Hertford House in Manchester Square, London. It is a national museum, which displays the artworks collected in the 18th and 19th centuries by the first four Marquesses of Hertford and Sir Richard Wallace, the son of the 4th Marquess (Wallace Collection 2020). It features important French 18th-century paintings, furniture, arms and armour, porcelain and Old Master paintings arranged into 30 galleries (ibid). The Wallace Collection opened to the public in 1900 in Hertford House and remains there to this day (ibid). It is a non-departmental public body, and admission is free (ibid).

The museum offers a package with a designed audio guide for BPSP and a large print floorplan (ibid). At the time of participants' visits to the museum, the website advertised audio guides (AG) specifically designed for BPSP (Lily, 11/2017; Fred 12/2017). As per the 27th of April 2021, the website does not advertise AG specifically designed for BPSP anymore (Wallace Collection 2021). Some galleries have large print labels, and there are arms and armour handling collection and wood marquetry handling materials available (ibid). Additionally, the gallery offers a series of multisensory events specifically designed for BPSP: 'Sensation!', 'Life drawing for Visually Impaired Visitors', and music sessions in partnership with Wigmore Hall and RNIB Family Day (ibid). These events are usually personalised experiences with a target audience, primarily elderly BPSP, and take place in designated

rooms away from the galleries (personal communication, 2017). It aims to make people comfortable in a dedicated space, create long-lasting relationships with the audience, and provide different multisensory experiences (personal communication, 2017). Technology is not usually employed during these events (personal communication, 2017).

6.2. Visitors Profiles

6.2.1. Visitors' demographics

Three participants visited the Wallace Collection, two males and one female. Fred and Lily were respectively British and Scottish. They were in their early thirties, held a university qualification, were all employed in managerial positions, and used technology for work purposes daily. Details of their work positions are not disclosed as they could make them identifiable. They both moved to London for work after university. Davide was Italian, but he lived in London at the time of the visit. During the interview, he explained that going to museums is a mainstream practice part of the London/British lifestyle. He compared his life in Italy, saying that he did not use to go to museums there, but only when he travelled abroad. He used to view it as a touristy activity rather than as part of his daily life. On the contrary, in London, he realised that museums are social spaces not only for tourists. He moved from Italy to London for work, and he stayed because he met his British partner James. He explained that he had to adapt to the new lifestyle with the difficulties of his sight deteriorating:

> It's already hard enough to deal with all the things. Things are very different here from home, and sometimes I feel like I have to make an extra effort. The fact that I'm losing my sight makes everything worse. You know, more difficult.

These difficulties seemed to come both from Davide's impairment and the circumstance that he moved to a different country and had to adapt to a different lifestyle. Sight deterioration is only one of the factors that made adapting to his life in the UK onerous. Table 6.1 presents

Table 6.1. Visitors' profile

	Fred	Lily	Davide
Gender	M	F	M
Nationality	British	Scottish	Italian/British
Occupation	IT developer and blogger	Education manager	Software developer
Highest educational qualification	BSc Computer science	BSc Mathematics	BSc Economy
Other museums visited[13]	V&A MoL	MoL	/

---

[13] As part of this research project.

participants' profiles, including gender, age, nationality, occupation, and highest educational qualification. Pseudonyms are used in writing for confidentiality. Fred visited the V&A first (chapter 5), the Wallace Collection and the MoL (chapter 7). Lily visited the MoL (chapter 7) as well.

6.2.2. Vision impairments

At the beginning of the interviews, I asked participants what type of vision impairment they had and how long they had been visually impaired. One participant, Lily, had been blind since birth. Fred had been impaired since birth, but his residual vision was 'still good enough, to the point that I can go around and do stuff almost like anyone else'. Likewise, Davide, who had been impaired since he turned eight years old, had enough residual vision and did not use a navigation aid.

Table 6.2 presents a summary of the different vision impairments of participants.

6.2.3. Visiting habits

Table 6.3 shows that all three participants are regular museum visitors[14]. As mentioned above (section 5.2.3), Fred typically visits museums two-three times per month, and he usually visits with friends, members of social groups, and on his own; Lily visits museums occasionally once every one/two month with her friends or with her partner; Davide occasionally visits museums mainly for special events with his partner or with his friends. Apart from Fred, who visited the Wallace Collection on his own on this occasion, the other two came with their usual companions.

6.3. The identified categories of the embodied practice

The analysis of participants' practice is presented following the same major categories of embodied practice identified in the previous chapter (Table 6.4). The category of co-touching is not present in this chapter as the Wallace Collection does not offer tactile opportunities in the main galleries, and participants did not touch objects. The identified categories addressed different aspects of the social context of the visit as follows: co-walking, scaffolding, identity formation, looking, and using resources.

6.4. Getting to the museum

During the recruitment process, all participants asked how to arrive at the museum, and they expressed different degrees of concern about the wayfinding. This section focuses on how participants arrived at the museum and the strategies they employed for navigation. Findings presented in this section come exclusively from interviews, as participants arrived at the museum on their own. Similar to chapter 5 (section 5.4), navigation elements and strategies that emerge in this sections are recurring as important factors throughout the next section 6.5 on walking in the museum environment.

During the interviews, I asked participants how they arrived at the museum and how their journey was. They explained in great details how they arrived and how their journey unfolded. Fred arrived at the Wallace Collection using the London underground. Similar to when he visited the V&A, he explained that he used the underground, and he did not have difficulties finding the place:

> Yeah, I'd already checked it out on City Mapper from my phone, and Google Street View, so I knew where I was going.

Table 6.2. Participants' vision impairments

	Vision impairment and residual vision	History of vision	Navigation aid
Fred	Diagnosis: Aniridia and Nystagmus. Issues: sensitivity to sunlight and glare; poor distance vision; shaky eyes, making it hard to focus on things unless they are close or enlarged.	Impaired since birth. Significant visual memory.	No aid Uses phone and monocular
Lily	Diagnosis: Blindness with some residual light perception	Blind since birth. No visual memory.	White cane
Davide	Diagnosis: Macular degeneration progressive vision impairment	Impaired since 8 years old Significant visual memory.	No aid

Table 6.3. Visiting habits

	Frequency	Typical companion	Companion on this occasion
Fred	Frequent	Friends; members of social groups; partner; alone	Alone
Lily	Frequent	Friends; partner	Friend (here called Ginny)
Davide	Frequent	Partner; friends	Partner (here called James)

---

[14] Definition from Merriman 1989, 49.

Table 6.4. Summary of the characteristics of sociocultural practice identified within each category

```
6.5 Co-walking
    • Planning
    • Co-presence and co-awareness
6.6 Scaffolding
    • Guidance and support
    • Shifting guidance
    • Intimacy and humour
6.7 Identity formation
    • Cultural identity
    • Social identity
6.8 Looking
    • Looking forward: expanding learning
    • Looking back: historic capital
    • Aesthetic capital
6.9 Using resources
    • Accessing content
    • Sharing meaning
    • Interest in new technology
    • Inclusive technical capital
```

He used the same strategy to arrive at the V&A (section 5.4). Again, he explained how he uses those navigation applications to check his routes in advance during his daily life. As I discussed in section 5.4, planning characterises Fred's navigation practice in his everyday life. He uses technology to plan his journeys through unfamiliar environments and to minimise difficulties related to his impairment. Findings from this section and the following one (6.5) further support that planning is a key element of Fred's embodied practice inside and outside the museum.

Davide came to the museum using the underground as well. He explained that he rarely has problems using the underground and that he uses it daily:

Oh I use the tube [underground] all the time. I think I never used a cab since I moved to London. [...] To be fair, I used it [the underground] in Milan too [where he used to live].

He mentioned that he only uses mobile applications to check the fastest route for his journey, as his vision is good enough to allow him to navigate a space without aids. He only checked the route to the Wallace Collection on the same day of the visit, and he admitted that he and his partner got lost on his way from Bond Street Underground Station to the museum:

[...] Sometimes it happens, and that's when I think I should check where things are before I just go. It's a bad habit. But to be fair it's not a big deal. James or I can just google where we are when we get lost [...] I use my phone and my computer for work all day every day, when I'm around I hate relying on it too much [...] I guess I'm fine with getting lost here and there. James is just a mess. He gets lost all the time, he just hates to use his phone.

While Fred and Davide have similar levels of residual vision, they described very different strategies and

activities that are part of their everyday practices. Based on my analysis, Fred seems to heavily rely on available technology tools like applications and navigation software to plan his journeys. Davide, on the contrary, is less inclined to use tools to plan his activities in advance. It is possible to look at their different uses of navigation aids to reach the museum and in general during their lives as everyday practices. I now turn to examine how these practices are applied in the context of the visit, particularly how they planned their visit.

Checking information and planning in advance was a recurring practice in Fred's visit. In the interview, he explained that he looked at the museum youtube channel and the instructions to use Smartify. He told in the interview that he looked at the website to check information about the collection, accessibility information, and he downloaded the floorplan online. He explained that this is something he would typically do for every museum he visits[15]:

I want to try all that stuff [resources mentioned on the website] out if I could. I check everything in advance or I would certainly miss some of that stuff on the day. [...] it [the website] looked very informative. There's all sorts of information there. It just made it look really enticing to come to. Very interesting. [...] I like to come prepared. It saves so much time if you already know where to go, what to ask for.

On the contrary, Davide did not plan his visit in advance. He and James did not check information on the website, but Davide mentioned that they had a look at the Wikipedia page of the Wallace Collection when I recruited them to be part of the research. During the interview, he mentioned several times how he does not mind 'getting lost' or 'taking longer' to get to places. He also described himself as 'chilled' and 'easy'. When I asked him to elaborate on that, he explained:

I'm losing my sight, it's fine. It's not like the biggest deal. And it's not like I can do anything about it. It's ok. Will it take me 1 hour instead of 30 minutes to get somewhere? Ok, fine. Will I miss something out? It's not the end of the world.

Although it is clear that there is an element in Davide's response that depends on his vision impairment and sight deterioration, it seems reasonable to argue that what emerges here is his personality and his personal preferences. 'Getting lost' or 'taking longer to get somewhere' is directly connected to his sight deterioration, but that is only one element of a more complex personality. He expressed his personal preference, which also unfolded during his museum visit.

Based on the comparison between the interview findings where Fred and Davide talk about the everyday practices of using technology tools and the way they use the tools

---

[15] These findings match with his previous experience at the V&A (chapter 5).

available in the museum context, it seems reasonable to argue that Fred seems to replicate the same successful strategies that are part of his everyday practices. Davide also seemed to replicate the same use of available tools and everyday practices, albeit those not consistently successful. Davide seemed to follow the same strategy of relying on his own (and his partner's) sense of orientation and accepting the risk of getting lost in the museum space.

Lily arrived at the museum using the underground as well. She explained that her partner drove from their home to the nearby underground station. They took the underground together, and they arrived at Bond Street station where she met her friend Ginny (with whom she visited the museum), and her partner left them to go to the museum together. Her partner picked her up again at the end of the visit directly from the museum. She and Ginny walked together to the Wallace Collection. Based on what she mentioned in the interview, she did not find the journey to the museum particularly difficult, thanks to the assistance of her partner first and her friend afterwards. Lily positively described her everyday practice of using the underground. She explains that it is easy for her to follow familiar routes and take the underground every day to go to work. However, while she expressed confidence in navigating familiar routes, she also mentioned discomfort and uncertainty when she faces unfamiliar routes. She explained how she would rely on her partner or friends to avoid unpleasant situations:

Yeah I go around on my own but it's easier when I'm with someone else. You've seen today. They didn't have anything for me [she refers to AG specifically designed for BPSP[16]]. If Ginny wasn't there, I wouldn't be able to do much. Maybe just a hot chocolate [in the café] […] It's the same outside. On the tube, you know. If something happens I don't want to be alone. It's so frustrating. I hope I get a guide dog soon[17].

In the interview, Lily often used the word 'frustrated' to describe how she feels when she cannot use the underground on her own or when she has difficulties navigating unfamiliar spaces. She used the same word in relation to when the front of house staff at the Wallace Collection was unable to find the AG specifically designed for BPSP[18]. These findings resonate with Jane's experience in section 5.4. Jane similarly expressed feelings of the frustration associated with navigating the underground, specifically due to her vision impairment.

Similar to Jane, Lily referred to her frustration every time she faced difficulties related to her disability. Whenever she faces this type of difficulties, she identifies herself with her disability, and her personality, independence, and confidence disappear. When she spoke about her use of the underground, she stated that she employs strategies to minimise frustration and unpleasant situations. She also

explained that she sometimes happens to face frustrating experiences on the underground as much as she tries to avoid them. She mentioned how she becomes very vocal about her rights as a disabled person. She said:

Don't get me wrong, I hate having to ask people to give me priority seat. I hate it. I used to be quiet and uncomfortable to avoid discussions. But now no more. If you see me with my cane, you either behave, or I'll tell you! […] That's why I prefer to be with someone. Things are rarely unpleasant with other people.

Lily's advocacy and being vocal about her rights as a disabled person helped me understand her identity as a disabled person. Lily showed signs of a developed social capital. She is a self-confident, empowered individual who is conscious of her rights as a disabled person, and she is willing to advocate for them. She employs her confidence and empowerment as a mean to encounter the space (in this case, the underground). By confidently encountering the space, Lily asserted her self-presence and became self-aware of her positioning within the environment as a disabled person and also in relation to other walking bodies. In this case, walking and navigating the underground can be seen as an empowering practice (Harris 2015). Lily enunciated herself in the space, becoming aware of her bodily reality and asserting her presence. Despite the difficulties, using public transport provides Lily with a higher sense of social freedom and diminishes the pressure on her social and cultural life.

Lily mentioned one of the 'tools' that she uses to be independent during her everyday life: 'being with a companion' to minimise the possibility of feeling unwelcome or uncomfortable. She used this tool as part of her technique of minimising the risk of facing frustrating inaccessible and uncomfortable situations, both on her way to the museum and in the museum itself. Minimising risks of encountering a frustrating situation seems a priority for Lily, as she also mentioned the desire to acquire a guide dog in relation to it. She seems to view the guide dog as a tool to navigate spaces and achieve independence.

This section has started to trace the strategies and personal preferences that participants employed as everyday navigation practices. These findings start to frame participants' behaviours and are a helpful foundation to analyse the different characteristics of participants' practice in the museum. The characteristics of everyday navigation practice examined here will be recurring elements in the next section 6.5 on the walking practice of participants during their museum experience.

6.5. Co-walking

In this section, I discuss how visitors walked in the museum in relation to objects, their companions, and other visitors. Similar to section 5.5, the discussion looks at the characteristics of walking in a museum and those of walking with a vision impairment. This section comprises two further parts, which explore the different

---

[16] I examine this further in section 6.9.
[17] Lily qualified for a guide dog shortly after her visit to the Wallace Collection.
[18] I examine this further in section 6.9.

characteristics that were identified as part of the walking practice of participants: planning (6.5.1); and co-presence and co-awareness (6.5.2).

6.5.1. Planning

Fred's experience in the Wallace Collection was similar to the one he had in the V&A (section 5.5.1). In the interview, he gave a detailed description of the planning that he did before the visit:

> I checked on the website the floorplan, the map. I check which way I had to go.

When he went to the V&A, he went to the information desk at the beginning of the visit to double-check the location of the gallery he intended to visit: 'to avoid getting lost'. Planning is a recurring element in Fred's museum visits. Figure 6.1 shows the route he took in the Great Gallery.

The route presented in figure 6.1 shows a sequential strategy to walk around the gallery. He chose a starting point and then explored every painting, objects and furniture piece, walking anti-clockwise. The video recordings show that he spent a similar amount of time in front of each painting (around 3 minutes), where he observed the painting itself and used digital tools to retrieve information. This visit strategy mirrors his desire to find out information about the paintings efficiently:

> Well, I knew what gallery I wanted to look at. So, I just wanted one of the big major ones. I knew it was a huge gallery, and again, there's so much going on in there. I want to try all that stuff out if I could and see all the paintings […] You need to know where things are to avoid wasting time or getting lost.

Fred's route and time spent in front of each painting mirrored his desire to learn and explore the museum content, to

aesthetically appreciate artworks, and to understand them in context. He spent almost 3 hours in the Great Gallery only. He looked at every artwork and only managed to explore the east side of the gallery, as the staff informed him that closing time was approaching. His walking practice in the Wallace Collection mirrors the one he had in the V&A, which suggests that Fred's practice is acquired and that he developed it as an experienced frequent museum visitor. His expertise as a practiced museum visitor provided him with the tools and strategies to read and make sense of the museum script (Rees Leahy 2012).

Fred was confident with his route and walking techniques, and he regularly employed them to achieve the goal of his visit. Fred's walking can therefore be considered a learning practice. He embraced the space and systematically engaged with cultural and digital tools. Meaning-making happened as he walked through the galleries. Hence, it is deeply connected with his walking practice. In this sense, if we look at planning as the element that enabled Fred to make meaning, we can consider planning as grounded in Fred's cultural practice (Gonzalez *et al.* 2005).

6.5.2. Co-presence and co-awareness

Several instances could be identified in Fred's visit where co-awareness emerged as a key characteristic of his walking practice. He had already expressed concerns about positioning his body in relation to objects in the V&A (section 5.5.2). Findings from interview responses, fieldnotes and video recordings (instance 6.1) show that he had similar concerns in the Wallace Collection:

> You've got to be careful not to touch it or anything because everything is quite nice and big and the lighting's good in there so I was very careful not to hit anything. So yeah, it was nice being able to get up close to stuff like that and you get a good feel for the - I mean

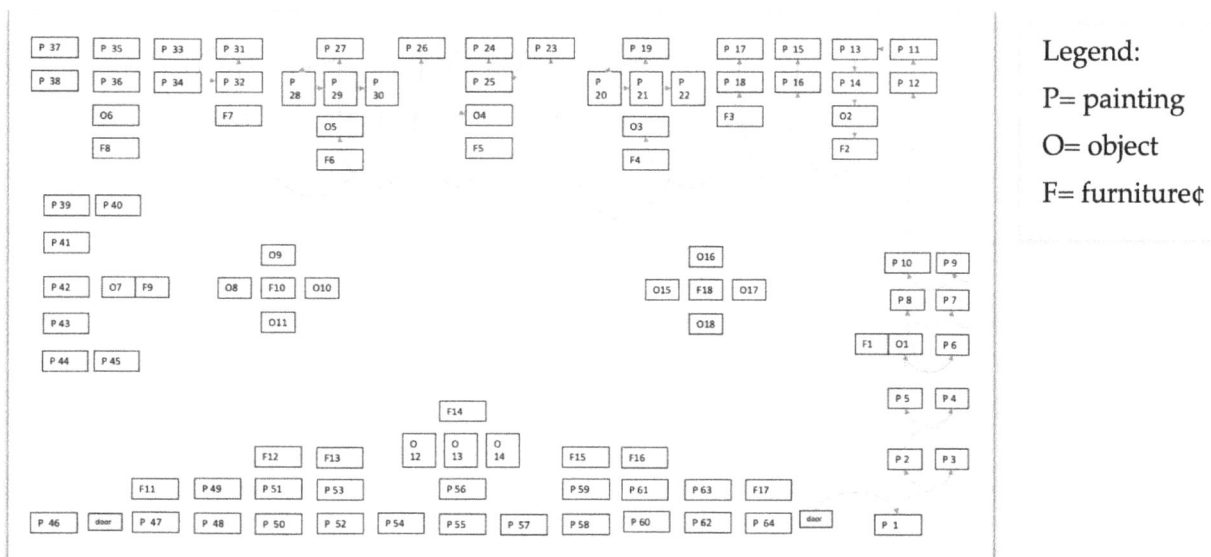

Figure 6.1. Route map of Fred's visit in the Great Gallery.

some of those paintings are huge so being able to stand right next to them you get a feel for the scale, it was brilliant.

Instance 6.1:

Source: video	Source: fieldnotes
	Fred observed each object in a similar way: he read information on Smartify, he looked at the object, and then he used his monocular to look at details.
The video shows that he kept a certain distance (about one meter) while reading and using his monocular (figure 6.2). Then, he got closer to observe objects when no other visitor was nearby (figure 6.3). He always remained further away when other people were observing the same objects (figure 6.4). He did not get closer even if other visitors were standing in his way and obstructing the view of the painting (figure 6.5).	

Figure 6.4. Fred keeping distance while another visitor looks at the objects.

Figure 6.2. Fred scanning an object with Smartify.

Figure 6.5. Highlight of the distance between Fred and the painting when other visitors stand in his way. The red line measures about one meter.

Figure 6.3. Fred looking closer at the object.

The sequence in figure 6.6 shows how he observed the bronze sculpture of a bull. He scanned it with Smartify to retrieve information (a), he read the information (b), then took a step back when other visitors got closer to observe it (c and d), and only when all the visitors left the area, he moved closer to observe the object (e and f).

In the interview, he also explained that he did not listen to the audio tracks from the Smartify application because he

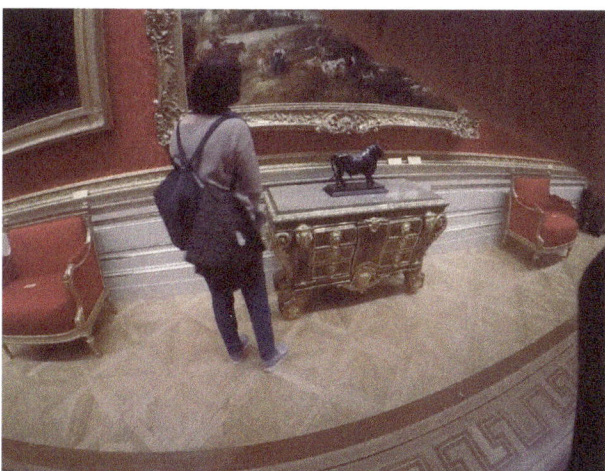

Figures 6.6abcdef. Sequence of Fred's interaction with the object.

'did not have headphones and he did not want to annoy other visitors. It would be very disturbing'.

These findings show Fred's awareness of other walking and standing visitors. As I have already discussed, Fred is an experienced museum visitor. In the two years before taking part in this research, he had visited several London museums and had familiarised himself with the museum context, content, and what kind of experience he wished to get out of his visits. He moved confidently in the environment, and he was always aware that his physical presence (he is considerably tall) could obstruct the view of paintings, sculptures and furniture for other visitors.

Despite visiting the museum on his own, Fred's visit was deeply social, as it was directly shaped by the social and physical environment where it occurred. He constantly negotiated and adapted his walking practice in relation to other walking bodies (Lageby 2013). Being co-aware of other bodies in the space triggered Fred's conscious response to those in his same perceptual range (Christidou and Diamantopoulou 2016; vom Lehn 2013). This supports my argument that Fred's embodied practice is acquired and culturally specific (section 5.5.2) (Rees Leahy 2012). As an experienced museum visitor, walking and standing were part of reading the museum script and respecting the museum's normative trajectories (Rees Lehay 2012). He let the co-presence of other visitors determine how he set his pace and negotiated spatial priorities (Harris 2015). In other words, he was constantly co-present in the space even if he visited alone (Theobo-Carlsen 2016). Fred was constantly reactive to the other moving bodies in his surrounding (Ingold 2011). Co-walking in the museum is, therefore, part of Fred's habitus as a learnt, acquired and culturally specific embodied practice (Ingold 2000).

Instances from Lily's visit suggest that co-presence and co-awareness were deeply linked with the perception she had of 'correct positioning' within the gallery and in relation to objects. Similar to Susan's visit in the V&A (section 5.5.2), Lily seemed constantly concerned about walking or standing in the 'right direction' and conforming to what she appeared to perceive as normative practices. In order to understand Lily's walking practice, it is important to present findings from Lily's self-reported concerns before the visit, which she expressed during the interview:

> [...] Well, how do you know that you're facing the right way? Even when you're listening to the device [AG] because you're kind of aware of that. Like you don't want to be standing in the wrong direction with your left-hand side facing a painting that the thing's telling you about, because it's a little bit awkward and you want to make sure you're getting the whole experience, that you're facing the painting like everyone else. You're just standing there with your audio guide like everyone else. And you're not kind of in the middle of the room listening to painting 118 that's somewhere way on the other side. I'd feel terrible. So embarrassed.

This quote shows how Lily perceives as 'incorrect positioning' would make her feel: she expressed discomfort, annoyance, and a feeling of 'missing out'. This feeling of 'missing out' shows how crucial correct positioning was for her and the importance she attributed to how other visitors may have viewed her. Lily seemed to perceive the museum visit as a 'performance' and wanted to 'perform' her part in the 'script'. She seemed to be aware that the 'performance' sits on a continuum and she wanted to be seen as an 'experienced performer'. In this quote, Lily spoke of getting 'the whole experience' in the space, which included what she perceives as correct positioning (Rees Leahy 2012).

This quote suggests that co-presence for Lily also included an element of how other people in the gallery see her. She was aware of her embodied presence and that of others in the space, and she was afraid that incorrect positioning due

to her vision impairment would make her look awkward or inexperienced. She explained that she did not want to be seen as inexperienced by others. She also emphasised several times how important it was for her to get an experience 'like everyone else', which included following those that she perceived as normative bodily practices, supposedly of sighted visitors. Despite her interest in going to museums is relatively recent, she seemed to have a defined idea of what normative bodily practices are supposed to be in a museum. Hence, during the interview, I asked her how she determined what the correct behaviour in the museum was:

> I mean, everyone knows that you can't touch stuff, and that you shouldn't go too close to paintings even if there isn't a rope. I guess I just feel I would look stupid standing far from a painting when I'm listening to the audio description of something that is far. Imagine being stuck in the middle of the room!

> [Prompt: have you had past experiences where someone told you not to touch an object or not to get too close to painting? Maybe as a child?]

> Not that I remember. I guess it's one of those things you just know.

From the findings presented so far, it becomes clear that Lily was aware of moving her body in the space throughout the visit in relation to other visitors. When she was observing paintings, she heavily relied on Ginny to position herself correctly. She folded her cane, linked her arm to that of Ginny, and they walked together. When they were standing in front of paintings, they often were one in front of the other, with their arms not linked as both were using the AG[19] and other digital tools. I now present an instance (6.2) that shows how her concern about correctly positioning her body in the gallery emerged during the visit:

Instance 6.2:

Source: video	Source: fieldnotes
Figures 6.8 abc show the sequence from the video	In front of 'Mrs Mary Robinson' painting by Gainsborough (figure 6.7) in West Room, while Ginny was checking the number for the audioguide, Lily did not realise she was standing very close to a chest of drawers. She accidentally leaned forward and hit the upper part of the object with her AG (attached to a lanyard around her neck). She grabbed the device, and she took a sudden step back. After this episode, she did not lean again towards an object, and even when standing, she linked her arm with her friend's or touched her elbow.

---

[19] Detailed discussion on the use of audio guides and other digital tools in section 6.3.5.

Figure 6.7. Mrs Mary Robinson by T. Gainsborough with chest of drawers. West Room, Wallace Collection.

Figure 6.8abc. Sequence of Lily's AG hitting the chest of drawers.

She later explained in the interview that she did that 'to understand where she was standing, to avoid feeling uncomfortable'.

Findings discussed above suggest that Lily's social practice was dependent on her social relation of co-presence with Ginny and others in the space, which, in turn, was dependent on the physical environment (Lageby 2013). Lily's response to the incident described in instance 6.2 was deeply grounded in her body's perceptual and social modalities. Lily's co-presence unfolded as she felt close to others to be perceived as she moved and walked (Goffman 1963). 'Being seen' by others who shared the same perceptual range made Lily aware of what her body indirectly communicated. She valued being viewed as a visitor who could perform 'correct' bodily techniques in the community of practice of art museum goers by adapting her practice to others (Ingold and Vergunst 2008). This was clear as she constantly made an effort to position herself at the correct distance from objects and to orientate herself in turn towards the paintings or towards Ginny. Positioning and orientating her body are part of Lily's participation framework (Goffman 1963). She used these strategies to monitor the co-presence of herself and Ginny by using non-verbal cues to engage in turns with Ginny and with objects. 'Correct' positioning and orientating enabled Lily to maintain control and negotiate their co-presence (Christidou and Diamantopoulou 2016). Lily's co-presence effectively enabled her to establish co-orientation and visual alignment with Ginny (Heath and vom Lehn 2002; -2004).

Lily's co-presence went beyond a form of awareness of others (Doxa 2001). Her embodied practice unfolded in a way that seemed to respond to external viewing and scrutiny constantly. Lily admitted to herself how 'terrible' and 'embarrassing' being seen as performing wrongly by others would be. Considering Lily's vision impairment, I argue that this was due to her lack of sight and thus to her sensory perception of co-awareness. This resonates with Kwon and Sailer's (2015) argument that co-awareness can be felt through all senses. Lily seemed to perceive the presence of others walking around them, and she kept pace with them. Therefore, sensory co-awareness can be seen as the foundation for Lily's practice (Ingold and Vergunst 2008). Co-awareness of those in the same perceptual range produced a response of concern, at times conscious, at times unconscious, from Lily (vom Lehn 2013). In section 6.7, I discuss further Lily's physical response to the possibility of being scrutinised by others, in relation to her identity development as a museum visitor and a disabled person.

Findings from this section suggest that positioning, museum etiquette, and perceived normative bodily practices played a key role in the participants' visit. If we look at walking as a cultural practice, the degree of ability to walk according to the museum's etiquette and position oneself in the space reflects the habitus of the visitor (Allen 2004a). The issue of co-presence and co-awareness raises the question of what participation means in this context. From the findings I presented so far, this research shows how BPS visitors' participation seems to happen through the body. The practice of learning how to position oneself in the space accounts for the evolving identity of the visitor and the increasing expertise through the bodily experience. Walking is a social and learning activity. I argue that this emerges in the space as, through walking, BPS visitors learn, and they change their perceived membership within the museum community: they learn how to use the space, use tools, and interact with the exhibit. Identities shifted as they increased expertise through bodily participation. It is important to make a link here between participation practices and how comfortable BPSP feel in museums both as visitors and in relation to their disability. Their participation through bodily practices is key to understand how they situate themselves within the exhibit and in social interactions, and how they perceive their body, and how self-conscious they are about how others perceive their body.

6.6. Scaffolding

Similar to the previous chapter, scaffolding elements were identified and discussed as part of all the categories presented in this chapter. However, in this section, I focus on two specific scaffolding characteristics identified and coded following Mai and Ash's (2012) theoretical framework of scaffolding in museums: 'guidance and support' (section 6.6.1) and 'intimacy and humour' (section 6.6.2).

6.6.1. Guidance and support

Davide and Lily's visits presented several instances of scaffolded meaning-making. Guidance and support were identified as key elements of the scaffolding activity. Several instances of shifting roles in guidance were identified in Davide's visit, similar to those identified when Susan and Sally, and Jane and Max touched objects together in the V&A (section 5.9.2). These are discussed below within Mai and Ash's (2012) scaffolding framework. While instances of shifting guidance were not observed in Lily's visit, her scaffolding activity with Ginny helps me discuss another element of the scaffolding activity: guidance fading. Findings discussed below suggest that while Lily's needs related to her vision impairment play an important role in their guiding dynamic, other factors (for instance, Ginny's familiarity with the museum and her expertise as a visitor) contribute to the scaffolding activity.

During the visit, Davide and James both used the application Smartify to access content about the paintings. They each used it on their own devices. While they moved together from one room to the other, they explored the content of each room independently.

James seemed to be more interested in the architectural features of the place, while David focused more on paintings and extensively used Smartify. Physical contacts, movements, and dialogues between the two are presented as scaffolding processes. The interactions mainly involved physical or verbal reciprocal guidance on 'read' certain exhibit elements. I now illustrate one instance (6.3) that includes a clear example of shifting guidance roles:

Instance 6.3:

Source: video	Source: fieldnotes
Davide looked at the painting 'Francesca da Rimini' (figure 6.9) in West Gallery III. He encountered difficulties when using Smartify to retrieve information (figure 6.10). Hence he called his partner, who was looking at another painting, asking for help (figure 6.11).	
	When James walked over, Davide explained the issue, and they both used their phones to understand why the application was not working. Davide seemed reluctant to get too close to the painting, and he gestured to James to bend and look at the label (figure 6.12). James read the label, took his phone out, typed on it and showed it to Davide. James explained to Davide from the Wikipedia page of the painting that there are several versions of the same painting, which is why the application was not recognising it.

Figure 6.9. Francesca da Rimini, by A. Scheffer. Great Gallery, Wallace Collection.

Figure 6.10. Davide using Smartify on his own, before he called James.

Figure 6.11. Davide calling James for help.

Figure 6.12. James reading the label, while Davide keeps his distance.

In this case, James took the lead in guiding Davide due to the difficulties Davide encountered. Instance 6.4 below show how guidance shifted within the same interaction:

Instance 6.4:

	While at the beginning Davide did not seem to notice the subject of the painting[20], after James explained the information on Wikipedia, he realised that the painting depicted a scene from the literature work Divina Commedia by the Italian poet Dante, which he had previously studied (he told this during the interview). The conversation between the two shifted to an explanation by Davide to James of the subject of the painting and the story of the poem. James asked questions about the historical context and the story of the characters depicted in the painting.
Together, they explored the painting itself, pointing at different features. Davide looked closely at the painting (figures 6.13 ab). He pointed at elements of the gilded frame and asked his partner to read aloud the Italian words engraved in the frame for him to translate them.	

Figure 6.13ab. Images showing how much closer Davide went to the painting compared to where he was standing in figures 6.10 and 6.12.

[20] Possibly due to either his vision impairment or the difficulty encountered using the application.

This instance (6.4) started with a scaffolding interaction in line with the traditional conceptualisation of scaffolding. James provided guidance to Davide when he encountered difficulty due to a combination of his vision impairment and the malfunctioning of the application Smartify. As the interaction progressed, guidance shifted from James to Davide as elements familiar to Davide emerged (the subject of the painting). Guidance can be seen as part of the scaffolding element of shifting roles conceptualised by Mai and Ash (2012). Davide was struggling in front of a painting and asked his partner for guidance. Guidance was then given, and James's support eventually faded, as progressively Davide became more confident and competent. However, the instance (6.4) shows that this is not the only moment when scaffolding occurred, but several others happen. The first instance of scaffolding is James guiding Davide; then, Davide positioned himself as an authority by guiding James in exploring the painting's subject. They kept taking the authority role at times, negotiating on their distributed knowledge (Ash *et al.* 2012). These instances show how shifting roles is a recurring element of their scaffolding practice, which allowed them to make sense of the exhibition.

This instance shows how part of the scaffolding and understanding the display together involves continuously engaging with each other in scaffolded meaning-making (Ash *et al.* 2012). It shows how the scaffolding practice includes instances in shifting roles. While the instance began with Davide asking for guidance, he then shifted his role, positioning himself as an authority by explaining the subject of the painting and translating words from his native language. The familiarity with the subject of the painting and the ability to translate the words engraved in the frame from Italian into English can be identified as the elements that enabled Davide to position himself as an authority and to guide James' scaffolding meaning-making. Additionally, while Davide at the beginning seemed reluctant to get closer to the painting to check the title, later, he eagerly and confidently bent over and got close to explore in more details the frame and the canvas. The fact that he knew the subject of the painting increased Davide's confidence in moving around the space and approaching objects.

Lily's impairment is different from Davide's. She had no residual vision and only minimal light perception. She used a white cane, and she often relied on the guidance of a sighted companion. In section 6.4, I presented quotes where she explained that she arrived at the Wallace Collection guided by her partner and her friend. 'Being with friends and family' is a tool of her mobility practice that allowed her to minimise the risk of negative experiences when navigating unfamiliar spaces. Going to museums was a relatively new activity in Lily's life. Hence, museums can be considered unfamiliar spaces for her. Visiting the space with Ginny gave her the confidence she would typically lack in an unfamiliar environment. Their interactions (instance 6.5) allow me to identify scaffolding activity in which Ginny gives guidance to Lily until she progressively develops confidence and guidance begins to fade, but never faded entirely.

Instance 6.5:

Source: fieldnotes
While walking, Ginny would either guide Lily with their arms linked, or Lily would grab Ginny's elbow with her hand. They never walked through the space without Ginny physically guiding Lily. At the beginning of the visit, Ginny would guide Lily and position her in front of paintings and objects. After visiting the Great Gallery and going into West Gallery III, Lily started to orient herself towards paintings and objects without Ginny's guidance. After the incident with the chest of drawers (instance 6.2), Lily stopped orienting her body towards the paintings and relied again on Ginny's guidance to position herself at a safe distance.

Lily seemed to perceive how complicated the environment was, as she explained during the interview that she preferred being guided by her companion:

> It's easier to let someone guide me around. Like I could use my cane, but it makes it easier [to be guided]. [...] And anyway, it's like quite difficult in here.

[Prompt: 'what do you mean?']

> Like, I don't think I can walk in here just with a cane. I always need someone to me. You see, even with a dog [a guide dog], it's hard. You get from A to B – fine. Here it's not like that.

This finding extends the existing definition of 'fading' within the scaffolding framework. Ginny's guidance diverted the traditional scaffolding guidance that fades as the expertise of the learner increases. Due to Lily's blindness, it is arguable that it would have been impossible for her to navigate the space entirely independently. Guidance not only never faded entirely, but it remained constant throughout the visit. Ginny's support was the tool that enabled Lily's practice: it seemed to give her confidence and to enable her to embrace the museum environment.

Lily's guiding experience can be placed halfway between Ravi's and Asif's experiences discussed in section 5.6.1. The following figure (6.14) summarises how Lily's scaffolding guidance evolved during the visit:

If we compare it to Ravi's (figure 5.11) and Asif's (figure 5.12), it seems clear that while Ravi's guidance faded and Ravi eventually took the lead, and Asif's guidance never faded, Lily's sit somewhere in between. Ginny's guidance eventually started to fade, allowing Lily to perform as an active contributor. The factors that played a role here were Lily's familiarity with the museum space and the type of relationship she had with Ginny. However, the guidance never entirely faded, and no instances were identified where Lily actively took the lead. If we consider that Ravi and Lily are both blind and have been impaired since birth, it seems clear that Lily's blindness cannot be considered the only reason why guidance never faded entirely. In fact,

Lily is a novice   observer   participant   active contributor

Guidance
is given ————————————————————→ Guidance
fades ————————————————————————→

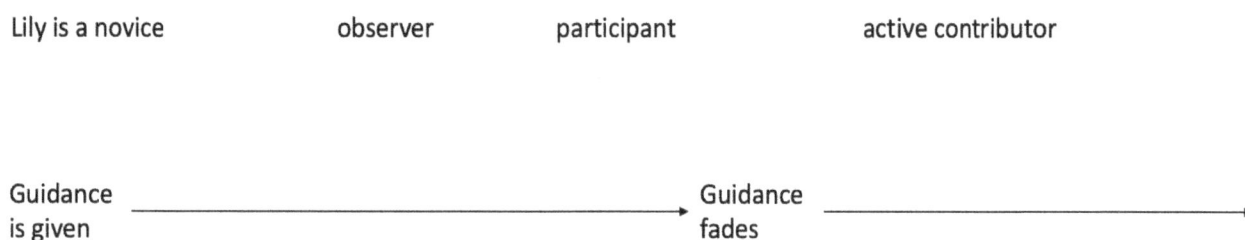

Figure 6.14. Progress of Lily's guidance.

as figure 5.11 shows, Ravi eventually took the lead of the visit as guidance faded.

Two reasons were identified to explain the difference in the evolution of guidance in Ravi's and Lily's case. Firstly, it is likely that Ravi's trained guide was trained to adapt guidance depending on the visitor's response they were guiding. While Ravi's guidance enabled him to take the lead and to become the scaffolder, Asif's guidance continued to guide him throughout the visit, responding to his needs. In Lily's case, Ginny was not a professional guide, and she was Lily's friend. Not only was she not trained to adapt her guidance to Lily's evolution as a visitor, but she also guided her in the same way she guides her on other social occasions.

An example of this is their interaction in the museum's café, where Ginny guided Lily to their table and facilitated the interaction with the café staff. Ginny seemed to be used to guiding Lily in a certain way to facilitate her friend's experience. She seemed to enact the same strategies in the museum space, and Lily appeared comfortable with her guidance. My research contributes to extending the scaffolding framework by highlighting the distinction between scaffolding and guidance between friendship groups and the dynamics and groups where one member acts in a professional capacity.

Additionally, the second reason why guidance never faded during Lily and Ginny's visit can be traced back to Ginny's expertise as a museum visitor. Lily described Ginny as a frequent, passionate, and experienced visitor. Lily explained that she started being interested in museums due to her friendship with Ginny. Consequently, it then seems reasonable to argue that Ginny's expertise and familiarity with museums put her in a different position than Lily, whom we can consider a novice museum visitor. In this case, the disparity of expertise facilitated Ginny's taking on a leadership role and maintained it throughout the visit. This analysis of scaffolding instances suggests that scaffolding is influenced by the nature of the relationship between the individuals that are part of the activity, their level of expertise, personal preference, level of confidence, and in this case, also their vision impairments. While vision impairment plays an important role in the guidance and supports dynamic, it is not the only factor that shapes the scaffolding activity.

6.6.2. Intimacy and humour

Davide visited the museum with his partner James. During the interview, Davide explained that they arrived at the museum together using the underground, and they got lost on their way from the underground station to the museum (section 6.4). When they arrived at the museum, they started to joke about the possibility of getting lost in there as well, hence James picked up a map from the front desk[21]. Based on the combination of video findings and the fieldnotes (instance 6.6), they kept joking, teasing, and laughing throughout the visit:

Instance 6.6[22]:

Source: video	Source: fieldnotes
	Davide and James walked into the Great Gallery and looked around. James elbowed Davide in the ribs and roared: 'This room is so big we could host the wedding with all of your family!' Davide burst into laughter so loudly that three other visitors turned around to look at them.
[In front of painting 'George IV' by Thomas Lawrence in the Great Gallery] Davide and James were standing in front of the painting, one next to the other, using Smartify to retrieve information on both their phones. After Davide finished reading, he turned towards James and started speaking to him,	
	and then positioned himself between James and the painting, imitating the peculiar pose of the king portrayed.
James laughed and teased him. They both laughed together.	

---

[21] This finding only comes from fieldnotes, as Davide was not wearing the recording equipment yet.

[22] This instance is a brief summary of a video-captured segment paired with fieldnotes. Screenshots of this segment could not be included, as one of the participants was identifiable.

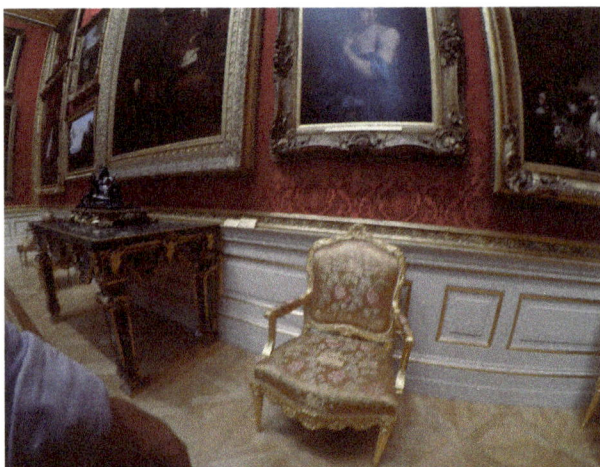

Figure 6.15. James standing next to Davide while holding hands (only part of James' arm is visible).

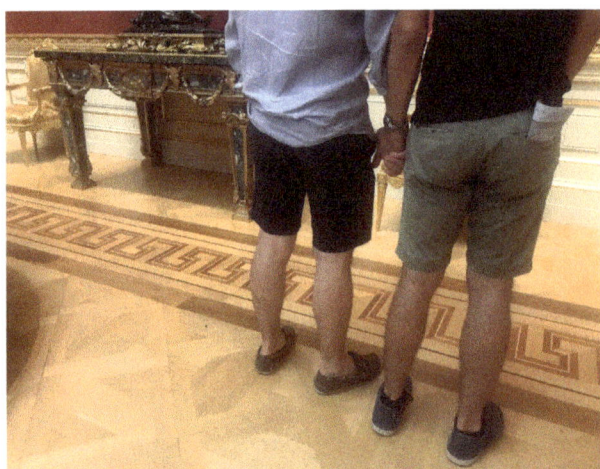

Figure 6.16. Davide and James holding hands.

The video also shows how they shared several moments of intimacy, such as kissing, holding hands (figures 6.15; 6.16), and embracing each other.

Davide and James began their visit by laughing at the possibility of getting lost. This carefree approach is consistent with Davide's self-reported personal preferences regarding navigation, which I discussed in sections 6.4 and 6.5. Laughing and joking illustrate how the couple scaffolded each other actions and ways of approaching the museum content. Instance 6.5 shows how part of understanding the exhibition together included laughing and joking together. It comprised a moment of figuring out together the content of the exhibit, which contained formal content, as well as jokes enacted through the body.

Davide and James' interactions were similar to those of Jane and Max in the V&A. Intimate physical gestures can be identified in both cases as elements that scaffolded the couple's activity and meaning-making (Mai and Ash 2012). As I have discussed in the previous chapter for Jane and Max, and as I discuss in this one for Davide and James, interactions facilitated by shared jokes and

intimacy presented a considerable level of 'emotional intimacy' and 'intuitive understanding' (Maybin *et al.* 1992, 23). Findings suggest that the more profound emotional interaction significantly contributed to how they scaffolded each other learning. In section 6.8, I present findings from the encounter of Davide and James with the paintings in the Great Gallery. While I present the instance in relation to Davide's visual practice, I also discuss further how the elements of intimacy and humour enabled their shared meaning-making.

The discussion showed how the interactions of both Lily and her friend and David and his partner included elements of social scaffolding. These intense social interactions created situated occasions in which both visitors made sense of the exhibit together. From the findings presented in this section, it is clear that the social practice was situated, dynamic, reciprocal, and involved scaffolded instances of intimacy and humour and shifting in the guidance and authority roles. Social interactions in the space formed the foundation of social practice, as they determined how the visitors responded together to the museum script.

6.7. Identity formation

This section presents findings from the category of 'identity formation'. Instances of identity formation are identified and discussed throughout this chapter. However, similar to section 5.7, this section contributes to the specific discussion on the correlation between identity development and practice. Here, I analyse how participants negotiated and refined their identities as museum visitors and disabled people. This section is divided into two further parts: identity and disability (6.7.1) and cultural and social identity (6.7.2).

6.7.1. Identity and disability

In section 6.5.2, I discuss Lily's co-presence dynamic in the space, presenting findings that suggest that she physically responded to the possibility of being scrutinised by others and thus negotiated her bodily practice accordingly. Here, I look at the incident where she accidentally hit a chest of drawers (instance 6.2), focusing specifically on how co-awareness of others, the feeling of being seen, and the potential visibility of her disability impacted Lily's identity formation as a disabled person in the museum.

Lily's experience appears to be similar to that of Susan in the V&A (section 5.7.1). Both participants verbally expressed concerns about the possibility of going against the museum etiquette because of their impairment. Susan described this possibility as 'embarrassing' and 'terrifying'. Lily used the words 'awkward', 'terrible', and 'embarrassing'. When both of them incurred incidents in the space, Susan with the pushchair (instance 5.7) and Lily with the chest of drawers (instance 6.2) seemed to attribute the incidents to their impairment and had a similar bodily reaction. Lily moved closer to Ginny, linked their arms and relied on her guidance. Susan did the same with Sally. Guidance was the tool that enabled them to physically react to the incident.

While 'being seen as disabled' is something that Susan started to experience later in life, Lily had experienced it since early childhood, as she was born blind. Being looked at or stared at seems to be an essential part of Lily's identity as a disabled person (Spirtos and Gilligan 2020). Her disability impacts her situated and ever-evolving sense of self in relation to how other people perceive her impairment (Alvesson and Willmott 2002). In this regard, the concept of dys-appearance (section 2.3) helps to understand how Lily's identity responded to the possibility of being stared at or being caught breaking the museum etiquette. If we look at identity as a social product that makes sense in the context and is expressed through the body (Schwarz *et al*. 2003), we can analyse which identity comes to mind when Lily and Susan faced difficulties in the space related to their disability. Navigation and movement-related difficulties while engaging in walking in the museum space were related to a certain degree to their lack of sight. Both Susan and Lily are familiar with the museum etiquette. They are frequent museum visitors, and going to museums is a social and cultural practice part of their habitus. They moved around comfortably for most of their visits and seemed at ease in the environment together with their companions.

Therefore, Lily's interpretation and physical reaction of the experienced difficulty triggered dys-appearance, as the relevant identity that emerged was mainly related to her disability (Imrie 2001). She seemed to associate her difficulty with her impairment rather than to the social and cultural barriers in the space (Paterson and Hughes 1999). This fact had a high impact on how she interpreted the difficulty and on which identities emerged. Her experience shows this clearly: the difficulty was interpreted as a product of how she sees her disabled body and how visibly disabled her body could appear to others. In this case, she reacted in a way that made sense for the interface between her view of her disabled body and what she thinks her disabled body means in context as a viewing subject. This situated reasoning (Oyserman 2015) influenced her choice, behaviour, and action: the difficulty was seen as solely dependent on the disability, and therefore the reaction became incongruent with her social identity as a museum visitor. In fact, after experiencing the difficulty, she took a passive attitude towards the museum content by heavily relying on Ginny's guidance, sitting down with Ginny, and chatting about non-related topics. Dys-appearance for Lily was a product of socio-spatial exclusion, which did not result from physical restrictions of the space, but from her perspective of her body as a viewing subject in a negative way that made her body insignificant and absent (Imrie 2001).

Davide and Fred instead seemed to interpret difficulties as part of the context and not solely in relation to their disability. In section 6.6.1 I discussed Davide and James'

scaffolding instance of guidance given in response to Davide's difficulty using the application Smartify. In section 6.5.2 I mentioned how Fred avoided using his phone to play audio tracks on Smartify since he did not have headphones and he did not want to disturb other visitors in his perceptual range by playing the audio track aloud. In both cases, they seemed to associate their difficulties with the accessible nature of the environment and of available resources:

- Fred did not have headphones, so he did not listen to commentaries on Smartify to avoid disturbing other people, and he stood away from paintings when other visitors were around to avoid obstructing the view for them.
- Davide had difficulties using Smartify with the painting 'Francesca da Rimini' and he turned to his partner for guidance.

Their interpretation of their disability, bodies, and context where they acted likely depended on how visible their disability was. Fred and Davide did not use navigation aids and had a good residual vision. At first glance, other visitors would have no apparent cues to hypothesise that they have an impairment. This played a significant difference compared to Lily's experience. Lily is blind with only a little light perception, and she used a white cane. Despite not using her cane in the museum, she is used to being seen using one during her everyday life. If we look at it in terms of practice, looking disabled and being seen as disabled can be identified as an everyday practice part of Lily's habitus. Despite not using a cane in the museum, the practice of being seen using one seemed consistent in her behaviour in the museum space.

It seems reasonable to argue that the perception that participants had of their disability and their body, together with the context in which they acted, influenced how they acted and described themselves (Oyserman 2001) and how they made sense of themselves and others while co-walking in the gallery (Hogg 2006; Oyserman 2001; - 2015; Oyserman *et al*. 2014). The development of identity through their relationship with the museum environment and cultural tools was related to a personal cultural journey rather than their vision impairment. Lily seemed more aware of how visibly disabled her body was, and she interpreted difficulties through her social identity related to her disability. On the other hand, Davide and Fred had a different understanding of their bodies and did not seem to associate difficulties solely with their impairment. They appeared to consider their actions in the space still as identity-congruent, so they interpreted difficulties as meaning that the action was 'for them', as well as meaningful and important in the situated context (Oyserman 2015).

6.7.2. Cultural and social identity

Lily's experience reminded that of Susan in many ways. Their experiences suggest a deep correlation between identity and practice (Wenger 1998b). Both Lily's and Susan's (section 5.7.2) identity formation in practice was enabled by the social participation in the museum visit and influenced by the 'negotiation of meaning' (Handley *et al.* 2006). Her social interaction had an equal impact on her perception of her disability on her practice and identity formation.

In order to understand the development of Lily's identity as a museum visitor in relation to her social participation, I present self-reported responses from Lily's interview and instances that exemplify how social participation unfolded. During the interview, I asked Lily why she decided to visit the Wallace Collection:

> It [the museums] is well known. So, I was quite intrigued to know what is it. I came with Ginny because she's an expert and it's great to visit with her. […] I like spending time with her. We'd normally go to a café, but this is something different.

This response illustrates that Lily valued that the museum offered her the possibility to spend time with her friend. She explained that spending meaningful time with her friend was something she valued and enjoyed doing during her everyday life. The way the visit unfolded shows how spending time together was a crucial element of their visit:

- They visited the museum's café before they started the visit. They ordered hot chocolate, and Lily later explained in the interview that having a hot chocolate is 'their thing'.
- During the visit, Lily asked Ginny twice if there were seats nearby to stop and sit. They sat on a couch in the Great Gallery (figure 6.17) and on a chair in West Gallery I (figure 6.18). They remained seated for respectively 35 and 10 minutes, and they engaged in conversations that started around the museum collection (two specific paintings) and continued to personal topics.

'Spending time with her friend', 'sitting down and chat', 'spending time in the café', 'having hot chocolate',

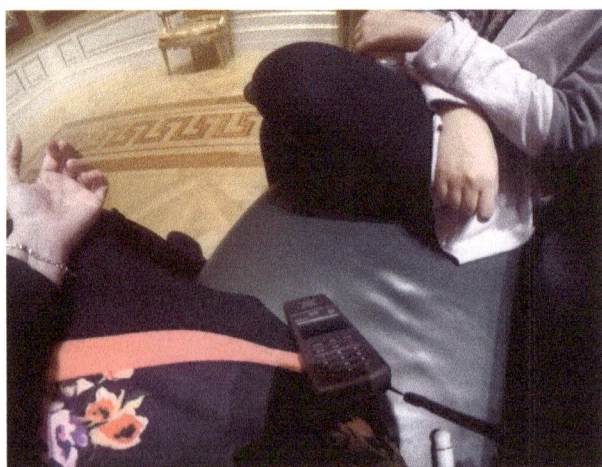

Figure 6.17. Lily and Ginny sitting on the couch in the Great Gallery.

Figure 6.18. Lily and Ginny sitting in the West Gallery I.

'chatting' are characteristics of Lily's social practice, which contribute to her identity formation. The element of going out with her friend was an important part of Lily's visit, as it was demonstrated by the fact that she actively looked for spots where she and her friend could sit down and talk before and during the visit. During the interview, she explained that she and her friend often meet in cafes to drink hot chocolate and chat about their lives. They replicated these same actions in the museum. One crucial element of Lily's experience was spending time with her friend and the visit's social opportunity. Lily developed meaning through the social interaction with Ginny and the situated learning opportunities of the visit (Wenger 1998b). Visiting the museum offered Lily the possibility to share a meaningful social experience with her friend and develop her cultural and social identity.

Another characteristic of Lily's social practice was the possibility of sharing an interest with her friend and engaging in activities to explore such interest together. During the interview, she explained that she became more eager to visit museums since she met Ginny, as museums are Ginny's favourite leisure-time activity:

> I think I've always been really interested in going to museums, but they've never been accessible. […] So sometimes I made an effort, but most of the times I would do other stuff that I know it's accessible like theatre or gigs. I've been going more since I met Ginny. She really likes going [to museums], and it's a lot easier as she can guide me, and she knows all the accessible things. […] I would not go by myself even if everything was fully accessible. I like that I can share this with her. We both enjoy art or history and it's nice to be able to do these things together. It's definitely something we have in common.

The painting Lily was most eager to see, as she told during the interview, was 'The Lady with a Fan' by Velazquez (figure 6.19). In the interview, she explained that Ginny is passionate about Velazquez too: 'It's something we have in common, we both like Spanish art!'.

Instance 6.7:

Source: video	Source: fieldnotes
When they both stood together in front of the painting, Ginny briefly described the features of the paintings: the subject, the colours, and the dimensions of it. Then, she told Lily the audioguide number, and Lily typed it on her device.	
	They listened together to the track, standing side by side.
At the end of it, they engaged in a conversation about the information they had just listened to, about the historical background, the provenance, the painting style of Velàzquez. They both contributed to the conversation by mentioning details about other paintings, other Spanish painters, and the aesthetic features.	

Figure 6.19. The Lady with a Fan, by Velazquez. Great Gallery, Wallace Collection.

It seems reasonable to argue that while Lily always had an interest in museums and their content, the general lack of accessibility discouraged her from actively visiting those spaces. She also explained that she would prioritise activities that interested her in the same way but that she knew were going to be accessible for her: theatre plays, and music gigs. Her friendship with Ginny then seemed the 'tool' that enabled her to explore her museum-related interests with her friend. Instance 6.7 describes only one of the several similar episodes that were recorded. From her responses and the way they interacted in instance 6.7, it seems clear that 'doing the exhibition together' and 'sharing an interest' was an important part of Lily's experience. 'Sharing the interest' unfolded during the visit in several instances: they looked at the paintings together, they chat about paintings and AG content, and Ginny facilitated the making of meaning by describing paintings

to Lily, by facilitating the use of technology tools, and by guiding her movements, pace, and walking.

Through her museum visits with Ginny, Lily seemed to have developed a mainstream understanding of art and, in general, collections, which is now part of her strong cultural identity. If we look at cultural identity through the lens of habitus, as coming predominantly from habits influenced by family and peers (Bourdieu 2010), Lily's identity as a museum visitor was encouraged by her social relation with Ginny. The act of attending the museum with Ginny is part itself of Lily's cultural identity. Lily looked at museums as places to develop meaningful relations rather than a repository of collections (Hayhoe 2017). Lily and Ginny used objects as a starting point for conversation relating to their own lives, experiences and emotions. By doing so, they created personally- and socially-referenced narratives about objects in a way that made the objects significant to their own lives (Paris and Mercer 2002). In doing so, they made meaning of objects, which then contributed to their identity formation. Their active construction of meaning directly depended on their knowledge, experience, interests, and social situation (Paris and Mercer 2002). Lily made sense of the painting by identifying features that reminded her of her personal experience and knowledge of the painter. In doing so, Lily recreated and embraced her memories and shared her meaning with Ginny (Paris and Mercer 2002).

6.8. Looking

This section presents findings on how participants made sense of the objects visually. The visual practice of participants was characterised by the understanding of visual culture (Hayhoe 2017, chapter 3 section 3.7). Participants' visual practice and interaction with elements of visual culture were influenced primarily by their vision impairment, residual vision and visual memory. However, the following sections show how other elements such as their personal preferences, education, aesthetic and cultural capital, social interactions with their companions, and their exposure to museums impacted participants' understanding of visual culture. This combination of factors is a major contribution that this study makes to the definition of embodied looking, expanding the traditional sense to encompass its meaning for BPSP. While in the previous chapter (chapter 5), I mainly presented findings about the tactile practice of visitors, in this chapter, I delve deeper into their visual practice, since participants did not interact with objects in a tactile way during their visit.

This section is divided into three parts, which analyse the different characteristics identified as part of the visual practice of participants. Different characteristics emerged from the analysis of the data from the Wallace Collection as compared to those discussed in chapter 5 (section 5.8), primarily owing to the nature of the museums' exhibits. While in the V&A, participants interacted primarily with 3D objects (albeit often behind ropes or in cases), in the Wallace Collection, they interacted mainly with 2D paintings. The characteristics identified were: residual vision and visual memory (6.8.1); beyond perception: aesthetic capital (6.8.2); and looking back: historical capital (6.8.3).

6.8.1. Residual vision and visual memory

In this section, I present findings about two key elements of the visual practice of participants: residual vision and visual memory. These findings are crucial to understanding how participants encountered objects, as that heavily depended on the nature of their sight loss, the type of vision impairment, the level of sight deterioration, and when they started to lose their sight. As discussed in chapter 3 (section 3.7), residual vision is the 'usable vision in an individual with congenital or acquired vision impairment' (APA 2018), while visual memory is understood as the ability to remember visual elements (complete or partial) from earlier life with more or less complex visual details (Hayhoe 2017, 141).

In section 6.5, I examined how Fred was aware of the co-presence of his body in the space and how he only moved closer to the objects when he was sure he would not obstruct the view of other visitors. When he went closer to the objects, he observed them from the 'safest' shortest distance possible, and he moved around the object, sometimes bending his head slightly to observe the object from every possible angle. The way he moved his body to see different parts of the paintings shows how he tried to use all of his remaining vision to look at different parts of the paintings and objects. This suggests that he moved his body to maximise the number of details he could grasp with his residual vision.

Findings from Fred's encounters with visual culture presented so far (section 5.8 and 6.8) challenge the assumption that BPSP cannot process visual concepts (Hayhoe 2017). Fred expressed his preference for historical details of the objects both in the V&A (section 5.8.2) and the Wallace Collection (section 6.8.3). However, his embodied practice of object fieldnotes suggests that Fred used his body to maximise the performance of his sight (Kleege 2018). Fred's embodied practice - like moving closer and positioning his body at a certain distance - contributed to his understanding of visual culture (Steier *et al.* 2015). This suggests that Fred's ability to perceive and make meaning of visual culture was grounded in his habitus just as much as it did in his sight abilities (Kleege 2018).

Fred employed well-established strategies from his everyday practice of looking at visual elements to access visual culture in the museum. The use of his monocular, together with interpretative resources like labels and the Smartify application, enhanced the impressions that Fred formed through his perception (even if impaired) (Kleege 2018). As an experienced and empowered museum visitor,

Fred did not necessarily suffer the lack of sight when he approached visual culture. Instead, he employed and relied on his learnt techniques (or funds of knowledge) to attend to his non-visual senses in different ways as during everyday practices (Kleege 2005).

Davide explained in the interview that his residual working vision allows him to make sense of images and that verbal or audio descriptions help to fill in any gaps from his immediate visual perceptions:

> I can still see quite well. It's getting worse, and it has certainly got worse in the past couple of years but thank God I can still see an image clearly enough. I miss details and there are gaps here and there. But things like audio descriptions help a lot to fill those gaps.

His vision impairment was progressive, and he started losing his sight when he was eight years old. However, he still retained a strong and vivid visual memory that allowed him to process complex visual details. He explained to me that when he was observing large paintings like 'George IV' by Thomas Lawrence (figure 6.20) in the Great Gallery, he could make sense of the subject of the painting:

> I could clearly see the face. It was a different colour from the rest of the painting. It was bright. The rest was quite dark and a bit blurry, but I think I could still see the shape of his [King George IV's] body.

These quotes show how he was able to process elaborate visual concepts like colours, light and shades. However, it also shows that his residual vision did not allow him to see finer details beyond shapes.

Findings from fieldnotes and video recordings interestingly provide insights into Davide's visual memory. In fact, he had a lively discussion with his partner in front of the painting 'George IV', as he remembered a visit to the Royal Pavilion in Brighton when he was a teenager, where he observed another portrait of the king - 'King George IV, Standing in Garter Robes' by Thomas Lawrence (figure 6.20)[23]:

> [...] It was very weird! I remembered that I went to Brighton as a kid, with school [...]. In the palace, the palace of the king, and there was this painting - a painting just like this one! It was huge, and the guy had a very funny face. He built the castle, I think? There was this huge painting, the same face – he looked like an idiot, with this weird white huge – how do you say it? Cloak? Cape? And a big necklace? I remember I was with my classmates and we made fun of it because it

---

[23] Davide did not remember the title of the painting in the Royal Pavillon (Brighton). From his description, I assumed it was 'King George IV, Standing in Garter Robes' by Lawrence. I later showed Davide a picture, and he confirmed that he was referring to that one.

looked very stupid. I think we were imitating the pose for the whole trip.

Davide used his bodily gestures to mimic the pose of the painting subject to James. He used his body to recall his visual memory of the episode and to narrate the story to James:

Instance 6.8:

Source: video	Source: fieldnotes
	Davide posed in front of James imitating the pose of the king in the portrait. He extended his neck and brought one leg forward and one hand on his chest[24]. He replicated the pose in the Wallace Collection for James, and they laughed about it together[25].
Davide remembered quite a few details from the painting, like the 'weird white huge cape' and the 'necklace'.	

Figure 6.20. King George IV, Standing in Garter Robes, by T. Lawrence (Author's own).

This set of findings shows two important things. The first is that Davide's vision at the time of his visit to the Royal Pavilion was good enough to observe small fine details in the painting. The way he spoke about the 'George IV' painting in the Wallace Collection is less elaborate, and he seemed to have missed most of the small visual elements of it. This shows how much his vision had deteriorated in the past twenty years. However, it also shows that his visual memory from the visit to the Royal Pavilion is strong and vivid: he can recall scenes from his earlier life with complex visual details. The scene he recalled in this instance is related to aesthetic visual concepts of the painting and the performance of imitating the pose of the king and the jokes and laughter he shared with his friends. Being in a similar situation with his companion and performing the same action allowed him to stimulate his memory and build a connection with the artwork. This interaction suggests that the development of a connection with objects through visual practice is more about personal and cultural journeys than sight loss.

Davide made meaning of the painting and demonstrated his interest by joining his partner to create a shared orientation to the work first and a mirroring one. Davide orientated his body to build a relation with the environment, the object, and his partner (Rees Leahy 2010). The embodied action of recreating the posture and the expression of a figure in a painting involved both an internally oriented cognitive function and a socially oriented representation that engaged others (in this case, his companion) in an interpretive process. Therefore, this specific instance of embodied practice can be seen as being part of Davide's habitus and contributing to how he made meaning of the painting (Bourdieu 2010; Rees Leahy 2012).

For instance, the interaction presented in instance 6.8 showed the role and meaning of familiarity and past experiences when he made sense of the painting in the social, situated and cultural context. Initial recognition of the subject triggered Davide's social interaction with the painting, and it was brought about through the social and embodied interaction of imitation. In this encounter, meaning-making was linked to Davide's identity and experience, and it was developed over a longer period than during this single visit. The meaning of the painting for him was valued as culturally relevant and personally significant. Davide's encounter with visual culture was an embodied and multisensory experience. This is consistent with Kleege's (2018) argument that BPSP can understand, conceptualise, and even perform visual concepts (section 3.7). Davide's interaction with the painting created a deep-seated situated relationship with the artworks, which formed a feeling of cultural ownership brought by the deep knowledge and the personal experience of it (Hayhoe 2017).

6.8.2. Beyond perception: aesthetic capital

I now turn to analyse how Lily made sense of visual concepts during her visit, despite her having no working residual vision - apart from light perception - and no visual

---

[24] It has to be noted that in the painting, the subject does not actually have a hand on his chest.
[25] Screenshots from the video are not included as the camera did not capture Davide's pose, but only James looking at him.

memory of visual concepts, as she was born blind. While these characteristics are entirely different from those of Fred and Davide, in this section, I present findings that suggest that Lily not only managed to made sense of visual concepts, but she also focused on the aesthetic characteristics of paintings, unlike Davide and Fred, despite their residual vision.

In the previous chapter (section 5.8.2), I presented the category named 'historical capital', which referred to the interest and preference of participants for the historic details of the objects they were observing. Here I discuss the category of 'aesthetic capital' (presented in chapter 3 section 3.7).

Lily seemed particularly interested in the aesthetic features of the paintings. She heavily relied on the verbal descriptions of the artworks provided by her companion and on the audio guide and, as the following instance shows:

Instance 6.9:

Source: video
When they both stood in front of the painting 'The Lady with a Fan' in the Great Gallery, Ginny briefly described the subject of the painting:

> 'it's a young very pale woman, probably 20 [years old]. She has a black veil that covers her hair and she is indeed holding a fan. It's number 208 [referring to the AG number]'.

They both stood in silence listening to the AG for about 3 minutes (figure 6.21). At the end of the track, they started talking:

Lily:	'so she was some French Duchess? What did he[26] say about the red and blue bow?'
Ginny:	'so, she has this watchcase with a blue bow on her arm. I only see blue really. Oh, wait no, there's a red thing on it, like a ribbon'.
Lily:	'Ah yeah he said that. So those are the only two colours? What is she wearing?'
Ginny:	'A brown dress. It's very dark brown. One of those big dresses of the 19th century. She has white gloves. The veil is black, and it covers her shoulders. She has a necklace. It's quite dark too. Almost black
Lily:	'but the veil?'
Ginny:	'Oh yeah sorry [laughs] yeah she's holding it with the left hand. Oh no wait, the right hand. It's brown. The same brown of the dress but with more light.
Lily:	'Yeah he said about the light. I remember that. I think he uses the white to make the light effect?'
Ginny:	'Yeah the face and the gloves are very white. But also, I think he uses lighter shades of the colour. I think that's what's going on with the fan. It's lighter where there's light'
Lily:	'mmm interesting'

Figure 6.21. Lily and Ginny listening to AG.

The audio guide provided a description of the painting grounded in visual language[27]. This was different compared to audio descriptions specifically designed for BPSP that use a more descriptive language. However, the conversation Lily had with Ginny about the visual concepts of the painting shows that the highly visual language did not confuse her. She engaged in a conversation about the information they had just listened to, not only about the historical background but also about the painting style of Velàzquez.

When Ginny mentioned details about colouring and light in the paintings, these details stimulated questions from Lily. I thought it was peculiar that she asked Ginny about using colour and light as a visual medium, due to the fact that she had previously mentioned that she had only minimal light perception. During the interview, I asked her the reason for that specific question, and she explained:

> Oh, I knew Velàzquez has this weird use of light. His paintings are usually some very dark colours with bright light. I think he uses white to make the effect. I've recently been to Spain on holiday, and we met this other couple and they had been to the Prado museum. We didn't go, but they told us that all the Spanish painters seem to adore painting with lots of light and shade contrasts.

These findings suggest that Lily made sense of the background information, details on shapes and colours, and historical details of the descriptions. She processed visual concepts through verbal imaging, according to her personal preference for the visual aesthetic features of the artworks, going beyond her lack of sight (Kleege 2018). She embraced the visual environment around her, and she actively resisted the challenges related to her lack of sight. Her disability did not trigger dys-appearance when facing visual culture (Imrie 2001), but instead she challenged

---

[26] The audio guide commentary has a male voice.

[27] At the end of the interview, I borrowed an audio guide from the museum and I listened to the track.

the difficulties she encountered, drawing on her funds of knowledge. She understood the visual element through her social participation through her body and the descriptions by her friend and from the audio guide. Although Lily could not see objects, she still desired to interact with them through visual practice. This clearly shows how visual practice goes beyond sight or the lack thereof (Hayhoe 2017).

Lily fought passive exclusion from museums owing to her blindness by developing an interest in technical features of aesthetic details, like the style, light and shades, the dimensions, and the colours. Her ability to engage with the content and visual concepts facilitated her inclusion. She seems to build her connection to the visual aesthetics in a non-visual way (Kleege 2018). However, although she developed an interest in the biographical status of the cultural tools, her primary focus seems to still be the aesthetic nature of artworks, as she often talks of visual elements. This allowed her to participate in a social experience of visual culture, making her feel included as a museum visitor. By making aesthetic sense of visual concepts, Lily acquired and developed highly formal cultural capital (Bourdieu 1986; Hayhoe 2017) and, specifically, aesthetic capital.

My research findings provide strong evidence to suggest that visual culture can be understood virtually and perceptually by all BPSP, irrespective of their impairment. Findings from Lily's experience of visual culture contradicts Hayhoe (2017) and Kleege's (2018) claim that BPSP tend to be drawn to the biographical value of the objects. They claimed that people with residual vision or usable visual memory tend to prefer the aesthetic nature of objects, while blind visitors tend to place greater importance on objects' historical and biographical details (Hayhoe 2017; Kleege 2018). Lily's experience shows the contrary: despite her complete lack of sight, the meaning she made with Ginny was heavily based on paintings' aesthetic capital. In the next section, I show how Fred and Davide's preference for the historic capital of objects also goes against Hayhoe and Kleege's argument. Despite both of them have usable residual vision and a strong visual memory, they primarily made sense of objects' historic capital.

6.8.3. Looking back

This section focuses on Lily's preference for aesthetic concepts to Davide and Fred's meaning-making of historical and biographical characteristics of objects. As I discussed in the previous section, despite Lily's lack of residual vision, she engaged in conversations about visual concepts and historical details. On the contrary, despite their residual vision is good enough to appreciate visual concepts visually, Davide and Fred clearly expressed their preference for historical and intellectual details of objects. This may be due to personal preference, alongside other factors, and further research is needed.

Davide's vision is deteriorating, as well as his ability to identify visual elements in the painting, and this was clear during the interview when I asked him to describe to me his interaction with the paintings in the Wallace Collection:

> I think I didn't look much at the paintings. I didn't think about it there, but now that you ask, I think I didn't even bother looking first. I scanned it with that app, read the descriptions and then I think I looked at them. It makes more sense to be fair. It's easier for me to look after I know what's there. Yeah, I think it makes sense. […] some descriptions [on Smartify] were really too short. I wished I could get some more details on things like painters, where they are from. You know, those kinds of things, about the history.

While Lily had a predominant interest in the aesthetic capital of objects, Fred focused on the sophisticated narratives of artworks as 'historical place markers' (Hayhoe 2017, 146). The meaning he made of them was intellectual, and, in some cases, personal and emotional:

> It's nice to be able to understand them and get the information about them [paintings]. It's interesting to read about it and then you read about how the artist had depression and committed suicide just after he painted it. It's crazy. Some quite sad stories behind these things as well. You get to hear about the artists. They do struggle sometimes. There are reasons behind why they paint what they do. So yeah, it's interesting to hear about all of these things. You feel emotional for them. They struggled so much but they produced these beautiful things and you feel a connection, you know?

This quote shows that he had a strong interest in historical details and valued the possibility of contextualising the subjects of the artworks. Additionally, he explained how getting to know information about the artists' lives enabled him to empathise with them and create an emotional connection with what he was seeing.

Fred emphasised how the intellectual, cultural development through the development of historic capital made going to museums a rewarding experience for him. While he seemed to appreciate the aesthetic quality, he expressed little aesthetic preferences, and he was significantly drawn to the historical context and intangible significance. In his interview, he described several of the paintings he observed. While he did not focus too much on aesthetic details, he explained to me the different historical information he obtained:

> You know, it's not all just sad [referring to artist's lives – previous quotes]. They tell you about the history of the painting itself. When it was made, how it got to the museum. The story of what was painted. I liked a lot the part about Greek mythology. Like about goddesses and gods of ancient times and things like that. I'm kind of vaguely aware of it. We never did it

in school very much, so kind of like hearing a bit about that. They're quite evil, some of these gods, sometimes. They're quite short-tempered. Like if they felt double-crossed or something, or if slighted in the smallest way or something, they just - yeah they're quite evil sometimes. It's quite fun though! It's like there's one goddess, I think she was discovered in a state of undress or something and so she turned this guy into a stag or something, and so his hunting dogs tore him to pieces. It's a bit much, but it's like, wow!

Fred was minimally interested in paintings as visually and aesthetic artworks, but he regarded them as cultural symbols representing a period. For him, these objects possessed little aesthetic capital, with value being primarily derived from being in their presence while learning about them (Hayhoe 2017). He made sense of visual culture not only through perception but mainly through interpretation (Hayhoe 2017). His lack of sight, paired with his outspoken preference for historic details of objects, allowed him to engage with objects on a deeper level (Hayhoe 2017). This opportunity created a situated context in which Fred developed historic capital and a feeling of cultural ownership, leading to forming a cultural identity beyond perception (Hayhoe 2017).

Fred and Davide's acquisition and development of historic capital enabled them to make sense of objects and establish a connection with their visual characteristics. From findings presented in previous sections, they seemed to have grown used to their impaired condition and rarely relied on residual vision alone to perform daily tasks involving visual elements, as residual vision can often be unreliable (Kleege 2018). Hence, they seemed to employ strategies from their funds of knowledge based on their everyday practices to encounter visual culture in the museum and make sense of objects' historical significance (Kleege 2018).

In summary, participants had different levels of residual visions and started losing sight at different stages in life. They all experienced different cultural and social engagement with museum objects as cultural tools to make sense of visual culture. They all used strategies and resources to access information about the objects: applications, audio guides, and verbal description by their companions. Some participants managed to interact with their surrounding visual culture as an intellectual practice; others managed to bring their visual practices to a deeper level. The findings presented in this section show that visual culture can be understood as BPSP visually and perceptually through visual practices. They show that participants developed an aesthetic, intellectual, and emotional connection with objects through perceptual and verbal engagement. While vision impairments influenced on a certain extent the aesthetic and intellectual meaning they made of objects, other elements of practice have greater effects. The habitus of the visitors seemed to

have a much more direct effect on cultural participation: education, background, familiarity with museums as institutions, values traditionally associated with museums, opportunity to visit museums during childhood, and vision each individual had of their disability. Participants with residual working vision (Fred and Davide) had a sense of an image, and the verbal content of the imaging can help fill in gaps missing from their immediate perceptions. Findings show that although their residual vision allowed them to get a sense of aesthetic features, they mainly found themselves drawn to the biographical status of the objects. Surprisingly, the only blind participant with no visual memory (Lily) engaged primarily with the aesthetic nature of objects, developing a higher level of aesthetic capital. This shows how meaning-making goes beyond sight and the lack thereof.

6.9. Using digital resources

This section focuses on how participants used resources, in particular digital ones. Contrary to the visits to the V&A (chapter 5), where only Fred and Susan used digital tools, at the Wallace Collection, all three participants engaged in digital interactions. The digital tools used by participants in the Wallace Collection were: audio guides provided by the museum, Smartify and Seeing AI used on personal mobile devices.

This section is divided into four sections, which explore the different characteristics identified in the way participants used resources to make meaning: interest in new technology (6.9.1); technical capital (6.9.2); inclusion tools (6.9.3); accessing content (6.9.4). This section presents several characteristics that were not identified in the previous chapter. This is due to nature and the number of resources offered by the museum and that all participants used them in different ways. Table 6.5 shows the tools participants used:

It is important to reiterate and emphasise that participants that visited the Wallace Collection are young professionals, with university degrees, who usually use advanced technology as part of their professions and during their everyday life.

6.9.1. Interest in new technology

In this section, I present one of the participants' digital interaction characteristics in the space: the interest in trying new technology. Fred explained during the interview that, even though he would still visit a museum if no resources were available, the availability of AG specifically designed for BPSP and the possibility to try out a new application (Smartify) made him more eager to visit the Wallace Collection:

I knew I wanted to try the Smartify app to get information on the paintings. I knew they had an advertisement on their website, they had an audio guide, which could

Table 6.5. Digital tools used by participants during their visit to the Wallace Collection

	AG	Smartify	Seeing AI
Description	The museum provides AG from the front desk at the cost of 4£. The AG is a handheld keypad device with no headphones. It is a push-button system operated by the visitor. The visitor enters the code assigned to the object, and the related content is provided[28].	Smartify is an independent external free application that enables visitors to scan works of art using their mobile devices and download additional information about the artwork. The Wallace Collection launched it in 2017 and advertised it on the website, on the museum floorplan leaflet, and at the front desk. It can be download before the visit or in the space. The museum offers free Wi-Fi.	Seeing AI is a free Microsoft application that uses AI software and mobile phones' cameras to describe people, text, currency, colour, and objects. It is used by BPSP during their everyday life to perform different tasks, and it is not specifically designed for or advertised by museums. The application has many functions: it speaks short text when it appears in front of the camera and provides audio guidance to capture printed pages. It also scans barcodes, recognises and describes people, facial expressions, as well as scenes.
Lily	Lily asked the museum in advance to have an AG for BPSP available at the front desk on her visit. When she arrived and asked for it, the staff could not find it and gave them two mainstream ones instead (free of charge). They used the AG for three paintings. Ginny checked and typed the numbers.	Ginny knew about the application and was keen to try it in the Wallace Collection. Ginny downloaded it in the museum on her phone and Lily's. Lily tried to use VoiceOver to convert text to speech, but it did not work. So they gave up and used the mainstream AG.	Lily had only begun to use Seeing AI. She uses it mainly to scan documents. For example, she used it to read a panel at the entrance of the Wallace Collection and one on the door of the Front State Room.
Fred	Fred saw on the website that the museum provided AG for BPSP. When he arrived, he asked for one at the front desk, but the staff did not know that they even had one. He was given a mainstream one (free of charge).	Fred read about it on the website. He downloaded it in advance using his home Wi-Fi and tried it at home to get familiar with the interface. After that, he used it for every painting, sculpture, and furniture he looked at.	Not used. In the interview, he mentions that he could have used to read the text of the labels.
Davide	Not used	Davide and James downloaded it on their devices using the museum Wi-Fi. After that, they used it separately on their mobile phones, even when looking at the same painting. Davide tried to use Voiceover, but it did not work well. Hence he just read the descriptions.	Davide uses the application daily for different tasks. He uses it to read signs and printed documents in non-accessible formats, scan barcodes, and help him navigate places. He used it to read large information panels and read the instruction on a leaflet to download Seeing AI.

tell you about things, for the visually-impaired, which I find quite useful. I want to try all that stuff out if I could. [...] Having apps or audio guides definitely makes me more eager, because it's easier to get access to the information then, rather than me struggling to look closely at a book or something.

Fred appreciated that new technology enables wider access to the museum content. He valued the possibility of accessing information in easier formats compared to more traditional tools like large print guides:

[Smartify] made it so easy. It's so easy just to go around and just say, 'Right, what's that?' Scan it. Seconds later you've got all the information there in front of you. It's ideal, it's brilliant. I can read it clearly on the screen. I could get it to speak to me if I wanted it to. Easy.

In section 6.5.1, I discussed how 'planning' is a key element of Fred's practice, which enabled him to make meaning in the space. This emerged again when he talked about the way he learned to use the Smartify app:

I downloaded it at home, before the visit, to make sure I knew how to use it. I didn't want to waste time here. I [...] downloaded it. [...] Then I tried it. I knew you could look at pictures of the objects from the museum on the website so I went on there and thought I could just try it. So I went to the Wallace Collection's website. I thought I'd try a few of their images. So I pulled them up on the screen and used the app to scan them and yeah, it was instant. Just worked instantly, so I knew it worked.

Planning was again the strategy he decided to employ to minimise the risk of disruption and avoid wasting time due to difficulties related to the technology. Similar to

---

[28] It has to be noted that as of 30th of May 2021, the website does not advertise an audio guide specifically designed for BPSP anymore.

the way he checked online the V&A digital audio guide before the visit (section 5.10.1), he familiarised himself in advance with the app's functioning. Planning this element of the visit reinforces the idea that planning is part of Fred's cultural practice (Gonzalez *et al.* 2005). Therefore, technology can be seen as one tool that enabled Fred to replicate successful everyday practices in the museum, which enabled meaning-making. Fred's cultural consumption and meaning-making were mediated by technology (Bourdieu's 1986). The technology was the mean that allowed him to make sense of the objects by developing historic capital.

Unlike Fred, Davide did not plan his visit, and he explained that he was pleasantly surprised at the idea of being able to try a new app:

> It was so cool. So we arrived and James says: look, we can get an audio guide. I swear to you, I thought 'oh God, please no, I already hate this'. I mean, cool – but I don't like using those things that they give you as audio guide. They always look old and bulky and you have to carry it around – it's so annoying. But you know, I didn't want to upset him because I know he likes it. Then he was like: 'oh look there's an app as well, I think we can scan paintings' and that sounded very cool. You know, I develop apps for work, but they're quite boring ones. So it's cool that I can try something new but that I understand. Even here [in the Wallace Collection]. It's cool because I can try to figure out how it works.

Davide's enthusiasm for the new application was clear in his physical response to the possibility of trying it out:

Instance 6.10:

Source: video	Source: fieldnotes
	At the front desk, when his partner suggested getting an AG, Davide smiled but did not reply. However, as soon as his partner mentioned the possibility to use Smartify, his facial changed, and it showed that he was interested and excited at the prospect of trying the app: he smiled widely and commented, 'that is so cool, what is it?'. He immediately reached to his pocket and got his mobile device – an iPhone – out, and he asked Siri – Apple's virtual assistant – to download the application (figure 6.22). Before starting the visit, James went to the toilet, and Davide remained at the entrance.
Davide spent the whole time that James was away installing and learning how to use Smartify (figure 6.23 ab).	

Figure 6.22. Davide downloading Smartify.

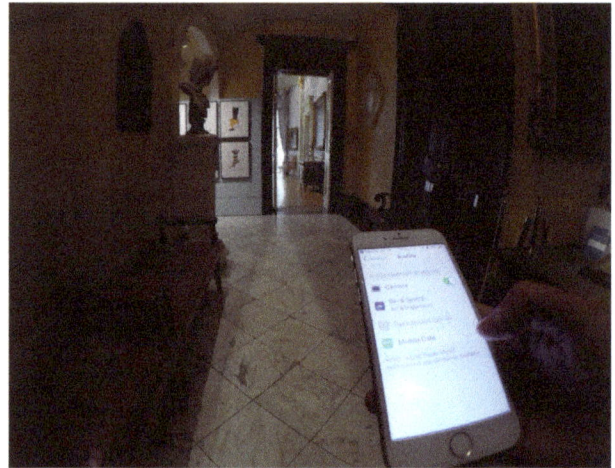

Figure 6.23ab. Davide learning to use Smartify.

The quote above and instance 6.10 show how technology played a meaningful role in Davide's experience. As an experienced, partially sighted person, he preferred to use his equipment rather than the audio guide. He was genuinely thrilled at the possibility of using his device to try out a new application. Davide was an application developer, and the possibility to try out the application seemed to recreate the comfort of his work. The possibility to use his mobile device to access the museum content allowed him to quickly develop the confidence to treat the potentially unfamiliar environment as his own. He seemed to be at ease and feel a physical and cultural connection with their environment, as he could use his mobile device as an everyday practice. In his case, the meaning resided not only in the content he accessed but primarily in the tool he used.

Additionally, Davide expressed excitement at the possibility of using new technology and testing the application for something fun, compared to the 'boring' work-related applications. He saw the museum collection to employ his skills by doing something he enjoys (trying out the new technology) while performing another activity (visiting the museum). Using his professional skills to make meaning of the museum collection put him at ease and enabled him to connect with the museum. Although Davide mentioned that visiting museums was not something he would regularly do, the possibility to use his familiar working skills allowed him to establish a relationship with the unfamiliar environment.

Davide's highly developed technical capital from his professional context enabled him to draw work-related competencies from his funds of knowledge and apply them in the museum (Yardi 2009). His mobile phone turned from an everyday device to a museum tool. It was a resource that allowed Davide to employ his technical capital to develop cultural capital by facilitating access and helping him navigate the collection (Hayhoe 2017). Going around the museum with his phone in his hand seemed to make Davide develop confidence and empower him in his walking practice. The elements of confidence and empowerment are strongly linked with Davide's professional identity. Developing an identity as a museum visitor and linking it to his professional one offered Davide a sense of belonging (Handley *et al.* 2006). Davide's identity had a substantial impact on his visit to practice (using his mobile phone) and meaning (his ability to experience the museum collection and environment). Identity, practice, and meaning had a substantial impact on Davide's overall learning experience. Following Wenger's framework, they can be seen as 'deeply interconnected and mutually defining' (1998b, 5). If we look at identity as the way learning changes who we are (Wenger 1998b), Davide's ability to make sense of the collection and environment through his everyday tools and funds of knowledge heavily impacted his learning experience. In the next section, I discuss in more detail the issue of technical capital in relation to the difficulties associated with the application.

6.9.2. Technical capital

The interest in trying out the application Smartify also brought up how familiar participants were with the use of technology, how developed their technical capital was, and how intuitive technology was to use. As previously mentioned, participants typically used advanced technology as part of their professions and everyday lives. Hence, their technical capital was highly developed, and it impacted how they decided to use technology in the space. In this section, I look at how their technical capital enabled them to use the technology successfully in the space, and I discuss the impact this had on meaning-making.

As I mentioned above, Smartify was a meaningful part of Davide's experience. He was both enthusiast at the idea of trying a new app, and the possibility to use his mobile device allowed him to feel confident as it made him perceive his visit as something in line with his professional identity. However, he also encountered difficulties in using the app, as I have already discussed in section 6.6.1 instance 6.3. In that instance, Davide was looking at the painting 'Francesca da Rimini' (figure 6.9) in West Gallery III. He used Smartify to retrieve information about the painting, but the application did not seem to work. Hence, he called James for help. In the interview, he explained what happened:

> The app did not seem to work at that point. It could not retrieve the correct information about the painting. It kept referring to a different painting that is actually a different version of the same painting by the same person, but that apparently is in the Louvre. He [James] figured it out from the Wikipedia page. There are more versions of the same painting around the world, so I think the wrong painting kept coming up on Smartify. They must all look the same. It happens with apps that use this type of AI features. It's like with Google Lens. It happens. The issue is also that the app is not very accessible. It doesn't let you modify the format of the text, and VoiceOver didn't work well. Other people with worse impairments would probably find it very difficult.

In this instance, he never seemed to associate his difficulty to his impairment but rather to the technology itself, probably due to his experience working with applications and his familiarity with how technology works. He seemed to perceive the difficulty he encountered as part of a meaningful experience and his actions to overcome it as identity-congruent (Oyserman 2015). Similar to Fred, his residual vision allowed him to use the app smoothly. However, he also pointed out that BPSP with different and more severe impairments would find it difficult to use the application features, as it did not allow to modify the format of the text, and it was not straightforward to use with VoiceOver or other screen reader software. It is also worth noting that, while Fred downloaded the application and learnt how to use it in advance, Davide did that directly in the gallery. In this case, this preference is related to Fred's planning strategy, while Davide has a spontaneous last-minute approach. However, it is also arguable that the ability to install, familiarise, and use a new application strongly depended on the person's technical capital (chapter 2, section 2.4.1).

Fred had a similar experience: his residual vision and familiarity with technology allowed him to use the application confidently in the gallery. He pointed his mobile device at paintings, allowed the application to scan and retrieve information, then moved the phone closer to his face to read. He used the application throughout the gallery:

> Actually, the app by default is white on black, which is ideal for me. There's no glare off the screen, then,

Figure 6.24. Fred trying to use the in-built magnifier to enlarge text of Smartify.

so it's easy enough to read. I tried increasing the font size (figure 6.24). You can increase the default font size on your phone, for apps that use the dynamic text size, but that app doesn't dial into that. So it just uses their text size that they give you. Which was good enough for me, because of the inverted colours, luckily. If it was black on white, it would have been more difficult, because it's harder for me to focus on it, because of the glare coming off of the white of the screen. So yeah, it would have been more of a strain on the eyes to read. It worked fine for me, but I guess it would have been a problem for people with different vision needs.

Fred's and Davide's predictions on the application's usability were partly proven correct during Lily's visit. Lily only briefly tried the app. She did not show particular interest in it:

It was mostly Ginny that wanted to try it. I'm not sure I really understand the concept. If I have to scan something, I can't really do it if I can't see it.

Ginny was keener to try the app, as she heard about it on social media. Hence, she convinced Lily to try it. They downloaded the application on the day of the visit on both their phones, and they used it together:

Instance 6.11:

Source: video
Ginny downloaded Smartify on her mobile phone and Lily's phone on the day of the visit. They tried it with two paintings in the Great Gallery (6.25ab). Ginny guided Lily when trying the app, but Lily never asked questions about the app and never seemed to express interest in it. She listened when Ginny read aloud the paintings' descriptions. Lily tried to use the in-built function VoiceOver to convert the text from the application into speech (figure 6.26ab). This did not work, as the application was not screen reader-friendly. They eventually gave up and went back to using the audio guide.

Figure 6.25ab. Lily using Smartify.

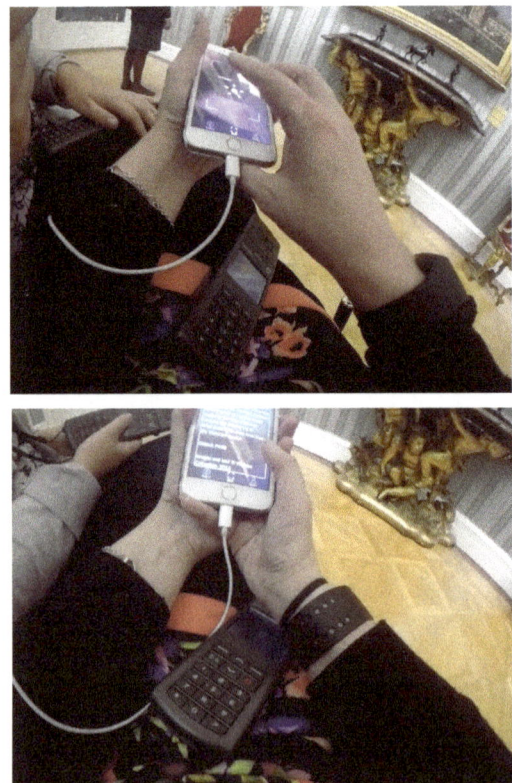

Figure 6.26ab. Lily trying to use VoiceOver with Smartify[29].

---

[29] Figure 6.26a shows the use of VoiceOver rotor. The rotor is the function that allows to choose between the different VoiceOver functions. The one displayed is 'Containers'. Figure 6.26b shows the software attempting to read the text: the white rectangular shape is the text that the software identified. Both functions did not work as expected with Smartify.

Lily expressed concerns during the interview, because she found it difficult to understand how Smartify worked, and because she would have had trouble to scan the objects during her visit, unless someone guided her in front of the painting at the correct height:

> So... I am still a bit confused for the concept that you don't need to take a picture [with the app], that you just hold out to scan the picture [the painting]. So, I guess I would need it to tell me that, I suppose, or yeah. So, I wasn't sure about that. [...] it doesn't tell you if you're scanning the right direction, like it doesn't tell you move left, move right. So, I would have no idea. I wouldn't know if I was in a room where that was even possible or if I was, I'd have no clue where I needed to aim. Like literally no clue. Like I could be holding it to someone's face trying to... and not know. So yeah, it needs to give some clear directions or like indications that you're in a room where that's possible and that it's on your left so you can hit that way.

Despite Lily having highly developed technical capital, she found it hard to access the app. This is because the application is not designed in an inclusive way, and it does not support accessibility functions in-built in the device. On the other hand, the application worked better for Fred and Davide for three main reasons. Firstly, their residual vision was relatively good enough to support the use of the application despite the fact that it was not entirely accessible. Secondly, their technical capital was probably more developed than Lily's due to their professions as IT and tech developers. Thirdly, they appeared more eager and interested in trying out the new technology than Lily, who was primarily interested in the social engagement with Ginny and accessing the collection with her.

The findings above illustrate that Smartify had the potential to fit into the definition of 'inclusive technology', as defined by Hayhoe (2014b, 2015b): 'Mainstream technology that can be used with either no or minimal adaption by a person with a disability as an accessible technology'. However, it required a significantly specialised technical capital, which not all BPSP (or sighted visitors) have. Davide's and Fred's technical capital came primarily from their professional experience, the availability and accessibility of technology in their networks, their familiarity with its use and their overall technical expertise (Yardi 2010; Brock *et al.* 2010). Together with their residual vision, these elements of technical capital were essential to use the application to make meaning effectively. This is consistent with Hayhoe's (2015b) argument that advanced technical capital enhances the possibility to develop further other capitals, in this case, cultural and historic capital (Hayhoe 2015b). Furthermore, Davide's and Fred's advanced technical capital enabled them to empower themselves

by accessing information that would have otherwise been unavailable to them (Brock *et al.* 2010; Yardi 2009).

The application was used with no adaptation by Fred and Davide, proving to be potentially accessible for BPSP with enough residual vision and an advanced technical capital. However, the issues identified by both Fred and Davide, and encountered by Lily, make the application non-inclusive for people who are blind, with minimal residual vision, or limited technical capital. The app, at the time, responded to the mainstream education needs of museums' visitors. However, it had the potential to become fully inclusive if it addressed education needs along with impairment ones.

6.9.3. Accessibility and inclusion tools

In this section, I analyse how the combination of technical capital and the accessibility and availability of digital tools enabled inclusive experiences or triggered exclusion.

When they were recruited, both Fred and Lily were enthusiastic about the idea of trying the Wallace Collection audio guide specifically designed for BPSP, as advertised on the museum's website. Fred asked for it on the day of his visit once he arrived at the front desk. Lily asked me to ask the museum in advance, to be sure to find it on the day of the visit. Despite I received a confirmation email saying that the audio guide specifically designed for BPSP would have been at the front desk for Lily, the staff could not find the device both in Lily's and Fred's case. In both cases, the staff at the front desk was not aware of resources for BPSP despite it being advertised on the website and advertised on the front desk wall. They tried to find out about the audio guide for BPSP, but they could not find anything. Finally, after 9 minutes in Lily's case and 11 minutes in Fred's case, the front desk staff apologised and offered them a mainstream audio guide free of charge.

It is interesting to look at Lily's physical reaction to this episode:

Instance 6.12:

Source: video	Source: fieldnotes
	Ginny asked for the audio guide at the front desk for both Lily and herself. Lily stood slightly back from the desk and let Ginny speak (figure 6.27). When Ginny called her forward, Lily explained that she had requested in advance an audio guide specifically designed for BPSP.
'we have sent an email asking for it and they said it was going to be at reception'.	

	When it became clear that the staff did not know about the special audio guide, she felt silent and took a step back again. Ginny often turned towards her (figure 6.28), but Lily did not intervene. Her hands seemed to be shaking, and she was nervously rubbing them together and rubbing them on her legs. Her right leg was shaking nervously as well[30].
This continued for 7 minutes until Ginny gave her the mainstream audio guide (figure 6.29).	

Figure 6.29. Ginny giving the AG to Lily.

During the interview, she described how this instance made her feel:

> I hate it when these things happen. It's so frustrating. There was no recognition or acknowledgement that we were there or had prearranged it. It's like we don't exist.

> [Prompt: 'I noticed that it was mainly your friend that spoke with the members of staff']

> Yeah, I thought she wanted me to talk, but I just couldn't. Sometimes I make an effort, you know, on the tube mainly. But it's really hard, because I'm just there, standing and kind of shaking. I get so nervous that it gets difficult to talk.

Figure 6.27. Ginny asking for the AG at the info desk. Lily is visibly behind.

She defined this experience as 'frustrating'. Her body reacted to the situation as she felt uneasy by enacting habits that showed her being jittery, tense, and shaky. She took a step back from the front desk, suggesting that she wanted to step away and put distance between her body and the situation that made her feel uncomfortable. Her reaction of not speaking up seemed to mirror the physical act of retracting from the situation. Despite her friend encouraging her to speak, her interview responses and her nervous gesturing made it clear that the experience immobilised her.

As seen in the previous section (6.9.2) and section 2.4.1, technical capital is formed through the availability and accessibility of technology in a network and the mobilisation of the resources to develop access to knowledge and acquisition of skills (Yardi 2009). The lack of accessible audio guides specifically designed for BPSP directly hindered Lily's possibility of developing technical capital. This directly influenced the possibility of developing further other capitals, like cultural, aesthetic, and historic capital (Hayhoe 2015b).

Figure 6.28. Ginny turning towards Lily.

---

[30] I did not observe Lily's hands or legs visibly shake in any other occasion, aside from the incident with the chest of drawers in the V&A.

Lily's reaction was deeply physical as her body responded to the lack of availability of advertised resources. Her body dys-appeared, as she seemed to associate the difficulty experienced with her impairment rather than the space's social and cultural barriers (Paterson and Hughes 1999). Technology, in this instance, reinforced and triggered Lily's exclusion. Lily's body effectively experienced a disabling cultural and socio-spatial experience (Imrie 2001). Her body directly felt the socially produced prejudice as an oppressive behaviour (Paterson and Hughes 1999; Valentine 1999). This was clear from her physical reactions and her words, 'it's like we don't exist'. Her body dys-appeared and felt like 'non-existing' in the sense that she could not participate in the social experience or contribute to the development of the social environment, and therefore she did not feel like she had a place in it (Edwards and Imrie 2003).

Fred's reaction to the same situation was of disappointment and annoyance. Unlike Lily, he was on his own when he approached the front desk to ask for the audio guide:

> I went to Reception, tried to get an audio guide first, for the visually-impaired, which they couldn't find. First member of staff went looking for it, but she still couldn't find it. She called someone else over, they couldn't find it. They called their manager down, they couldn't find it. So eventually, I said: 'Well, just give me an ordinary audio guide, and I'll take that with me'. [...] I was expecting the audio guide, because it says it on the website. They didn't seem to know if they should have had one or not. They knew they had audio guides there, but she seemed to be a bit surprised that they might have one for a visually-impaired person. And even though she acknowledged it was on the wall next to us, she said, 'Oh, it's on the wall there, so we should have one'. And it's on the website, because I saw it there. She said, 'Well, there should be one there', but she didn't know where it was or what to look for, she didn't know if it was part of the main audio guide, you just selected a different option or something. So yeah, she didn't seem to know how to do it. I thought: I'm not going to get it am I? Which is a shame.

I asked him to describe how the situation made him feel:

> Well, frustrated. Because it's advertised as being there. They made a big deal on their website about how accessible the place is. The YouTube channel has a British Sign Language video introducing you to the museum, and they're making a big song and dance about it. You walk into Reception, they don't know how to give you the audio guide they're advertising. So it is disappointing and frustrating, because I was looking forward to using that. So that was a shame.

Fred's response to the situation presented three key aspects. Firstly, he expressed his frustration due to the lack of accessibility resources in general, but also due to unavailability of the audio guide, despite the fact that it was advertised on the website. Secondly, he seemed annoyed that members of staff did not know that they had resources for BPSP and that they appeared surprised that they even had one. He seemed particularly annoyed because of the museum's claim to be accessible on the website and social media platforms. Finally, he seemed genuinely upset because he was eager to use the resource to access the museum content. He eagerly anticipated its use, and the lack of it made him feel like he was 'missing out'. The lack of resources, the lack of acknowledgement, the fact that the museum seemed to break the 'promise' of accessibility, which he seemed to see as part of a social contract. The issue of 'missing out' contributed to a dys-abling experience, which partially triggered exclusion (Imrie 1999). Fred drew from his funds of knowledge as an experienced visitor to fight the exclusion and find alternative ways to access information and develop historic capital (namely, his monocular and Smartify).

Audio guides are perceived as a mainstream technology in museums (Hutchinson and Eardley 2020). Even less experienced visitors are aware of the possibility of using one in most museums (Fryer 2016). Experienced BPS museum visitors tend to be familiar with the difference between a mainstream audio guide and one that contains non-visual audio descriptive language specifically designed to facilitate the visit of BPSP (Hutchinson and Eardley 2020). This type of audio guide is popular among BPSP (Cock *et al.* 2018; Hutchinson and Eardley 2020). They provide BPSP with broader access to information and allow them to understand the tangible and intangible features of objects (Fryer 2016). It is not surprising then that both Lily and Fred, as experienced visitors, were thrilled at the idea of trying one at the Wallace Collection. It is even less surprising that they could not use them deprived them of the experience they were looking forward to and had considered meaningful. This triggered exclusion. Ironically, the audio guide, a tool designed to make collections more accessible, turned out to passively exclude all the BPS participants who decided to use it. It has to be noted, however, that this could be a symptom of wider access issues across the museum environment as well as of lack of relevant training offered to its staff rather than an Issue with the technology itself, as both Fred and Lily had successfully used audio guide in other museum visits.

6.9.4. Accessing content

In section 6.8.3, I presented findings about Fred's and Davide's preference for historical details of objects. In this section, I look at how they used technology to access those details, to develop historic capital, and to make meaning of objects. Fred used Smartify to access information about the objects he was looking at:

Instance 6.13:

	Source: video	Source: fieldnotes
		Fred looked at every painting in the Great Gallery. He stood in front of each object.
	He: a. scanned the object using Smartify (figure 6.30a); b. read the description on the application (figure 6.30b); c. stepped closer to observe it (figure 6.30c); d. used his monocular to observe it even closer (figure 6.30d).	
		He repeated this sequence for each object.

During the interview, Fred explained that although he could have used the mainstream audio guide he was given or a large print book available in the gallery, he decided to use only Smartify on his phone:

You know, I could have magnified with my phone [to read the large print booklet] or used a handheld magnifier if I wanted to or something, but it's easier on my phone. I could not carry the book, the phone, the audio guide, my monocular, the magnifier... it's just really overkill. [...] So, yeah, I basically just end up using the app all the way around. [...] The phone was giving me plenty of information so that was ideal. So I just carried it around like that really, just looking at each page [page retrieved on Smartify] as I spent a nice bit of time on each one just there's so much detail on all of them [...] it gave you a bit of a description of the page and says who was in it, who it was by, the background behind it, a bit about the artist if it was relevant. How it was acquired as well, by the Marquesses, who used to own the place. So yeah, it was a nice bit of detail there. Not overly complicated. It wasn't too much. Just a nice amount really, yeah. It was quite interesting.

These findings suggest that Smartify allowed Fred to make sense of objects and develop historic capital. The possibility to easily access this information on his phone was the main reason why Fred decided to try the technology. He used the digital resource as a learning tool. Similar to when he used the digital audio guide in the V&A (section 5.10.1), his highly developed technical capital enabled Fred to develop historic capital and make meaning of objects. The technology's usability also enabled him to effectively

Figure 6.30abcd. Sequence of how Fred looked at objects.

move around the space. In fact, he seemed to prefer the possibility to use his mobile device to access information compared to bring around bulky resources like large print booklets.

Davide used Smartify to scan paintings and retrieve information, but he also used the application Seeing AI to scan and read panels. He explained that he uses Seeing AI daily, and why and how he decided to use it in the museum. Davide described himself as a frequent user of the app:

> Oh it's the holy grail of apps. I use it to read panels, printouts, things like documents that I get in non-accessible formats. Sometimes, when my eyes are very tired, I use it to scan barcodes in supermarkets or to read signs on the underground. It has made my life a lot easier since it came out[31].

From his response, the application seemed to be an essential element in his daily routine, and he used it to perform several everyday practices. The way he used Seeing AI in the museum space (as shown in the above screenshots) in the same way he uses it during his everyday routine, shows that Davide decided to replicate successful everyday practices during his visit. The video showed that Davide avidly used the application during his visit as well:

Instance 6.14:

Source: video
Davide switched continuously between Smartify and Seeing AI, depending on what function he needed. In front of paintings, he used Smartify to retrieve information (figure 6.31). When he encountered panels, he used Seeing AI to read them in the Great Gallery and West Room I (figure 6.32). He also used it to scan some labels at the beginning of his visit on the ground floor (figure 6.33).

Figure 6.31. Davide using Smartify.

[31] Seeing AI was released in the Uk in November 2017.

Figure 6.32. Davide using Seeing AI on a door panel.

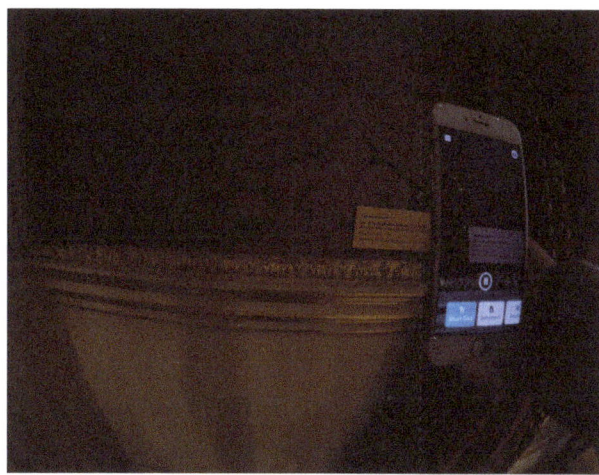

Figure 6.33. Davide using Seeing AI on a label.

Smartify and Seeing AI both have the potential to fit in Hayhoe's (2014a) definition of 'inclusive technology', as they are available for everyone in the same space and can be used by sighted and non-sighted visitors with little or no adaptation. They are not 'special' technologies that draw attention and identify disabled people in mainstream settings (Hayhoe 2014a). To truly be considered an inclusive technology, Smartify would have to adapt to the needs of people with no residual vision and needs to work with in-built accessibility features of mobile devices.

The case of Seeing AI is slightly different from that of Smartify; however, it still fits within this 'inclusive technology' framework. While Smartify was an application specifically designed for the museum content, advertised by the museum, used primarily in the museum context, and for every visitor, Seeing AI is an application specifically designed for BPSP, designed to be used in their everyday practices and not specifically related for the museum context. This description seems to exclude Seeing AI from the definition of 'inclusive technology', as it is not a mainstream application also used by BPSP with little or no adaptation (Hayhoe 2015a). It is used solely by people with vision impairment. However, it can also be argued that the software itself is not the only aspect of the technology that needs to be addressed. To illustrate this point, I would like to draw attention to my findings which suggest that what makes the technology inclusive is the possibility of participants to use their own mobile devices in the space, rather than having to carry around 'special' equipment. Therefore, the software (the app) and the vehicle (the mobile device) must be addressed as one, making the technology genuinely inclusive.

If we follow Hayhoe's model of ITC (Hayhoe 2015a), the findings I have presented in this section suggest that Smartify and Seeing AI can be considered inclusive traditional and mainstream technologies that promote inclusion through facilitating forms of cultural and social capital in museums. In fact, in Davide and Fred's experiences, they seemed to provide, in different ways, equality of opportunities achieved through equal access to information. Davide used the digital resources to replicate successful strategies he employed in his everyday professional life. This enabled him to develop a sense of belonging and make sense of the environment and the collection. Similarly, Fred developed historic capital by using the Smartify app, which enabled him to use his mobile device to access information quickly and effectively.

These findings demonstrate further the ITC model's assumption that literacy of technology (in particular digital ones) is crucial to assist social inclusion of disabled people. Fred and Davide's highly developed technical capital had a crucial impact on how they used technology to develop further forms of capital. However, technology alone is not enough to trigger inclusive practices. My research shows that participants' expertise in museum visits combined with their familiarity with mainstream technology triggers social and cultural inclusion in a mainstream context like museums.

While it is incontrovertible that the participants' experience was facilitated and enhanced by using these applications, it is necessary to bear in mind who these participants are. As I mentioned at the beginning of this section, participants who took part in this study are young professionals who use technology as part of their jobs and everyday lives. Technology is a strong component of their habitus. They own expensive mobile devices and use mainstream and specifically designed applications to perform in different contexts of their lives. Visitors of different ages and different technical capital do not necessarily respond in the same way to technology in galleries. There are currently no studies that look into the technical literacy of visitors (or non-visitors) coming from different backgrounds and less privileged habitus.

6.10. Conclusion

In this chapter, I presented five major categories of embodied practice: co-walking, scaffolding, identity formation, looking, and using resources. The 'touching' category was not identified as participants were not allowed and did not touch objects in the museum.

This chapter started by presenting findings about the profile, background, visit frequency, and usual companions of the Wallace Collection participants (section 6.2). This was followed by a brief analysis of how participants arrived at the museum (section 6.4). Section 6.5 discussed findings from the co-walking category. The research showed how participants seemed to replicate successful mobility strategies from their everyday practice inside the museum. They repeated successful guidance, navigation, and positioning strategies. From the findings presented in this section, walking was recognised as a cultural activity and a social practice. Participants made sense walking together with their companions and 'doing the exhibition' together. In particular, this section highlighted how positioning was a prominent characteristic of participants' embodied practice. All participants seemed to be aware of supposed 'correct' ways of navigating and positioning in relation to objects and other people in the galleries. Furthermore, they all appeared to value the idea of conforming to these set of 'normative rules', in some cases, to avoid standing out because of their disability. Findings highlighted how participants' perception of their disability and their body, together with the context in which they act, influenced how people saw and described themselves and how participants were aware of their bodies and other bodies while walking in the gallery.

Section 6.6 discussed how visitors' bodies interacted with others in scaffolded meaning-making of the museum content and environment. Key findings showed that scaffolding guidance in the museum space was determined not only by participants' vision impairment but also by their personal preferences, type of guidance and level of confidence. In Lily's case, guidance never faded, both because of her impairment and because the scaffolder, Ginny, constantly guided the visit owing to her higher expertise as a frequent visitor. Additionally, findings showed that part of scaffolding the exhibition included instances of humour and intimacy and shifting roles. Deep emotional interaction seemed to contribute significantly to how participants and their companions scaffolded each other learning.

Section 6.7 on identity formation contributed to the understanding of the correlation between identity and practice. Key findings showed that the museum visit contributed to developing social and cultural identities and the negotiation of participants' identities as disabled people. The act of attending the museum was analysed as part of the social and cultural identity of visitors. The act of 'being seen' in the space and potentially 'being seen as disabled' impacted the embodied practice of Lily, who faced several difficulties due to her impairment. Lily seemed to associate her difficulty with her impairment rather than with the social and cultural barriers in the space (Paterson and Hughes 1999). Guidance appeared to be the tool that enabled her to resist dys-appearance and continue her visit.

Section 6.8 discussed the category of looking and how participants encountered and made sense of visual culture. Findings slightly differed from those from the V&A due to the nature of the collection. In the Wallace Collection, participants mainly encountered paintings. Findings showed that the understanding of visual culture was influenced primarily by their vision impairment, their residual vision and visual memory, and other elements such as their personal preferences, their education, their aesthetic and cultural capital, and the social interactions with their companions. I introduced a discussion of the concept of aesthetic capital developed by Hayhoe (2017). Findings from Lily's experience of visual culture showed that despite being fully blind, she could still make some sense of visual concepts by creatively understanding visual culture.

Section 6.9 ended the chapter by discussing the way participants used digital resources. Findings showed that participants used digital tools to access content and to make meaning of objects. Values attributed to digital tools were different: participants were interested in trying the new technology, while others looked at them as inclusion tools or tools to access content and information. The findings I have presented in this section showed that the audio guide, a mainstream tool designed to make collections more accessible, turned out to passively exclude all the participants who decided to use it due to a more general access issue of the museum and its staff rather than to the technology itself. Findings also suggest that Smartify and Seeing AI can be considered inclusive technology that promotes inclusion in museums' further forms of cultural and social capital. They seemed to provide, in different ways, equality of opportunities achieved through equal access to information. It was clear that technology alone is not enough to trigger inclusive practices. Findings showed that participant's expertise of museum visits combined with their technical capital triggered social and cultural inclusion in a mainstream context like museums.

Museum of London

7.1. Introduction

This chapter presents findings from the third and final case study, namely the Museum of London (MoL). The analysis is based on the post-visit interviews and fieldnotes. As previously mentioned in chapter 4, while the V&A and the Wallace Collection allowed me to conduct interviews, collect field notes, and use the body camera, the MoL did not give the authorisation to record videos in the galleries. Hence, findings are presented draw on interviews and fieldnotes. Three participants agreed to visit the MoL between February 2018 and June 2018: Fred, Lily, and Anna. According to her preferences, one participant's interview (Anna's) was carried out in Italian and English, and the parts in Italian were transcribed and then translated into English.

7.1.1. Description of the museum

The Museum of London (MoL) is a historical museum located in the Barbican complex of buildings in Barbican, London. It is a local museum that displays the largest urban history collection globally, with more than six million objects (Museum of London 2020a). The museum comprises a series of chronological galleries about archaeological finds, the built city, urban development and London's social and cultural life, with multisensory and interactive displays and activities (ibid). It is located by the ancient Roman London Wall, still visible from the museum's windows. The museum is free, and it opened to the public in 1976 (ibid). It undertook a redevelopment, which was completed in 2010, and in 2015 it was announced that the museum would move from its Barbican site to nearby Smithfield Market by 2023 (ibid).

As of 2017, due to the lack of a dedicated accessibility manager, accessibility issues are managed by the head of the learning department in collaboration with people from every other department in the museum (personal communication, 2017). This management strategy led to creating rich multisensory exhibits accessible for BPSP and the wider public. No specific technological resources have been employed specifically only for BPSP in the galleries (personal communication, 2017). However, BPSP can book in advance a one-to-one guided tour with a trained guide (Museum of London 2020b). While it might not be viewed as the most accessible approach, it is undoubtedly one of the most inclusive, as resources are available for everyone, without distinctions for individual abilities. In addition, the museum website advertises 'large print guides for the permanent galleries and major exhibitions are available at the Information Desk' (Museum of London 2020b).

7.2. Visitors profiles

This section provides a summary of demographics information of the three participants that visited the MoL.

7.2.1. Visitors' demographics

This section presents findings on visitors' demographics. Three participants visited the MoL, one male and two females. Fred is British, Lily is Scottish, and Anna is Italian. Fred visited the V&A first (chapter 5), the Wallace Collection (chapter 6), and then decided to visit the MoL. Lily visited the Wallace Collection first (chapter 6) and then the MoL (chapter 7). Anna only visited the MoL.

Table 7.1 summarises participants' profiles, including gender, age, nationality, occupation, and highest educational qualification. Pseudonyms are used in writing for confidentiality.

As mentioned in chapters 5 and 6, Fred and Lily were respectively British and Scottish. They moved to London for work after university. Anna was Italian and lived near Milan. She visited London several times a year as part of her family lived in the city. She fluently spoke English and Italian. All participants had an undergraduate qualification. Fred and Lily had jobs in managerial positions; Anna was a full-time athlete, motivational speaker, and collaborated with several disability charities. Details of their work positions and sport discipline are not disclosed as these could make participants identifiable.

Table 7.1. Visitors' profile

	Fred	Lily	Anna
Gender	M	F	F
Nationality	British	Scottish	Italian
Occupation	IT developer and blogger	Education manager	Athlete, coach, advocate, motivational speaker
Highest educational qualification	BSc Computer science	BSc Mathematics	BSc Sports Science
Other museums visited[32]	V&A MoL	MoL	/

---

[32] As part of this research project.

7.2.2. Vision impairments

At the beginning of interviews, participants were asked what type of vision impairment they had and how long they had been visually impaired. I presented Lily and Fred's impairment in the previous chapter (section 6.2.2). Anna has been impaired since birth. She can 'see a bit from [her] left eye, but nothing else'. Similar to findings from the V&A (chapter 5) and the Wallace Collection (chapter 6), the diversity of vision loss and needs impacted several aspects of the museum experience.

Table 7.2 presents the different vision impairments of participants.

7.2.3. Visiting habits

Table 7.3 shows that Fred, Lily and Anna are regular museum visitor[33]. In the interview, Anna explained that she 'visit[s] museums way more when she is in London, as there are not many museums where I live [in Italy]. Only a tiny one'. As in the previous visits (section 5.2.3; 6.2.3), Fred visited the MoL on his own; Lily visited with the same friend, Ginny, with whom she visited the Wallace Collection (section 6.2.3); Anna visited with two friends, Sonia and Elena, on this occasion, as she explained in the interview:

> By the way, I normally come to London to visit my family, [...] I have been to museums here [in London] with them sometimes. [...] [This time] I came with these two friends from Italy. They [play sport] with me. It's a girls trip. [...] [Prompt: do you go to museums with them in Italy] Oh yeah we did once or twice.

Table 7.2. Participants' vision impairments

	Vision impairment and residual vision	History of vision	Navigation aid
Fred	Diagnosis: Aniridia and Nystagmus. Issues: sensitivity to sunlight and glare; poor distance vision; shaky eyes, making it hard to focus on things unless they are close or enlarged.	Impaired since birth. Significant visual memory.	No aid. Uses phone and monocular
Lily	Diagnosis: Blindness with some residual light perception	Blind since birth. No visual memory.	White cane
Anna	Diagnosis: Glaucoma. Severe vision impairment	Impaired since birth. No visual memory	White cane/ guide dog

Table 7.3. Visiting habits

	Frequency	Typical companion	Companion on this occasion
Fred	Frequent	Friends; members of social groups; partner; alone	Alone
Lily	Frequent	Friends; partner	Friend (here called Ginny)
Anna	Regular	Family; friends	2 friends (called here Sonia and Elena)

Table 7.4. Summary of the characteristics of sociocultural practice identified within each category

7.5 Co-walking
- Planning
- Co-presence and co-awareness

7.6 Scaffolding
- Guidance and support

7.7 Identity formation
- Identity and disability
- Social and cultural identity
- Sense of place

7.8 Looking
- Looking back: historic capital
- Beyond perception: aesthetic capital

7.9 Touching
- Learning through touch
- Co-touching
- Forbidden touch

7.10 Using resources
- Inclusion tool
- Accessing content
- Social engagement tool

7.3. The identified categories of the embodied practice

The analysis of participants' practice is presented following the same major categories of embodied practice identified in the previous two chapters. The identified categories addressed different aspects of the social context of the visit as follows: co-walking, scaffolding, identity formation, looking, touching, and using resources.

7.4. Getting to the museum

Similar to the previous two chapters (5 and 6), participants talked during the interviews about how they arrived at the museum. These findings help contextualise how participants walked in the museum space (section 7.5), which answers RQ2. Findings presented in this section come primarily from interviews, as I only met the participants directly at the museum. However, I observed

Lily's behaviour when she arrived at the space in front of the museum: due to security checks, she and her friend spent time in the queue to enter the museum. Hence, partial fieldnotes findings are presented here as well.

Similar to his previous two visits to the V&A (section 5.4) and Wallace Collection (section 6.4), Fred used the underground, and he used the applications Google Maps, CityMapper, and Google Street View to check his route and the museum entrance in advance:

> [Thanks to the apps] I can just walk to it with confidence, knowing that I already know the route.

He, again, emphasised how he uses typically these applications in his daily life to check every route in advance to minimise the risk of getting lost. He explained that if he had not done that, he would have had serious difficulties finding the museum entrance, as it is not directly accessible from the road:

> So now I knew I was coming here, I properly looked, and I managed to kind of see where the escalator and the lift was to come up, because it's not really easy to spot.

Fred checked the information and planned his visit using all available tools for his museum visit; he planned his route to get there in the same way. Planning was a recurring element in his three visits, and it is a deeply ingrained practice in his everyday life. This everyday practice gives him confidence and empowers him to move independently in the space.

Lily used the underground as well. Lily's partner escorted her to the underground, and he guided her to the museum entrance, where she met her friend Ginny who was waiting for her. Instance 7.1 illustrates the dynamic between Lily and Ginny while they were waiting to enter the museum. While several characteristics of Lily's identity as a disabled person emerged in the previous chapter (section 6.4), findings from this interaction help better understand what 'looking disabled' meant for Lily.

Instance 7.1:

Source: fieldnotes and interview
[To enter the museum, there was a long queue due to security checks] Ginny suggested going to the front of the queue and asking to be given priority because of Lily's impairment. While suggesting that, she also acknowledged that Lily did not need to be given priority on that occasion: 'It's not like on the tube'. Lily said that she would rather avoid doing so, and the two stood in the queue for around 10 minutes until they reached the entrance.

Lily seemed very reluctant to disclose her disabled status. She seemed uncomfortable at the idea of 'using her impairment' for something that she did not perceive as necessary. When I asked her about it during the interview, she explained:

> Queueing was not a big deal. I would have asked for a seat on the tube, but this was so unnecessary. I need a seat on the tube for balance because it moves. I hate when people see you skipping a queue. There's always someone who asks why. I'd probably ask if I were pregnant or I couldn't stand.

Her response suggests that she was concerned about being seen as disabled and as someone who needs assistance. The issue of 'being seen as disabled' came up again during Lily's visit to the MoL, and I analyse it in section 7.7.1. In section 6.4, I discussed Lily's empowering and self-confidence attitude when she seemed unafraid to advocate for her rights on public transport. While she could have skipped the queue due to her vision impairment on this occasion, she preferred not to do so and wait in line. From her response, this choice seems to come from two different reasons. The first, most straightforward one is that waiting in line did not have a negative impact on Lily's body in the same way a moving train might do. However, the main reason seemed to be Lily's reluctance to disclose her impairment and make her disability visible to avoid public's scrutiny and confrontation. She seemed to choose a different response about disclosing her impairment than when she uses public transport in relation to the social context of waiting in line with other museum-goers. This suggests that Lily was aware of her positioning in relation to the other members of the community of practice of museum-goers, and she decided to act in a way that put her on the same level, rather than standing out due to her disability.

This is consistent with studies showing how young disabled people resist external viewings of their disability, being conscious of how their action may or may not disclose their impairment (Hutchinson *et al.* 2018; Spirtos and Gilligan 2020). In this case, Lily openly stated how she wanted to avoid mainstream ableist society perceptions of negative bias towards her disability, possibly due to negative past experiences ('there is always someone who asks). In doing so, she decided to momentarily distance herself from a disability identity by not disclosing her impairment (Frances 2014). Being seen as disabled, in this case, was part of the process in which Lily defined herself in relation to her position within the social group, which has an impact on the development of her social identity and sense of belonging (Hutchinson *et al.* 2018). From this section, it seems clear that the reluctance to 'being seen as disabled' is part of Lily's identity just as much as her advocacy displayed in section 6.4. While the two may appear as divergent, Lily does not seem to consider them in contrast. Both attitudes are part of her identity as a disabled person, and each is situated within different situations and social contexts.

Anna did not use the underground and shared an Uber with her two friends. She explained that they could have taken the tube, but they were out for brunch before the visit, they lost track of time, and they realised that they would have been late otherwise. In the interview, she also mentioned how that is something that regularly happens to her:

> Thank God for Uber and MyTaxi[34]. It's crazy. I'm always late. I even put alarms to try to make it on time. I always end up being late. We're on holiday, so it's even worse, you know?

Anna did not seem too concerned with the possibility of arriving late to agreed meetings, as she seemed to rely on shared transport services a lot. When prompted, Anna spoke about how she moves around in London and her hometown in Italy:

> If I can take public transports, I do because it's slightly cheaper. I take the bus back home a lot. In London I can use the tube pretty well to be honest. But I'm also never alone, you know? My family is with me. And in Italy I have my guide dog. I don't bring him here [in London]. It would be awful. He stays at home. I use the white cane, which helps. But at the same time, I am never fully independent because I'm not used to it. I think that's also why we came with uber. The underground would have been fine, you know? But also, not really [she laughs]

The tone of Anna's response in the last quote changed as she started talking about her everyday navigation practices. While at the beginning she seemed to be careless about the possibility of arriving late to meetings, and she initially attributed the choice to use Uber services to the distraction of her and her friends, later she acknowledged that that choice came primarily from navigation needs and preferences. She spoke of navigation aids as essential to her independence. Her familiarity with moving around with her guide dog seems at the core of her ability to travel independently in Italy. On the contrary, the relative lack of practice with the white cane seemed to concern her if she had to move around unescorted.

I end this section by reflecting on how participants' everyday navigation practices analysed as part of getting to the museum are deeply rooted and heavily influence participants' sense of independence. Elements like planning, technology, being with friends or family members, guide dogs, and travelling independently are part of participants' practices. Due to the challenges posed by their impairments, participants seem to master navigation techniques and how to use aids. These elements of everyday navigation practice are recurring in the next section, where I examine how participants' walking unfolded during the visit.

---

[34] Uber and MyTaxi are two applications that provide on-demand shared transit service.

7.5. Co-walking

In this section, I discuss participants' walking practice in relation to their companions, other walking visitors, and objects. This section is divided into two parts: planning (7.5.1), and co-presence and co-awareness (7.5.2).

7.5.1. Planning

Planning was again a recurring element of Fred's visit, similar to his previous visits to the V&A (section 5.5.1) and the Wallace Collection (section 6.5.1). He carefully planned his visit in advance, finding information on the museum website. Following the information on the website, Fred decided to follow the chronological order of the museum:

> I saw on the maps on the website it was chronological. So I thought well it'd be a good idea to follow that. And the woman at reception when I went up there suggested that and she handed me the map as well. So that's what I did, I just followed the exhibition through from there. And it just helped to build up the history bit by bit as you go through, which is quite nice.

He seemed to appreciate how the chronological narrative helped him put the objects and the different periods into context. This resonates with his preference for historical details of objects and his highly developed historic capital explored in the previous chapters (section 5.8.2 and 6.8.3). Figure 7.1 shows how he began his visit in the temporary exhibition space, which at the time was exhibiting the 'Fatberg!' temporary exhibition, and then continued directly towards the Roman London gallery.

When I asked in the interview why he did not start form the 'London before London' gallery, he answered:

> I didn't see it. I'll definitely go back then.

While it is clear that planning still played an important role in Fred's visit, it seems reasonable to argue that the chronological layout of the museum is what enabled him to make meaning of his visit. Contrary to his previous visits, this time, Fred did not decide which gallery to visit but rather let the museum space guide his visit. This is supported by the fact that he did not notice the first gallery, 'London before London'. In the previous visits, he knew precisely which gallery he wanted to visit and how to reach them. In this case, the chronological nature of the museum layout provided him with the confidence of visiting the space following the order of the exhibits rather than planning a specific route.

Anna had a different experience in the space. She visited the MoL specifically to see the 'London 2012 Cauldron' gallery. When she and her friends arrived, they asked for directions at the information desk to reach the gallery first and begin their visit there. Figure 7.2 shows that Anna spent 48 minutes in the London 2012 Cauldron gallery.

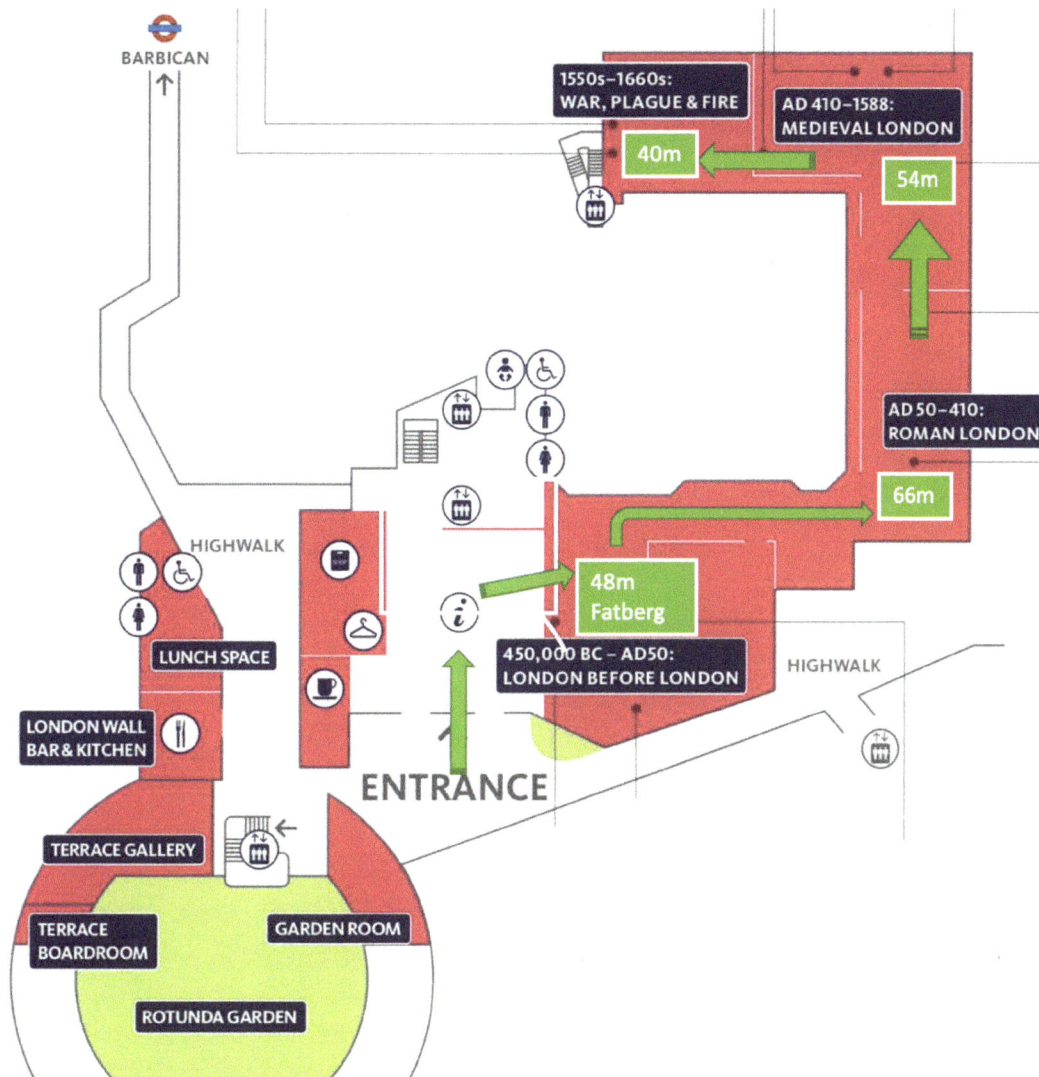

Figure 7.1. Route map of Fred's visit.

It also shows that the time they spent in the London 2012 Cauldron gallery is significantly superior to that spent in the galleries they visited after. Their route and the time spent in the galleries show Anna's strong desire to experience that specific piece of the museum collection.

She commented in the interview:

> The rest of the museum is interesting as well. Very nice stuff indeed. But we came for the Cauldron. I was really excited to see it. I planned this since forever. I checked the website a million times. I checked it on YouTube and Instagram. […] I knew this was the room I wanted to visit.

Anna mentioned how she planned the visit specifically to visit the 'London 2012 Cauldron' gallery. Planning was therefore connected to the main reason why she and her friend decided to visit the museum. While in the space, they took their time to make the most out of the gallery. The time spent in the gallery and the priority given to it,

as they visited it first, allowed them to explore the space, connect with the objects, and make meaning together. Planning, gathering information from a different number of sources enabled Anna to achieve the main aim of her visit.

Therefore, Anna employed the strategy of planning in advance in a similar way to Fred. She planned her visit in order to maximise her time in the space, to identify the gallery she was interested in and to be able to dedicate to it enough time, attention and priority. While planning in Fred's experience seems to be, at least partially, connected to his vision impairment, in the case of Anna, it seems connected to her strong desire to visit the London 2012 Cauldron. Accordingly, rather than a strategy commonly employed by BPSP to minimise difficulties related to their impairment, we look at a common visiting strategy with more to do with a specific visiting preference than sight loss. Fred's planning can be considered a strategic part of his knowledge as an experienced visitor and a BPS person (Gonzalez *et al*. 2005). Anna's planning seemed to

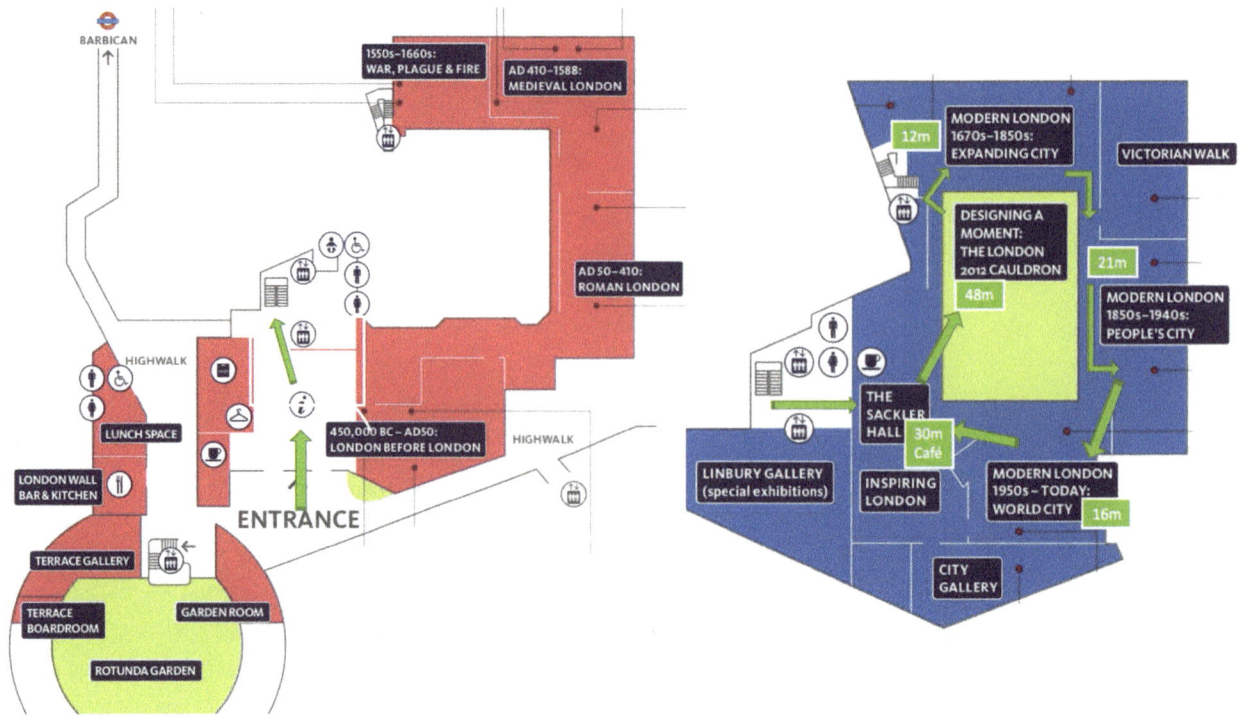

Figure 7.2. Route map of Anna's visit.

be a more situated practice with a specific visiting aim, eventually expanding to become part of her social practice.

7.5.2. Co-presence and co-awareness

Consistently with findings from previous chapters (section 5.5.2 and 6.5.2), co-presence was identified as a key characteristic of Fred's walking practice. The following two instances suggest that 'correct positioning' and awareness of other looking and walking bodies were a constant concern throughout Fred's visit.

Instance 7.2:

Source: fieldnotes
Fred spent around 12 minutes listening to a talk about the Fatberg temporary exhibition. During the talk, he moved from the front of the group, where he was standing at the beginning, to the back. After the talk, the group of people that gathered to listen to it moved to look at the 'Fatberg' objects inside cases. Fred waited for around 3 minutes before getting closer to the cases. When he did, only the other two people were looking at them at the same time.

Instance 7.3:

Source: fieldnotes
In the 'Roman London' gallery, Fred stopped to watch the video 'Public London'. The video had subtitles. He stood on the left of the screen for approximately the first 2 minutes, quite far away from the screen. A group of three other visitors was watching the video at the same time.
After the video ended, the group left while Fred remained. He walked closer to the screen and re-watched the video from the beginning to the end, standing very close in front of the screen.

In the interview, Fred explained that he did not have difficulties watching the video. However, he needed to stand close to the screen in order to read the subtitles:

> I waited until those people left [to get closer and read]. You know, if I stand in front of a screen, they won't see anything!

Similar instances were observed throughout Fred's visit. Due to his vision impairment, Fred needed to get very close to objects and panels to look at them and to read information. However, he always stood back and waited for other visitors to leave before getting closer to objects and panels. Instance 7.2 and 7.3 show how Fred was aware of the physical characteristics of his body and how his height can affect other people's in the space. When he moved from the front of the group to the back of it, it seems reasonable to say that he did so in order to minimise visual inconvenience for other visitors due to his height.

Similarly, after the end of the talk, he waited until other people observed the cases and left before getting closer. Presumably, he did so to avoid standing in the way of other visitors. He regulated his co-presence cautiously through his shifts in posture and positioning. He only occupied the space around the exhibits when his co-visitors moved on with their visit, carefully positioning himself where others did not occupy space.

Findings from this section further support my argument (section 5.5.2 and 6.5.2) that Fred's embodied practice is acquired and culturally specific (Rees Leahy 2012) and that co-walking is part of his habitus as a learnt, acquired and culturally specific embodied practice (Ingold 2000). Fred was aware of the physical characteristics of his body and his needs related to his vision impairment, and he constantly negotiated and adapted his practice in relation to those and the presence of others. These bodily techniques of attentive viewing and self-restrained movements were consistent throughout the three visits and are part of Fred's habitus as an experienced museum visitor (Ingold 2011; Rees Lehay 2012). In addition, Fred negotiated how to read the 'script of the display' in relation to others (Rees Lehay 2012).

Lily's instances of co-presence differed from those identified in the Wallace Collection since she and Ginny had a different type of visiting experience in the MoL. Being guided by a trained guide for the first part of their visit enabled different dynamics in relation to the presence of others.

In the Roman gallery (instance 7.4), Lily's guide made Lily touch several tactile objects, as well as touch three objects that visitors are generally not allowed to touch: the 'Stone Figure of a Soldier' (figure 7.3), the 'Reconstruction of Donkey Mill', and the 'Sculpture of Four Mother Goddesses':

Instance 7.4:

Source: fieldnotes
When they started touching the 'Stone Figure of a Soldier' (figure 7.3), Ginny expressed her concerns as she realised it was not a tactile object. Lily immediately stopped touching the sculpture, took a step back and moved her head from her right side to her left side, seemingly to look if others were around. The guide reassured her that they had leeway to touch objects other than tactile ones during the special tour. Lily relaxed her posture, took a step closer to the object and started touching it again.

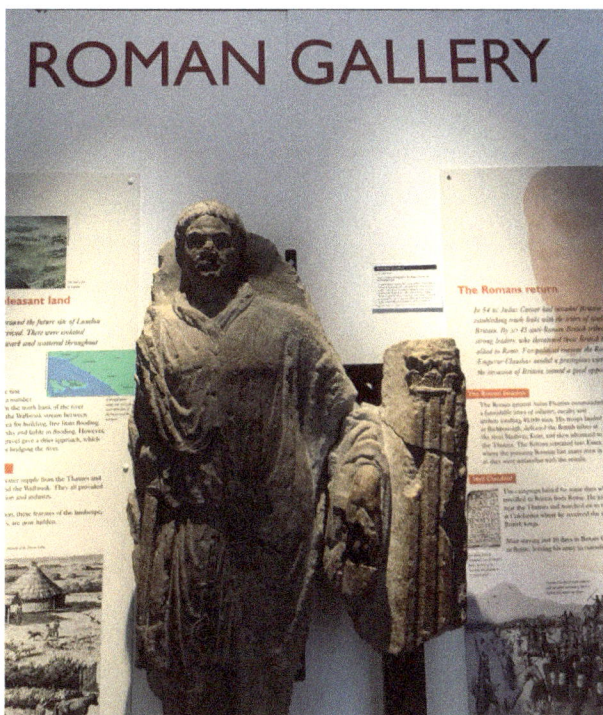

Figure 7.3. Stone Figure of a Soldier.

Lily enjoyed being able to touch objects usually not available for touch, as she mentioned in the interview. However, she still expressed concerns about how other visitors viewed and judged her for touching those objects. The presence of the guide, which Lily viewed as a symbol of the museum authority, seemed to enable Lily to set aside her concerns and to enjoy the tactile experience. Given how important 'not to stand out' was for her, this was a crucial aspect of her visit. The following transcript shows how the presence of the guide can be seen as an empowering tool that enabled Lily to interact with objects:

> She [the guide] made me touch some Roman stones that most people can't touch. I loved it, it was great. I mean I was worried because you know, other people see you and it's awkward. What will they think? I don't know, it's strange, maybe they can guess I'm blind… I don't know. I don't like it. But you know, I was with a guide, she could have explained. I mean, she decides what I can or can't touch, so oh well… I thought it was great.

Lily seemed to enjoy the possibility of touching objects that visitors usually are not allowed to touch, as she has frequently mentioned in the interview how much she values being able to touch objects and how negatively not being able to touch something impacts her experience. While I explore this further when I discuss her tactile practice in section 7.9, it is important to focus on the other characteristic that emerges from these findings: Lily's concern that other visitors were seeing her touching non-tactile objects. This concern of 'being seen doing something wrong' was already discussed as a recurring element of Lily's visit to the Wallace Collection (section 6.5.2).

Lily extensively explained how she valued 'correct positioning' in relation to objects. She seemed aware that touching 'forbidden' objects was not following museums' 'normative practices' (Harris 2015). In this case, she touched the objects because her guide was present and enabled the interaction. Her bodily reaction to Ginny's concerns about touching objects labelled with 'please do not touch' suggests that she was still aware of the presence of other bodies in her perceptual range. She reacted similar to when she hit the chest of drawers in the Wallace Collection: she removed her body from the object's proximity, and she 'looked around' to 'see' if others had seen her performing in that specific way. Co-awareness of other visitors' presence was still a key element of Lily's practice, despite the presence of the guide. Lily seemed to perceive the presence of her guide as an enabler, yet she remained aware of others and how her actions could be viewed or perceived.

Co-awareness and the consciousness of being the subject of other visitors' observation made Lily negotiate and regulate her positioning in a socially organised 'choreography' of bodies in the space (vom Lehn *et al.*

2001). Through co-presence, Lily developed a level of awareness of herself and her body as a viewing subject. She was aware of her visibility as others could have stared at her and questioned her behaviour since she behaved in a way that went against the museum's official script (Rees Leahy 2012). Lily became aware of her spacial relationship to objects as she started sensing that her performance was the object of external scrutiny. Lily started to perceive herself as a viewing subject and an audience, and she acted accordingly (Bagnall 2003). Findings presented above suggest that she feared 'being looked at' due to elements connected to her disability. She feared being put on the spot by going against the museum script, despite being enabled to do so by her guide, who represented the museum authority. In section 7.7, I expand further on how this impacted Lily's identity development as a disabled person and as a museum visitor.

7.6. Scaffolding

7.6.1. Guidance and support

In section 7.5, I examined how Lily walked through the museum together with her guide and her friend Ginny. I look at scaffolding instances in Lily's practice, and I compare how scaffolding guidance unfolded between Lily and Ginny in the Wallace Collection (section 6.6.1).

At the beginning of the visit, the guide offered her arms to Lily, and they walked together with their arms linked. Ginny followed them, usually positioning herself on Lily's free side. The walking dynamic was completely different from the way the two walked together in the Wallace Collection. In that case (section 6.5), walking together enabled a deep social interaction between the two. In the case of the MoL, the presence of the guide inhibited them from verbally or physically interacting as much. Only when the guide left them after more than two hours of the guided tour did the two friends interact the same way they did in the Wallace Collection.

However, despite these differences, instances of scaffolding guidance seemed to occur similarly. In the Wallace Collection, Lily relied entirely on Ginny for navigation. Ginny decided where to go, where to stop and positioned Lily at the 'correct' distance from objects. The two of them linked their arms for most of the visit. Similarly, the museum guide seemed to guide Lily throughout the guided tour.

The elements of guidance observed were:

- Lily and her guide had arms linked during the visit at all times.
- The guide directed Lily by walking slightly in front of her while Lily followed.
- The guide stopped and positioned Lily in front of each object.
- When they walked down the stairs at the end of the 'War Plague and Fire' gallery, the guide placed Lily's hand on the handrail after Lily asked to walk down the stairs instead of taking the lift.

Certain scaffolding characteristics resemble those identified in other studies (for example, guiding hands on objects) (Mai and Ash 2012). My research shows other characteristics that are specific to the experience of BPS visitors, such as guidance for positioning in front of objects, and guidance while walking through the space. Guidance never seemed to fade during the guided tour. In the middle of the tour (in the Roman gallery) and towards the end of the tour, near the middle of the Medieval Gallery, Lily seemed to lose interest in the tour. Several elements that suggested boredom were observed:

Instances 7.5:

	Source: fieldnotes
Before	**After**
Lily asked question when touching objects.	Lily stopped asking questions.
Lily actively conversed with her guide, trying to include Ginny in the conversation. Lily often turned towards Ginny to speak to her.	Both Lily and Ginny felt silent, and they did not interact with each other or with the guide.
Lily energetically followed her guide without ever slowing down.	When looking at objects that could not be touched, Lily did not seem to follow her guide: she looked away, stood further from the object and the guide (despite the linked arms), and looked like she was being 'dragged' by her guide.

Lily's body reacted to the situation. Lily seemed to passively accept her guide's guidance during these moments. This suggests that the lack of interest in the content or the tour format was detrimental to guidance fading. While in the Wallace Collection (section 6.6.1), Ginny's guidance to Lily did not fade because of Lily's vision impairment and the well-rehearsed guiding dynamic between the two, in this case, it is reasonable to say that it did not fade because of a lack of interest/ boredom. Lily mentioned 'boredom' as an element of the visit during the interview:

> The tour was very long. I wasn't expecting it to be that long. At the beginning I told her [the guide] that I was interested in an overview of the museum. We did basically everything instead. It was very long. And a bit boring when I could not touch things. I don't really see the point if I can't touch something. And the historical part is interesting of course, but I like to know more other things. Things like colours, or shape.

The elements of boredom and lack of interest can be seen as additional reasons why guidance did not fade during Lily's visit, together with the reasons already discusses in section 6.6.1, namely Lily's needs related to her vision impairment, Ginny's lack of professional training, and Ginny's higher level of expertise as a museum visitor.

Anna's walking practice was deeply influenced by her two friends' presence and the fact that she did not have her guide dog with her. As explored in sections 7.2.2, she usually walked accompanied by her guide dog while in Italy, but she did not bring her dog with her when she travelled to London. The lack of aid provided by the guide dog limited Anna's mobility independence. Hence, Anna walked into the museum on her own and with her friend Sofia's assistance:

Instance 7.6:

Source: fieldnotes
When they arrived at the museum, Sofia guided Anna through security and walked with her to the information desk. They did not link arms. Instead, Sofia guided Anna by putting her hand on Anna's back. Anna kept her white cane folded in her left hand.
Anna asked at the information desk directions to the 'London 2012 Cauldron' gallery in English.
While Anna verbally guided them, Sofia physically guided Anna down the stairs to the lower ground floor of the museum, to the 'London 2012 Cauldron' gallery. Anna walked with her right arm linked to Sofia's left arm.
When they reached the gallery, Anna unlinked her arm from Sofia's, unfolded her white cane and walked independently around the gallery using her white cane. She traced the edges of the balustrade that surrounds the Cauldron (figure 7.4, yellow arrow) with her white cane, and she leaned over closer to the torches until she could reach them (figure 7.4, red arrow). She touched one of the torches while her friends stood back.
Anna called both Elena and Sofia to get closer to the Cauldron, but they did not touch the torches.
After they looked at the Cauldron, they moved back and watched the video of the Opening Ceremonies of the Olympic and Paralympic games. While they watched the videos, Anna held both Elena and Sofia's hands.
Anna always walked, linking arms or grabbing Sofia's elbow. She was never guided by her other friend Elena. For the rest of the visit, Anna folded her white cane and let Sofia guide her.

When I asked why only Sofia guided her and not Elena, Anna explained in the interview that Sofia guided her because she was used to it as she regularly helps her during training sessions:

Sofia and I train together. That's why. She knows how I walk, we're comfortable. It's just easier. I think we didn't really think about it, you know. It just came automatic. I think I mostly rely on Sofia even outside of here [the museum].

The findings presented above show the scaffolding nature of the guidance instances. Five moments of shifting guidance roles were identified:

1. Sofia guided Anna to the information desk
2. Anna asked for directions to the 'London 2012 Cauldron' gallery and verbally guided Sofia and Elena.

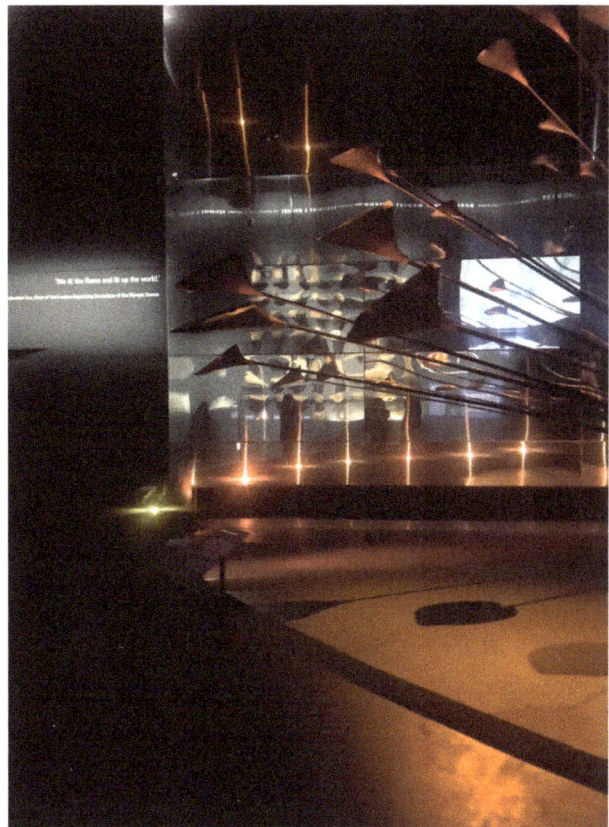

Figure 7.4. Edges of the balustrade that surrounds the Cauldron (yellow arrow), and the torches (red arrow).

3. Sofia physically guided Anna to the 'London 2012 Cauldron' gallery, following her verbal directions.
4. Anna explored the gallery independently and guided her friends towards the Cauldron.
5. Sofia guided Anna for the rest of the visit.

Anna took on leadership roles and guided her friends when she felt confident. She asked for directions, being the only one who spoke fluently English. Additionally, she seemed confident and at ease in the 'London 2012 Cauldron' gallery because of the deep emotional collection with the objects on display. This growing confidence due to this emotional connection seemed to allow her to explore the unfamiliar environment of the 'London 2012 Cauldron' gallery independently.

Her emotional connection to the display allowed her to grow confident and empowered her to move independently in the space. This growing confidence and independent walking created scaffolding instances of shifting of authority roles. Sofia and Anna constantly re-negotiated each other guidance role throughout the visit. The quote above shows how Anna was at ease with Sofia's guidance. This was clear as she allowed Sofia to guide her for the rest of the visit, where they explored together objects that she was interested in but did not seem to develop an emotional connection with them.

Findings in this section contribute to the understanding of walking as part of the embodied practice and as a deeply social and cultural practice. The continuous scaffolded guidance and the confidence triggered by the emotional connection with objects enabled Anna to make meaning in a situated social context.

7.7. Identity formation

This section discusses findings from the category of 'identity formation'. While instances of identity formation are presented and analysed throughout the chapter, I discuss specifically the correlation between identity development and practice. This section is divided into three further parts: identity and disability (7.7.1), cultural and social identity (7.7.2), and sense of place: 'Londoners' identity (7.7.3). This third characteristic of identity formation did not emerge in data from the other two case studies. It is specifically related to the content of the museum – that is, the history of London. I analysed instances related to participants' identity as Londoners through the theoretical framework of sense of placemaking (chapter 3, section 3.7.3).

7.7.1. Identity and disability

This subsection looks at two instances that influenced participants' development of their identity as disabled people. In the case of Lily, I discuss one instance where her bodily practice made her uneasy about the way her guide interpreted her disability. Second, in the case of Anna, I look at how the encounter with the London 2012 Olympic Cauldron enabled her to further develop her identity as a disabled person and athlete.

Lily reported in the interview how a specific guidance instance made her feel 'uneasy' during the visit:

> [The guide] was very nice, don't get me wrong. But at some point, she was sort of insinuating that I needed to take the lift instead of the stairs for some reason. I had the impression that she thought I couldn't do stairs. I felt chilling. I literally froze. Super uneasy really. I'm sure she didn't mean it in a bad way though.

Instance 7.7 offers a better understanding of how Lily's body reacted to this guidance attempt:

Instance 7.7:

Source: fieldnotes
[At the end of the 'War Plague Fire' gallery, to continue the visit to the 'Modern London' galleries, it is necessary to go from the ground floor to the lower ground floor of the museum. This can be accessed by a flight of stairs or by a lift.]
The guide suggested to Lily to take the lift to 'make things easier'. Lily declined and asked to take the stairs instead. Lily was vocal about the fact that she 'had no problem at all in doing the stairs.' After this, the guide placed Lily's hand on the handrail and offered her arm to Lily. Lily walked down the stairs alone, rejecting the guide's arm support. She linked again to her guide's arm only at the bottom of the stairs.

This instance resonates with Hayhoe's (2017) discussion around passive exclusion in museums when BPSP's agency is denied, and their identity is associated with their impairment only. Lily's guide's misunderstanding of physical needs led to a moment of dys-appearance, which Lily resisted (Imrie 2001). Lily openly admitted how she felt the effect of the dys-abling experience through her body: 'I felt chilling. I literally froze'. This aligns with Paterson and Hughes' (1999) argument that the oppressive socially constructed barriers or dys-abling practices are felt through the body. Lily's body felt the socially constructed prejudice, which she interpreted as oppressive behaviour (ibid). Thus, the body momentarily dys-appeared (Imrie 2001).

It is important to highlight how the dys-appearance was temporary. In fact, instance 7.7 shows how Lily, after an initial moment of bewilderment, actively resisted the dys-abling experience. She verbally asserted her physical abilities and distanced herself from the dys-abling and prejudiced interpretation of her impairment offered by her guide. Additionally, she took control of her bodily movements by walking down the stairs unassisted and openly refuting her guide's support. As Lily primarily saw her visits to the museum as having a social and cultural purpose, she did not seem to want to be associated with her disability. This desire seems part of Lily's practice both outside and inside the museum. She wanted to identify with a more mainstream, social and cultural identity in the museum, where she is not seen as impaired and needs different to those of others (Hayhoe 2017).

As previously mentioned, Anna visited the MoL to specifically look at the Cauldron from London 2012 Olympic and Paralympic games. The London 2012 Olympic and Paralympic games seemed to be a symbolic milestone in Anna's life as an athlete. She often remarked how her sport is not only a job but her main interest and her passion. In the interview, Anna explained what the games represented to her, what it meant to her to see the Cauldron, and she described her excitement:

> It [the Olympic and Paralympic 2012 games] was the biggest thing. Seriously I lived it as if I was there. [...] Being an athlete or a coach is already a difficult life. It's a lot of hard work you know? You always train, you always work. It's actually not just a work, it's your passion, your entire life. As a disabled athlete and coach, it's even harder I would say. Not so much the [sport she practices], but the fact that you have to constantly prove that you can. [...] The games were the biggest recognition. Seriously. Paralympics have always been a thing, but never as much as during the London 2012 games. We felt the importance. There was recognition.

Anna walked up close to the Cauldron while her friends stood back, and then she gave in to the urge to touch it. While I discuss further what touching the Cauldron meant for Anna and how that impacted her meaning-making of the exhibition, I focus on how being in the presence of the Cauldron and establishing a connection with it contributed to her identity development as a disabled person and athlete. The following quote shows Anna's desire to get close to the object despite the museum's regulations:

> I couldn't stop. Everyone knows you can't touch stuff in museums. […] But you know what? I just had to. It wanted to touch it so badly. […] It felt amazing. […] I truly felt a connection. I couldn't believe I was there in front of it. I brought back all the memories and the emotions

Instance 7.8 shows how she reacted to the video of the Paralympic Games opening ceremony:

Instance 7.8:

Source: fieldnotes
Anna and her friends watched the videos of the Paralympic and Olympic games ceremonies. When the Paralympic game opening ceremony started, Anna gasped with her mouth wide open in an expression of surprise. As the video was playing, Anna had tears in her eyes. Her friend Sofia noticed it, and she walked close to her. Anna kept standing with her face towards the screen, but she took Sofia's hand and held it tightly. Her friend Elena walked close to them, and Anna placed a hand around her shoulder.

Anna further explained what it felt like to be in the presence of the Cauldron, what it meant to re-watch the opening ceremonies, and what it meant to be able to touch the Cauldron:

> I just couldn't believe I was there. It's huge exactly like I thought […] And the room. I swear I could not see a thing, but I felt it. […] There was a certain atmosphere. Like you knew that there was the Cauldron there. The same one of the Olympic games. I was there next to it. It just meant so much. And even touching it, even if I couldn't do it really. Just meant so so much. I felt represented. I thought I was only going to find the Cauldron and then information about the Olympics. But no! A whole section was dedicated to the Paralympics as well! I was very surprised when the video started playing.

The 'ambience' or 'atmosphere' provided by the gallery's environment and facilitated by the proximity to the Cauldron and the tactile experience enhanced Anna's emotional connection to it. Her connection to the object itself and what it represented dates back to her experience of the Olympic and Paralympic games in 2012. Her experience at the museum strengthened, enhanced, and developed this connection. Anna created a connection with the Cauldron by making sense of it both as a 'perceptually aesthetic object' (Hayhoe 2013, 7) and as an object that embodied intellectual, historic and emotional meaning. She made sense of the object by being in the presence of

it. Her embodied experience of the object brought together the intellectual and emotional spheres. The relationship she built with the object through visual understanding and touch allowed her to get emotionally closer to it. This emotional connection allowed her to gain cultural and social capital (Bourdieu 2010).

Anna's identity as a disabled person was deeply influenced by the fact that she is a disabled athlete. Her disability identity comprised personal and community dimensions (Cunningham *et al.* 2019). The personal identity was mainly connected to how she viewed herself as a person with a disability (ibid). The community dimension was associated with how she viewed herself as connected to the community of disabled athletes and, in general, disabled people (ibid). Therefore, it seems reasonable to argue that how the museum represented the disability narrative of the Paralympic games contributed to shaping Anna's identity within the museum visit.

Feeling 'represented' was a crucial aspect that enabled Anna's sense of belonging, participation, and identity formation. Her embodied reaction of surprise to the video of the Paralympic opening ceremony signifies that she did not expect it to be included. The issue of representation of disability-related narratives did not emerge at any other point in my study. However, Anna's experience is significant and paradigmatic. The Paralympics narrative adopted by the museum was a positive one. Disability was represented through association with determination, empowerment, inclusivity, independence, and extraordinary athletic performance. Being acknowledged and represented as an athlete and as a disabled person enabled Anna to re-live the emotions and feelings associated with the Paralympic games of 2012 and establish a deep and meaningful connection with the object and the museum.

Anna's embodied and cognitive response to the exhibition suggests that the museum succeeded in representing what disability has meant, means, and could mean to society within the framework of the Paralympic games (Sandell *et al.* 2005, 5). The Paralympic narrative succeeded in challenging 'reductive stereotypes', presenting the diversity of disability experience (ibid). In doing so, the exhibition enabled Anna to feel included, to develop a sense of belonging, and to re-define her identity as a disabled athlete.

7.7.2. Social and cultural identity

Throughout this chapter, I present instances in which Lily and Anna made meaning with their friends and companions during their visit. Their social interactions in the space support my discussion of museums as places to develop a social and cultural identity in section 6.7.2. Lily's development of identity as a museum visitor was again enabled by her social relationship with Ginny, similar to her visit to the Wallace Collection. Lily again explained how much she valued the possibility that the museum offers to go out and spend time with her friend. She explained further how her friendship with Ginny enabled her to visit museums which otherwise she would consider 'out of her reach':

> I've always felt like museums were quite out of my reach. […] Well normally I kind of go in and become a bit lost and get overwhelmed and go home. […] Here I come with Ginny and we have a great time with no fuss. […] Being able to go with friends is quite great. I would not come to museums without her. It would be overwhelming. Also, it's just great that I can do something I like and be with my friend at the same time.

From these responses, it is clear how taking part in the museum visit with her friend has a dual value for Lily. On the one hand, she values the fact that her friend's expertise and familiarity with museum environments enabled her to pursue her cultural interests in museums. On the other hand, she valued how the museum offered the optimal opportunity for her to be with her friend, spending enjoyable time together. The friendship with Ginny seems to be the tool that enables Lily to explore museums, while at the same time, going to the museum together seems to be the tool that enables the two of them to share a pleasurable and meaningful social experience and to negotiate their identity as museum visitors.

Albeit differently compared to Lily, visiting the museum and sharing the experience with her friends contributed to Anna's identity development as an athlete and as a museum visitor. Anna explained what it meant for her to visit the Cauldron gallery with her friends and to share this interest with them:

> We are friends, but not just that. Sofia is an athlete as well. We train together. […] Sofia and I coach [a group of young athletes]. It's our world. […] Elena is not an athlete, but she is really passionate. She works for [the sport centre where they train], that's how we became friends. It's a passion for all of us. The sport is what we have in common. That's why we were so excited to be here and to see it [the Cauldron].

Anna's response shows that being an athlete and the sport, in general, are not just professional activities for her and her friends. Being an athlete is a passion that they have in common. Visiting the museum, and specifically, the galleries related to the London 2012 games, represented an occasion to share their primary interest, as well as reconnecting to the Paralympic games. Their choice to visit the MoL was grounded in the possibility of exploring their common interest, and sharing such interest was a crucial part of their social practice.

If we consider the Paralympic games as an abstract space, Anna established a connection with it in the act of placemaking through the Cauldron (Budge 2020). The Paralympics was a metaphorical place of importance to Anna, and this meaningfulness was tied to what it represented. As Anna walked and moved her body through the physical place, she made meaning of it and the intangible significance of the Paralympics, establishing a sense of belonging (Cresswell 2015). The abstract meaning she made of the games was deeply situated through the ongoing situated interaction with the environment (Kyle and Chick 2007), where the physical encounter held a level of significance (Budge 2020, 14).

7.7.3. Sense of place: 'Londoners' identity

A placemaking element of cultural and social identity formation was identified in the visits of Fred and Lily. Both of them expressed how the museum made them feel connected with the city of London and enabled the development of their identity as 'Londoners'. Both Fred and Lily moved to London during their adult life. They both mentioned a strong connection with the city and the values it embodies. The occasion of the visit to the MoL allowed them to explore and strengthen this connection further. Both participants expressed a strong sense of place and attachment to the city, and their encounter with the museum collection seemed to strengthen place attachment and meaning.

In the interview, Fred explained why the content of the museum resonated so much with him and his personal experience of London:

> I really love this city. I'm a big London fan. I love living here and since I moved here, I have tried to explore it as much as possible. And being able to learn about all this history, you know the past, all the history of the place and how it used to be. It's just great. It's great. There is so much to learn. So much history. […] I will definitely come back and look at the rest of the museum. I can't wait.

Fred indeed went back to visit the museum shortly after his visit for this research project, and in his blog he reiterated his strong connection to the city of London:

> I was really looking forward to exploring it, as I've always loved the city since I was a child visiting relatives here, and I'm now very happy to be actually living here. […] [The museum] makes you appreciate all the more just how special and amazing the place is. [Quote extracted from Fred's blog]

Fred had recently moved to London and explained that exploring the city was one of his favourite activities during all three interviews. He described how the act of visiting museums allowed him to fit in and to feel part of the London community. The museum's content spoke to him as a visitor and as a Londoner. The historic capital he developed allowed him to develop an embodied emotional connection and sense of place with the museum collection. Being in the museum and learning about London's historical past strengthened his sense of belonging to the city.

In the previous chapter (section 6.8.2), I analysed how Lily and Ginny shared an artistic interest in Spanish painters and how going to museums allowed them to explore their shared interest together. In the MoL, while Lily expressed a general interest in history and archaeology, she never went into details about a specific period or type of objects during the interview. However, she mentioned several times her and Ginny's shared interest and passion for London:

> Well I'm a massive London fan. I've lived in London for seven years and I've never been [to the MoL]. And I'm a bit sort of London-centric, like I love the history, I love reading stuff about London and watching programs and you kind of have to go to the Museum of London, right? […]
>
> […] She [Ginny] and I met in London shortly after she moved here. Our friendship is basically based about London. London is very important for both of us. It's something we have in common. We really like living here […].
>
> […] Coming here together is very nice because we're not tourists really. We love the city, the history, we explore the city together all the time. It's like exploring the city in the past. When you recognise places like St Paul or old London you feel like you belong here because you have been.

Fred and Lily came to the MoL with their own understanding about the city of London. This allowed them to make meaning from exhibitions as they look through the lens of their own experiences and identity as Londoners (Doering and Pekari 1996; Silverman 1995). The 'Londoner' identity participants added to their museum experience and helped to supply their side of meaning-making (Stainton 2002). Over their time living in the city, Fred and Lily developed layered, lived experiences of London as a place (Budge 2020). Their identity as Londoners developed through a series of daily negotiations as they navigate physical spaces through situated and 'reiterative' social practices (Cresswell 2004). This occurs in an embodied form through mobility, movement, and the experiences that unfold through place and mobility, as they moved their bodies around London as an everyday practice, coming to understand the place and establishing a sense of belonging. (Cresswell 2015). Fred and Lily brought these experiences with them in the museum, and the physical encounter with the environment and the collection enabled them to connect with and negotiate their identity and sense of place as they moved their bodies through the museum, establishing a sense of belonging (Budge 2020). Their social engagement with the city through the museum visits reflected the place as meaningful (Budge 2020).

The sociocultural context of their visits can be seen as a helpful place to see how Fred and Lily were in dialogue with the museum content and how they engaged with their own experience as Londoners to make meaning of the collection (Stainton 2002). The museum itself became the tool that enabled conversations about the city of London, and the development of the identity of visitors as Londoners.

7.8. Looking

7.8.1. Looking back

Similar to the previous visits to the V&A and Wallace Collection, Fred clearly expressed his interest and preference for the historical and intellectual details of the objects. This preference influenced the way he physically approached each object. Unlike his previous visits, in the MoL, he did not use digital or non-digital accessibility resources to access information for each object. Hence, he resorted to using his resources (his mobile phone and his monocular) to access objects' labels and information panels, as instance 7.9 shows:

Instance 7.9:

Source: fieldnotes
Fred stopped in front of each object and each panel he encountered, and he read all the information panels and labels and looked at objects. He used the same sequence to approach each object: he looked at the label briefly, observed the object for 10–20 seconds, went back to the label to read it in full, and then observed the object for 20–30 more seconds. He spent between 1 and 3 minutes looking at each object.

Fred specified in the interview:

> So it's interesting to see how London's kind of grown, and then kind of gone into ruins, and then grown again. It's kind of got this, had peaks and troughs all the way through history. So yeah, it's been really interesting to see all that. […] I kind of learnt more detail about the history was really interesting definitely. It kind of just helped to fill in lots of the gaps and just make it feel like a more, it's like a story I suppose the way it progressed. I really enjoyed learning about the history.

Fred seemed to rely on the perception of what remains of his vision together with his accessible resources in order to develop historic capital about the objects. While he observed the objects, his attention focused primarily on the historical and biographical information provided by panels and labels. His experience in all three museums was entirely non-tactile and non-perceptual. The meaning he made can be understood through the lens of historical capital. Fred focused on information about objects to access the intellectual discussion about their significance. While his interest encompassed the aesthetic qualities of the objects, his bodily approach to the objects and the information labels and panels suggest that the aesthetic qualities are secondary in value compared to the historical ones. He made meaning during his visit through the development of historic capital. This allowed him to look at objects in terms of their historical and intellectual significance. Because of his sight loss, through the historical narrative, Fred had a different relationship with objects. He evolved an alternative 'narrative of learning' about them (Hayhoe 2017). Such narrative comes from his own historical understanding of political, cultural, and social periods that the object represents and that he associated with it (ibid).

Fred's desire to learn about objects' historical significance comes back in section 7.10, where I look at the frustration and feeling of exclusion triggered by the lack of mainstream or assistive resources to access information in the museum.

7.8.2. Beyond perception: aesthetic capital

Similar to her experience in the Wallace Collection, Lily expressed her interest in the aesthetic characteristics of objects and her desire to make sense of visual content beyond verbal knowledge, despite her lack of visual perception. However, her visit to the MoL unfolded differently compared to that in the Wallace Collection. The presence of her guide seemed to be an obstacle to Lily's development of aesthetic capital. The following instances and Lily's interview responses support this claim.

At the beginning of the tour, the guide asked Lily what kind of tour she wanted. Lily replied that she wanted a general tour of the museum and to learn about the collection. She did not mention any aspect of the objects in which she was specifically interested. During the tour, the guide equally focused on tactile objects as well as objects behind cases. She gave a verbal description of objects, briefly mentioning their shapes, and then focused on historical details. The following two instances (7.10 and 7.11) show Lily's different response to verbal descriptions for objects behind cases and tactile objects:

Instance 7.10:

Source: fieldnotes
At the beginning of the tour, in the 'London before London' gallery, the guide stopped in front of several objects behind cases. In particular, she guided Lily in front of two stone Maceheads from 2500BC (figure 7.5). The guide began describing the object by briefly reading the label (figure 7.6), giving quick information about the intricate decoration pattern. Then she immediately switched the focus on the historical meaning of the objects, talking about the symbolic significance they had in terms of power and status. At the end of the description, Lily asked her guide what colour the Maceheads were, but the guide seemed confused by the question and turned to Ginny. Ginny replied, 'black with marble-like shades of white and grey'. Lily turned her body to face Ginny and kept asking questions to Ginny about the shape and the texture of the Maceheads. After this episode, Lily did not ask any other question related to the aesthetic properties of the objects behind cases they stopped at.

Figure 7.5. Stone Maceheads from 2500BC.

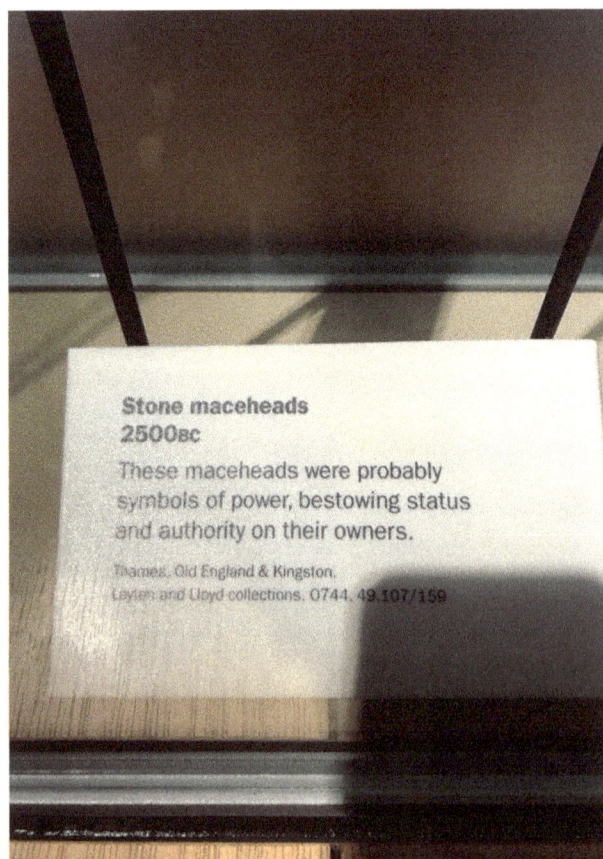

Figure 7.6. Label of stone Maceheads from 2500BC.

128

Instance 7.11:

Source: fieldnotes
Lily, Ginny and their guide encountered a reconstruction of Roman mosaic pavements. The guide began to explain that mosaics were used as decorative floor pavements in noble Roman houses, and she gave details about the manufacturing and use of mosaics in Roman society. The museum offered touch mosaics reconstructions (figure 7.7ab); hence Lily started touching them while the guide was talking.   When the guide stopped talking, Lily turned to Ginny and asked her how the mosaics appeared, explicitly asking if they looked like Pompeii mosaics. The two engaged in a conversation about the colours of the mosaics and compared them to Pompeii mosaics. In particular, Lily asked questions about the geometrical patterns and the use of the colour red.

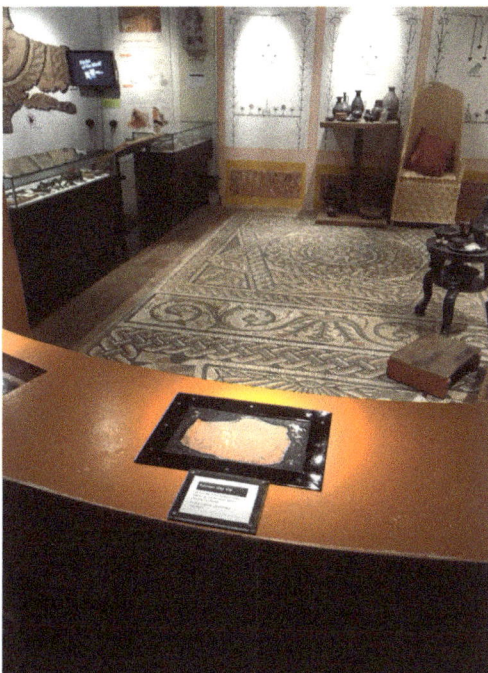

Figure 7.7ab. Roman mosaics' tactile reconstruction.

In the interview, Lily explained that touch helped her visualise details like shape, material, and the way the objects felt:

> Yes that [touch] helps a lot because you can picture in your head what something looks like, because you can touch it and you can feel the shape and what it's made of. I feel how it feels. So that helps. But for things like colours and drawings, it's not ok. I can't touch something and know what colour it is. And that's the interesting part!

It is interesting to draw a parallel between instance 7.10 and Lily's encounters with paintings in the Wallace Collection (section 6.8.2). Due to the lack of accessible audio descriptions designed for BPSP in the Wallace Collection, Lily was forced to use a typical audio guide device in the space. Such device had brief visual descriptions and mainly focused on the historical narratives of paintings with heavily visual language. This in appearance may sound similar to her experience in the MoL, as her guide did not provide specific audio descriptions of objects. However, as analysed in section 6.8.2, the lack of audio descriptions did not prevent Lily from developing aesthetic capital. In the Wallace Collection, the highly visual descriptions did not confuse Lily, but rather the deeply social interaction Lily had with Ginny in front of Velazquez paintings (section 6.8.2) enabled the development of aesthetic capital. Lily took in the paintings from the exhibition comfortably, as her social interaction with Ginny enabled her.

In the MoL, the lack of familiarity between Lily and the guide and the guide's misunderstanding of Lily's preferences seemed to discourage Lily from asking questions and pursuing her interests for aesthetic visual concepts. In the interview, she explained how those historic-dense descriptions made her feel:

> It was a bit boring to be fair. All that history felt boring. I don't even know what she was talking about most of the times. I know the history already. I studied it in school, it was not that. […] I could not imagine what she was talking about. I don't know what some of the objects were. [Prompt: why didn't you ask to get a more visual description?] I mean, I kind of tried. But if that's the tour she knows.

The lack of visual description did not allow Lily to develop aesthetic capital because she did not feel connected to the objects. The mere historical notions did not resonate with her interest in aesthetic features. As Lily enquired about visual details of the objects, the guide was not sure if and to what extent the objects and their visual qualities were noticeable to the Lily. The overly historical narrative proposed by her guide as a consequence of this uncertainty triggered feelings like boredom which hindered the meaning-making process and consequently made Lily passively excluded. The social and embodied interaction with Ginny appeared to be Lily's tool to resist this exclusion. She verbally asked questions about the aesthetic features of objects, and she also moved her body to direct her attention towards Ginny, somehow living the guide out of their interaction. 'Doing the exhibition together' is part of Lily and Ginny's shared repository of funds of knowledge. Lily drew from it during the visit to resist the boredom and the consequent exclusion.

It is interesting to draw a parallel between the previous instances and section 7.7.1, where I discuss how the interaction between Lily and her guide triggered the dys-appearance of Lily's body and the consequent resistance. In that particular episode, the guide actively made a dys-abling remark on the ability to walk down the stairs. In this case, Lily mentioned that she had the impression that the guide focused on historical and biographical details of objects because she assumed that as a blind person, she would have been less interested in the aesthetic details:

> I guess she thought that I'm blind so I can't really see things like colours or decorations. So why bother describing it? Which is a shame because I really like it.

Lily suggested that assumptions about her disability could have influenced her guide's guiding style. Lily actively tried to express an interest in aesthetic qualities and visual concepts, but the guide did not change her guiding style. This strengthened her feeling that her disability was used to restrict normalised notions of enjoying the visual arts and encountering the environment (Hayhoe 2017). These instances show the effects of Lily's embodied, social, and cultural experience on her feelings of inclusion through the museum. Engaging with mainstream forms of visual culture and adhering to what she perceived as correct bodily practices made Lily feel a sense of belonging and ownership of the museum. Visiting the museum in a 'mainstream' way significantly contributed to Lily's development of a cultural form of identity and a sense of belonging to the community of museum-goers. Guidance from her guide did in those two instances did not scaffold but somewhat hindered Lily's meaning-making.

The following section broadens the perspective and shows how Lily's meaning-making in the MoL happened primarily through the embodied practice of touching objects. Touch seemed to allow Lily to regain agency on the visit, shift the focus on elements that interested her and develop aesthetic capital. The physical connection to objects seemed to make Lily actively shift and focus the conversation on aesthetic features. Touch seemed the mean to facilitate making sense of the objects both physically, through tactile exploration of shapes and materials, as well as cognitively, as it gave Lily the confidence to shift the conversations.

7.9. Touching

This section presents and discusses findings about how visitors made sense of the museum collection through touch. The museum provides tactile objects in each gallery for everyone to touch. These objects are part of the narrative and the storytelling of the galleries. Lily and Anna touched several objects during their visit, while Fred did not, similar to his visit to the V&A.

This section is divided into three parts, which analyse the different characteristics that were identified as part of the tactile practice of participants: professional guidance (7.9.1), co-touching (7.9.2), and forbidden touch (7.9.3). The latter characteristic refers to two instances in which Lily and Anna intentionally touched objects that were not meant to be touched without authorisation from the museum. No other participants touched non-tactile objects during the other visits.

7.9.1. Learning through touch

As I briefly mentioned in section 7.8.2 when referring to Lily's development of aesthetic capital, Lily touched several objects both with her guide and with her friend Ginny. Unlike the professional tactile guidance provided in the V&A by the specifically trained guides, in the MoL, the guide only guided Lily's hand on top of the objects and let her explore them by herself. While the lack of video findings makes it difficult to analyse how Lily touched each object, fieldnotes still provide interesting insights. Instances 7.12 and 7.13 below show how, despite the presence of the guide, it was Ginny that scaffolded Lily's meaning-making, by physically guiding her tactile exploration.

Instance 7.12:

Source: fieldnotes
In the 'Roman London' gallery, Lily and Ginny touched the replicas of two Roman Mortaria (figure 7.8). The guide explained both the use of mortaria and how they were manufactured. Lily touched one of the mortaria starting from the rim, exploring the inside and the outside. She commented with Ginny how grit the inside felt, and they joked about making pesto with it. Ginny laughed and commented that it was probably used in the same way in Roman times, and that the gritty inside was necessary to grind things up with a pestle, like for pesto.

Figure 7.8. Replicas of two Roman Mortaria.

Instance 7.13:

Source: fieldnotes
In the gallery 'London before London', Lily's guide made her touch two replicas of wooden objects used for magical and ritual purposes (figure 7.9). While the guide explained the beliefs related to different wood types, Lily touched the objects on her own with two hands. She seemed to struggle with the shape of the Dagenham idol while the guide was verbally describing it, as Lily did not seem to understand its shape. The guide mainly focused on the historical details of the object, so Ginny jumped in and guided Lily's hand on the features of the wood piece. She placed Lily's finger on each feature of the objects and described them while guiding Lily's fingers.

Figure 7.9. Replica of a wood club of Alder (left) and of a Dagenham idol (right).

I asked Lily whether she had encountered any difficulty when touching the objects:

> No not really they were all pretty easy. I guess maybe only with the wooden one the one looking like a person. That was weird. I didn't get it. She explained it, but it was difficult because I didn't understand the shape. Ginny helped.

Lily did not seem to encounter difficulties when touching the majority of the tactile objects they encountered. These objects had common and simple shapes, easy to explore and to understand, like the mortarium. On the

other hand, when she approached a more complicated object like the wooden replicas (figure 7.9), she seemed to require guidance as she seemed confused by their shapes and features. When looking for guidance, she instinctively turned towards Ginny rather than asking her guide. This resonates with the analysis of instances 7.10 and 7.11 in section 7.8.2: Lily asked questions about visual aesthetic properties of the objects she was touching to Ginny rather than to her guide. Her familiarity with Ginny and their well-tested practice of 'doing museums together' gave Lily the confidence to turn to her friend to obtain specific guidance without asking for it. Their shared interest in aesthetic characteristics of museum objects (as seen in section 6.8.2) allowed Lily to develop the confidence to approach the museum's objects and pursue her interests.

The two instances above present two elements of Lily and Ginny's scaffolding activity. The first instance shows that Lily did not experience difficulties while touching the mortarium. She did not require formal guidance to touch the object or to make sense of its physical characteristics. Instead, she joked with Ginny about the function of the mortarium and how it could be used today to 'make pesto'. Ginny responded by laughing and saying that it probably had a similar function in Roman times. This interaction shows how meaning-making was facilitated by jokes and laughter (Mai and Ash 2012). Lily's joke and Ginny response presented a certain degree of 'intuitive understanding' (Maybin *et al.* 1992, 23). This interaction shows how meaning-making started with Lily's action of touching the object and progressed through jokes and laughter, as ultimately, Lily and Ginny scaffolded each other's learning. Similar to the case of Jane and Max (section 5.6.2) and Davide and James (section 6.6.2), jokes and humour were a key part of Lily and Ginny's scaffolding and understanding the exhibition together (Mai and Ash 2012). Joking about objects together was part of the complex and intense social activity that enabled shared meaning-making by mixing object-related and non-object-related talk effortlessly (Mai and Ash 2012).

The second instance presents a different scaffolding moment, where Ginny provided physical guidance in response to Lily experiencing difficulties making sense of the object. In section 6.6.1, I have discussed how Ginny guided Lily throughout the visit, scaffolding her meaning-making, with the element of guidance never entirely fading. In the MoL, Lily relied less on Ginny's guidance due to the presence of the guide. However, when she experienced difficulties, Lily turned to Ginny rather than her guide for help. Ginny's guidance can be seen as part of their shared funds of knowledge, which they draw from to 'do the exhibition together' (Gonzalez *et al.* 2005). Similar to her visit to the Wallace Collection (section 6.6.1), relying on Ginny's guidance seemed to be one of the tools that enabled Lily to make meaning during her visit.

This analysis shows clearly the social impact of guidance on Lily's tactile experience. Due to issues in communication or the guide's confusion (potentially due to the lack of training) Lily's guide did not determine how Lily experienced the objects. Rather the guide simply added to Lily's tactile experience by offering descriptions of what she saw. On the contrary, Ginny effectively communicated to Lily how she experienced the display both tactually and verbally. In turns, Lily communicated her perspectives, providing information (both verbally and physically) that allowed Ginny to align with her experience by observing Lily's tactile exploration of the objects and listening to her descriptions. Lily and Ginny's interaction and experience of touching objects together resembled the way in which two sighted visitors would make sense of objects together through touch (vom Lehn 2010, 765).

7.9.2. Co-touching

The previous section focused on the scaffolding instances of guidance identified while Lily touched objects. This section discusses one specific instance in which Lily and Ginny made meaning of an object, an Anglo-Saxon mud-house, together in a practice of co-touching. Instance 7.14 below shows how Lily and Ginny physically encountered the Anglo-Saxon mud-house by stepping in it and co-touching its features:

Instance 7.14:

Source: fieldnotes
In the Anglo-Saxon part of the Medieval London gallery, Ginny noticed the reconstruction of an Anglo-Saxon mud-house (figure 7.10) and asked the guide if they were allowed to step inside. The guide assented, and Ginny took Lily's arm and guided her to the middle of the reconstruction. The guide read aloud the label of the reconstruction. Ginny then described the inside of the mud-house, giving details on the fireplace, the walls, and the construction. Ginny guided Lily towards the walls of the reconstruction and made her touch the woven woods. They then proceeded to touch the fireplace at the centre of the mud-house. Afterwards, they sat down in silence on the bench inside the reconstruction, and they stood there for around 30 seconds listening to the sounds coming from the speakers inside the reconstruction. Then Lily mentioned how this reminded her of a mud-house she visited when she was in Kenya, and she and Ginny looked for similar elements between the reconstruction and Lily's memories of the Kenyan mud-house, like the outer mud coating, the central fireplace and the woven wood parts. They touched these parts together, and Lily described to Ginny her experience in Kenya.

In the interview, she explained further how touching the mud-house with Ginny enabled her to remember details of her trip to Kenya and to make connections:

Yeah and again a similar kind of thing where it made me think of times when I'd been in the Maasai Mara in Kenya. And they welcomed me into their homes, and we saw how the homes were designed and it was very similar and yeah, making those connections it's great.

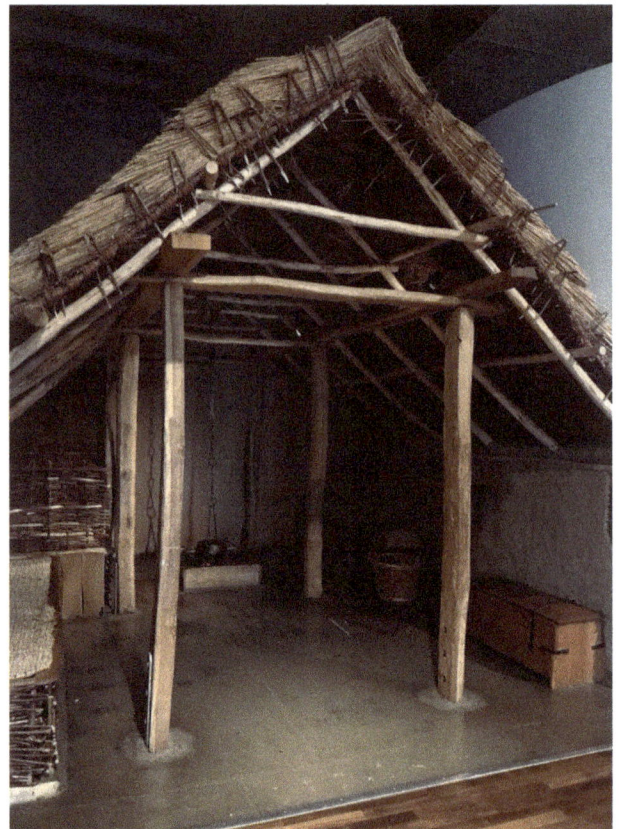

Figure 7.10. Reconstruction of an Anglo-Saxon mud-house.

They were mud-houses too […] We spoke a bit about my trip in Kenya. Ginny has never been, so I did most of the talking. I described something and Ginny said that there was something similar there, like the fireplace!

The quote clearly shows how being inside the reconstructed Anglo-Saxon mud-house triggered Lily's memories. Lily was able to touch the reconstruction, and she could stand inside hearing sounds and feeling the atmosphere of the mud-house. The combination of these haptic sensations and Ginny's description of the environment allowed Lily to understand the space and make a parallel with her visit to a Kenyan mud-house. Touch and ambience enabled these connections that Lily made between archaeological objects and objects from episodes of her personal history. These connections enabled meaning-making, as Lily constructed her knowledge from her past experiences that she brought to the museum. She made meaning by connecting her experience with what she experienced in the situated context. The museum became the social, cultural and physical context in which she and Ginny 'engaged with, made sense of and learnt from their recent past' through their bodily encounter with material culture (Moussouri and Vomvyla 2015, 99).

Similar to when she encountered the painting 'Lady with a Fan' by Velazquez (section 6.7.1), Lily made sense of the reconstruction by identifying features that reminded her of her personal experience. Making these connections enabled Lily to elaborate and develop an understanding of her own identity (Paris and Mercer 2002). Lily verbally took the lead of the visit, and she guided Ginny through her story-telling about her trip to Kenya. This enabled them to identify and touch together features of the mud-house in the process of co-creation and story-telling. Ginny enabled Lily's tactile exploration by guiding her hands and by touching features with her. On the other hand, Lily enabled shared meaning-making by co-touching and linking it to her story-telling of her past experience. The mud-house allowed Lily to recreate and embrace her memories, express her ownership of the experience, and share her meaning with Ginny (Paris and Mercer 2002, 406).

Their practice of co-touching went 'beyond touching for the sake of touching', to figure out what the object was (Rowe and Kisiel 2012, 74). It was a prolonged and socially mediated interaction. Through co-touching the mud-house, Lily was reminded of her personal experience and shared with Ginny how the mud-house intertwined with her life (Wyman *et al.* 2011). Therefore, the mud-house represented the ideal setting for sharing memories and strengthening their relation (Alvarez 2005). Similarly, in the following section, I discuss how the 'Pleasure Gardens' gallery and the experience of co-touching objects there represented the ideal setting for Lily and Ginny to make sense of the objects together. However, while the mud-house is a multisensory tactile reconstruction that visitors are allowed to touch, Ginny and Lily co-touched non-tactile objects in the 'Pleasure Gardens' gallery, defying the MoL's regulations.

7.9.3. Forbidden touch

This section presents findings from Lily and Anna's visits where they specifically touched objects that the museum did not allow visitors to touch. I argue that this 'forbidden touch' (category that emerged during the data coding) strengthened the relationship with their companions and objects and enabled the development of identity and a sense of ownership.

In section 7.5.2, I mentioned how Lily's guide allowed her to touch non-tactile objects that visitors are generally not allowed to touch in the Roman gallery. After the end of the guided tour, Lily and Ginny explored the lower ground floor of the museum. When they entered the Pleasure Gardens gallery (a closed room with only one door for entrance and exit), they realised that they were alone, and that no other visitor could see them. This encouraged them to touch objects despite they were not marked as 'tactile'. The following instances (7.15 and 7.16) describe their 'forbidden touch' interaction Lily and Ginny had in the Pleasure Gardens gallery:

Across the two visits that Lily and Ginny had at the Wallace Collection and the MoL, these instances in the 'Pleasure Gardens' gallery were the first and only time when Lily and Ginny did not seem concerned about the museum etiquette of correct positioning and the 'do not

Instance 7.15:

Source: fieldnotes
Lily and Ginny entered the gallery, which was empty and remained empty for the whole time. Lily followed Ginny with their arms linked. They reached a bench in the middle of the gallery, and they sat down for approximately 5 minutes. They chatted about the guided tour, and then Ginny briefly described the room's atmosphere and what the Pleasure Gardens were in the Victoria times. Ginny then described the video that was being displayed on the walls, and they remained seated in silence to listen to the actors in the video. At the end of the video, they stood up, and Lily followed Ginny around the room again with their arms linked. Ginny briefly described the clothing of the mannequins behind the glass cases. Ginny then made Lily stop in front of the mannequin of a 'Masked Lady' with antlers and a dark gown with gold stars (figure 7.11). Ginny briefly described it and mentioned that the mannequin was not behind a case. Lily asked if it was possible to touch, and Ginny replied with a mischievous tone that no sign allowed or explicitly forbade touch. Lily laughed, she furtively moved her head left and right to look around, and they started to touch it together. Ginny guided Lily's hands to reach the antlers of the mannequin, and they touched them together, making comparisons with reindeers. Lily touched the rest of the mannequin independently. Rather than focusing on the mannequin itself, Lily seemed to be more interested in the details of the dress. She discussed with Lily the hem of the low-cut neckline, the corset shape of the waistline, and the details of the metal stars.

Figure 7.11. Mannequin of 'A Masked Lady'.

touch' policy. It seems reasonable to say that this was because the guide had previously let her touch non-tactile objects and that when they visited the gallery, it was empty, and no one entered the space while they were

Instance 7.16:

Source: fieldnotes
After finishing touching the mannequin of the 'Masked Lady', Ginny told Lily that there were two more mannequins adorned with costumes that were not behind cases. Lily exclaimed 'let's see', and Ginny guided her to the mannequin of a Harlequin (figure 7.12). Lily again started touching it, mainly concentrating on the diamond-shaped pattern of the clothing. They touched it together and talked about how the silk material felt, and Ginny described the colours. Lily mentioned that she heard of Harlequin masks at the Venice Carnival. After finishing touching the Harlequin, they moved on and touched the mannequin of the 'Turkish Ambassador' (figure 7.13). Lily mainly focused on touching the turban, while Ginny described the colours of the dress

Figure 7.13. Mannequin of 'Turkish Ambassador'.

Figure 7.12. Mannequin of 'Harlequin'.

there. The secluded atmosphere of the gallery encouraged and enabled them to seek a more intimate interaction with the objects. This is in line with the findings from sections where Lily's concerns for what she perceives as 'correct behaviour' seemed to be mainly related to how others saw her behaving in the space. The lack of people in the 'Pleasure gardens' gallery seemed to allow Lily to become less tense, disregard her concerns for 'normative practices', and make meaning of the objects by co-touching them with Ginny.

From the findings presented so far, it is possible to argue that Lily is a knowledgeable museum visitor. She was aware of certain restrictions (like the widespread

'do not touch' policy), adapted to perceived normative bodily practices. She developed this understanding of normative practices through her visiting activity with Ginny, an experienced museum visitor. As seen in section 7.5.2, through co-presence, Lily developed awareness of her body as a viewing subject. She feared being scrutinised if defying the museum script, 'being seen doing something wrong'. This concern arose specifically when she was given the opportunity to touch non-tactile objects by her guide. They arose due to Lily's co-awareness of the presence of other bodies in the same perceptual range (Christidou and Diamantopoulou 2016).

Interestingly, her bodily reaction to co-presence related to touching non-tactile objects was the same in the Roman gallery (section 7.5.2, instance 7.4) and the Pleasure Gardens gallery. Lily moved her head as if she were looking for others in her same perceptual range. Lily could not have seen people due to her blindness. This suggests that her bodily gesturing was connected to her awareness of the presence of other bodies in her perceptual range, despite her impairment. Therefore, her embodied response to co-awareness can be seen as a deeply situated modality of engagement and communication (vom Lehn and Heath 2007; Steier *et al.* 2015).

Lily elaborated further in the interview how touch enabled her to make sense of the dresses she was touching:

So, it was really nice to be able to feel those costumes. But also, feel them on a mannequin. Just touching would be quite confusing because you can't really tell how [the dresses] are made. They're too elaborate. Whereas at least on the mannequin, you're like, "Oh, okay, that's the waist coat, that's the trousers, the hem, the turban". Like in a shop. If I understand the shape and how it is made, I can focus on other things too, the colour, the shape, because I don't have to just spend time figuring out the thing.

Lily made sense of objects in a variety of ways in the Wallace Collection and the MoL. She adapted her learning practice to the situated context and the resources available. In the Pleasure Gardens gallery in the MoL, touch enabled Lily and Ginny to make their meanings together by learning directly from contact with the objects (Clavir 1996; Spence and Gallace 2008). Touch can be considered a standalone learning tool that enabled the social interaction between Lily and Ginny and their shared meaning-making.

Despite the mannequins cannot be fully classified as 'sculptures', they present an analogy with neoclassical sculptures of human bodies due to their three-dimensional nature. In this sense, we can apply Hopkins' (2003) argument that sculptures are the ideal form of museum object for BPSP to make sense of through a multisensory interaction. Hopkins (2003) argued that sculptures offered equality of access, as they stimulate all the senses beyond sight. While Lily had to employ strategies to make sense of paintings in the Wallace Collection, as they were created primarily for vision, the mannequins in the MoL offered a more democratic form of aesthetic. Hopkins (2003, 26) argued that 'sculptures' fundamental source is our awareness of our possibilities for movement and action'. That awareness derives from the possibility of a form of engagement which does not come from sight or touch, but rather from a 'complex mixture of the sensory with our awareness of our bodies, and their possible interactions with the world' (Hopkins 2003, 26). Lily's act of touching the mannequin did not aim to create a mental image or access visual concepts despite her lack of sight. Her tactile exploration aimed to make sense of the objects' spatial reality, materials, and how they felt (Davidson *et al*. 1991), beyond the objects' 'visual nature' (Levent and Pascual-Leone 2014).

Despite the museum not letting visitors touch the objects in the Pleasure Gardens gallery, it seems reasonable to argue that touch was a key valuable way of learning, enjoying and investigating the collection for Lily (Candlin 2004). From an institutional perspective, tactile restrictions would have hindered and limited the meaning-making process if Lily and Ginny had not defied the museum script by going against correct normative behaviours. Through tactile exploration, Lily developed a higher form of aesthetic capital that she would not

have had access to otherwise, thus leading to passive exclusion.

Anna's experience offers a different perspective on 'forbidden touch'. As mentioned above in sections 7.6.1

Instance 7.17:

Source: fieldnotes
While in London 2012 Cauldron gallery, Anna walked very closed to the Cauldron, up until the edge of the Cauldron's base, while her friends stood farther. No one else was present in the gallery. Anna traced the edges of the balustrade that surrounds the Cauldron (figure 7.14, yellow arrow) with her white cane. She folded her cane, and she kept it in her left arm. Anna stretched her hand to reach the Cauldron; then she paused, turned to look at me, and asked, "Can I touch it?". In order to minimise the effect of my presence, I replied, "please, do whatever you feel like doing as if I was not here". Sofia laughed, and Elena protested that it was better not to touch it. Anna turned back to face the Cauldron. She bent and leaned over the balustrade and stretched her hand to reach one of the torches (figure 7.14 red arrow). She couldn't reach them, so she leaned and sat on the balustrade until she could reach them. She touched one of the torches with one hand. She only placed her hand on the torch; she kept it there for about 20 seconds while she closed her eyes. Her friends at the back were giggling and nervously looking around. After 20 seconds, she slightly moved her hand on the surface but only 2–3cm left and 2–3cm right. She stopped, and she moved back to join her friends.

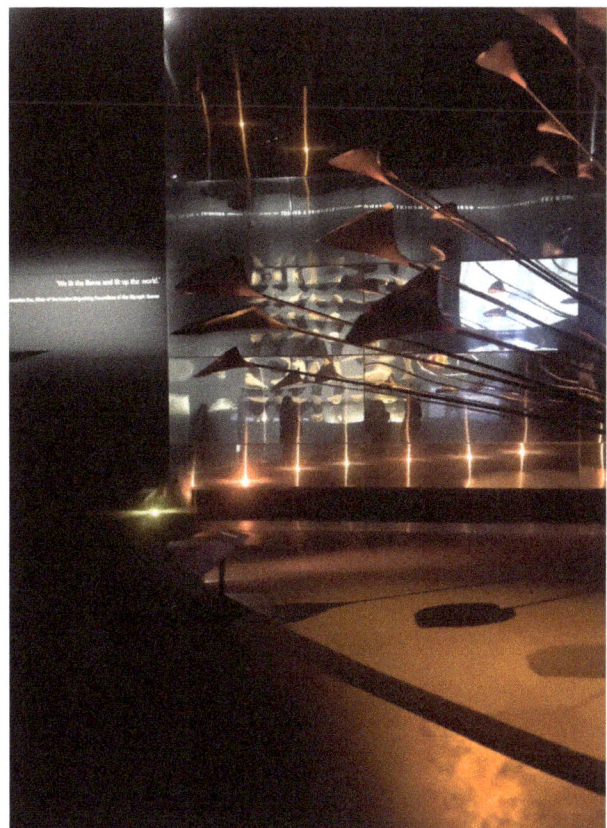

Figure 7.14. Image of the edges of the balustrade that surrounds the Cauldron.

and 7.7.1, Anna decided to touch the London 2012 Cauldron despite it is forbidden to touch the object (instance 7.17):

> I couldn't stop. Everyone knows you can't touch stuff in museums. Or at least, you can't until they tell you that you can. But you know what? I just had to. It wanted to touch it so badly. No one was there, so I did. […] I know I should be ashamed but I'm not. I guess also it's not like I damaged it. It felt amazing. I could 'feel' it [makes the gesture of inverted commas with her hands].

Anna was aware of the museum's policy about touching. She was also aware that, as a general rule, most museums operate a 'do not touch' policy. Nevertheless, she decided to ignore that rule and to touch the Cauldron. Her decision seemed to derive from her strong desire to build a physical connection with the object and the fact that the gallery was empty apart from her friends and me. Similar to Lily's experience in the Pleasure Gardens gallery, the secluded nature of the gallery enabled Anna to touch the 'forbidden' object without having to worry about the presence of other visitors.

The encounter with the London 2012 Cauldron was a highly emotional experience for Anna. Anna felt connected with the object before coming to the museum, as it represented a significant event in her life as an athlete, the Olympic and Paralympics games of 2012. The Cauldron seemed to embody for Anna the event itself and everything it represented. Physical proximity and touch were an expression of her emotional closeness to the object. Anna's eagerness to get close to the object was evident even before entering the gallery when she planned her visit (section 7.5.1).

Anna still had the perception of shapes, some forms, and some colours. However, due to the dim light in the gallery, she could only see a blurry outline of the Cauldron by getting very close. The dim light of the 'London 2012 Cauldron' gallery created an evocative ambience, but at the same time, it made it difficult to see in the gallery, even without a vision impairment. However, despite the environment being not ideal for someone with severe vision impairment, vision difficulties were not why Anna touched the Cauldron. The tactile interaction in instance 7.17 does not suggest an exploration to find out details of the object that she was not detecting visually. Instead, placing the hand on the torch and not moving suggests a desire to establish emotional contact with the object. Touch seemed to enable Anna to take ownership of her relationship with the Cauldron and, by association, with what it represented. While Lily's forbidden touch performance came from the desire to touch together, understand the objects, and develop aesthetic capital, Anna's performance derived from her desire to be emotionally close and take ownership

of the object, and only secondarily because of her lack of sight. Anna's most important need during her visit was to be in proximity to the Cauldron and to be able to establish a connection with it, which she did by touching it. Proximity to the Cauldron gave Anna greater cultural value and affirmed her identity, as well as a higher need beyond verbal understanding (Hayhoe 2017). Touching the Cauldron meant for Anna a personal, cultural symbolic meaning beyond perception.

Touching the Cauldron provided an opportunity to interact with artworks on a deeper level. This opportunity allowed Anna to establish a deep-seated situated relationship with the object and a sense of cultural ownership. Following Merlau-Ponty's (1962) embodiment framework, this means that Anna perceived and made sense of the Cauldron through her body, both through touch and through proximity. Her body held an 'intentional perspective' (Merlau-Ponty 1962), meaning that Anna did not experience the Cauldron through its appearance or the tactile exploration only, but rather through a holistic multisensory perception of the intangible values it represented. Anna's body made sense and established a connection with the intangible values associated with the Cauldron through its imagined materiality.

Touching the object was deeply connected to Anna's identity development, as discussed in section 7.7.1. Her physical defiance of the museum's 'do not touch policy' was a form of authoritative speech and affirmation of self-presence (Butler 1993). Her resistance to the museum script and normative behaviours was an exercise of binding power and a form of political resistance. Anna reclaimed their right as a disabled athlete to participate and enact a re-appropriation of the space (Rees Leahy 2010).

7.10. Using digitals resources

This section turns to the analysis of how participants used digital resources to make meaning of the collection. This section is divided into three further parts, which look at the different characteristics that were identified as part of the digital practice of participants: accessibility and inclusion tool (7.10.1), accessing content (7.10.2), and social engagement tools (7.10.3).

The MoL website provided detailed accessibility information about navigation and mobility in the space, access to the museum content, and access events. The website provided information about the low lighting levels in the 'Galleries of Modern London' (figure 7.15). Additionally, it included a section on access resources for BPSP (figure 7.16). The museum did not offer audio guides, either mainstream or designed explicitly for BPSP. However, it did offer Large Print guides that could be collected from the Information Desk. Despite not being highlighted in the accessibility section on the website, the museum offered built-in touch screen, video, and audio devices, as well as tactile objects in most galleries.

Lighting

Please note that the lighting in the Galleries of Modern London is lower than in our other galleries.

Figure 7.15. Website information about the low lighting levels in the 'Galleries of Modern London' (Museum of London 2020b).

Access for visitors with visual impairments

- Access guide dogs are welcome in all areas of the museum
- Magnifying glasses are available from the Information Desk
- Large print guides for the permanent galleries and major exhibitions are available at the Information Desk

Figure 7.16. Website information about access resources for BPSP (Museum of London 2020b).

7.10.1. Inclusion tool

In the interview, Fred explained how he thoroughly navigated the MoL website before his visit to plan his experience, the best route, and which accessible resources to use. As seen in his visit to the V&A (section 5.5.1) and Wallace Collection (section 6.5.1), carefully planning every aspect of his visits in advance and using digital resources are key parts of his museum visiting practice. When he arrived at the museum, similar to when he visited the V&A and the Wallace Collection, he stopped at the information desk to ask for the large print guides advertised on the website. He stood waiting for around 7 minutes at the information desk while the member of the reception staff went to find the information he needed. She came back with only a large print map of the museum, apologising for not finding the large print guides. He decided not to take it with him, and left the information desk to start the visit. During the interview, he explained what happened and on how that made him feel:

That is very disappointing, as I've found [large print guides] to be really useful in other museums to help me kind of read things. Because some things in there you can't read very easily […] I don't know if she knew [whether they had large print guides or not], she said she would look. She wasn't sure. Which didn't fill me with confidence, admittedly. But she went and had a look but she, she came back saying they haven't got any large print guides for the galleries.

[Prompt: Did you tell her that the website says they're there?]

I didn't tell her, I probably should have done, really. It's frustrating. I mean in other museums, they're just sort of in each exhibition. You just go inside the door and

they're on the wall like. Here you have to pick them up from the desk, which suggests they perhaps haven't got quite so many available, maybe. Perhaps they ration them slightly, I don't know. It was very disappointing. […] I knew I had my binocular, my telescope on me. And I had my phone, so I knew I'd be able to read things with that. I still wish it was easier.

Similar to when he could not get an accessible audio guide in the Wallace Collection (section 6.9.3), Fred expressed feelings of frustration and disappointment. While in the Wallace Collection, he managed to use Smartify to access information, the lack of large print guides in the MoL had a severe impact on the way he accessed content. The large print guides would have been the only accessible resource available for BPSP, as the museum did not offer audio guide or other types of assistive resources. Fred was left on his own to figure out how to access information, and he had to heavily rely on his residual vision and his tools (instance 7.18):

Instance 7.18:

Source: fieldnotes
In the galleries, he used his monocular, and he went very close to the panels and labels to read them. Additionally, at times he used his phone to take pictures of the panels. He then opened the picture on his phone, and he would enlarge it to read the content.

Fred heavily relied on his residual vision and everyday practices to access inaccessible information. He managed to employ strategies that are part of his everyday life to 'do the exhibition'. His ability to find alternative routes to access the museum content depended on the fact that he was a practiced museum visitor, experienced in the difficulties that reading the museum script entailed for someone with low vision. The difficulty he encountered (the lack of accessible resources) did not relate to his disability but rather to the museum practice. This did not make Fred's body dys-appear like in the case of Lily in the Wallace Collection (section 6.9.3). He expressed frustration and disappointment, but then he immediately reacted, and he drew from his funds of knowledge to identify strategies to go about his visit.

Fred's feeling of frustration was amplified because said resources were advertised as available on the website. He perceived the lack of accessible resources as unwelcoming and exclusionary. The fact that resources that were not available were advertised as available on online platforms made Fred's first experience of the museum even more inaccessible and exclusionary.

Fred recognised the museum's effort to broaden accessibility to the collection. However, he also explained how the current resources are not suitable for his needs:

> It's brilliant to see that they do accessible tours involving audio description and British sign language for a start. The audio description tours are mostly during the week though, so I would have to get half a day off work for something like that. Which I can do sometimes, but it's not always going to be convenient.

This quote refers to a common access problem that several museums experience. Museums tend to offer accessible special events dedicated to disabled people, making the museum space more accessible and inclusive. While these resources are ideal for many, they do not accommodate the needs of all disabled people, and they do not always encourage disabled visitors to take ownership of their visit and visit the space independently. As an experienced visitor, Fred did not need a private tour to be guided or shown around. All three experiences in the V&A, the Wallace Collection, and the MoL showed how his experience enabled him to visit the space independently and make his meaning. Attending an organised (possibly audio described tour) seemed appealing to him; however, he expressed his concern for the timing of those tours. These tours, especially in London museums, tended to happen during working hours; hence they tended to cater to an older audience, as younger disabled people often work during those hours. The visits of the participants in this study support this. Ten out of eleven visits occurred during the weekend or evening hours (Jane at the V&A). Only Asif, who at the time was not in employment, visited the V&A during the week. Therefore, the availability of accessible resources is necessary to offer an inclusive and independent experience to all visitors, including disabled people.

7.10.2. Accessing content

Despite Anna not asking for assistive resources, she experienced difficulties in reading panels and labels in the London 2012 Cauldron room. The lighting level was very low (as reported on the museum website), and her residual vision did not seem enough to read the white-on-blue writings (figures 7.17 abc). In order to overcome the

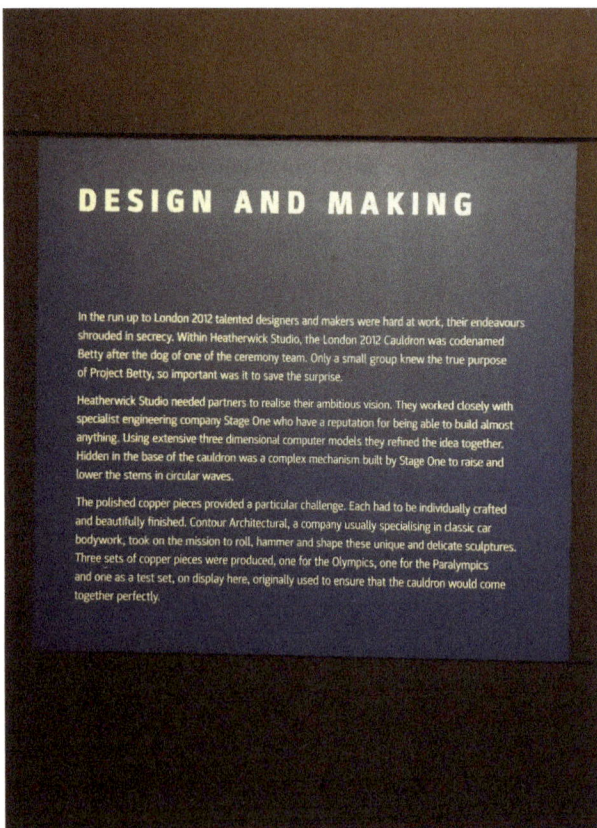

Figure 7.17ab. White-on-blue text of the labels and the panels.

difficulties, she decided to use the text to speech function of Seeing AI. Instance 7.19 shows how she approached the text:

Instance 7.19:

Source: fieldnotes
Sofia guided Anna in front of the label of the Cauldron. Anna bent and tried to read it, but she did not seem to be able to do so. Sofia read the label aloud for her. Anna went on her own close to the wall where the torches moulds are displayed (figure 7.18). She went very close to all of the torches until she reached the panel on the left of the display. She took her phone out of her pocket, put a headphone in her right ear, opened Seeing AI, opened the text to speech function, pointed the camera at the panels. The phone flashed to capture the picture and then presumably read the text back to Anna via the headphone.

Figure 7.18. Torch moulds of the Cauldron.

In the interview, Anna explained why she used Seeing AI to read the panel:

> You know, yeah … they could have read it to me. But you know what it's boring to always ask. I don't know I didn't think about it. It was easier to just use my phone. I use it for other things as well, like reading signs, documents, books, and so on.

Similar to the way Davide used Seeing AI in the Wallace Collection, Anna decided to use it for two reasons. Firstly, it allowed her to overcome the difficulty due

to the dim light and the panel format. Secondly, she expressed the desire not to ask her friends to read for her. Seeing AI was once again used as a resource to navigate the content of the exhibition and access resources independently. Independence appeared to be a value for both Davide and Anna. This did not seem to be connected specifically to the museum experience. The use of Seeing AI (as well as the highly developed technical capital) was something part of their daily practices and funds of knowledge.

As argued in the previous chapter (section 6.9.4), despite being an application specifically designed for BPSP, Seeing Ai still fitted the description of inclusive technology by Hayhoe (2015a). In Anna's experience with the app, what made the technology inclusive was the opportunity it offered Anna to navigate the content independently, without relying on her friends, and to access inaccessible panels. This contributed to the general ethos of Anna's experience. Anna's experience was, in fact, one of empowerment, confidence, independence, profound emotional connection, and development as a disabled person and athlete. The way the application supported her to access content independently contributed to her independence and empowerment. The inclusive capital of the technology resided in the fact that it allowed Anna to independently develop other forms of capital, mainly cultural and human. This enabled her to develop a sense of belonging and to make sense of the environment and the Cauldron.

7.10.3. Social engagement tool

From my findings, it was clear that participants used technology as social engagement tools. The literature on social media use by young BPS adults is limited and little can be found on its use in museum contexts. One example is McMillen and Alter's (2017) work on digital museum access, which looked at how museums can connect, engage and socially include disabled people through social media. However, the specific use of social media for museum engagement by young BPS adults has not be researched yet. Findings from this study are limited and do not aim to offer a comprehensive account of social media use in museums by young BPS adults. However, findings clearly show how this is an important part of their experience and needs to be researched further.

While Anna and Fred did not engage in any low- or high-tech interactive activity proposed by the museum, they both used their mobile phones as social engagement tools during the visit. They took several pictures of their visit, and they shared them with their followers on social engagement platforms. Anna shared images on social media platforms like Instagram and Facebook. Fred posted images on his Facebook page, his Instagram account, and his blog. On his blog, he also shared a detailed summary of his visit. Anna primarily took pictures of the Cauldron, of herself and her friends. Fred only took pictures of the exhibition.

Instance 7.20 and 7.21 show how Anna used her mobile phone to take photos of the London 2012 Cauldron:

Instance 7.20:

Source: fieldnotes
After Anna looked at and touched the Cauldron, she read the labels using Seeing AI, watched the videos, and went around the room with her friends. After she finished looking at the exhibition, she took her phone from her pocket, and took pictures for around 15 minutes. She took: • Several pictures of the Cauldron from different angles. • Pictures of all the labels and panels. • Selfie pictures of herself with the Cauldron as background. • Selfie pictures of herself and her friends with the Cauldron as background. • Pictures of her friends with the Cauldron as background. Her friends also took pictures of her with the Cauldron as background.

Instance 7.21:

Source: fieldnotes
Anna took mostly serious self-portrait (selfie) and portrait pictures of herself and her friends. However, Sofia took three 'funny' pictures of Anna while she pretended to 1. kiss one of the torches, 2. kneel to light up one of the torches (like it happened in the actual opening ceremony), 3. look at the Cauldron with 'dreamy eyes' (her eyes facing upwards and her lips smiling) while sitting on the ground.

She explained in the interview the value she attributed to pictures:

> You know, I really use these pictures. I take them for Instagram and I post them on Facebook as well. I have an account where I show my trainings and a bit of my life. So I want to show this [the Cauldron] because it's so cool. […] So, before this trip I posted on my stories some videos from the Paralympic ceremony. You know, it exploded. Everyone was like 'this is great' 'I remember it'. So I told my followers I was coming here and I was going to see it. It's big, you know? It was a big thing the whole ceremony and, you know, how visible they made it. Paralympic games were big. Just as big as the other games. It was one. […] I think it's important to remind it sometimes, and you know, I feel Instagram is a community in a way. So, if I share it, and then I show how much sport helps, then people can relate.

As well as sharing her experience with her two friends during her visit also mentioned how she shared her experience on social media before, during, and after the visit. Anna appeared to use social media to share her experience with the companions that physically went to the museum with her and other people in her life that followed her on social media. She seemed to value the possibility that social media offered her to share her experience with her friends and followers, connect with others, and explore their shared interest together. After Anna's visit to the MoL, I monitored her social media accounts, and in the evening after the visit, Anna shared an Instagram and a Facebook post with several pictures of herself and her friends with the Cauldron. I monitored the posts for the following days, and I noticed an enthusiastic interaction between Anna and her followers, where she answered questions about her visit, the Cauldron, the museum, and her emotions in the space. Such interactions under the MoL posts were similar to other interactions she had with her followers on other posts about her training, her travels, and her activities as a disability rights advocate. Anna used pictures as a channel to empower people by reminding them of the value and the goals achieved during the 2012 Paralympic games.

Social media platforms enabled her to share through her pictures her experience among her online community of practice of disabled people and athletes. Sharing pictures through social media and creating engagement enabled sharing her meaning with her followers and friends by telling her own story. Anna made sense and refined her meaning of the Paralympic and its role in her life by engaging about her visit on social media platforms. Pictures contained meaning for Anna, as they represented the connection she made with the Cauldron.

Through the social media interactions, she established a connection between the physical place of the museum and the abstract space of her community of practice (Seamon and Sowers 2008). Through her body, Anna made meaning of the Cauldron, understood the museum place, and established a sense of belonging (Cresswell 2015). The pictures enabled her to communicate her meaning with others. Through her digital social media posts, Anna marked both the physical place of the museum as the site of the Cauldron and the abstract 'space' of the Paralympic games as meaningful (Budge 2020). By sharing her pictures and the museum's location, Anna did not simply visit the museum, but she communicated and showed to others that 'she was there'. In doing so, she used the pictures and the tags as markers of identity, and she laid a symbolic claim to the museum and the Paralympics (Boy and Uitemark 2017)

Instance 7.21 shows how Anna used bodily humour to challenge the museum's power and authority and claim the space as her own. This act can be considered part of Anna's agency, which involved identity work (Kozinets *et al.* 2017). Anna expressed her agency and identity through re-appropriating the space by performing a bodily affirmation of self-presence through physical humour (Burness 2016; Kozinets *et al.* 2017).

As mentioned above, Fred took pictures of labels and panels to read them through his enlarged phone screen better. Additionally, he also took pictures of the exhibition. Fred expressed a desire similar to Anna to share his experience with his friends and followers and to advocate for the needs of BPSP through his blog:

> I do yeah. I mean I post them on Facebook and things like that and I show them on Instagram and my blogs and things like that. I kind of share what I've been up to. Because a lot of people can't come here and they don't live near here. So it's nice to show them what I've seen. And sometimes it might tempt them to come here as well. So you know I've had people say 'oh I should come here as well like you know it looks really good'. I can help other visually impaired people by showing what's out there.

Fred used photos and his blog account as an advocacy tool to communicate details about his visit to other BPSP who followed him. He used pictures (along with blog posts) to communicate details of the visit and accessibility tips to those interested in visiting the museum. Additionally, he presented his narrative of the museum and its content for people that do not have the opportunity to visit.

Fred's use and sharing of the images showed his agency, authority, and desire to communicate and share his perspective and meaning (Budge and Burness 2018). Fred's posts can be considered a creative act, which contributed to the dynamic social nature of his visit and helped him refine his meaning. Taking the pictures of the elements he identified as meaningful in the galleries and taking the time to write the blog post can be seen as expressions of Fred's agency (Budge 2020; Burness 2016). Both taking pictures and writing about it were creative acts of capturing the experience of visiting the museum in a way that allowed Fred to connect with his community of practice of online audience (Budge 2020). Both in the case of Fred and Anna, the choice for a visual medium and of mainstream platforms were emancipatory ones.

While this book did not aim to provide an encompassing discussion of the embodied use of social media in museums among BPSP, the analysis presented above feels like a good closing point, as it acts as a reminder that this is an emerging area of research within a rapidly evolving technology framework. These findings are an interesting starting point for future research on the role of digital museum experiences and digital collections, as well as on the interaction among online communities of practice for BPS and disabled museum visitors.

7.11. Conclusion

The analysis of findings in the MoL was consistent with the two previous chapters. I identified the same six significant categories of embodied practice as in the V&A: co-walking, scaffolding, identity formation, looking, touching, and using resources.

Section 7.5 discussed the practice of co-walking. Key findings showed a major similarity with the previous two chapters: the predominant importance of 'correct' positioning for participants. While all participants seemed to be aware of 'normative' positioning in the environment, two participants seemed at ease with the possibility of 'breaking the rules' for the first time. Both Lily and Anna touched objects that were not available to touch. Participants seemed to be constantly aware of others and of how their actions could be viewed or perceived. When Lily and Anna found themselves alone with their companions in secluded galleries, they put aside their concern for 'correct' behaviours and decided to touch the objects.

Scaffolding instances were identified in the experiences of Lily and Anna and discussed in section 7.6. Lily's experience was similar to her experience in the Wallace Collection. She heavily relied on guidance, of her guide first, and her friend after. The guidance provided by the museum guide was different from the guidance offered to Ravi and Asif in the V&A. The guide did not seem to have specific training to perform audio descriptions, and Lily found the content boring at times. The element of boredom was one of the reasons why guidance did not fade during her visit. In Anna's visit, I identified several instances of shifting guidance roles between her and her friends. Anna took the lead of the visit several times, empowered by the emotional connection she developed with the Cauldron and the exhibit. This connection allowed her to grow confident and to move independently in the space.

Section 7.7 contributed to understanding how participants developed identities while interacting with the environment, the collection, and other visitors. In line with previous chapters, key findings highlighted how meaning was developed through social relationships and shared identities. However, two surprising findings emerged in this chapter. A peculiar finding that had not previously emerged was the development of identity in relation to placemaking. Fred and Lily both expressed how the museum enabled the development of their identity as 'Londoners' by making them feel connected with the city. Participants brought with them to the museum their 'Londoner' identity, which added to their museum experience and enabled meaning-making (Stainton 2002). Their social engagement with the city through their museum visits reflected the place as meaningful (Budge 2020). The museum allowed Fred and Lily to develop their identity as Londoners and feel part of the city's wider community. Anna's experience also offered a perspective on identity which had not been identified before. Anna's identity as a disabled person was deeply connected to her being a disabled athlete. Visiting the museum's exhibition about the Paralympic games of 2012 and being metaphorically acknowledged and represented as a disabled athlete allowed Anna to form a meaningful connection with the object and the museum. Therefore, feeling 'represented' was a key factor that enabled Anna's sense of belonging, participation, and identity formation. The museum positively represented the disability narrative of the Paralympic games and positively shaped Anna's identity within the museum visit.

Section 7.8 discussed how participants developed aesthetic and historic capital from their encounter with visual culture. Findings from this section were in line with those from previous chapters and from Hayhoe's findings about aesthetic and historical preferences of BPSP in museums (2013; -2017). They actively challenged the idea that aesthetic capital is inferior to historic capital in the experience of BPSP (Hayhoe 2017; Kleege 2018). While the different levels of vision influenced how participants visually approached objects in the MoL, their personal preferences and interests shaped the visual relationship they established. Rather than their vision impairments, the museum's social experience allowed them to develop capital, knowledge, and an emotional connection with objects.

Section 7.9 presented findings from the category of 'touching'. From the findings presented in this section, it is clear how touch was not merely an act of exploration to compensate for vision loss. It was a sociocultural practice, and it developed social, cultural, and human capital. Unlike previous findings from the V&A and the Wallace Collection, in the MoL, two participants, Lily and Anna, touched objects despite the museum 'do-not-touch' policy. By going against the museum's 'normative' behaviour, touch seemed to be the tool that enabled meaning-making in the space and enabled them to develop an emotional connection to objects.

This chapter ended with a discussion of how participants used resources, particularly digital ones, in section 7.10. Similar to the findings from the Wallace Collection, key findings showed that the lack of assistive resources (of any kind) negatively impact the experience of disabled people and actively hinders meaning-making. Museums have the social and moral responsibility to cater to diverse audiences' needs and fulfil their promises about accessibility resources usually displayed on their websites. Another critical finding emerged during Fred and Anna's visit, where social media and blog platforms were used for the first time as a tool to share the visit live with people outside the museum through online interactions by posting pictures and writing about their visit. These digital interactions appeared to be a tool to share the experience, engage in conversations, and feel connected with the broader communities of disabled people, London-enthusiasts (in the case of Fred), and disabled athletes (in the case of Anna). Museums seemed to be perceived as a fulfilment of social need and a form of intellectual recreation.

8

Conclusions and Implications

8.1. Introduction

This research aimed to explore the complexities of the embodied practice of BPS museum visitors. To achieve that, I employed a qualitative methodology and analysed instances of embodied practice through video recordings, interviews, and fieldnotes. This analysis acknowledged the multimodality and situated nature of meaning-making and identity formation. The research aim was not to reach universal meanings, but rather to draw understanding by linking visitors' embodied practice to their meaning-making process and identity formation.

In this final chapter, I argue that contextualised analysis and comparison of the three case studies allowed me to answer my specific research questions and enabled me to draw general conclusions regarding the primary research question: 'How do BPS visitors' social embodied practice contributes to meaning-making and identity formation in museums?'. This was achieved by employing an interpretative phenomenological framework, looking at BPS participants' own accounts of their visit, observing them during the visit through fieldnotes and video recordings, and analysing the findings. Six categories helped build a framework around the key general themes of embodiment, meaning-making, and identity formation.

As museums are traditionally considered visual institutions and the act of visiting is often linked to the performance of sight, the place of BPS visitors has been contested and misunderstood (Hayhoe 2017). My research concurs with previous studies that have demonstrated that BPSP visit museums, enjoy them, and have meaningful and fulfilling experiences within them (Candlin 2010; Hayhoe 2017; Kleedge 2018). These studies have also suggested that museums offer more experiences than those just involving visual perception. Several participants took part in the study by going on guided tours. Others visited the museums with friends or partners. One visited all three museums on his own. My findings showed that all the participants enjoyed, made meaning and obtained value from their visits. They all participated in the learning culture of the museum.

Although this research considered a relatively small number of participants, the dataset collected was particularly rich because the research was carried out in three different museums, the participants presented different types of visual impartments and residual vision levels, and the findings were discussed and compared against previous research. My findings and conclusions can, therefore, be used as a general framework for considering BPS visitors and their needs. In the following section (8.2), I reflect in detail on the methodology I employed and its contribution to the wider debate of qualitative analysis of the museum experience. In order to reveal the implications for future research and professional practice, I present an overview of the findings of this research from the three case studies, following key overarching themes, and considering them in relation to aspects of museums and disability research and practice. Particular emphasis is given to the social and ethical responsibilities of museums as spaces of inclusion and empowerment.

8.2. Key findings

My interpretative phenomenological methods of data collection allowed me to explore my research questions related to the embodied experience, meaning-making, and identity formation. In this section, I summarise and outline these three key themes by bringing together and comparing the core findings from chapters 5–7. Based on the research questions, data coding, and analysis, I identified six categories characterising the practice of BPSP: (i) co-walking, (ii) scaffolding, (iii) identity formation, (iv) looking, (v) touching, (vi) using resources. Each category encompasses instances of embodiment, meaning-making, and identity formation. In particular, while I consider identity formation one of the key overall themes, I also considered it as a stand-alone category. This allowed me to analyse specific instances related to participants' sociocultural identity and their identity as disabled visitors. Other instances related to identity formation were also found within the other categories.

8.2.1. Embodiment

One of the book's aims was to understand the embodied practice of participants. The starting point was the idea that due to the lack of sight, the embodied practice of BPSP through the unfamiliar, complex, and non-linear environment of museums presented differences compared to that of sighted visitors. The theoretical framework outlined in chapter 2 set the goal of this book to research the role of the body in the situated learning activity by integrating approaches of situated learning and embodiment. The sociocultural nature of learning, and therefore of activity, is of paramount importance within situated learning theory. Consequently, situated activity is largely a process of forming and mediating sociocultural relationship between individuals and the surrounding environment. In this book, I argued that the embodied nature of situated learning activity could not be disregarded, as the learning activity cannot be understood without considering the body and its implications.

The role of the body, in this research, referred to the embodied practice in relation to objects, resources, and other individuals in the learning environment. The interactions between participants and their companions were a meaningful aspect of the learning activity. Learning was a highly social process in which participants and their companions constantly negotiated means of communication with each other. Participants frequently used the body to communicate during social interactions. For example, by pointing at a specific object or guiding their companions' hands while co-touching an object, participants intended to draw the attention of their companions to clarify what they were referring to. Activity (whether meaning-making or identity formation etc.) can therefore be seen as both sociocultural and deeply embodied.

My research showed that as they walked through the space, participants experienced both a feeling of self-presence (Rees Leahy 2012) and co-presence (Lageby 2013). The former enabled them to develop a higher awareness of their bodies within the environment. The latter allowed them to develop an awareness of other walking and looking bodies in their perceptual range and to negotiate their embodied presence in the space in relation to others (Christidou and Diamantopoulou 2016). They encountered their companions and other visitors in a situated context of interaction (Giddens 1984).

Fred's experience clearly showed how walking in museums is a social activity even if someone is walking alone (Thobo-Carlsen 2016). This was clear when he approached objects in all three museums which other visitors were standing nearby and looking at (sections 5.5.2, 6.5.2, 7.5.2). Fred's embodied response to other visitors' presence showed that he was constantly aware of them as well as his own body and his vision needs. He consistently stood back to avoid obstructing views of objects, and he only moved closer to observe objects and read panels when other visitors had left his perceptual range.

The findings from this research demonstrate further that walking bodies are physically and sensorially reactive to the other bodies co-present in the surrounding environment (Ingold 2011). Sensory perceptions of other bodies and their movements were defined as co-awareness (Doxa 2001; Kwon and Sailer 2015). An example was Susan's co-awareness of other visitors entering the space she was in with Sally which made her employ 'involvement shields' to minimise social contact with, and create a barrier between the other co-walkers (Goffman 1963) (V&A, section 5.5.2). Another example was Lily's embodied reaction to the incident with the chest of drawers (section 6.5.2) and to the possibility of being seen touching 'forbidden objects' (sections 7.5.2 and 7.9.3). She moved her head as if she was 'looking around' to 'see' if others had seen her behave 'incorrectly'. The combination of walking and feeling self-present and co-present served as a means to encounter the space. Participants negotiated their walking practice in relation to other co-present bodies while becoming aware of their own embodied reality. Interactions of co-presence

among participants supported the argument that visiting an exhibition is a deeply social activity as they were all constantly responsive to the presence and movements of others in the same perceptual range (Christidou and Diamantopoulou 2016).

Participants' walking practice and their ability to adapt to that of others were also discussed as symptomatic of cultural competence and the ability to read the museum script (Rees Leahy 2012). I discussed this within Rees Leahy's (2012) framework of 'normative practices', namely the bodily techniques and behaviours that the experienced visitor employs to 'correctly' read the museum script. Fred and Lily's aforementioned correct positioning in response to co-awareness are examples of normative practices. Whether they were experienced museum visitors or not, all participants seemed to be more or less aware of touching policies, distancing from others and objects, what to look at and for how long, appropriate walking routes etc. In several instances, they affirmed self-presence and claimed ownership of objects and space by openly defying these. Such was the case of Jane in the V&A, when she enacted her own walking narrative despite perceiving the museum environment as hostile and 'not for her', and of Anna and Lily in the MoL, when they touched objects thereby defying the 'do not touch' policy. Findings showed that these normative techniques are inscribed in the body and build the now-experienced visitor's self-awareness as a viewing subject within the museum (Rees Leahy 2012).

In order to respond to these perceived normative practices and to better read the museum script, participants employed a variety of strategies which responded to different needs, mainly related to vision impairments, social and cultural preferences, and everyday practices. I analysed the element of guidance through the lens of scaffolding refined and developed by Mai and Ash (2012). The experience of scaffolding guidance of Ravi (V&A), Asif (V&A), and Lily (Wallace Collection) offer an interesting comparison and a surprising finding. A typical element of scaffolding guidance is that it fades over time and eventually ends as the learner acquires competence and develops confidence. The visits of the three participants presented different levels of guidance fading. In the case of Ravi, guidance eventually faded completely, and he actively contributed to meaning-making, taking ownership of his visit. In the case of Asif, it never faded, and he continued to be guided by the scaffolder as a passive recipient rather than an active maker of meaning. In the case of Lily, guidance faded at times, but never entirely. It remained constant throughout the visit, and it seemed to be the tool that enabled Lily's meaning-making. These findings showed that scaffolding guidance in the museum space was determined not only by participants' vision impairment but also by their personal preferences, type of guidance, and level of confidence. In fact, while all three participants were blind with no residual vision, guidance faded (or did not fade) in three different ways. Asif and Lily's lower levels of confidence and guiding styles impacted on guidance fading. In fact,

Ravi's level of confidence in the space developed pretty fast, and his guide (professionally trained) adapted her guiding style to it, letting Ravi take charge. The disparity of expertise between Lily (a casual visitor) and Ginny (an experienced visitor) facilitated the fact that Ginny took on a leadership role and maintained it throughout the visit. The most surprising finding was that Lily was a considerably more experienced visitor compared to Ravi, and yet in her experience, guidance still did not fade entirely. My research clearly shows that scaffolding is deeply influenced by the nature of the relationship between the learner and scaffolder that are part of the activity.

Across the three case studies, I also discussed embodied resistance to socio-spacial inclusion, referred to here as dys-appearance. Previous studies suggested how Bourdieu's concept of habitus could reveal how social status, class, poverty and disadvantage are integral to the embodied experience of dys-appearance (Allen 2004a; -2004b; Imrie 2000). Findings from my study suggest that another of the variables that could incline some impaired peopleto resist dys-abling experiences and socio-spatial exclusion was their expertise as museum visitors. A clear example is the different way in which Fred and Lily responded to the lack of availability of audio guides in the Wallace Collection. While they both expressed feelings of frustration and disappointment, their embodied response was different. Fred, an experienced museum visitor, quickly employed strategies that form part of his everyday life to read the museum script, drawing from his funds of knowledge to find alternative ways to access the museum content. Lily, on the contrary, experienced a deeply dys-abling physical response, as she seemed to locate the difficulty experienced with her impairment rather than pin it to the social and cultural barriers in the space. Her body dys-appeared as she felt excluded from contributing to the social experience of the space.

8.2.2. Meaning-making

In this research, meaning-making was discussed as arising from bodily interactions with others and the environment. Therefore, it was grounded in participants' embodied practice. Meaning-making was analysed primarily as a way of developing shared meaning and different forms of cultural capital through the lens of scaffolding and funds of knowledge.

Participants scaffolded a shared understanding of the museum experience. Social interaction played a central role in the way participants made sense of the collection and of the environment. Meaning-making was a continuous and situated process that involved the participants, their companions, and others who happened to share the same perceptual space. Participants brought to the museum a shared understanding of the world that they constantly negotiated and refined during their experience.

Following Mai and Ash's (2012) scaffolding framework, I identified several instances of shifting guiding roles among participants which enabled meaning-making. Davide's interaction with his partner James in front of the painting 'Francesca da Rimini' in the Wallace Collection showed how several scaffolding interactions occurred where they kept passing back and forth the authority role, thereby negotiating their shared distributed knowledge. Similarly, Anna's experience in the MoL was enhanced by shifting scaffolding interactions with her friends, which facilitated meaning-making. Anna took the lead several times, empowered by the emotional connection she developed with the Cauldron and the exhibit. She guided her friends, and she made her own meaning through touch, through the social interaction with her friends, and later through digital post-visit interactions with her online community.

Objects and resource-based encounters constituted the basis for shared meaning-making. My findings suggested that visual culture is potentially understandable perceptually by all BPSP, irrespective of their type and level of vision impairment. The experiences of Fred, Susan, and Davide showed how residual vision and visual memory, paired with audio descriptions and other resources, enabled them to make some sense of visual concepts like colour, shapes, visual depth etc. The experiences of Ravi, Asif, and Lily showed that, despite being fully blind, they too could make some sense of visual concepts by creatively understanding visual culture. In the case of Asif in particular, aesthetic exclusion and difficulties in making sense of elaborate visual concepts, rather than the vision impairment itself, was what made it hard to access the complex artwork.

A surprising finding was that participants with significant residual vision developed a higher historic capital despite their significant residual vision, while participants who have no residual vision focused their attention on the aesthetic details of objects, developing a higher aesthetic capital. Participants seemed to build their meanings of visual aesthetics in non-visual ways. Key findings showed that the meaning participants made of visual culture was influenced not only by their vision impairment and their residual vision and visual memory but also by other factors like personal preferences, their education, and the social interactions with their companions. The analysis of participants' embodied perceptions contrasted with the cultural experiences of their blindness and vision loss. Overall, the development of historic and aesthetic capital was of paramount importance for the making of their own meaning and the feeling of inclusion in the visual culture of the museum. Embracing the visual culture of the museum, participants actively resisted the challenges related to their sight loss and negotiated their membership in the museum's community.

Finally, my findings provided evidence that bodily practice was an effective tool in developing forms of cultural capital and understanding 'abstract' concepts. Participants wanted to interact with objects through visual practices despite not being able to fully see them. The development of forms of cultural capital like historic and aesthetic capital and the understanding of visual concepts and material culture were critically affected by the embodied status of proximity and co-touching. While not all participants engaged in tactile explorations, touch appeared to be one of the primary senses used to access objects due to the 'higher conscious awareness' that participants learnt to interpret tactile perceptions with (Kleege 2018). This finding is in line with previous studies with BPSP (Candlin 2010; Hayhoe 2017; Kleedge 2018; vom Lehn 2010, among others).

I developed the concept of co-touching to analyse how the social element of touch created situated opportunities where participants and their companions made meaning of the objects while they touched them together. Key findings from the V&A and the MoL showed that touch has a role in expanding socially-mediated interactions and fostered stronger connections between participants and companions. Touch enabled them to make their own meaning, be reminded of personal memories, and share with companions the way certain museum objects intertwined with their lives. Co-touching enabled sharing memories and strengthening relations. Hence, the museum became the social, cultural, and physical context in which participants engaged with and made meaning of their recent past through their bodily encounter with material culture. Because of their sight loss, participants created a different relationship with objects, often developing alternative narratives of learning which drew from their own meanings and understandings of political, cultural, and social values embodied and represented by objects.

Another key finding demonstrated the higher value associated with touching objects for participants. Unlike previous findings from the V&A and the Wallace Collection, Lily and Anna touched objects in the MoL thereby defying the museum policy. The secluded atmosphere of the galleries, together with the fact that no other people were present, encouraged and enabled them to seek a more intimate interaction with the objects. By going against the museum's 'normative' behaviour, touch seemed to be the tool that enabled meaning-making in the space together with their companion and also enabled them to develop an emotional connection to objects. These experiences of 'forbidden touch' made participants develop higher forms of cultural capital, as well as highly emotional connections. While Lily touched the objects to inform her understanding of visual concepts, Anna desired to be emotionally close and take ownership of the object and, by association, with what it represented. In brief, this study helped demonstrate the value of touching objects in creating a socially inclusive environment, where democratic and participatory practice is enabled, and disabled people can participate equally in the shared production of knowledge in their social group.

8.2.3. Identity formation

Another significant aspect of this volume was to understand the development of participants' identities as museum visitors and as disabled people. The museum provided visitors with space to develop and negotiate individual and collective identities through their social encounters with companions, other visitors, and the collections. Different identities emerged during the same visit situated in the social context in which they occurred.

In chapter 2 (section 2.5.1), I discussed identity within the situated learning theoretical framework. In situated learning, the emphasis is mainly placed on the social and tool-mediated nature of learning (Brown *et al.* 1989; Lave and Wenger 1991). Learning is chiefly conceptualised as a process socially situated in activity, in which an (active) formation of identities takes place (Lave 1991). However, the formation of identities in relation to the body has essentially been overlooked in situated learning theories (Packer and Goicoechea 2000). Rather than looking at learning as an identity development process, it was sometimes relegated to a process of cognitive change (Packer and Goicoechea 2000). Hence, this research drew directly from Wenger's (1998b) definition of identity and analysed participants' identity formation in relation to embodied practice and participation.

Key findings showed that museums are social spaces in which community membership and identity are developed and solidified. Findings demonstrated that museums play a key role in developing cultural capital and subsequently a cultural form of identity. The relationship which participants developed with the museum and its objects was sophisticated, personal, deeply situated, and beyond the act of simply visiting for pleasure, inclination, or habit. The act of attending the museum itself formed participants' cultural identity which was based on a personal cultural journey of identity and self-esteem, rather than mere sight loss. Participants made sense of the direct relationships they developed with the objects (both through visual practice and tactile practice) as a symbol of cultural identity. For some, coming to the museum was a significant part of their cultural and social identity. In particular, they valued the pleasurable and meaningful social experience offered, which enabled them to negotiate their identity as museum visitors with their companions.

Another significant finding was how touching objects contributed to the normalisation process of sight loss and of acceptance of disability-related identity, in line with Candlin's (2010) study. Findings suggested that the fact that tactile objects both in the V&A and the MoL were on open display and could be explored by BPSP as well as by companions contributed to the normalisation process, allowing participants to avoid feeling excluded or marginalised. Attending museums actively reinforced wellbeing, and participants felt that they could share their experience, enabling them to feel part of a normalised notion of enjoying the museum. This allowed participants to make and share their own meaning and to feel a sense of belonging and ownership of the museum. BPSP's identity is always partially associated with their sight loss, what it represents, and its implications. Being able to equally participate in mainstream activities like museum visits defined participants social and cultural identity and preserved their sighted cultural identity or created an alternative non-visual identity. The act of visiting museums constituted a rejection of the impact and imposition of sight loss. These visits avoid a sense of exile from a former sighted self and develop a sense of continuity and inclusion. Visiting museums allowed participants to keep in touch with a visual society of family, friends, and peers.

The development of identity as a disabled person was deeply connected with the embodied practice. Through the co-present act of being a viewing subject, participants developed a deep awareness of their bodies (and of their disability) as a viewing subject. Some feared to be looked at and scrutinised if they defied the museum script or were 'seen doing something wrong'. Across the chapters, findings showed how participants faced difficulties related to their disability had an impact on their practice and identity formation, and therefore on learning. Disability had an impact on participants' situated and ever-evolving sense of self, in particular in relation to how other people perceived them and their impairment in the social context of the museum. In response to the co-presence of other visitors, some participants tended to resist external viewings and scrutiny of their disability by acting in a way that made their embodied practices resemble that of non-disabled people. In some cases, experiencing disability-related difficulties in the museum lead to dys-appearance. This happened when they seemed to associate difficulties with their impairment rather than to the social and cultural barriers in the space. Participants tend to use tools like companions' guidance, resources, and interactions with objects to resist dys-appearance and socio-spatial exclusion.

Other key findings demonstrated how participants' identity as disabled people developed positively in the museum. The case of Anna in the MoL was paradigmatic. Anna's experience at the museum strengthened, enhanced, and developed her connection with the Olympic and Paralympic games of 2012 through the highly emotional and personal connection she developed with the Cauldron. Findings showed how the way the museum represented the disability narrative of the Paralympic games contributed to positively shape and develop Anna's identity as a disabled athlete. The representation of disability through empowering and inclusive narratives made Anna feel acknowledged and represented as an athlete and as a disabled person, allowing her to re-live the emotions and feelings associated with the Paralympic games of 2012, and to establish a deep and meaningful connection with the object and the museum. These findings further suggest that museums play a key role in reframing, informing and enabling how society perceives and understands disability (Sandell *et al*. 2010).

8.3. Concluding recommendations and a view on the future

This book substantially contributes to museum studies and disability studies by exploring issues around disability and embodiment in museums. Several existing studies have examined embodiment in relation to various fields and in multifaceted ways in relation to disability (Imrie 2000; Oliver 1990; Paterson and Hughes 1999, among others). This research's analysis of the embodied practice of BPSP in relation to meaning-making and identity formation provided an original contribution to the entangling of the embodiment, museums and disability framework. In this section, I reflect on the implications of the findings of this book for museum practice, and offer recommendations for developing accessible and inclusive exhibitions and programmes.

One distinctive characteristic of this study, which I acknowledged throughout the analytical chapters, was the participants' social class. All but two participants were highly educated (from undergraduate to doctoral level), in full-time employment, and middle- to upper-class people. The remaining two participants were a student and a volunteer, and could still be included in the middle-class category. While the participants' social class was not part of the criteria during the recruitment of participants, the fact that all of them came from a specific background felt like a limitation at times. However, it also contributed to understanding how social class and education backgrounds (not only vision impairment) impact the museum experience. People from higher education backgrounds were significantly more empowered and independent in this space. Participants' level of education facilitated a greater intellectual engagement and understanding of collections and the development of cultural capital, which partially negated their vision impairment, whether they were fully blind or partially sighted. Going forward, it is necessary to look at the elements of habitus and social class and the disabled identity only. This is because people from a less privileged education background may be less likely to access to higher forms of cultural education when older.

The backgrounds of my participants are consistent with findings from Hayhoe's (2017) study on the profile of BPSP who visit art museums: educated individuals from middle- and upper-class backgrounds. However, they are not in line with findings drawn from national statistics on sight loss (section 1.2). Statistics show that 39% of BPSP of working-age experience mild or severe financial hardships and only 27% are currently in employment (RNIB 2021). This prompts critical reflections for both academics and practitioners. It shows the need to expand academic research on BPSP to participants from different social classes and less privileged educational and professional backgrounds. It is necessary to adapt and adopt methodological frameworks aimed at reaching those BPSP who are left out of current research (and potentially of museums). It is also necessary to adopt frameworks from similar studies of other under-represented and less privileged groups and communities that would allow us to understand their perspectives, explore their meanings, and amplify their voices.

Practitioners face a similar struggle. The demographic of BPSP that currently visit museums is not consistent with the demographic of BPSP in the UK. BPS visitors tend to be elderly (often retired) people from middle- and upper-class backgrounds who have usually lost sight later in life and tend to visit museums to maintain habits and interests from their lives before sight loss. Younger BPSP that visit museums are generally children and teenagers who are part of organised groups (usually visiting with schools or families), or highly empowered, independent, and educated people like the participants of my study. If museums are to remain (or better, become) relevant to the broader demographic of BPSP, new access, marketing, and interpretation strategies should be employed.

Exploring the embodied and social interactions of BPSP in the museum can facilitate communication between visitors and the museum. Different sociocultural modes of performance and participation come to the foreground through the analysis of embodied and social practices. By doing this, my research contributes to the understanding of the way BPSP visitors physically respond to the museum content and environment. Furthermore, by focusing specifically on BPSP's perspective, listening to their voices, and presenting their lived experiences, this research sets to help museums understand a traditionally excluded audience. They then have the knowledge to build accessible resources and promote inclusive environments which can empower BPS visitors.

Findings from this book demonstrate that creating an accessible and inclusive visit experience for BPSP is a long process and cannot be addressed with tokenistic approaches or short-term quick fixes. My research is of help to museum teams coming together to address tangible and intangible exhibition elements while keeping in mind the needs of BPSP. Examples of possible ways forward were offered directly by the experiences of three participants in this study. Fred expressed his difficulty attending special tours for BPSP provided by the museum due to inconvenient times since they are typically held during weekly working hours. This, combined with the occasional lack of accessible resources made it difficult to visit the space independently. He had to draw from his everyday strategies and his experience as a museum visitor to have a meaningful experience. Davide pointed out in section 6.9.2 that the technology resources offered are not always compatible with the accessibility needs of BPSP. He noted how people with lower technical capital or more severe sight loss would face significant difficulties using non-inclusive technology (following Hayhoe's (2014a) definition). Finally, Anna's experience with the 2012 Olympics and Paralympics' Cauldron (section 7.7.1) sheds light on the importance of representation to create an inclusive environment. Being represented in the collection as a disabled athlete through the positive narrative around the Paralympic Games empowered Anna as a disabled person and enabled her to establish a deep and meaningful connection with the object and the museum.

My findings show the impact that information provided to visitors before entering the museum has on their visit.

BPSP use the museum website to plan their visit, their activities in the museum, what to do, where to go and how to access resources. Museums should ensure that information on websites are accurate, constantly updated, and consistent with what is offered to BPSP once they enter the space. This allows BPSP to plan their visit in a way that is smoother and more successful. Similarly, another element crucial for the successful planning of the visit is the training of front of house staff. In several instances, participants encountered difficulties as staff members were not aware of resources the museum offered and they were not able to adequately provide assistance. The combination of clear and accurate information on museum websites and specialist staff awareness training is essential to ensure that BPSP can smoothly start their museum journey.

The provisions that the three case study museums offered to participants evidence tangible, if imperfect, efforts towards making collections accessible. In particular, my findings show that engaging with multisensory and interactive tactile opportunities provides different levels of understanding and processing information. Tactile opportunities are often offered in museums in the form of tactile tours, special tactile permission for BPSP to touch objects that cannot be touched commonly, tactile objects on open display for everyone to touch, and tactile replicas like casts or 3D prints. This book provided detailed accounts of how participants interacted with several of these resources, focusing on how they made meaning through touch and the kind of feelings and connections that tactile exploration enabled. Different types of collections and displays allow for various degrees of tactile opportunities. Although this research does not aim to provide exhaustive recommendations on best practice for producing tactile resources, it does provide significant insights that museums should consider when offering these opportunities.

First and foremost, tactile opportunities are generally considered a valuable way of accessing collections as they provide insights that verbal descriptions and visual examinations alone cannot offer. However, findings from this research show that touch alone is often not enough for BPS visitors to make sense of objects. Therefore, museums should provide tactile objects paired with interpretation that facilitates the understanding of the object and the social experience of co-touching. Additionally, while the offer of private tactile tours (one form of interpretation) was valued, special provisions offered only to BPSP can alienate them from the social context of the visit. Provision needs to be inclusive and allow BPS visitors to negotiate how they make sense of the objects together with their group. Therefore, I argue that museums should offer a plurality of tactile opportunities paired with a plurality of interpretation and guiding resources to respond to the needs and preferences of all visitors.

Similarly, my findings on visitors' preferences for historic and aesthetic details of objects and their interests in museums' specific themes and collections, suggest the need to offer a wide variety of content and information in a plurality of formats. For example, participants in this study used audio guides, audio descriptions, guided tours, large print booklets, and mainstream labels and panels. They all used different formats and resources based on 1) their personal preferences, 2) the needs associated with their vision impairment, and 3) what was available in the gallery. Hence, my study suggests that museums should offer accessible resources to provide the widest variety of content possible, to attend to visitors' different needs and preferences.

An effective way of doing this can be offered by mainstream digital guides provided both in the form of headsets and available through personal devices, either from a mobile application or via the museum website. Ideally, digital guides would incorporate a wide variety of accessible formats to choose from such as large print transcripts, audio content, visual content etc., and a wide variety of content, covering aesthetic visual descriptions and historic information. Several solutions were investigated in the past years to offer digital access to content both in the museum and online. This book examined the application Smartify and the digital audio guide provided by the V&A through their website. Other application examples are the guides provided in adjustable formats by Bloomberg Connect (2021) and Google Arts and Culture (2021). Another example is the digital guide provided by the Wellcome Collection through the use of QR codes for the exhibition 'On Happiness – Joy and Tranquillity', partially developed following findings from this research (Wellcome Collection 2021b). In addition, several museums are experimenting with similar content available through their websites in different formats. While this book does not recommend a specific format or software that can create a universal digital guide, I argue for the need to provide these solutions in fully accessible formats. As seen both in the case of Fred's visit to the V&A and the experiences with Smartify in the Wallace Collection, digital resources can be significantly detrimental to the experience of BPSP if something goes wrong or proves to be challenging to use. Therefore, BPSP must be consulted at all stages of the product development process, and solutions must be adequately tested for compatibility with all major accessibility settings and software. In this sense, this research contributes to recent debates around the development of accessible resources, assistive technology, and museums' role in providing inclusive and welcoming environments through digital innovation.

These recommendations clearly show that considering BPSP at all stages of the exhibition and programme developments should become part of how the whole museum operates, rather than the responsibility of a single team or only factored in at an audience research level. This can be achieved by employing one or more access lead people who can help teams understand the importance of researching and consulting with BPSP throughout the decision-making process. Such role would allow to advocate and offer guidance on good practice to help teams ensure that individuals and groups can fully contribute their expertise and experience. In doing so, the access lead would work with teams to help them reframe and refine their practice to embed audiences' perspectives into their work. In addition, they would advise and train staff on the physical, sensory, and intellectual needs of BPSP, managing the visitors-facing element of the museum and its learning strategies. Having one or more people working in this capacity across the museum's teams and the directory would ensure that BPSP's voices are heard and represented throughout each stage of the process.

The analysis of interview responses, fieldnotes, and video recordings suggests that BPSP extensively use tactile and audio resources if provided in clear, accessible and intuitive formats. Additionally, my research also shows how the possibility of being guided by a sighted companion or a purposely trained guide significantly enhances the experience of BPS visitors. These findings indicate the importance of offering a plurality of accessible and inclusive resources that can facilitate access to the collection, social interactions, and independence. Organised tours and digital resources should take into account demographic aspects like age, types and level of vision impairments, and related needs. Museum professionals should also reconsider the ways disability and the lived experiences of disabled people are represented in their collections (Dodd *et al.* 2010). Museums can provide BPSP with opportunities to develop social, cultural, and human capital and a sense of belonging, independence, and empowerment. A plurality of resources developed by the understanding of the individuality of the experience of disabled people, as well as by addressing the uncomfortable 'difficult' stories related to disability in the collections, has the potential to overcome the close relationship identified by Bourdieu (1984) between cultural capital and class position.

8.4. A note on the COVID-19 pandemic

After finishing the data collection and during the writing up stage of this research, the Coronavirus (COVID-19) pandemic erupted and took a significant toll on museums and museums visitors all over the world. Public health measures like social distancing regulations, one-way navigation systems, and hand sanitising rules affected the embodied practice of visitors inside the museum when they re-opened in England after the first and second lockdowns (March–May 2020 and October–December 2020 (IFG 2021). During the first period in England, I decided to create a further layer of analysis and to resume my conversations with BPS friends and colleagues and some participants from my PhD, whom I approached via email and invited for a follow up video-call interview. The purpose of this new layer of data collection was to investigate how the pandemic, and the consequent change of everyday embodied practices due to social distancing, had and would influence the way they approached and used physical and digital museum spaces in the long term.

I published my analysis in the Journal of Conservation and Museum Studies in the special collection 'COVID-19 and the Museum' (Cecilia 2021a). Findings showed how participants seemed to be increasingly worried that new regulations would hinder access to the environments and the collections (Cecilia 2021a, 1). In particular, elements like navigation, wayfinding, correct distancing and positioning in relation to objects and other visitors caused concern (Cecilia 2021a, 3). These findings are in line with findings from this volume, which already identified those elements as key factors in the embodied experience of participants. Similarly, participants expressed concern about the potential future lack of availability of tactile opportunities which was described as 'totally discouraging' (Cecilia 2021a, 4). This is in line with the findings presented in this book, as touch was employed by several participants as an important way to develop cultural capital, make meaning of objects with their companions, and establish emotional connections. The lack of tactile resources would be perceived as a significant step back for inclusive experiences.

Among these concerns related to physical access, the development of accessible digital content and access to online collections was highlighted by several participants as a positive experience during the lockdown periods (Cecilia 2021a, 5). These opportunities allowed BPSP to socialise and participate in cultural activities from home, removing physical barriers (Cecilia 2021a, 5).

The COVID-19 pandemic offers a unique opportunity to research further the way physical restrictions impact the embodied experience of BPSP and of disabled people more generally. Additionally, it provides an opportunity to expand and adapt the new digital experiences in a way that are accessible and meaningful for all. Further research on the way BPSP physically respond and adjust to the new 'normative' practices embedded in the post-COVID physical and digital museum script is of the utmost importance and must be placed at the forefront of the agenda.

Bibliography

Abberley, P., 1987. The Concept Of Oppression And The Development Of A Social Theory Of Disability. *Disability, Handicap & Society* 2, pp. 5–19.

Ainscow, M., and Sandill, A., 2010. Developing inclusive education systems: the role of organisational cultures and leadership. *International Journal of Inclusive Education* 14/4, pp. 401–416.

Alibali, M. W., and Goldin-Meadow, S., 1993. Gesture-Speech Mismatch and Mechanisms of Learning: What the Hands Reveal about a Child's State of Mind. *Cognitive Psychology* 25/4, pp. 468–523.

Allen, C., 2004a. Merleau-Ponty's Phenomenology And The Body-In-Space Encounters Of Visually Impaired Children. *Environment And Planning Disability: Society And Space* 22, pp. 719–735.

Allen, C., 2004b. Bourdieu's Habitus, Social Class And The Spatial Worlds Of Visually Impaired Children. *Urban Studies* 41/3, pp. 487–506.

Allen, S., 2002. Looking for Learning in Visitor Talk: A Methodological Exploration. In G. Leinhardt, K. Crowley, and K. Knutson, (eds.), *Learning Conversations in Museums*. Mahwah, N.J.; London: Lawrence Erlbaum Associates, pp. 259–303.

Alvarez, A., 2005. Please Touch: The Use of Tactile Learning in Art Exhibits. *Proceedings form J. Paul Getty Museum Symposium, "From Content to Play: Family-Oriented Interactive Spaces in Art and History Museums,"* June 4–5.

Alvesson, M., and Willmott, H., 2002. Identity Regulation as Organizational Control: Producing the Appropriate Individual. *Journal of Management Studies* 39, pp. 619–644.

American Association of Psychology (APA)., 2018. *Residual Vision*. Retrieved on 12 March 2020 from World Wide Web: https://dictionary.apa.org/residual-vision

Anderson, R. G. W., 2003. *Enlightening the British: knowledge, discovery and the museum in the eighteenth century*. London: British Museum Press.

Appleton, J., 2001. *Museums for the People*. London: Signet House.

Asakawa, S., Guerreiro, J., Ahmetovic, D., Kitani, K., and Asakawa, C., 2018. The Present and Future of Museum Accessibility for People with Visual Impairments. *ASSETS '18: Proceedings of the 20th International ACM SIGACCESS Conference on Computers and Accessibility*, pp. 382–384.

Ash, D., 2004. Reflective scientific sense-making dialogue in two languages: The science in the dialogue and the dialogue in the science. *Science Education* 88/6, pp. 855–884.

Ash D., Lombana J., and Alcala L., 2012. Changing Practices, Changing Identities as Museum Educators. In E. Davidsson, A. Jakobsson, (eds.), *Understanding Interactions at Science Centers and Museums*. Rotterdam and Boston: Sense Publishers, pp. 23–44.

Axel, E. S., and Levent, N. S., (eds.), 2003. *Art beyond sight: A resource guide to art, creativity, and visual impairment*. New York: Art Education for the Blind and AFB Press.

Baga, J., 2012. E-resource round up: Emerging technology as assistive technology: Conference report. *Journal of Electronic Resources Librarianship* 24/1, pp. 46–48.

Bagnall, G., 2003. Performance and Performativity at Heritage Sites. *Museum and Society* 1/2, pp. 87–103.

Ballarin, M., Balletti, C., Vernier, P., 2018. Replicas in cultural heritage: 3d printing and the museum experience. *International Archives of the Photogrammetry, Remote Sensing & Spatial Information Sciences* 42/2, pp. 55–62.

Barnes, C., and Mercer, G., 2002. *Disability*. Oxford: Blackwell Publishers Ltd.

Barnes, C., and Mercer, G., 2010. *Exploring Disability*. Cambridge: Polity Press.

Barnes, C., Mercer, G., and Shakespeare, T., 1999. *Exploring Disability: A Sociological Introduction*. Cambridge: Polity.

Barnes, C., Oliver, M., and Barton, L., (eds.), 2002. *Disability Studies Today*. Cambridge: Polity.

Barron, B., 2006. Interest and Self-Sustained Learning as Catalysts of Development: A Learning Ecology Perspective. *Human Development* 49/4, pp. 193–224.

Barsalou, L. W., 2003. Situated simulation in the human conceptual system. *Language and Cognitive Processes* 18/5–6, pp. 513–562.

Barsalou, L. W., Niedenthal, P. M., Barbey, A. K., and Ruppert, J. A., 2003. Social embodiment. In: B. H. Ross, (ed.), *The psychology of learning and motivation*. San Diego, CA: Academic Press, pp. 43–92.

Barton, L., 1998. Sociology, Disability Studies and Education. In: T. Shakespeare, (ed.), *The Disability Reader: Social Science Perspectives*. London: Cassell, pp. 53–65.

Barton, L., and Armstrong, F., 2001. Disability, Education and Inclusion: Cross Cultural Issues And Dilemmas. In: G. L. Albrecht, K. D. Seelman, and M. Bury, (eds.), *Handbook Of Disability Studies*. Thousand Oaks, Ca: Sage, pp. 693–710.

Belland B. R., 2014. Scaffolding: Definition, current debates, and future directions. In: J. M. Spector, M. D. Merrill, J. Elen, M. J. Bishop, (eds.), *Handbook of research on educational communications and technology*. New York, NY: Springer; pp. 505–518.

Belova, O., 2012. The event of seeing: A phenomenological perspective on visual sense-making. In S. Dudley, (ed.), *Museum Objects: Experiencing the properties of things*. Hoboken, New Jersey: Taylor and Francis, pp. 117–133.

Bennett, T., 1995. *The Birth of the Museum: history, theory, politics*. London, New York: Routledge.

Bennett, T., Savage, M., Silva, E., Warde, A., Gayo-Cal, M., and Wright, D., 2009. *Cultural, Class, Distinction*. London: Routledge.

Bertelson, P., and De Gelder, B., 2004. The Psychology of Multimodal Perception. In: J. Driver and C. Spence, (eds.), *Crossmodal space and crossmodal attention*. Oxford, UK: Oxford University Press, pp. 142–143.

Black, G., 2005. *The Engaging Museum: Developing Museums for Visitor Involvement*. Oxford: Routledge.

Bloomberg Connects., 2021. *Arts and Culture on demand*. Retrieved on 07 August 2021 from World Wide Web: https://www.bloombergconnects.org

Bourdieu, P., 1977. *Outline of a Theory of Practice*. Cambridge University Press.

Bourdieu, P., 1984. *Distinction: A Social Critique of the Judgment of Taste*. London: Routledge.

Bourdieu, P., 1986. The Forms of Capital. In J. Richardson, (ed.), *Handbook of Theory and Research for the Sociology of Education*. Westport, CT: Greenwood, pp. 241–258.

Bourdieu, P., 1990. *The Logic of Practice*. Stanford: Stanford University Press.

Bourdieu, P., 1993. *The Field of Cultural Production*. Cambridge: Polity Press.

Bourdieu, P., 2005. *The Social Structures of The Economy*. Cambridge: Polity Press.

Bourdieu, P., 2006. Cultural Reproduction and Social Reproduction. In D. Grusky and S. Szelényi, (eds.*), Inequality: Classic Readings in Race, Class, and Gender*. Oxon: Routledge, pp. 257–272.

Bourdieu, P., 2010. *Distinction*. London: Routledge Classics.

Boy, J., and Uitermark, J., 2017. Reassembling the City through Instagram. *Transactions of the Institute of British Geographers* 42, pp. 612–624.

British Museum., 2021. *Accessibility at the Museum*. Retrieved on 26 March 2021 from World Wide Web: https://www.britishmuseum.org/visit/accessibility-museum

Brock, A., Kvasny, L., and Hales, K., 2010. Cultural Appropriations of Technical Capital: Black women, weblogs, and the digital divide. *Information, Communication & Society* 13/7, pp. 1040–1059.

Brown, J. S., Collins, A. and Duguid, P., 1989. Situated cognition and the culture of learning. *Educational Researcher* 18/1, pp. 32–42.

Buck, E. G.,1997. Museum bodies: the performance of the Musée Gustave Moreau. *Museum Anthropology* 20/2, pp. 15–24.

Budge, K., 2020. Visually Imagining Place: Museum Visitors, Instagram, and the City. *Journal of Urban Technology* 27/2, pp. 61–79.

Budge, K., and Burness, A., 2018. Museum Objects and Instagram: Agency and Communication in Digital Engagement. *Continuum* 32/2, pp. 137–150.

Burness, A., 2016. New Ways of Looking: Self-Representational Social Photography in Museums. In T. Stylianou-Lambert, (ed.), *Museums and Visitor Photography: Redefining the Visitor Experience*. Edinburgh: MuseumsEtc.

Bury, M., 1991. The sociology of chronic illness: a review of research and prospects. *Sociology of Health & Illness* 13/4, pp. 451–68.

Butler, J., 1993. *Bodies that Matter*. London and New York: Routledge.

Cahagan, J., 1984. *Social Interaction and its Management*. London and New York: Routledge.

Campbell, F. K., 2019. Precision Ableism: A Studies in Ableism Approach to Developing Histories of Disability and Abledment. *Rethinking History* 23/2, pp. 138–156.

Campbell, J., and Oliver, M., 1996. *Disability Politics: Understanding Our Past, Changing Our Future*. London: Routledge.

Candlin, F., 2003. Blindness, art and exclusion in museums and galleries. *The International Journal of Art Design* 22/1, pp. 100–110.

Candlin, F., 2004. Don't touch! Hands off! Art, blindness and the conservation of expertise. *Body & Society* 10, pp. 71–90.

Candlin, F., 2006. The Dubious Inheritance of Touch: Art History and Museum Access. *Journal of Visual Culture* 5/2, pp. 137–154.

Candlin, F., 2007. Don't touch! Hands off! Art, blindness and the conservation of expertise. In: E. Pye, (ed.) *The power of touch: handling objects in museum and heritage contexts*. London: UCL Institute of Archaeology Publications, pp. 89–106.

Candlin, F., 2010. *Art, Museums and Touch*. Manchester: University of Manchester Press.

Cappella, J. N., and Planalp, S., 1981. Talk and Silence Sequences in Informal Conversations III: Interspeaker Influence. *Human Communication Research* 7, pp. 117–132.

Carr, D., 2001. A museum is an open work. *International Journal of Heritage Studies* 7/2, pp. 173–183.

Carroll, N., Moore, M., and Seeley, W.P., 2012. The philosophy of art and aesthetics, psychology, and neuroscience. In A.P. Shimamura, and S.E. Palmyre (eds.) *Aesthetic science. Connecting minds, brains, and experience*. New York: Oxford University Press, pp. 31–62.

Cavazos Quero, L., Iranzo Bartolomé, J., Lee, S., Han, E., Kim, S., and Cho, J., 2018. An Interactive Multimodal Guide to Improve Art Accessibility for Blind People. *Proceedings of the 20th International ACM SIGACCESS Conference on Computers and Accessibility (ASSETS '18)*, pp. 346–348.

Cazden, C., 2001. *Classroom discourse: The language of teaching and learning*. Portsmouth, NH: Heinemann.

Cecilia, R. R., 2018. *Gravegoods project. Evaluation of the Room 64: Early Egypt Gallery*. Internal Report, Supplemental Material. London: The British Museum.

Cecilia, R. R., 2019. "Please Do Not Touch": Risk Mitigation and the Efficacy of Touching Deterrents. *University of Cambridge repository*, 5, 1–72, p, ill.

Cecilia, R. R., 2021a. Covid-19 Pandemic: Threat or Opportunity for Blind and Partially Sighted Museum Visitors? *Journal of Conservation and Museum Studies* 19/1–5, pp. 1–8.

Cecilia, R. R., 2021b (in press). Blind and partially sighted people's motivation to visit museums: a London-based case study. In: *Inklusion in der Archäologie*. Berlin: Forum Kritische Archäologie.

Celani, G., Zattera, V., de Oliveira, M., and Lopes da Silva, J., 2013. "Seeing" with the hands: Teaching architecture for the visually impaired with digitally fabricated scale models. In J. Zhang and C. Sun, (eds.), *Global design and local materialization*. Berlin: Springer.

Chadwick, A., n. d. *Defining impairment and disability*. Disability Studies, University of Leeds.

Charmaz, K., 2010. Studying the experience of chronic illness through grounded theory. In G. Scambler and S. Scambler, (eds.), *New Directions in the Sociology of Chronic and Disabling Conditions: Assaults on the Lifeworld*. London, New York: Palgrave Macmillan, pp. 8–36.

Chartrand, T. L., and Bargh, J. A., 1999. The chameleon effect: The perception–behavior link and social interaction. *Journal of Personality and Social Psychology* 76/6, pp. 893–910.

Chatterjee, H. J., 2008a. Introduction. In H. J. Chatterjee, (ed.), *Touch in museums: policy and practice in object handling*. Oxford: Berg, pp. 1–8.

Chatterjee, H., (ed.), 2008b. *Touch in Museums: Policy and Practice in Object Handling*. Oxford: Berg.

Chrisley, R. and Ziemke, T., 2002. Embodiment. In: *Encyclopedia of Cognitive Science*. London: Macmillan Publishers, pp. 1102–1108.

Christidou, D., 2012. *Does "pointing at" in museum exhibitions make a point? A study of visitors' performances in three museums for the use of reference as a means of initiating and prompting meaning-making*. Unpublished Ph.D. thesis. University College London.

Christidou, D., 2013. Bringing Meaning into Making: How Do Visitors Tag an Exhibit as Social when Visiting a Museum. *The International Journal of the Inclusive Museum* 6/1, pp. 73–85.

Christidou, D., 2016. Social Interaction in the Art Museum: Connecting to Each Other and the Exhibits. *The International Journal of Social, Political and Community Agendas in the Arts* 11/4, pp. 27–38.

Christidou, D., and Diamantopoulou S., 2016. Seeing and Being Seen: The Multimodality of Museum Spectatorship. *Museum & Society* 14/1, pp. 12–32.

Clancey, W.J., 1997. *Situated cognition: On human knowledge and computer representations*. Cambridge: Cambridge University Press.

Clark, A., 1997. *Being there. Putting brain, body, and world together again*. Cambridge, MA: MIT Press.

Classen, C., 2005. *The Book of Touch*. Oxford: Berg.

Classen, C., 2007. Museum Manners: The Sensory Life of the Early Museum. *Journal of Social History* 40/4, pp. 895–914.

Classen, C., 2012. *The Deepest Sense: A Cultural History of Touch*. Champaign, IL: University of Illinois Press.

Classen, C., 2016. *The Museum of the Senses: Experiencing Art and Collections*. London: Bloomsbury Academic.

Classen, C., and Howes, D., 2006. The Museum as Sensescape: Western Sensibilities and Indigenous Artefacts. In E. Edwards, C. Gosden and R. Phillips, (eds.), *Sensible Objects: Colonialism, Museums and Material Culture*. Oxford: Berg, pp. 199–222.

Clavir, M., 1996. Reflections on Changes in Museums and the Conservation of Collections from Indigenous Peoples. *Journal of the American Institute for Conservation* 35 /2, pp. 99–107.

Cock, M., Bretton, M., Fineman, A., France, R., Madge, C., and Sharpe, M. (2018). *State of museum access 2018*. Retrieved on 15 March 2021 from World Wide Web: https://vocaleyes.co.uk/state-of-museum-access-2018

Coleman, J. S., 1988. Social Capital in the Creation of Human Capital. *American Journal of Sociology* 94, pp. 95–120.

Connors, C., and Stalker, K., 2007. Children's Experiences of Disability: Pointers to a Social Model of Childhood Disability. *Disability & Society* 22/1, pp. 19–33.

Corbin, J., and Strauss, A., 2008. *Basics of Qualitative Research: Techniques and Procedures for Developing Grounded Theory.* Los Angeles; London; New Delhi; Singapore: Sage Publications.

Cox, A., 2018. Embodied Knowledge and Sensory Information: Theoretical Roots and Inspirations. *Library Trends* 66, pp. 223–238.

Creswell, J. W., 1998. *Qualitative inquiry and research design: Choosing among five traditions.* Thousand Oaks, CA: Sage Publications.

Creswell, T., 2002. Bourdieu's Geographies: In Memoriam. *Environment and Planning D Society and Space* 20/4, pp. 379–382.

Cresswell, T., 2004. *Place: A Short Introduction.* Malden, MA: Blackwell.

Cresswell, T., 2015. *Place: An Introduction.* Malden, MA: Wiley-Blackwell.

Croft, E., 2020. Experiences of Visually Impaired and Blind Students in UK Higher Education: An Exploration of Access and Participation. *Scandinavian Journal of Disability Research* 22/1, pp. 382–392.

Crossley, N., 1995. Merleau-Ponty, The Elusive Body and Carnal Sociology. *Body & Society* 1, pp. 43–63.

Crossley, N., 1996. Body-subject/body-power: agency, inscription and control in Foucault and Merleau-Ponty. *Body and Society* 2/2, pp. 99–116.

Crotty, M., 1998. *The foundations of social research: Meaning and perspective in the research process.* Thousand Oaks, CA: Sage Publications.

Cunningham, C., Barker, J. B., and Slater, M. J., 2019. The relationship between disability-related identities and well-being in elite para athletes. In International Paralympic Committee, (ed.), *VISTA 2019 Conference Proceedings.*

Curtis, E., 2008. Walking Out of the Classroom: Learning on the Streets of Aberdeen. In T. Ingold, and J. L. Vergunst, (eds.), *Ways of Walking. Ethnography and Practice on Foot.* Farnham: Ashgate, pp. 143–154.

Daly, K., 1992. The Fit Between Qualitative Research and Characteristics of Families. In: J. Gilgun, K. Daly, and G. Handel, (eds.), *Qualitative Methods in Family Research.* Thousand Oaks, CA: SAGE Publications, pp. 22–39.

Davidhizar, R., and Bowen, M., 1992. The dynamics of laughter. *Archives of Psychiatric Nursing* 6/2, pp. 132–137.

Davidson, B., Heald, C. L., and Hein, G., 1991. Increased Exhibit Accessibility through Multisensory Interaction. *Curator* 34/4, pp. 273–290.

Davis, J., 2008. Are museums deliberately blind to the needs of the blind? *Tahoma West Literary Arts Magazine* 12/1.

Dawson, M., 2014. Embedded and Situated Cognition. In L. Shapiro, (ed.), *The Routledge Handbook of Embodied Cognition.* Abingdon: Routledge, pp. 59–67.

De Coster, K., and Loots, G., 2004. Somewhere in between Touch and Vision: In Search of a Meaningful Art Education for Blind Individuals. *International Journal of Art & Design Education* 23, pp. 326–334.

Denzin, N., and Lincoln, Y., 2005. *The SAGE handbook of qualitative research.* Thousand Oaks, CA: Sage Publications.

Descartes, R., 2008 [1637]. *Meditations on first philosophy* (Trans. by M. Moriarty). Oxford: Oxford University Press.

Disability Rights UK., 2021. *Brexit and the Equality Act?.* Retrieved on 03 April 2021 from World Wide Web: https://www.disabilityrightsuk.org/brexit-and-equality-act

Dodd, J. and Sandell, R., 2001. *Including Museums: Perspectives on Museums, Galleries and Social Inclusion.* Leicester: RCMG University of Leicester.

Dodd, J., Sandell, R., Delin, A., and Gay, J., 2004. *Buried in the footnotes: the representation of disabled people in museum and gallery collections.* University of Leicester Report. Retrieved on 07 May 2021 from World Wide Web: https://hdl.handle.net/2381/33

Dood, J., Sandell, R., Jolly, D., and Jones, C., 2008. *Rethinking Disability Representation in Museums and Galleries.* Leicester, UK: Research Centre for Museums and Galleries (RCMG), University of Leicester.

Dodd, J., Jones, C., Jolly, D., and Sandell, R., 2010. Disability reframed: Challenging visitor perceptions in the museum. In R. Sandell, J. Dodd, and R. Garland-Thompson, (eds.), *Re-Presenting Disability: Activism and agency in the museum.* London and New York: Routledge, pp. 92–111.

Doering, Z. D., and Pekarik, A. J., 1996. Questioning the entrance narrative. *Journal of Museum Education* 21/3, pp. 20–22.

Doxa, M., 2001. Morphologies of Co-presence in Interior Public Space in Places of Performance: The Royal Festival Hall and the Royal National Theatre of London. *Proceedings of 3rd International Space Syntax Symposium, Atlanta, U.S.A: Georgia Institute of Technology*, pp. 16.1–16.15.

Drodge, E. N., and Reid, D. A., 2000. Embodied cognition and the mathematical emotional orientation. *Mathematical Thinking and Learning* 2/4, pp. 249–267.

Dudley, S., (ed.), 2010. *Museum Materialities: Objects, Engagements, Interpretations*. Abingdon, UK: Routledge.

Dunn, D. S., and Burcaw, S., 2013. Disability Identity: Exploring Narrative Accounts of Disability. *Rehabilitation Psychology* 58/2, pp. 148–157.

Durham-Wall, M., 2015. What are you looking at?: Staring down notions of the disabled body in dance. *Choreographic Practices* 6/1, pp. 25–40.

EBU., 2020. *About blindness and partial sight*. Retrieved on 17 April 2021 from World Wide Web: http://www.euroblind.org/about-blindness-and-partial-sight/facts-and-figures

Edwards, C., and Imrie, R., 2003. Disability And Bodies As Bearers Of Value. *Sociology* 37/2, pp. 239–256.

Eisenhauer J., 2007. Just Looking and Staring Back: Challenging Ableism through Disability Performance Art. *Studies in Art Education*. 49/1, pp. 7–22.

Equality and Human Rights Commission., 2019. *The public sector equality duty*. Retrieved on 03 April 2021 from World Wide Web: https://www.equalityhumanrights.com/en/corporate-reporting/public-sector-equality-duty

Equality and Human Rights Commission., 2021. *Our Brexit work*. Retrieved on 03 April 2021 from World Wide Web: https://www.equalityhumanrights.com/en/our-brexit-work

Farnell, B., 1999. Moving bodies, acting selves. *Annual Review Anthropology* 28, pp. 341–373.

Fenwick, T. J., 2003. Reclaiming and re-embodying experiential learning through complexity science. *Studies in the Education of Adults* 35/2, pp. 123–142.

Firestone, W., 1987. Meaning in Method: The Rhetoric of Quantitative and Qualitative Research. *Educational Researcher* 16/7, pp. 16–21.

Fleming, D., 2001. The Politics of Social Inclusion. In: J. Dodd and R. Sandell, (eds.), *Including Museums*. University of Leicester: Research Centre for Museums and Galleries, pp. 17–19.

Fleming, D., 2002. Positioning the Museum for Social Inclusion. In: R. Sandell, (ed.), *Museums, Society, Inequality*. London: Routledge, pp. 213–224.

Fontana-Giusti, G. K., 2007. Urban strolling as the measure of quality. *Architectural Research Quarterly* 11/3–4, pp. 255–264.

Frances, J., 2014. Damaged or unusual bodies: Staring, or seeing and feeling, *Body, Movement and Dance in Psychotherapy* 9/4, pp. 198–210.

Fryer, L., 2016. *An introduction to audio description: A practical guide*. Oxford: Routledge.

Gadoua, M. P., 2014. Making Sense through Touch. *The Senses and Society* 9/3, pp. 323–341.

Gallace, A., and Spence, C., 2008. A Memory for Touch: The Cognitive Psychology of Tactile Memory. In: H. J. Chatterjee, (ed.), *Touch in museums: policy and practice in object handling*. London: Bloomsbury, pp. 163–186.

Garip, B., and Bülbül, M. S., 2014. A Blind Student's Outdoor Science Learning Experience: Barrier Hunting at METU Science and Technology Museum. *Eurasian Journal Physics & Chemistry Education* 6/2, pp. 100–109.

Garland-Thompson, R., 2000. Staring Back: Self-Representations of Disabled Performance Artists. *American Quarterly* 52/2, pp. 334–338.

Garland-Thompson, R., 2009. *Staring: How We Look*. New York and Oxford: Oxford University Press.

Garoian, C. R., 2001. Performing the Museum. *Studies in Art Education* 42/3, pp. 234–248.

Gerges, M., 2018. So What if Selfies are Narcissistic?. *Canadian Art*. Retrieved on 21 April 2021 from World Wide Web: https://canadianart.ca/features/so-what-if-art-selfies-are-narcissistic/

Gibbons, P., 2015. *Scaffolding language, scaffolding learning*. Portsmouth: Heinemann.

Giddens, A., 1984. *The Constitution of Society: Outline of the Theory of Structuration*. Cambridge: Polity Press.

Gilman, B. I., 1916. Museum Fatigue. *The Scientific Monthly* 2/1, pp. 62–74.

Ginley, B., 2013. Museums: A Whole New World for Visually Impaired People. *Disability Studies Quarterly* 33/3.

Giudice, N. A., and Legge, G. E., 2008. Blind Navigation and the Role of Technology. In A. Helal, M. Mokhtari and B. Abdulrazak, (eds.), *The Engineering Handbook of Smart Technology for Aging, Disability, and Independence*. Hoboken, New Jersey: John Wiley & Sons, Inc., pp. 479–500.

Gkatzidou, S., and Pearson, E., 2009. The potential for adaptable accessible learning objects: A case study in accessible podcasting. *Australasian Journal of Educational Technology* 25/2, pp. 292–307.

Goffman, E., 1963. *Behavior in Public Places*. New York: Free Press.

Goffman, E., 1981. *Forms of Talk*. Philadelphia: University of Pennsylvania.

Goldin-Meadow, S., Nusbaum, H., Kelly, S., and Wagner, S., 2001. Explaining math: Gesturing lightens the load. *Psychological Science* 12, pp. 516–522.

Gombrich, E. H., 1984. *The sense of order: Studies in the psychology of decorative art*. London: Phaidon Press.

Gonot-Schoupinsky, F. N., Garip, G., and Sheffield, D., 2020. Laughter and humour for personal development:

A systematic scoping review of the evidence. *European Journal of Integrative Medicine,* pp. 101144.

Gonzalez, N., Moll, L., and Amanti, K., 2005. *Funds of knowledge: theorizing practices in households, communities, and classrooms.* Mahwah: Lawrence Erlbaum.

Goodley, D., 2004. Who is Disabled? Exploring the Scope of the Social Model of Disability. In J. Swain, S. French, C. Barnes, C. Thomas, (eds.), *Disabling Barriers, Enabling Environments.* Thousand Oaks, Ca: Sage, pp. 118–133.

Google Arts and Culture., 2021. *Google Arts and Culture.* Retrieved on 07 August 2021 from World Wide Web: https://artsandculture.google.com

GOV.UK., 2021. *Equality Act 2010.* Retrieved on 03 April 2021 from World Wide Web: https://www.legislation.gov.uk/ukpga/2010/15/contents

Grandjean, G., 2000. The Blind And Museums: Choosing Works Of Art For Tactile Observation. In: Fondation de France & ICOM, (eds.), *Museums Without Barriers: A new deal for disabled people.* London: Routledge, pp. 101–106.

Granott, N., 2005. Scaffolding dynamically toward change: Previous and new perspectives. *New Ideas in Psychology* 23/3, pp. 140–151.

Grosz, E., 1994. *Volatile Bodies: Toward a Corporeal Feminism.* Bloomington: Indiana. University Press.

Guarini, B., 2015. Beyond Braille on toilet doors: Museum curators and audiences with vision impairment. *Media-Communications Journal* 18/4.

Handley, K., Sturdy, A., Fincham, R., and Clark, T., 2006. Within and beyond communities of practice: Making sense of learning through participation, identity and practice. *Journal of Management Studies* 43/3, pp. 641–653.

Harbison, R., 2000. *Eccentric Spaces.* Cambridge, MA: MIT Press.

Harris, J., 2015. Embodiment in the Museum – What is a Museum?. *ICOFOM Study Series* 43b, pp. 101–115.

Hay, R., 1998. Sense of place in a developmental context. *Journal of Environmental Psychology* 18, pp. 5–29.

Hayhoe, S. J., 2013a. A practice report of students from a school for the blind leading groups of younger mainstream students in visiting a museum and making multi-modal artworks. *Journal of blindness innovation and research* 3/2, pp. 1–11.

Hayhoe, S. J., 2013b. A review of the literature on the use of mobile tablet computing as inclusive devises for students with disabilities. In *Proceedings of the Current Trends in Information Technology 2013 Conference,* Dubai, December 2013. New Jersey: IEEE.

Hayhoe, S. J., 2014a. An enquiry into passive and active exclusion from sensory aesthetics in museums and on the Web: Two case studies of final year students at California School for the Blind studying art works through galleries and on the web. *British Journal of Visual Impairment* 32/1, pp. 44–58.

Hayhoe, S. J., 2014b. The need for inclusive accessible technologies for students with disabilities and learning difficulties. In L. Burke, (ed.), *Research, reflections & arguments on teaching & learning in a digital age.* Melton, Suffolk: John Catt Publishing.

Hayhoe, S. J., 2015a. Utilising mobile technologies for students with disabilities. In A. Robertson and R. Jones-Parry, (eds.), *Commonwealth education partnerships—2015* (Vol. 16). Cambridge: Commonwealth Secretariat & Nexus Strategic Partnerships.

Hayhoe, S. J., 2015b. A pedagogical evaluation of accessible settings in Google's Android and Apple's iOS mobile operating systems and native apps using the SAMR model of educational technology and an educational model of technical capital. In *Proceedings of INTED2015 9th International Technology, Education and Development conference, March 2015.* Valencia: IATED.

Hayhoe, S. J., Roger, K., Eldritch-Böersen, S., and Kelland, L., 2015. Developing Inclusive Technical Capital beyond the Disabled Students' Allowance in England. *Social Inclusion* 3/6, pp. 29–41.

Hayhoe, S. J., 2017. *Blind visitor experiences at art museums.* London: Rowman & Littlefield.

Hayhoe, S. J., 2018. *How a blind artist is challenging our understanding of colour.* The Conversation March 23, 2018. Retrieved on 26 May 2020 from World Wide Web: https://theconversation.com/how-a-blind-artist-is-challenging-our-understanding-of-colour-93872

Heath, C., Luff, P., vom Lehn, D., Hindmarsh, J., and Cleverly, J., 2002. Crafting Participation: Designing Ecologies, Configuring Experience. *Visual Communication* 1/1, pp. 9–33.

Heath, C., and vom Lehn, D., 2002. Misconstruing interactivity. *Paper presented at the Interactive Learning in Museums of Art and Design.*

Heath, C., and vom Lehn, D., 2004. Configuring reception: (Dis-)regarding the 'spectator' in museums and galleries. *Theory, Culture & Society* 21/6, pp. 43–65.

Hefferson, K., and Gil-Rodriguez, E., 2011. Methods: Interpretative phenomenological analysis. *The Psychologist* 24, pp. 756–759.

Heidegger, M., 1962 [1927]. *Being and Time.* Oxford: Blackwell.

Heller, M. A., Kennedy, J. M., Clark, A., McCarthy, M., Borgert, A., Wemple, L. A., Fulkerson, E., Kaffel, N., Duncan, A., and Riddle, T., 2006. Viewpoint and orientation influence picture recognition in the blind. *Perception* 35/10, pp. 1397–1420.

HESA., 2019. *Higher Education Student Statistics: UK.* Retrieved on 07 April 2021 from World Wide Web: https://www.hesa.ac.uk/news/27-01-2021/sb258-higher-education-student-statistics

Hetherington, K., 2003. Accountability and disposal: visual impairment and the museum. *Museum and Society* 1/2, pp. 104–115.

Hillier, B., 1996. *Space is the Machine.* Cambridge: Cambridge University Press.

Hillis, C., 2005. *Access for blind and partially sighted people to outdoor heritage sites.* London: RNIB.

Hirose, N., 2001. An ecological approach to embodiment and cognition. *Cognitive Systems Research* 3, pp. 289–299.

Hirose, N., 2011. Affordances, Effectivities, and Extension of the Body. In W. Tschacher, and C. Bergomi, (eds.), *The implications of embodiment: Cognition and communication.* Charlottesville (USA), Exeter (UK): Imprint Academic, pp. 231–252.

Hodkinson, P., Biesta, G., and James, D., 2007. Understanding Learning Culturally: Overcoming the Dualism Between Social and Individual Views of Learning. *Vocations and Learning* 1, pp. 27–47.

Hogg, M. A., 2006. Social identity theory. In P. J. Burke, (ed.), *Contemporary social psychological theories.* Stanford, CA: Stanford University Press, pp. 111–136.

Hogg, L., 2011. Funds of knowledge: An investigation of coherence within the literature. *Teaching and Teacher Education* 27, pp. 666–677.

Hohenstein, J., and Moussouri, T., 2018. *Museum Learning. Theory and Research as Tools for Enhancing Practice.* London & New York: Routledge.

Hooper-Greenhill, E., 1994. *Museums and Their Visitors.* London: Routledge.

Hooper-Greenhill, E., 1995. *Museum, Media, Message.* London: Routledge.

Howes, D., 2014. Introduction to Sensory Museology. *The Senses and Society* 9/3, pp. 259–267.

Hughes, B., 1999. The Constitution of Impairment: Modernity and the Aesthetic of Oppression. *Disability & Society* 14/2, pp. 155–172.

Hughes, B., and Paterson, K., 1997. The Social Model of Disability and the Disappearing Body: toward a Sociology of Impairment. *Disability & Society* 12/3, pp. 325–340.

Hutchinson, K. A., Roberts, C., and Daly, M., 2018. Identity, Impairment and Disablement: Exploring the Social Processes Impacting Identity Change in Adults Living with Acquired Neurological Impairments. *Disability & Society* 33/2, pp. 175–196.

Hutchinson, R. S., and Eardley, A. F., 2019. Museum audio description: the problem of textual fidelity. *Perspectives: Studies in Translation Theory and Practice* 27, pp. 42–57.

Hutchinson, R. S., and Eardley, A. F., 2020. The Accessible Museum: Towards an Understanding of International Audio Description Practices in Museums. *Journal of Visual Impairment & Blindness* 114/6, pp. 475–487.

Imrie, R., 1996a. Equity, Social Justice and Planning for Access and Disabled People: An International Perspective. *International Planning Studies* 1/1, pp. 17–34.

Imrie, R., 1996b. *Disability and The City.* London: Paul Chapman Publishing.

Imrie, R., 1999. The Body, Disability and Le Courbusier's Conception of The Radiant Environment. In R. Butler and H. Parr, (eds.), *Mind and Body Spaces: Geographies of Illness, Impairment and Disability.* London: Routledge, pp. 25–45.

Imrie, R., 2000. Disabling Environments and The Geography of Access Policies and Practices. *Disability & Society* 15/1, pp. 5–24.

Imrie, R., 2001. Barriered And Bounded Places and The Spatialities of Disability. *Urban Studies* 38/2, pp. 231–237.

Imrie, R., 2012. Universalism, Universal Design, and Equitable Access to The Built Environment. *Disability and Rehabilitation* 34/10, pp. 873–882.

Ingold, T., 2000. *The Perception of the Environment.* London: Routledge.

Ingold, T., and Vergunst, J. L., 2008. *Ways of Walking. Ethnography and Practice on Foot.* Farnham: Ashgate.

Ingold, T., 2011. *Being Alive: Essays on Movement, Knowledge and Description.* London: Routledge.

Institute for Government (IFG)., 2021. *Timeline of UK coronavirus lockdowns.* Retrieved on 29 April 2021 from World Wide Web: https://www.instituteforgovernment.org.uk/sites/default/files/timeline-lockdown-web.pdf

Iverson, J.M., 1999. How to get to the cafeteria: gesture and speech in blind and sighted children's spatial descriptions. Developmental Psychology 35, pp. 1132–1142.

Iverson, J., and Goldin-Meadow, S., 1997. What's Communication Got to Do With It? Gesture in Children Blind From Birth. *Developmental Psychology* 33/3, pp. 453–467.

Iverson, J., and Goldin-Meadow, S., 1998. Why people gesture when they speak. *Nature* 396, p. 228.

Iverson, J., and Goldin-Meadow, S., 2001. The resilience of gesture in talk: Gesture in blind speakers and listeners. *Developmental Science* 4, pp. 416–422.

Jacobs, J., 1989 [1961]. *The Death and Life of Great American Cities*. New York: Vintage Book.

Janes, R. R., and Sandell, R., (eds.), 2019. *Museum Activism*. London and New York: Routledge.

Jewitt, C., and Price, S., 2019. Family touch practices and learning experiences in the museum. *The Senses and Society* 14/2, pp. 221–235.

Johnson, D. W., and Johnson, R. T., 2008. Social Interdependence Theory and Cooperative Learning: The Teacher's Role. In R. M. Gillies, A. F. Ashman, and J. Terwel, (eds.), *The Teacher's Role in Implementing Cooperative Learning in the Classroom*. Boston, MA: Springer US, pp. 9–37.

Johnson, M., 1987. *The body in the mind: the bodily basis of meaning, imagination and reason*. Chicago: University of Chicago Press.

Jones, A., 2007. *Memory and Material Culture*. Cambridge: Cambridge University Press.

Joppke, C., 1986. The Cultural Dimensions of Class Formation And Class Struggle: On The Social Theory Of Pierre Bourdieu. *Berkeley Journal of Sociology* 31, pp. 51–78.

Keary, A. M., 2009. Do we? Can we look at the disabled body? In L. Hartley, (ed.), *Contemporary body psychotherapy: The Chiron approach*. London: Routledge, pp. 164–176.

Keller, H., 2005. *The story of my life*. New York: Pocket Books.

Kendon, A., 2004. *Gesture: Visible action as utterance*. Cambridge: Cambridge University Press.

Kennedy, J. M., 2008. Metaphoric pictures devised by an early- blind adult on her own initiative. *Perception* 37/11, pp. 1720–1728.

Kennedy, J. M., and Juricevic, I., 2006. Blind man draws using diminution in three dimensions. *Psychonomic Bulletin and Review* 13/3, pp. 506–509.

Kirshenblatt-Gimblett, B., 1998. *Destination Culture: Tourism, Museums, and Heritage*. Berkeley: University of California Press.

Kirshenblatt-Gimblett, B., 2000. The Museum as Catalyst (Keynote Address) *Museums 2000: Confirmation or Challenge, ICOM Sweden, the Swedish Museum Association and Swedish Travelling Exhibitions/ Riksutställningar,* 29 September 2000, Vadstena, Sweden.

Kitchin, R., 1998. 'Out Of Place', 'Knowing One's Place': Space, Power and the Exclusion of Disabled People. *Disability & Society* 13/3, pp. 343–356.

Kleege, G., 1999. *Sight Unseen*. New Haven and London: Yale University Press.

Kleege, G., 2005. Blindness and Visual Culture: An Eyewitness Account. *Journal of Visual Culture* 4/2, pp. 179–190.

Kleege, G., 2013. Some touching thoughts and wishful thinking. *Disability Studies Quarterly* 33/3, pp. 37–41.

Kleege, G., 2018. *More than Meets the Eye: What Blindness Brings to Art*. New York: Oxford University Press.

Kozinets, R., Gretzel, U., and Dinhopl, A., 2017. Self in Art/Self as Art: Museum Selfies as Identity Work. *Frontiers in Psychology* 8/731, pp. 1–12.

Krantz, G., 2013. Leveling the participatory field: The Mind's Eye program at the Guggenheim Museum. *Disability Studies Quarterly, 33*/3. Retrieved on 03 April 2021 from World Wide Web: http://dsqsds.org/article/view/3738

Kwon, S. J., and Sailer, K., 2015. Seeing and being seen inside a museum and a department store. A comparison study in visibility and co-presence patterns. In: K. Karimi, L. Vaughan, K. Sailer, G. Palaiologou, and T. Bolton, (eds.), *Proceedings of the 10th Space Syntax Symposium (SSS10)*. London: Space Syntax Laboratory, The Bartlett School of Architecture, University College London, pp. 24:1–24:15.

Kyle, G., and Chick, G., 2007. The Social Construction of a Sense of Place. *Leisure Sciences: An Interdisciplinary Journal* 29/3, pp. 209–225.

Lageby, A., 2013. *Patterns of co-presence Spatial configuration and social segregation*. Stockholm: KTH Architecture and the Built Environment.

Laird, J., Wagener, J., Halal, M., and Szegda, M., 1982. Remembering what you feel: Effects of emotion on memory. *Journal of Personality and Social Psychology* 42, pp. 646–657.

Lalli, M., 1992. Urban-related identity: Theory, measurement, and empirical findings. *Journal of Environmental Psychology* 12, pp. 285–303.

Lancioni, T., 2006. Toccare ma non guardare. La semiotica e il problema della trasposizione tattile delle arti visive. In: R. Farroni *et al.*, (eds.), *L'arte a portata di mano*. Roma: Armando Editore, p. 5764.

Larkin, M., Eatough, V., and Osborn, M., 2011. Interpretative phenomenological analysis and embodied, active, situated cognition. *Theory & Psychology* 21/3, pp. 318–337.

Latham, K., 2012. Numinous experiences with museum objects. *Visitor Studies* 16/1, pp. 3–20.

Lave, J., 1991. Situated learning in a community of practice. In: L. B. Resnick, J. M. Levine and S. D. Teasley, (eds.), *Perspectives on socially shared cognition*. Washington: American Psychological Association.

Lave, J. & Wenger, E., 1991. *Situated learning. Legitimate peripheral participation*. Cambridge, UK: Cambridge University Press.

Leder, D., 1990. *The Absent Body*. Chicago, Chicago University Press.

Levent, N., and Pascual Levone, A., (eds.), 2014. *The Multisensory Museum: Cross-Disciplinary Perspectives on Touch, Sound, Smell, Memory, and Space.* New York: Rowman & Littlefield.

Levine, J. M., and Resnick, L. B., 1993. Social foundations of cognition. *Annual Review of Psychology* 44, pp. 585–612.

Lin, N., 2001. *Social Capital: A Theory of Social Structure And Action.* New York: Cambridge University Press.

Locker, D., 1983. *Disability and Disadvantage: The Consequences of Chronic Illness.* London, New York: Tavistock.

Lund, K., 2012. Landscapes and narratives: Compositions and the walking body. *Landscape Research* 37/2, pp. 225–237.

MacDonald C. M., 2004. A chuckle a day keeps the doctor away: therapeutic humor and laughter. *J Psychosoc Nurs Ment Health Ser.* 42/3, pp. 18–25.

Mai, T., and Ash, D. B., 2012. Tracing our Methodological Steps. In: D. B. Ash, J. Rahm, and L. M. Melber, (eds.), *Putting Theory into Practice. New Directions in Mathematics and Science Education.* Rotterdam: Sense Publishers, pp. 97–117.

Manduchi, R., and Kurniawan, S., 2011. Mobility-Related Accidents Experienced by People with Visual Impairment. *Insight: Research and Practice in Visual Impairment and Blindness* 4/2, pp. 44–54.

Martiny, K. M., 2015. How To Develop A Phenomenological Model Of Disability. *Medical Health Care and Philosophy* 18, pp. 553–565.

Marty, P. F., 2008. Introductions. In P. F. Marty and K. Burton Jones, (eds.), *Museum Informatics People, Information, and Technology in Museums.* New York and London: Routledge Ltd, pp. 1–25.

Mascolo, M. F., 2005. Change processes in development: The concept of coactive scaffolding. *New Ideas in Psychology* 23, pp. 185–196.

Mason, M., 2007. Critical Thinking and Learning. *Educational Philosophy and Theory* 39/4, pp. 339–349.

Mauss, M., 1973. Techniques of the Body (trans. Bill Brewster). *Economy and Society* 2, pp. 70–88.

Maybin, J., Mercer, N., and Stierer, B., 1992. 'Scaffolding': learning in the classroom. In: K. Norman, (ed.), *Thinking Voices: The work of the National Oracy Project.* London: Hodder & Stoughton, pp. 186–195.

McGlone, F., 2008. The Two Sides of Touch: Sensing and Feeling. In: H. J. Chatterjee, (ed.), *Touch in museums: policy and practice in object handling.* London: Bloomsbury, pp. 41–60.

McNeill, D., 1992. *Hand and mind: What gestures reveal about thought.* Chicago: University of Chicago Press.

Meltzoff, A. N., 2002. Elements of a developmental theory of imitation. In: A. N. Meltzoff and W. Prinz, (eds.), *The imitative mind. Development, evolution, and brain bases.* Cambridge: University Press, pp. 19–41.

Merleau-Ponty, M., 1962. *Phenomenology of perception (Originally 1945).* London: Routledge.

Merleau-Ponty, M., 1963. *The Structure of Behavior (Originally 1942).* Boston, MA: Beacon Press.

Merriman, N., 1989. Museum visiting as a cultural phenomenon. In: P. Vergo, (ed.), *The New Museology.* London: Reaktion Books, pp. 149–171.

Mesquita, S., and Carneiro, M., 2016. Accessibility of European museums to visitors with visual impairments. *Disability & Society* 31, pp. 1–16.

Miles, C., Tait, E., Schure, M. B., and Hollis, M., 2016. Effect of Laughter Yoga on Psychological Well-being and Physiological Measures. *Advances in Mind-body Medicine* 30/1, pp. 12–20.

Moll, L. C., Amanti, C., Neff, D., and Gonzalez, N., 1992. Funds of knowledge for teaching: Using a qualitative approach to connect homes and classrooms. *Theory Into Practice* 31/2, pp. 132–141.

Montarzino, A., Robertson, B., Aspinall, P., Ambrecht, A., Findlay, C., Hine, J., and Dhillon, B., 2007. The Impact of Mobility and Public Transport on the Independence of Visually Impaired People. *Visual Impairment Research* 9/2-3, pp. 67–82.

Morcom, V., 2015. Scaffolding social and emotional learning within "shared affective spaces" to reduce bullying: A sociocultural perspective. *Learning, Culture and Social Interaction* 6, pp. 77–86.

Moussouri, T., 2007. Implications of the Social Model of Disability for Visitor Research. *Visitor Studies* 10/1, pp. 90–106.

Moussouri, T., and Vomvyla, E., 2015. Conversations about Home, Community, and Identity. *Archaeology International* 18, pp. 97–112.

Museum Association., 2020. *There is a strong feeling among disabled people that we have been losing ground.* Retrieved on 03 April 2021 from World Wide Web: https://www.museumsassociation.org/museums-journal/opinion/2020/11/there-is-a-strong-feeling-among-disabled-people-that-we-have-been-losing-ground/#

Museum in a Box. 2021. *About,* 2021. Retrieved on 05 March 2021 from World Wide Web: https://museuminabox.org/about/

Museum of London. 2020a. *About us.* Retrieved on 07 May 2020 from World Wide Web: https://www.museumoflondon.org.uk/about-us

Museum of London. 2020b. *Accessibility.* Retrieved on 07 May 2020 from World Wide Web: https://www.

museumoflondon.org.uk/museum-london/plan-your-visit/museum-accessibility

NFB., 2019. *Blindness Statistics.* Retrieved on 17 April 2021 from World Wide Web: https://nfb.org/resources/blindness-statistics

NHS., 2021. *Blindness and vision loss.* Retrieved on 03 April 2021 from World Wide Web: https://www.nhs.uk/conditions/vision-loss/

Nirje, B., 1969. The normalization principle and its human management implications. In R. Kugel, and W. Wolfensberger, (eds.), *Changing patterns in residential services for the mentally retarded.* Washington, D.C.: President's Committee on Mental Retardation.

Noordegraaf, J., 2004. *Strategies of Display: Museum Presentation in Nineteenth- and Twentieth-century Visual Culture.* Rotterdam: NAi Publishers.

Oliver, M., 1990. *The Politics of Disablement.* London, Macmillan.

Oliver, M., 1996. *Understanding Disability: From Theory To Practice.* London: Macmillan.

Oliver, M., 1998. Theories of Disability in Health Practice and Research. *BMJ* 317, pp. 1446–1449.

Oliver, M., 2013. The social model of disability: thirty years on. *Disability & Society* 28/7, pp. 1024–1026.

O'Loughlin, M., 1998. Paying attention to bodies in education: theoretical resources and practical suggestions. *Educational Philosophy and Theory* 30/3, pp. 275–298.

Ostrove, J. M., and Crawford, D., 2006. "One lady was so busy staring at me she walked into a wall": Interability Relations from the Perspective of Women with Disabilities. *Disability Studies Quarterly* 26/3.

Ostrow Seidler, C., 2011. Fighting Disability Stereotypes with Comics: "I Cannot See You, but I Know You Are Staring at Me". *Art Education* 64/6, pp. 20–24.

Owens, J., 2015. Exploring the critiques of the social model of disability: the transformative possibility of Arendt's notion of power. *Sociology of Health and Illness* 37, pp. 385–403.

Oyserman, D., 2001. Self-concept and identity. In A. Tesser and N. Schwarz, (eds.), *Blackwell handbook of social psychology.* Malden, MA: Blackwell Press, pp. 499–517.

Oyserman, D., 2015. Identity-Based Motivation. In R. A. Scott and S. M. Kosslyn, (eds.), *Emerging Trends in the Social and Behavioral Sciences.* New York: John Wiley & Sons, Inc.

Oyserman, D., Smith, G. C., and Elmore, K., 2014. Identity-based motivation: Implications for health and health disparities. *Journal of Social Issues* 70, pp. 206–225.

Packer, M. J., and Goicoechea, J., 2000. Sociocultural and constructivist theories of learning: Ontology, not just epistemology. *Educational Psychologist* 35/4, pp. 227–241.

Painter, J., 2000. Pierre Bourdieu. In M. Crang And N. Thrift, (eds.), *Thinking Space.* London: Routledge, pp. 239–259.

Paris, S. G., and Mercer, M. J., 2002. Finding Self in Objects: Identity Exploration in Museums. In G. Leinhardt, K. Crowley, and K. Knutson, (eds.), *Learning Conversations in Museums.* London: Routledge, pp. 401–423.

Paterson, K., and Hughes, B., 1999. Disability Studies and Phenomenology: The Carnal Politics Of Everyday Life. *Disability & Society* 14/5, pp. 597–610.

Pea, R. D., 2004. The social and technological dimensions of scaffolding and related theoretical concepts for learning, education, and human activity. *Journal of the Learning Sciences* 13/3, pp. 423–451.

Pierroux, P., 2003. Communicating art in museums. *Journal of Museum Education* 28/1, pp. 3–7.

Port, R. F., and van Gelder, T., (eds.), 1995. *Mind as motion: Explorations in the dynamics of cognition.* Cambridge, MA: The MIT Press.

Price, S., Jewitt, C., and Moussouri, T., 2021. Supporting Family Scaffolding and Collaboration through Digital Interactive Tabletop Exhibits. *Visitor Studies.*

Proctor, N., 2005. Providing deaf and hard-of-hearing visitors with on-demand, independent access to museum information and interpretation through handheld computers. *Conference Proceedings Museums and the Web 2005.* Vancouver: Archives & Museum Informatics Place.

Pye, E., (ed.), 2007. *The Power of Touch: Handling Objects in Museum and Heritage Contexts.* Walnut Creek, CA: Left Coast Press.

Rambusch, J. and Ziemke, T., 2005. The Role of Embodiment in Situated Learning. In B. G. Bara, L. Barsalou, and M. Bucciarelli, (eds.), *Proceedings of the 27th Annual Conference of the Cognitive Science Society.* Mahwah, NJ: Lawrence Erlbaum, pp. 1803–1808.

Rauch, J., 2018. *Generation next, Millennials will outnumber baby-boomers in 2019.* The Economist, [internet]. Retrieved on 21 February 2020 from World Wide Web: https://web.archive.org/web/20190313195431/http://te.tbr.fun/generation-next/

Rees Leahy, H., 2007. Walking for pleasure? Bodies on display at the 1857 Manchester Art-Treasures exhibition. *Art History* 30/4, pp. 545–565.

Rees Leahy, H., 2010. Watch Your Step: Embodiment and encounter at Tate Modern. In S. H. Dudley, (ed.), *Museum Materialities: Objects, Engagements, Interpretations.* London: Routledge, pp. 162–172.

Rees Leahy, H. R., 2012. *Museum Bodies: The Politics and Practices of Visiting and Viewing*. Farnham: Taylor & Francis Group.

Reich, C., 2014. *Taking Action Toward Inclusion: Organizational Change and the Inclusion of People with Disabilities in Museum Learning*. Boston: Boston College.

Resnick, P., 2002. Beyond Bowling Together: SocioTechnical Capital. In J. M. Carroll, (ed.), *HCI in the New Millennium*. New York: Addison-Wesley, pp. 247–272.

Rickard, C., 2013. *Multimodal Cues in the Socialization of Joint Attention in Young Children with Varying Degrees of Vision: Getting the POINT Even When You Can't See It*. Unpublished Ph.D. dissertation, University of Colorado, Boulder, CO, USA.

Rickard, C., Strother, M., Fox, B., and Raymond, C., 2019. Scaffolding Embodied Access for Categorization in Interactions between a Blind Child and Her Mother. *Languages* 4/2, pp. 1–14.

Rizzolatti, G., Fadiga, L., Fogassi, L., and Gallese, V., 2002. From mirror neurons to imitation: Facts and speculations. In: A. N. Meltzoff and W. Prinz, (eds.), *The imitative mind. Development, evolution, and brain bases*. Cambridge: Cambridge University Press, pp. 247–266.

RNIB., 2019. *Key information and statistics on sight loss in the UK*. Retrieved on 03 April 2021 from World Wide Web: https://www.rnib.org.uk/professionals/knowledge-and-research-hub/key-information-and-statistics

RNIB., 2021. *Eye health and sight loss stats and facts*. Retrieved on 03 April 03 2021 from World Wide Web: https://www.rnib.org.uk/eye-health-and-sight-loss-stats-and-facts

Rodriguez, G., 2011. Power and agency in education: Exploring the pedagogical dimensions of funds of knowledge. *Review of Research in Education* 37/1, pp. 87–120.

Rogoff, B., 1990. *Apprenticeship in thinking – cognitive development in social context*. New York: Oxford University Press.

Rogoff, B., 2003. *The cultural nature of human development*. New York and Oxford: Oxford University Press.

Rogoff, I., 2005. Looking Away: Participations in Visual Culture. In G. Butt, (ed.), *After Criticism: New Responses to Art and Performance*. Oxford: Blackwell Publishing Ltd, pp. 117–134.

Rohrer, T., 2007. The Body in Space: Embodiment, Experientialism and Linguistic Conceptualization. In J. Zlatev, T. Ziemke, R. Frank, R. Dirven, (eds.), *Body, Language and Mind, vol. 2*. Berlin: Mouton de Gruyter.

Romanek, D., and Lynch, B., 2008. Touch and the Value of Object Handling: Final Conclusions for a New Sensory Museology. In: H. J. Chatterjee, (ed.), *Touch in museums: policy and practice in object handling*. London: Bloomsbury, pp. 275–286.

Roth, W. M., 2002. From action to discourse: The bridging function of gestures. *Journal of Cognitive Systems Research* 3, pp. 535–554.

Roth, W. M. and Lawless, D. V., 2002. How does the body get into the mind? *Human Studies* 25, pp. 333–358.

Rowe, S., 2002. The Role of Objects in Active Distributed Meaning-Making. In: S. Paris, (ed.), *Perspectives on Object-Centered Learning in Museums*. Mahwah (NJ): Lawrence Erlbaum Associated Publications, pp. 19–35.

Rowe, S., and Kisiel, J., 2012. Family engagement at aquarium touch tanks—Exploring interactions and the potential for learning. In E. Davidsson, and A. Jakobsson, (eds.), *Understanding interactions at science centers and museums*. Rotterdam: Sense Publishers, pp. 63–77.

Rowlands, M., 2010. *The new science of the mind: From extended mind to embodied phenomenology*. Cambridge, MA: The MIT Press.

Rueff-Lopes, R., Navarro, J., Caetano, A., and Silva, A. J., 2015. A Markov Chain Analysis of Emotional Exchange in Voice-to-Voice Communication: Testing for the Mimicry Hypothesis of Emotional Contagion. *Hum Commun Res* 41, pp. 412–434.

Sandberg, R., 2016. *3D printing for blind people: The future potential of a cutting edge technology*. Retrieved on 15 February 2018 from World Wide Web: https://www.incobs.de/articles/items/3d.html

Sandell, R., 1998. Museums as agents of social inclusion. *Museum Management and Curatorship* 17 /4, pp. 401–418.

Sandell, R., 2002. Museums and the combating of social inequality: roles, responsibilities, resistance. In R. Sandell, (ed.), *Museums, Society, Inequality*. London and New York: Routledge, pp. 3–23.

Sandell, R., 2007. *Museums, Prejudice and the Reframing of Difference*. London and New York: Routledge.

Sandell, R., 2017. *Museums, Moralities and Human Rights*. London and New York: Routledge.

Sandell, R., Delin, A., Dodd, J., and Gay, J., 2005. Beggars, freaks and heroes? Museum collections and the hidden history of disability. *Journal of Museum Management and Curatorship* 20/1, pp. 5–19.

Sandell, R., Dodd, J., and Garland Thomson, R., 2010. *Re-Presenting Disability: activism and agency in the museum*. London and New York: Routledge.

Sandell, R., and Nightingale, E., (eds.), 2012. *Museums, Equality and Social Justice*. London and New York: Routledge.

Saunders, J., 2014. Conservation in Museums and Inclusion of the Non-Professional. *Journal of Conservation and Museum Studies* 12/1–6, pp. 1–13.

Scherer, M. J., 1996. Outcomes Of Assistive Technology Use On Quality Of Life. *Disability And Rehabilitation* 18/9, pp. 439–448.

Schwandt, T. A., 2000. Three epistemological stances for qualitative inquiry: interpretivism, hermeneutics, and social construction. In N. K. Denzin, and Y. S. Lincoln, (eds.), *Handbook of qualitative research.* Thousand Oaks, CA: Sage, 189–213.

Schwarz, N., Bless, H., Wänke, M., and Winkielman, P. 2003. Accessibility revisited. In G. Baudenhausen and A. Lambert, (eds.), *Foundations of social cognition.* Mahwah, NJ: Erlbaum.

Seale, J., Garcia Carrizosa, H., Rix, J., Sheehy, K., and Hayhoe, S., 2021. A participatory approach to the evaluation of participatory museum research projects, *International Journal of Research & Method in Education* 44/1, pp. 20–40.

Seamon, D., and Sowers, J., 2008. Place and Placelessness, Edward Relph. In P. Hubbard, R. Kitchen, and G. Vallentine, (eds.), *Key Texts in Human Geography.* London: Sage, pp. 43–51.

Shakespeare, T., 1994. Cultural Representation of Disabled People: Dustbins For Disavowal. *Disability & Society* 9, pp. 283–299.

Shakespeare, T., (ed.), 1998. *The Disability Reader: Social Science Perspectives.* London: Cassell.

Shakespeare, T., 2005. Disability Studies Today And Tomorrow. *Sociology Of Health & Illness* 27, pp. 138–148.

Shakespeare, T., and Watson, N., 2001. The Social Model Of Disability: An Outdated Ideology?. In S. N. Barnart and B. M. Altman, (eds.), *Exploring Theories And Expanding Methodologies: Where We Are And Where We Need To Go.* Bingley, UK: Emerald Group Publishing Limited, pp. 9–28.

Silverman, L., 1995. Visitor Meaning-Making in Museums for a New Age. *Curator* 38/3, pp. 161–170.

Silverman, D., 2006. *Interpreting Qualitative Data: Methods for Analyzing Talk, Text and Interaction.* London: Sage.

Silverman, L. H., 2010. *The Social Work of Museums.* London: Routledge.

Smith, E. R., and Collins, E. C., 2010. Situated cognition. In L. Feldman Barrett, B. Mesquita, and E. R. Smith, (eds.), *The mind in context.* Guilford: New York, NY.

Smith, H., J. L., Ginley, B., and Goodwin, H., 2012. Beyond compliance? Museums, disability and the law. In R. Sandell, and E. Nightingale, (eds.), *Museums, Equality and Social Justice.* London: Routledge, pp. 59–71.

Smith, J. A., and Osborn, M., 2003. Interpretative phenomenological analysis. In J. A. Smith, (ed.), *Qualitative Psychology: A practical guide to research methods.* London: Sage, pp. 51–80.

Smith, J. A., Flowers, P., and Larkin, M., 2009. *Interpretative Phenomenological Analysis: Theory, Method and Research.* Los Angeles: Sage.

Solnit, R., 2001. *Wanderlust. A History of Walking.* London: Verso.

Soren, B., 2009. Museum experiences that change visitors. *Museum Management and Curatorship* 24/3, pp. 233–251.

Spence, C., 2007. Making Sense of Touch: A Multisensory Approach to the Perception of Objects. In: E. Pye, (ed.), *The power of touch: handling objects in museum and heritage contexts.* London: UCL Institute of Archaeology Publications, pp. 45–62.

Spence, C., and Gallace, A., 2008. Making Sense of Touch. In: H. J. Chatterjee, (ed.), *Touch in museums: policy and practice in object handling.* London: Bloomsbury, pp. 21–40.

Spirtos, M., and Gilligan, R., 2020. 'In your own head everyone is staring': the disability related identity experiences of young people with hemiplegic cerebral palsy. *Journal of Youth Studies*, pp. 1–17.

St Julian, J., 1997. Explaining learning: The trajectory situated cognition and the implications of connectionism. In: D. Kirshner and J. A. Whitson, (eds.), *Situated Cognition: Social, semiotic, and psychological perspectives.* Mahwah (NJ): Lawrence Erlbaum Associates.

Stainton, C., 2002. Voices and Images: Making Connections Between Identity and Art. In G. Leinhardt, K. Crowley, and K. Knutson, (eds.), *Learning Conversations in Museums.* London: Routledge, pp. 213–257.

Steier, R., 2014. Posing the question: Visitor posing as embodied interpretation in an art museum. *Mind, Culture, and Activity* 21/2, pp. 148–170.

Steier, R., Pierroux, P., and Krange, I., 2015. Embodied interpretation: Gesture, social interaction, and meaning making in a national art museum. *Learning, Culture and Social Interaction* 7, pp. 28–42.

Stokowski, P. A., 2002. Languages of place and discourses of power: Constructing new senses of place. *Journal of Leisure Research* 34, pp. 368–382.

Streeck, J., 2009a. Gesturecraft: The manu-facture of meaning. Amsterdam: John Benjamins Publishing.

Streeck, J., 2009b. Depicting gestures: Examples of the analysis of embodied communication in the arts of the West. *Gesture* 9/1, pp. 1–34.

Swarts, D., 1997. *Culture and Power: The Sociology of Pierre Bourdieu.* Chicago: The University of Chicago Press.

Thobo-Carlsen, M., 2016. Walking the Museum – Performing the Museum. *The Senses and Society* 11/2, pp. 136–157.

Thomas, C., 2010. Medical sociology and disability theory. In G. Scambler, and S. Scambler, (eds.), *New Directions in the Sociology of Chronic and Disabling Conditions: Assaults on the Lifeworld*. London, New York: Palgrave Macmillan.

Thomas, P., Gradwell, L., Markham, N., 1997. *Defining Impairment within the Social Model of Disability*. Retrieved on 15 March 2021 from World Wide Web: https://disability-studies.leeds.ac.uk/wp-content/uploads/sites/40/library/thomas-pam-Defining-Impairment-within-the-Social-Model-of-Disability.pdf

Tiwari, R., 2010. *Space-Body-Ritual: Performativity in the City*. Lanham, Maryland: Lexington Books.

Turner, B., 2001. Disability and The Sociology of The Body. In G. Albrecht, K. Seelman, and M. Bury, (eds.), *Handbook of Disability Studies*. Thousand Oaks, Ca: Sage, pp. 252–266.

Tzortzi, K., 2014. Movement in Museums: Mediating between Museum Intent and Visitor Experience. *Museum Management and Curatorship* 29/4, pp. 327–48.

Udo, J. P., and Fels, D. I., 2010. Enhancing the entertainment experience of blind and low-vision theatregoers through touch tours. *Disability & Society* 25/2, pp. 231–240.

V&A., 1997. *Balaustrade*. Retrieved on 18 June 2020 from World Wide Web: https://collections.vam.ac.uk/item/O3665/balustrade-lane-danny/

V&A., 2002. *Fallen Angel*. Retrieved on 18 June 2020 from World Wide Web: https://collections.vam.ac.uk/item/O70792/the-fallen-angel-group-rodin-auguste/

V&A., 2007. *Portrait of Honoré de Balzac*. Retrieved on 18 June 2020 from World Wide Web: https://collections.vam.ac.uk/item/O135951/honore-de-balzac-bust-rodin/honor%C3%A9-de-balzac-bust-rodin/honor%C3%A9-de-balzac-bust-rodin/

V&A., 2019. *Disability and Access*. Retrieved on 16 March 2019 from World Wide Web: https://www.vam.ac.uk/info/disability-access

V&A., 2020. *About us*. V&A, [internet]. Retrieved on 29 May 2020 from World Wide Web: https://www.vam.ac.uk/info/about-us

V&A., 2021. *Disability and Access*. Retrieved on 26 March 2021 from World Wide Web: https://www.vam.ac.uk/info/disability-access

Valentine, G., 1999. What It Means To Be A Man: The Body, Masculinities And Disability. In: R. Butler and H. Parr, (eds.), *Mind And Body Spaces: Geographies Of Illness, Impairment And Disability*. London: Routledge, pp. 167–180.

Varela, A. H., Thompson, E., and Rosch, E., 1991. *The embodied mind: Cognitive Science and human experience*. Cambridge, MA: MIT Press.

Vogelzang, J., Admiraal, W., and van Driel, J., 2019. Scrum Methodology as an Effective Scaffold to Promote Students' Learning and Motivation in Context-based Secondary Chemistry Education. *Eurasia Journal of Mathematics, Science and Technology Education* 15/12.

vom Lehn, D., and Heath, C., 2005 Accounting for new technology in museum exhibitions. International Journal of Arts Manage 7/3, pp. 11–21.

vom Lehn, D., 2010 Discovering 'Experience-ables': Socially including visually impaired people in art museums. *Journal of Marketing Management* 26/7–8, pp. 749–769.

vom Lehn, D., 2013. Withdrawing from Exhibits: The Interactional Organisation of museum visits. In P. Haddington, L. Mondada and M. Nevile, (eds.), *Interaction and Mobility: Language and the Body in Motion*. Berlin: De Gruyter, pp. 65–90.

vom Lehn, D., and Heath, C., 2007. Social Interaction in Museums and Galleries: A Note on Video-Based Field Studies. In R. Goldman, R. Pea, B. Barron, and S. Derry, (eds.), *Video Research in the Learning Sciences*. Mahwah, NJ: Lawrence Earlbaum Associates, pp. 287–301.

vom Lehn, D., Heath, C., and Hindmarsh, J., 2001. Exhibiting interaction: Conduct and collaboration in museums and galleries. *Symbolic Interaction* 24/2, pp. 189–216.

Vygotsky, L. S., 1978. *Mind in Society: The Development of Higher Psychological Processes*. M. Cole, V. John-Steiner, S. Scribner, E. Souberman, (eds.), Cambridge, MA: Harvard University Press.

Wallace Collection 2020. *About us*. Retrieved on 24 May 2020 from World Wide Web: https://www.wallacecollection.org/about-us/

Wallace Collection 2021. *Access*. Retrieved on 16 March 2021 from World Wide Web: https://www.wallacecollection.org/visit/access/

Walsh, P. K., 1992. *The representation of the past: museums and heritage in the post- modern world*. London, New York: Routledge.

Wang, H. C., Katzschmann, R. K., Teng, S., Araki, B., Giarre, L., and Rus, D., 2017. Enabling independent navigation for visually impaired people through a wearable vision-based feedback system. *2017 IEEE International Conference on Robotics and Automation (ICRA)*.

Wellcome Collection., 2021a. *Accessibility*. Retrieved on 26 March 2021 from World Wide Web: https://wellcomecollection.org/pages/Wvm2uiAAAIYQ4FHP

Wellcome Collection., 2021b. *Joy and Tranquillity digital guide*. Retrieved on 10 August 2021 from World Wide Web: https://wellcomecollection.org/pages/YLCu9hEAACYAUiJx

Wenger, E., 1998a. *Community of Practice: Learning as a Social System*. Retrieved on 07 December 2020 from World Wide Web: https://thesystemsthinker.com/communities-of-practice-learning-as-a-social-system/

Wenger, E., 1998b. *Communities of practice. Learning, meaning and identity*. Cambridge, UK: Cambridge University Press.

Wenger, E., 2009. *Communities of practice. A brief introduction*. Retrieved on 7 December 2020 from World Wide Web: https://www.ohr.wisc.edu/cop/articles/communities_practice_intro_wenger.pdf

Wenger E., 2010. Communities of Practice and Social Learning Systems: the Career of a Concept. In: C. Blackmore, (eds), *Social Learning Systems and Communities of Practice*. London: Springer, pp. 179–198.

Williams, P., Jamali, H.R., and Nicholas, D., 2006. Using ICT with people with special education needs: what the literature tells us. *Aslib Proceedings* 58/4, pp. 330–345.

Wilson, F., 1994. The silent message of the museum. In J. Fisher, (ed.), *Global Visions: towards a new internationalism in the visual arts*. London: Kala Press in association with the Institute of International Visual Arts, pp. 152–60.

Wilson, M., 2003. Six views of embodied cognition. *Psychonomic Bulletin and Review* 9/4, pp. 625–636.

Wilson, K., 2016. Critical reading, critical thinking: Delicate scaffolding in English for Academic Purposes (EAP). *Thinking Skills and Creativity* 22, pp. 256–265.

Wilson, P. F., Stott, J., Warnett, J. M., Attridge, A., Smith, M. P., Williams, M. A., 2018. Museum visitor preference for the physical properties of 3D printed replicas. *Journal of Cultural Heritage* 32, pp. 176–185.

Wilson, P. F., Griffiths, S., Williams, E., Smith, M. P., and Williams, M. A., 2020. Designing 3-D Prints for Blind and Partially Sighted Audiences in Museums: Exploring the Needs of Those Living with Sight Loss. *Visitor Studies* 23/2, pp. 120–140.

Wintemute, R., 2016. Goodbye EU Anti-Discrimination Law? Hello Repeal of the Equality Act 2010?. *King's Law Journal* 27/3, pp. 387–397.

Wojton, M. A., Heimlich, J., and Shaheen, N., 2016. Accommodating Blind Learners Helps All Learners. *Journal of Museum Education* 41/1, pp. 59–65.

World Health Organization. 2001. *International Classification of Functioning, Disability and Health (ICF)*. Retrieved on 15 March 2021 from World Wide Web: https://www.who.int/classifications/international-classification-of-functioning-disability-and-health

Worth, N., 2013. Visual Impairment in the City: Young People's Social Strategies for Independent Mobility. *Urban Studies* 50/3, pp. 574–586.

Wood, D., Bruner, J., and Ross, G., 1976. The role of tutoring in problem solving. *Journal of child psychology and psychiatry* 17, pp. 89–100.

Wyman, B., Smith, S., Meyers, D., and Godfrey, M., 2011. Digital Storytelling in Museums: Observations and Best Practices. *Curator: The Museum Journal* 54, pp. 461–468.

Yardi, S., 2009. Social learning and technical capital on the social web. *Crossroads* 16/2, pp. 9–11.

Yardi, S., 2010. A Theory of Technical Capital. *Position Paper TMSP Workshop*, pp. 11–14.

Ziebarth, B., 2010. *What visitors with vision loss want museums and parks to know about effective communication*. Bloomington: Indiana University.

Ziemke, T., 2002. Introduction to the special issue on situated and embodied cognition. *Cognitive Systems Research* 3, pp. 271–274.

Lightning Source UK Ltd.
Milton Keynes UK
UKHW051144060223
416527UK00008B/204